Does the Center Hold?

Text and Illustrations
by
Donald Palmer

Does the Center Hold?
An Introduction to Western Philosophy

Donald Palmer
College of Marin

Mayfield Publishing Company
Mountain View, California
London • Toronto

Library of Congress Cataloging-in-Publication Data

Palmer, Donald.
    Does the center hold? : an introduction to western philosophy /
    Donald Palmer
        p.   cm.
    1. Philosophy — Introductions.   I. Title
BD21. P24 1990
190 — dc20
ISBN 0-87484-911-X

                                                          90-34877
                                                          CIP

Manufactured in the United States of America
10 9 8 7

Mayfield Publishing Company
1240 Villa Street
Mountain View, California 94041

Sponsoring editor, James Bull; managing editor, Linda Toy; production
editor, Sondra Glider; manuscript editor, Sylvia Stein Wright; text
and cover designer, Jeanne Schreiber; hand lettering, Robin Mouat
illustrations, Donald Palmer.

The text was printed on 50# Finch Opaque by Edwards Brothers, Inc.
Text credits are on a continuation of the copyright page, p. 519.

Contents

8-16
19-23
30-35
37-42

45 Total

81-234

46

239-246
250-270
274-284

37

406-439

27

436-475
483-498

62

To Leila

Preface

I think most people, if they are lucky, end up in a professional field to which they were attracted because they had some special affinities, talents, or skills. (I advise my students, "Do what you do best, what you do better than most, and what you love doing"; and I trust that in their case, I am not advocating great criminality.) At least that must be true of philosophy majors. I've met students whose parents pressured them to go to law school or medical school, but I can't remember meeting students whose parents insisted that they become philosophy majors. Certainly, nobody ever went into this field motivated by greed, unless he or she was laboring under a serious misapprehension. Plato may have gone into philosophy impelled by a frustrated lust for power, but few make that mistake anymore. So you and I in our youth must have found philosophy somehow <u>inherently</u> <u>interesting</u> and in some way a "natural" for us. Unfortunately, as I'm sure you've noticed, not all students agree with us about philosophy's native charms.

I must admit, based on my own experience as a student (at the College of Marin, the University of California at Berkeley, the University of Madrid, and the University of Navarre), that philosophy can be made to seem tremendously exciting or deadly boring, depending on how it's taught. (This is probably true of all fields, but somehow it is more true of philosophy.) If we make the reasonable assumption that not every college student has the natural philosophical skills and talents we think we had as philosophy students, then we cannot rest assured that the field of philosophy in itself is inherently attractive to all our students. Philosophy is not everybody's cup of tea, as amazing as that may seem to us. (I was shattered this week in an office hour when a student asked me, "Does this class get more interesting later?" I _wanted_ to say, "How dull your soul must be. This is _philosophy_!") We philosophy teachers believe that our topic offers something important even to those students for whom philosophy has no intuitive attraction. But it is up to us to prove it. Without guidance, some people do not see the relevance to their lives of the medieval debate over the status of the universals. (I'm serious, you know. What if there is truth in the last line of Eco's novel, _The Name of the Rose_? "The Rose exists by virtue of its name. We have only names." What if Shakespeare is wrong, and that which we call a rose by some other name would _not_ smell as sweet? This _matters_.)

_So_, I've written this book in the hope that it is a contribution toward a more interesting, perhaps more exciting, and certainly more _fun_ philosophy class. I've tried to write it in a lively and engaging manner without watering down difficult ideas too much and without pandering to simplicity. The vocabulary may sometimes be just a notch beyond the students' familiarity, but not so much as to be a "turnoff." Students want to be challenged, after all. Do I need to justify using cartoons and jokes in order to make the book more entertaining? I hope not. Philosophy should be fun. Thoughts are good to think. That goal also explains why, unlike the authors of many philosophy texts, I've taken personal positions on most of the topics I discuss. This procedure probably needs more of a justification than do the cartoons. Well, frankly, a philosophy book that simply lays out end to end the various alternative ideas in a purely antiseptic way is a book I find inherently dull _and_ suspect. (I don't mind if a cafeteria lays out food that way, but then I don't like cafeterias much either.) You'll no doubt disagree with some of my conclusions, but at least I don't think you'll find them doctrinaire. I'm a hopeless eclectic — or perhaps a Jamesian. (If it works, use it!) Not only that, but according to my experience as student and teacher, part of the dynamics of a philosophy course, unlike courses in Spanish or biology, consists in _slight_ antagonisms between the text and the class. Think of this as an opportunity! I'm sure I've given you plenty of fodder.

I hope one of the strengths of this book is found in the connections it makes between philosophy and other fields in which your students are interested, especially art, literature, physics, sociology, psychology, and psychoanalysis. Philosophy may no longer be the queen of all the disciplines, but she is certainly their consort.

In spite of some appearance to the contrary, the text is fairly conventional in the selection of its material. The topics here are themes typically taught in introductory philosophy courses on this continent. I think the chapter divisions and subdivisions speak for themselves in this respect. I try to establish continuity throughout the book both by providing a Glossary with a system of cross-references and by keeping certain themes alive from chapter to chapter so that ideas once learned do not simply evaporate. (Here, too, "use it or lose it.")

And now to the acknowledgments. If a long list of names bores you, skip this last paragraph because I intend to pay my debts here and thank many of the people who participated in the construction of this book (most without their knowledge or consent). First, the philosophers.... well, that's all the philosophers I've ever studied, but particularly Wittgenstein, Kierkegaard, Sartre, Marx, Freud, Nietzsche, Plato, Descartes, Spinoza, and Hume; you'll hear from them again. (Some may be rolling over in their graves.) Next, my own teachers, including Virginia Orkney, Cornelius Weber, George Duncan, Howell Breece, John Searle, Stanley Cavell, Benson Mates, Stephen Pepper, Jerry Clegg, Juan Rodríguez Rosado, Leonardo Polo, and (by osmosis) Charles Addams and Virgil ("Vip") Partch. Next, thanks to all my students over a twenty-five year period at the College of Marin — all five thousand of them. (When I reach seven thousand, I'll retire.) Then to Robin Mouat, my calligrapher, and to my angels at Mayfield Publishing Company: Sondra Glider, Jean Mailander, Kirstan Price, Jeanne Schreiber, Pam Trainer, and Silvia Stein Wright. And particularly to my editor, Jim Bull, who not only suffered all this, but actually solicited it, as he did my first book, Looking at Philosophy. And to my very helpful reviewers: Charles Page, Lane College; Richard Payne, San Jose State University; and Don Porter, College of San Mateo. Also, though it may seem odd, I want to thank the great American desert, where many thoughts were hatched and pages written — the Smoke Creek Desert, the Black Rock Desert, the Mojave, the Organ Pipe National Monument, the Anza-Borrego, and therewith (of course) the late Edward Abbey, wherever you may be. Finally, let me thank my true source of energy, inspiration, and love, the person to whom this book is dedicated, my wife, Leila May. Without her, even philosophy would be worth much less to me.

Introduction

Introductions are meant to introduce. They establish relations between people and other people or between people and ideas or places. But that's the purpose of this whole book, which is an introduction to philosophy. This book is meant to introduce people to other people (most of whom are dead, unfortunately), people to ideas (living, I hope), and people to a place (the high country of the mind — though there are a few bogs, sinks, and badlands here as well, I fear). So such a book should not need much of an introduction, which would be merely an introduction to an introduction.

Still, a few preliminary comments are appropriate. First, a word about the style. Everybody's style is both unique and imitative. Consciously or unconsciously, I've imitated the styles of my teachers and of the philosophers I've studied. (I've thanked them in the preface.) This book is written in something of a unique style in spite of all these influences. I hope philosophy teachers, philosophy students, and the occasional general reader will find my style compatible with their own styles of teaching, learning, thinking, and enjoying. My style attempts to be both lighthearted and serious at the same time. It is lighthearted because of my deep conviction that joy and knowledge are not mutually exclusive (Nietzsche's "joyful wisdom"). I hope you'll find at least some of the jokes funny without being distracting. I dare to hope that a few of them might be illuminating. But the book is also serious because it asks serious questions. The philosophers Jean-Paul Sartre and Martin Heidegger tell us that to be human is to confront the world with questions. And all of our smaller questions are framed by the bigger questions, questions like: "What is reality?" "What is knowledge?" "What is value?" "What is it to be human?" These are philosophical questions. They are what philosophy (and life) are about. What annoys some people about philosophy is that these questions never seem to receive a final answer. Each generation appears to answer them; then each new generation rephrases them in such a way as to require new answers. But that's also what is annoying about life (and what's exciting about it as well).

Nevertheless, I have been so presumptuous as to try to draw my own tentative conclusions at the end of each chapter. This isn't always done in introductory philosophy books because students are supposed to be allowed to draw their own conclusions — but I suspect that one way or another students will manage to survive my conclusions (especially with the help of their professors!). And if you don't want to be contaminated by my conclusions, just skip them. (Although who's fooling whom? Writers' conclusions are usually subconsciously smuggled into the formulation of the questions they pose. Be on guard!)

Another feature of this book to which students should be alerted is its exclusively Western orientation. The philosophers and philosophies studied here are all in the Greco-Roman-European tradition. There have been rich philosophical veins in other cultures, but I do not have the expertise to mine them. Not only are most of the philosophies set forth in this book Western philosophies, but they are systems of thought that have been put forward for the most part by males. This is a weakness in my book for which I am only partly at fault. I agree with the feminist philosophers who claim that in the past women have been systematically discouraged from attempting to participate in the history of philosophy and that when such attempts were made, they were marginalized or even suppressed. I am heartened to note that today the system of barriers that has discouraged women from a philosophical vocation is being dismantled.

Now, what about the title of the book, "Does the Center Hold?" I borrowed the idea from the poet William Butler Yeats, who, in "The Second Coming," says, "Things fall apart; the centre cannot hold." Yet in prereflective thought (life before philosophy), the center certainly _seems_ to hold most of the time for most of us. The world we inhabit presents itself to us in a fairly orderly and predictable manner in both its physical and social manifestations. But occasionally natural or social disasters burst forth (such as earthquakes and wars), the order and reasonableness of things disappear, and there is chaos. Also, at some point in their lives, most individuals suffer bouts of "minimadness," where the center does not seem to hold. (Such an experience may have inspired Yeats' poem.) Furthermore, as Descartes reminds us, every night we each slip into a dreamworld that is madder than madness. Then we wake up and minimize the experience of unreason by relegating it to a sphere of unreality.

When I was a child, I liked to go to Playland at the Beach in San Francisco (now covered over with townhouses). One of my favorite spots was the Dizzy Dish. You sat at the center of a large disc, which slowly began rotating. As it moved faster and faster, only the person sitting at the exact center, marked by an orange circle, was safe (by virtue of centripetal force). All others inevitably began sliding off the disc, first inch by inch; then suddenly, amid much shrieking, they were hurled to the perimeter (centrifugal force). When you first felt yourself slipping, you clawed to reach the middle, but it seemed to pull away from you inexorably. The center did not hold. I suspect that the onset of insanity sometimes provokes similar sensations, but so does the study of philosophy. Under the philosophical scrutiny of thought, knowledge, reality, and values, the commonsensical center and normal orderliness of the world seem to slip away. As Nietzsche said, while philosophizing we sometimes feel as though we have cut our moorings and that we are floating off into the cold darkness of outer space.

And yet philosophy is not just a skeptical undertaking whose point is to dethrone the normal and the commonplace. It is also an attempt to achieve a view of "the bigger picture" — to see whether sense can be made of the totality of experience. The book's title, "Does the Center Hold?" asks whether a scrutiny of human experience reveals some kind of unity, or does it plunge us into chaos? Each of the chapters in this book attempts to be an aid to the student in answering that overarching question, each by scrutinizing a different feature

4

of experience. Of course, students must draw their own conclusions. Mine, flavored with what I hope is a healthy skepticism, is that the center does hold, but only _roughly_. Some
days it seems to hold better than others.

Chapter I

What Are We Doing in This Class?

Is Philosophy Possible?

There are very few academic courses in which a big part of the class time is spent agonizing over what the subject matter of the course is and over whether the discipline to be studied even exists. Yet such is the case in philosophy. Philosophy poses a series of questions that it tries to answer, and one of these questions is "what is philosophy?" This fact itself tells us something about philosophy because it informs us of philosophy's <u>self-reflective</u> nature.

Yes, but <u>is</u> there such a thing as anatomy?

ANATOMY 1A
Prof. Zwerbling

Philosophy is a form of thought that thinks about itself. In fact, one might say (rather pompously) that philosophy is the human mind thinking about itself. It is this perhaps overly introspective aspect of philosophy that annoys some people and causes them to think of philosophers the way they think of neurotics and psychotics — who also spend a

Thought thinking about itself

lot of time creating bizarre, convoluted explanations of how they relate to the world and to themselves (Indeed, we shall see that the line between philosophy and madness is sometimes very thin indeed, and more than one philosopher has come to the conclusion that what is needed is a <u>cure</u> for philosophical problems rather than a solution to them.)

The thin line between philosophy and madness

The Origins of Philosophy

One way of trying to understand philosophy is to look at its origins, both linguistic and historical. The word "philosophy" is from the Greek _philosophia_, meaning "the love of wisdom." Plato took this definition very seriously and saw the philosopher as a kind of lover; hence Plato spent a lot of time trying to determine the meaning of love in order to demonstrate that _true_ lovers _always_ love wisdom. But the activity we call philosophy went back hundreds of years before Plato. It is generally agreed that the first recorded philosopher in the Western tradition was THALES OF MILETOS (c. 580 B.C.). Looking briefly at what _he_ had to say may reveal something about the nature of philosophy, though it might also prove to be a bit disappointing because Thales' main theory is so obviously false (his theory : _everything is water_ !)

Everything is water

and because his "activity" does not seem so unusual — at least not to us. It is known that while visiting Egypt, Thales formulated a hypothesis to explain why the Nile, unlike almost every other known river, tended to dry up in the winter and flood in the summer. Thales' hypothesis was that winds were the cause of these phenomena. What's so remarkable about this theory (other than the fact that we now know it to be false)? What catches our attention is that all of Thales' predecessors had tried to explain these facts about the Nile by attributing them to supernatural events. Thales, rather than talking about miracles or the will

8

of the gods, explained the one natural phenomenon (the flooding of the Nile) in terms of other natural phenomena (the desert winds). Even his outrageous claim that everything is water is also an attempt to explain natural phenomena in terms of natural phenomena (and not so outrageous a claim — the leap from "Everything is water" to "Everything is atoms" is smaller than it may seem, and this leap took only a hundred years).

The leap from "Everything is water" to "Everything is atoms"

From the point of view of our desire to learn something about the nature of philosophy, Thales' erroneous answer is much less significant than his question (namely, "what is everything composed of?"), and what is even more interesting than either Thales' question or his answer are the presuppositions behind his question. Like most Greeks, Thales was acutely aware of the dramatic changes that took place in the observable world: day changes to night, then back to day again; summer changes to winter, then to summer again; hot changes to cold and then to hot again. And there was that most mysterious of all changes, life to death, which somehow produced life again. Thales' question assumes that if

9

there is change, then there must be something behind change that itself does not change. Thales also observed that the world was composed of many individual things: rocks, lizards, toothpicks, rainbows, and people. Yet the world was somehow a _whole_ and not just a loose collection of unrelated objects. Thales'

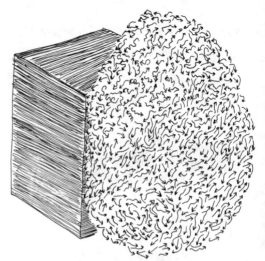

Something behind change that itself does not change

question assumes that _if there is "many," then somehow there must be a "one" behind the "many."_ Furthermore, Thales' question assumes that the human mind is capable of fathoming that unchanging One behind the many, and once having fathomed it, the mind would understand what makes the center hold, would understand the sense in which things hang together. This was Thales' concern and continues to be the concern of philosophers twenty-six hundred years later.

Once again, it is important to stress that for Thales, the answer to his question would have to be a _natural_ one, not a supernatural one. This is primarily what separates Thales' mode of thinking from the _mythic_ form of thought that preceded him. Myths explain why things are the way they are by tracing these things to their origins. In this respect, MYTHOS (the mythic way of thought) is no different from LOGOS (the philosophical/scientific way of thought). But myth traces the origins of things to supernatural time, sometimes called "strong time" by mythologists, and to supernatural ancestral beings. The order of the social and natural worlds is explained by showing how these worlds relate to "strong time" and to the divine beings that inhabited that time. Myths are usually conservative. They justify the status quo by revealing its relation to "strong time" ("We do these things because our ancestors did them...."). Myths very often begin with a formula that refers to the beginning of the world ("Once, a long, long time ago, when the earth was very young...."). The recitation of the myth removes the speaker and his audience from natural time and returns them to "strong time." Furthermore, the ritual surrounding the recitation of a myth reconstitutes the social and natural worlds. The mythical mind believes that if these myths were not recited, if these rituals were not performed, the world would fall into chaos, the center would not hold, things would fall apart. Societies based on myth are traditionally

The center does not hold. Things fall apart.

"unhistorical." They do not record history because "history" implies change, and myth-oriented societies deny change. The only change was the fall from strong time into daily time. Nothing has changed since then.

Like mythical explanations, Thales' "philosophical" theory traces things to their origin — not to their chronological origin, but rather to their <u>ontological</u> origin, that is, to their origin <u>in being</u>. What must be the nature of things for them to exhibit the forms they do exhibit and to undergo the changes they do undergo? Thales' hypothesis contains no reference to "strong time" or supernatural entities

The fall from strong time

(though one curious fragment from his book says, "All things contain gods"). It involves logical analysis of the observable facts drawn from observation. The Greeks were aware of the four elements: earth, water, air, and fire. Thales concluded that one of these must be more basic than the others and asked himself which of the four was

capable of taking on the greatest number of forms. Water seemed to be the most likely candidate. When heated, water changed to steam, then to air. When frozen, it changed to a solid. It disappeared both down into the earth and up into the sky and then bubbled back up from the earth and fell from the sky. Thales saw that rivers deposited deltas at their mouth and (incorrectly) deduced that water was being turned to earth. He saw dew on the ground in the morning and (incorrectly) deduced that earth was being changed to water. He saw the Mediterranean phenomenon called "the sun drawing water" (in which, during certain kinds of storms over the sea, clouds seem to swirl in a vortex around the sun), and he incorrectly deduced that the fire in the sun was fed by water. Then water it was! And not supernatural water — though perhaps very <u>super</u> natural water.

The distinction between <u>mythos</u>

and _logos_ is helpful in determining the nature of philosophy, but it is not without its problems. First, the viability of the distinction itself has been questioned by some. The psychologist C. G. Jung and the anthropologist Claude Lévi-Strauss have both argued that so-called _logos_ is simply our modern, Western way of mythmaking and is in some respects inferior to other forms of _mythos_. In this vein, Robert Pirsig, in his _Zen and the Art of Motorcycle Maintenance_, writes:

> The term _logos_, the root word of "logic," refers to the sum total of our rational understanding of the world. _Mythos_ is the sum total of the early historic and prehistoric myths which preceded the logos. The mythos includes not only the Greek myths but the Old Testament, the Vedic Hymns and the early legends of all cultures which have contributed to our present world understanding. The mythos-over-logos argument states that our rationality is shaped by these legends, that our knowledge today is in relation to these legends as a tree is in relation to the little shrub it once was. One can gain great insight into the complex overall structure of the tree by studying the much simpler shape of the shrub. There is no difference in kind or even difference in identity, only a difference in size.... [M]ythos [is] the huge body of common knowledge that unites our minds as cells are united in the body of man. To feel that one is not so united, that one can accept or discard this mythos as one pleases, is not to understand what this mythos is.[1]

Scholars have pointed out that many of the philosophers who followed Thales still displayed decidedly mythical trends in their thought. For example, Thales' immediate philosophical descendent, ANAXIMANDER of Miletos (c.545), criticized his master's theory, saying that if any one of the four elements were fundamental, then long ago everything would have collapsed back into that element. So for him there must be an aboriginal, nameless, formless element behind all things, and he called this primordial stuff "the Indeterminant" or "the Unlimited."

The most famous fragment still extant from Anaximander's lost book says:

> From what source things arise, to that they return of necessity when they are destroyed; for they suffer punishment and make reparation to one another for their injustice according to the order of time.

Some say that in using moral categories such as "injustice" and "reparation" to explain the world, Anaximander is clearly pursuing a form of explanation not unlike that of the

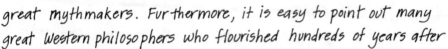

great mythmakers. Furthermore, it is easy to point out many great Western philosophers who flourished hundreds of years after Anaximander and who had recourse to divine beings in their philosophical accounts of reality. (See Chapter 5.) So the rejection of supernatural explanation cannot be the essence of philosophy.

Water suffering punishment for its injustice

Another problem with the <u>mythos</u> / <u>logos</u> distinction is that even if one accepts it as delineating the difference between myth and "rational thought," it still cannot be used to distinguish between philosophy and other forms of rational thought such as science. (And indeed, Thales does seem to be the first entry in both histories of Western philosophy and histories of Western science.) Some writers accept this fact and, stressing the _speculative_ nature of philosophy, claim that science is what happens when certain branches of philosophy find a way of becoming _experimental_ and _empirical_. For example, Sir Isaac Newton, whom we consider an exemplary scientist, titled his main work _The Mathematical Principles of Natural Philosophy_. And in truth, much of what was once touched only by philosophers' speculation has been taken over today by physicists, sociologists, and psychologists.

In spite of this, designating philosophy as simply immature science not only diminishes philosophy, but misses much of what is interesting about it. I suspect (but cannot prove) that there are many philosophical questions that by their very nature can _not_ be made experimental — particularly those having to do with _values_. (When the first Soviet cosmonauts communicated to earth that they had surveyed the skies and discovered that there was no god to be found up there either, one must think that either they were joking or that they badly miscon- strued the problem of God's existence.) Furthermore, philosophical questions often arise _within_ science. When

physicists claim that certain particles are fundamental, the question comes up, by what criteria do we determine that something is "fundamental"? Or what criteria shall we use in medicine for determining death? What counts as the confirmation of a theory? These kinds of philosophical queries, which constantly crop up in science, cannot be ignored; and they prove that philosophy is not just unenlightened science. One influential twentieth-century philosopher, MARTIN HEIDEGGER (1889-1976), in trying to draw a distinction between science and philosophy, claimed that science is a kind of degenerate philosophy and that it has

MARTIN HEIDEGGER

had a bad effect on the history of philosophy. Though Heidegger's view is extreme, it is worth summarizing. He believed that the central problem in philosophy is what might be called "the mystery of Being" and that Thales and his followers (known collectively as the "pre-Socratics") asked what is still the correct philosophical question, namely, "What is the being of Being?"

Heidegger thought that later philosophers (starting about with Plato) betrayed the primary question and asked rather, "What is the being of _beings_?" For example, in Chapter 4, we will see the seventeenth-century French philosopher René Descartes divide the world up into two substances, minds and bodies, and attempt to define and characterize each independently of the other. According to Heidegger, Descartes' project has already abandoned the real question, which concerns the revelation of

Being itself, and has taken up the more shallow question of the nature of specific beings (minds and bodies). For Heidegger the existentialist, the openness to Being was Thales' concern, and it must still be ours to the extent

We must remain open to Being.

that we aspire to philosophical goals.

I think our brief journey to the historical origin of philosophy has been helpful, though not definitive. A number of features of philosophy will probably not get addressed by simply returning to philosophy's Greek source. Another approach, which will get at some of those features, is to list and characterize the various branches of philosophy that are generally recognized today.

Contemporary Branches of Philosophy

If you pick up the catalogue of a typical four-year college or university in the United States and look under the "philosophy" heading, you are likely to find courses offered in the following areas, among others: epistemology, ontology (or metaphysics), logic, ethics (or moral philosophy), political philosophy, and aesthetics, along with a group of courses whose titles begin with the words "philosophy of ____," for example, "philosophy of science," "philosophy of religion," "philosophy of psychology," "philosophy of sport." Let's take a look at what you would study if you signed up for these courses.

Epistemology

Epistemology is theory of knowledge. It concerns questions like these:

What is knowledge, and how does it differ from opinion? Does knowledge require certainty, or can something be known without being known for certain? Does knowledge in fact exist, or must we be satisfied with mere opinion? If there is knowledge, how do we come by it?

(Notice that these questions are conceptual rather than experimental. Only the last of these questions could be made the object of an experiment, strictly speaking, and hence could be claimed to be the dominion of psychology; yet we shall shortly see that even this question is not exclusively, or even mostly, experimental.)

Ontology

Ontology is theory of being. (Some writers prefer to call this "metaphysics.") It concerns the following questions:

What is it for something to be real? What is the nature of existence? What is the difference between appearance and reality?

(Notice that these questions are not experimental because you would already have to have made some tentative decision about them before you could begin any

19

experiment. The questions "Do minds exist?" and "Are prime numbers real?" are not like the questions "Do unicorns exist?" and "Are ghosts real?" To answer the latter questions, experiments and explorations can be imagined. But there are few field trips in philosophy because there is no place to go — or, to put it more accurately, no matter where you are, you are already _there_!)

Philosophy field trip

Logic

Logic is the most specialized branch of philosophy. It is sometimes defined as the science of valid inference. This science, which was founded by Aristotle in the fourth century B.C., is a purely _formal_ study. That is to say, it wants to know what forms of argumentation are valid, and it does not concern itself with the truth status of the argument's conclusion or with the various parts of the argument. For example, the argument:

> All men are mortal.
> Socrates is a man.
> Therefore Socrates is mortal.

is a _valid_ argument and would be so even if it turned out that the first or second line (or "premise") of the argument were false. Even if we discovered that some men are immortal and that Socrates was actually a fish, the argument would be valid purely because of its _form_, which is the following:

All As are Bs.
S is an A.
Therefore S is a B

How old are you, anyway?

9,627 years old.

Then obviously you are _not_ Socrates.

All men are mortal.
Socrates is a man.

The next three branches of philosophy — ethics, political philosophy, and aesthetics — are all versions of AXIOLOGY, which is the study of value. Ethics is the study of moral value, political philosophy is the study of social value, and aesthetics is the study of artistic value, or more widely, the study of beauty.

Ethics

Ethics, or moral philosophy, asks questions like these:

What is the good life? Are there such things as moral duties and obligations that bind us? That is, is there something we truly _ought_ to do? Are some moral arguments "better" than others, or are all of them equally valid or invalid? Are values absolute, or are they relative to time and place?

(Again, notice that these questions are not experimental or empirical. Psychologists may be able to tell us why people hold the moral values they do hold. Sociologists and anthropologists may tell us whether any values are held by all cultures and what the social consequences are of holding certain values. But these are not the same

Look, I'm not saying I *disapprove* of your values or that mine are *better*. I'm just saying that mine are *different*!

questions philosophers ask, though empirical information about values provided by the social sciences may be pertinent to the philosophical questions about morality.)

Political Philosophy

Political philosophy asks questions about social values. It asks:

Can the idea of government be rationally justified, or must all governments be irrational? Do humans have any political duties or social obligations? Under what conditions? Are there such things as natural social rights? Can such rights be justifiably removed as a form of punishment?

(Once more, notice that these questions are *related* to questions asked by political scientists, and sometimes they overlap them — as in the question "Are some forms of government superior to others?" But generally they are not identical to the questions asked by political scientists, the latter of which are basic-ally empirical.)

Aesthetics

The philosophy of fine art, or AESTHETICS, asks about the nature of artistic or aesthetic value. It wants to know the source and justification of aesthetic judgment and whether there are certain necessary features of art or perception that make some artwork or perceptions objectively more valuable than others. Aesthetics

also wants to see how artistic activity fits in conceptually with the rest of human activities.

As mentioned earlier, besides these traditional branches of philosophy, one will also find in college catalogues courses called "Philosophy of X," where X is some field or ac-tivity that itself is <u>not</u> philosophy, such as science, law, sport, religion, or even love and sex. (In fact, aesthetics is such a branch when it is defined as "philos-ophy of fine art," for art itself is <u>not</u> philosophy. Yet it is pos-sible to philosophize about art, and when one does that, one engages in aesthetics.) The reason such fields as these are possible has to do with a feature of philosophy that has been called its "second order" level of analysis. Take a look at this attempted definition of philosophy by William Capitan. I think it fails as an exhaustive definition (they all do!), but it does have the virtue of revealing the side of philosophy we are discussing now. Capitan says philosophy is "rational inquiry into the structure of any thought system, its presuppositions, concepts, and the status of its claims." [2] This definition shows why it is possible to have the "philosophies of ____" and also shows why a course on Marx or Freud might well be taught in a philosophy department even though neither Marx nor Freud is thought of primarily as a philosopher. Freud, for instance, employs certain key concepts, like "sublimation," "projection," "trans- ference," "displace- ment," and "reaction- formation"; and psy-

Marx and Freud are discovered in a philosophy class.

choanalysts look for instantiations of these concepts in human behavior. This is <u>first</u> <u>order</u> analysis. Philosophers do not engage in this "hands on" approach, but take a step back and ask "second order" questions like "What is the logic of these concepts?" "What presuppositions do these concepts make about the mind, knowledge, and value?" "What would count as establishing a case for or against these claims?" Capitan's definition stresses what we can call the analytical or critical aspect of philosophy, what has already been designated here as its "second order" status. A tendency to emphasize this analytical feature of philosophy is also seen in the

24

definition of Stuart Hampshire, a well-known contemporary British philosopher. According to Hampshire, "Philosophy is a free inquiry into the limits of human knowledge, and into the most general categories applicable to experience and reality."[3] With the term "_free_ inquiry," I take it that Hampshire is laying out an _ideal_ condition for philosophy — that its inquiry should be unconstrained by the dictates and requirements of politics, religion, personal advantage, or the demands of other "special interests." I say it is an _ideal_ condition because surely a great deal of what passes for philosophy has bowed one way or another to the demands of extraphilosophical agenda. This "ideal" seems to imply that there is, or ought to be, such a thing as pure reason, or pure logic, and that philosophy should be the pursuit of this unfettered rationality. But in truth it is not likely that the human mind ever functions purely objectively and disinterestedly, independent of nonphilosophical encumbrances, at least concerning issues of any importance. Nevertheless, Hampshire is right — philosophy must engage in self-vigilance and be suspicious of its own motives if it is even to approximate its goal.

Hampshire's definition refers to "the most general categories applicable to experience and reality." This intentionally vague part of his characterization calls attention both to the fact that there are certain key categories of interest to philosophy (such as time, space, existence, sociality, beauty, love, and death) and to philosophy's interest in their _general_ character. By their general character, Hampshire means something like this: I may ask you what time it is, and in doing so, I am certainly not asking a philosophical question. Or you may tell me that it takes less time to fly from San Francisco to Reno than from Reno to St. Louis, and in doing so, you are not making a philosophical

Pardon me, sir. Can you tell me what time it is?

Ooooh. A philosopher!

assertion. But if I ask you not "What time is it?" but "What is time?", then I am asking a general question that is probably a philosophical question (unless, for example, I am simply asking you for the dictionary definition because my English isn't too hot, and I'm not familiar with the word "time"). Similarly, if I ask you what it means for something to be located in space, I am asking a philosophical question, but not if I ask how many chairs will fit around the dining room table.

In this book, I call these general questions the "_big questions._" This is slightly pompous, but not quite as pompous as calling them "the most important questions," as some philosophers do. (It should be admitted forthwith that what makes a question "important" are the circumstances in which it is asked.) One could also call these philosophical questions _deep_ questions, but they are deep not in some presumptuous sense, but in a metaphorically archeological sense, or geological sense. They are deep in the sense that they lie beneath other questions and support them. When I talk about the amount of time it takes to get from point A to point B, then underlying my meaning is some general conception of time, and philosophy critically investigates that underlying general conception.

Let me add yet another attempt to define philosophy.

This one is from Professor Craig Channell. According to him, philosophy is the "ongoing critical activity of developing theories to describe, explain, or account for certain aspects of human experience."[4] Though the last part of his definition is so vague as to be practically useless, his reference to philosophy as an "activity of developing theories" emphasizes a feature of philosophy that the other definitions have understressed — philosophy's _constructive_ and _creative_ side. Some philosophers (especially in the first half of the twentieth century) have thought that philosophy should not develop theories, but should be satisfied with engaging exclusively in criticism and analysis; but, as we shall see, the history of philosophy abounds with grand theoretical schemes trying to show how everything relates to everything else. Almost all of philosophy's "greats" developed such schemes. _This_ feature of philosophy is well captured in Wilfrid Sellars' perhaps slightly facetious definition of philosophy as "an attempt to see how things, in the broadest possible sense of the term, hang together, in the broadest possible sense of the term."[5]

So why are there so many _attempts_ to define philosophy? Why not a straightforward, definitive statement made once and for all? After all, we can do that with words like "triangle." "A triangle is a three-sided closed figure." Anything that is a triangle has those features, and anything that has those features is a triangle. Anything that lacks them is _not_ a a triangle — PERIOD! The reason

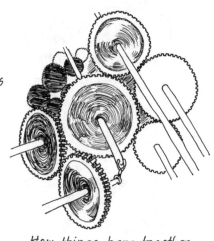

How things hang together

we can give an exhaustive definition of "triangle" but not "philosophy" is probably that the former is a _closed_ concept, and the latter is an _open_ concept. That is, we can state the conditions that are both _necessary_ and _sufficient_ for something's being a triangle, but probably such conditions do not exist for something being a piece of philosophy. Philosophy is not the _only_ open concept. Some of the best are — such as "love" and "art." Let me illustrate. A few years ago I was in a museum of modern art on an uncrowded weekday morning. I wandered into a large room and saw that

The Gravel Pile

it had only a pile of gravel in the middle. At first I thought I had mistakenly trespassed into a room where construction was going on. I started to back out when I noticed that there was a small engraved card on a stand in front of the heap of rock. It contained the words "The Gravel Pile." There were some museum visitors strolling around the pile quietly contemplating this "work." Others were scoffing at it. The question has to come up — "Is this ART?" Only the most arbitrary definition can decide that question for us.

Art has recently gone through a critical period of exuberance and self-doubt. The outer edges of the concept expand and contract and sometimes seem to break. This is perhaps as it should be (more on this in Chapter 11). But even if we are unsure about works on the periphery, that does not prevent us from recognizing cases at the center of the concept. There may be doubt about Robert Barry's conceptual art (his work: _All the things I know but of which I am not at the moment thinking_ — 1:36 P.M.; 15 June 1969, New York), but there can be no doubt about Vermeer's _Girl with Turban_.

The case is similar with philosophy. Most of the questions we will examine are at the center of the concept, but a few will be on the periphery. We will discover that there is no _one_ characteristic, or set of characteristics, that must be necessarily present and when present are sufficient to guarantee that we are doing philosophy and when absent are sufficient to guarantee that we are _not_ doing philosophy. Rather, philosophical inquiries will have what Ludwig Wittgenstein called "family resemblances" when he tried to show what an "open concept" was like. He wrote the following about the open concept "game":

> And we can go through the many, many other groups of games in the same way; can see how similarities crop up and disappear.
> And the result of this examination is: we see a complicated network of similarities overlapping and criss-crossing: sometimes overall similarities, sometimes similarities of detail.
> I can think of no better expression to characterize these similarities than "family resemblances"; for the various resem-

blances between members of a family : build, features, colour of eyes, gait, temperament, etc. etc. overlap and criss-cross in the same way. — And I shall say "games" form a family.[6]

Family resemblance

The Philosophy of Socrates

Let us make one last attempt to understand what philosophy is by trying something different. We will turn to ancient Greece once more and examine the activity of one of the earliest and most famous philosophers, SOCRATES, and hope thereby to gain some insight into the nature of philosophy itself.

Socrates (469 – 399 B.C.), who spent his entire life in Athens, did not give lectures or write treatises. Not only did he not write treatises, he was opposed to writing philosophy in any form be-cause he thought that the letter kills the spirit. Philosophy for Socrates was a kind of social activity, a kind of discourse be-tween two or more people who were looking for the truth. There-fore, his philosophizing took place in the streets of Athens and

SOCRATES

in its shops and parks, where Socrates would engage anyone who was interested in conversation about "higher things." Socrates' wife, Xanthippe, sometimes found Socrates' habits annoying because she would send him on a simple errand, and he would remain for long stretches of time pursuing his philosophical interests. Sometimes he would return hours later without the item he'd been sent out for. According to one story, Socrates had been stumped by a question posed to him during one of these conversations, and he remained standing on the spot all night, chin in hand, thinking. According to another (probably apocryphal) story, Xanthippe, in exasperation, hid his robe so he could not go out and philosophize with the boys. But Socrates slipped out nude, and his disciples began bringing an extra robe in case Socrates arrived naked.

Fortunately, Socrates' brightest disciple, Plato, did not heed his master's advice concerning the written word. Plato wrote down everything he could remember Socrates having said. He transcribed Socrates' words in the same conversational style in which he had heard them, and the result is about twenty famous "Platonic dialogues." If it were not for these, and for the briefer and less philosophical writings of another

Socrates arriving for a philosophy discussion

contemporary, Xenophon, we would know very little of Socrates' teachings. As it is, there are certain problems that students of Socrates have to deal with. How can we be sure that Plato is really giving us the thoughts of Socrates and not his own thoughts? After all, even though Plato's philosophy is an expansion of Socratic thought, we know that Plato developed his own philosophy far beyond Socrates' formulations. There is probably no ultimate solution to this problem; but as a rule of thumb, we can say that the earlier the dialogue, the more authentic the record, and, the later the dialogue, the more likely that Plato is simply using the figure of Socrates as his own spokesman.

Each of the main Platonic dialogues emphasizes one philosophical theme – for example, the nature of truth, beauty, justice, virtue, courage, piety, friendship, or the art of governing. It has been demonstrated that the typical Platonic dialogue of the early period can be schematically divided into three segments. In the

(1)	(2)	(3)

first segment, Socrates meets a young man who claims to _know_ something about one of the aforementioned "big" topics. Socrates flatters the young man and compliments himself on his luck at having found someone who actually _knows_ something that he, Socrates, has been seeking for fifty years — and a _young_ man at that, usually of eighteen, nineteen, or twenty years of age. Socrates begs the young man to impart to him his wisdom. When the young man does so, Socrates acts deeply impressed — sometimes awe-struck. The young man's head begins to swell.

What we can call the second segment of the dialogue begins when Socrates seems to notice some apparently minor problem

How wonderful that you know what virtue is — and to think, you're only 20 years old!

with the formulation of the youth's argument. The young man thinks a simple cosmetic job can cover the blemish, but we readers know that Socrates' objection will become the small thread that, when pulled, unravels the garment. By the end of this second segment, the young man

is confused and admits ignorance. In some of the dialogues, Socrates' cross-examination is quite gentle; in others, it is quite harsh. In one dialogue, the protagonist ends up in tears.

What we call the third and final segment of the dialogue begins when both Socrates and his

SOCRATES! what have you done to me?

? ?

partner have admitted ignorance. The young man does not know what "X" is (virtue, beauty, truth, etc.), and Socrates does not know either. At this point, Socrates will say to his despairing companion something like this: "Look, here we are, two ignorant men, yet two men who _desire_ to know. I am willing to pursue the question seriously if you are willing." And in a certain sense, the real philosophizing begins at this point. It is as if, before any real philosophy can exist, the young man's earlier claim to knowledge had to be shown for what it was — an arrogant, blustering sort of defense mechanism whose function was to disguise the man's ignorance from himself and from others. This is the negative, destructive side of Socrates' method. Then the constructive side comes about in the third part of the dialogue, where Socrates and the young man try out numerous hypotheses meant to discover the truth. Yet in almost every case, the truth remains undiscovered. The Socratic dialogues end inconclusively. Why is this? Before we can answer this, we will have to say more about "Socratic ignorance."

During Socrates' trial for impiety, teaching false doctrines, and corrupting the youth, Socrates tells the jury the story of his friend Chaerephon, who had gone to the temple of Apollo at Delphi to worship and had asked the god (through the oracle, who was the god's spokesperson) who was the wisest man in the world. The oracle answered that Socrates was the wisest. Socrates claimed to be absolutely perplexed by this response because he knew nothing, so how could he be the wisest man in the world? But eventually

Socrates lectures the jury.

Socrates came to realize that in some sense, he was wiser than others. Others knew nothing but _thought_ they knew something; Socrates knew nothing, and _knew_ that he knew nothing. Therefore, he knew more than others.

How seriously are we meant to take this story? It is obviously loaded with irony; Socrates is using it to inform his 501 jurors and his accusers both that they were wrong to charge him with teaching false doctrines (because he knows nothing, he teaches nothing) and wrong to believe that they were in a position to judge him (because as ignorant people, they were in a position to judge no one). And indeed, Socrates' discourse is full of irony. It is clearly part of his method of philosophizing to communicate ironically, indirectly, using flattery, insult, humor, overstatement, understatement, misstatement, poetic allusion, and "old wives' tales" ("old husbands' tales"?). Professor Robert Paul Wolff, in his book _About Philosophy_, has a simple but ingenious analysis of "Socratic ignorance" that we will borrow.[7] Wolff says that we can think of the Socratic dialogue as having three audiences. The first audience is the most naive audience and is usually represented by the young man with whom Socrates discourses. When Socrates says, "I am ignorant," the young man takes this assertion literally and contrasts it with his own supposed state of wisdom. The second audience is more sophisticated and is represented either by characters who appear in the dialogue in some peripheral way or by the readers of the dialogue. This audience thinks, "He is _not_ ignorant. His claim of ignorance is purely ironic." And in some sense, this second audience is surely right. Socrates obviously _does_ know things and knows more than those to whom he professes ignorance. But there is yet a third audience, the most sophisticated one of all, represented, it is hoped, by the most sophisticated readers of the dialogue (namely you and me).

35

This audience says, "He _is_ ignorant." That is to say, in terms of the rigorous standards to which Socrates holds himself and others, he truly does not know. There is a _deep_ sense of knowledge in which the true knower can give an exhaustive account of what he knows, and he understands how that knowledge relates to all other knowledge. Also, the knower has incorporated that knowledge into his life in ways that have transformed him. In other words, for Socrates, he who truly _knows_ justice becomes just, he who knows truth becomes truthful, and

I am ignorant.

He _is_ ignorant.

FIRST AUDIENCE

He is _not_ ignorant.

SECOND AUDIENCE

He is ignorant.

THIRD AUDIENCE

The three audiences

[
TRUTH (trōōth): verity, conformity with fact. Honesty, integrity.
]

he who knows beauty becomes beautiful. There is a kind of knowledge in which one understands how all things are linked, and in this sense, when one knows anything, one knows everything. When one achieves this

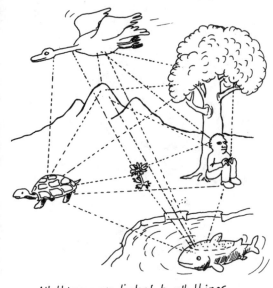

knowledge, one achieves human excellence — <u>aretê</u> in Greek — and one becomes an excellent human being. This is the knowledge Socrates has sought all his life, but it has always eluded him. And in this sense, Socrates does not know. He is <u>ignorant</u>. The irony thickens here, of course,

All things are linked to all things.

because both the least sophisticated and most sophisticated audiences agree that Socrates is ignorant, but for very different reasons.

Now we can return to the question of why the Socratic dialogues all end inconclusively. They <u>must</u> do so. If at the end of the various dialogues, Plato had made Socrates finally define "X" (again, truth, justice, beauty, etc.), this would have been completely misleading, for it would have implied that knowledge could be purely formal — that we could arrive at a dictionary-type definition and memorize it. Then once we had memorized it, we could say we <u>knew</u> it, even though this "knowledge" had in no way affected our lives.

Yet Socrates went to his death still pleading ignorance and claiming at the same time that "the unexamined life is not worth living." At the end of his trial, he bade farewell to his accusers and the jury with these words: "The hour of departure has arrived, and we go our ways — I to die, and you to live. Which is better God only knows." And when asked in his execution room what he would do in the afterlife, if indeed there was an afterlife, he said he would continue doing in death what he had done in life. He would ask the shades in Hades if they had any knowledge. So is this not discouraging — that one of the greatest philosophers and deepest thinkers of all time went to his grave never achieving the knowledge he had spent his life seeking, a knowledge whose search is called "philosophy," and that we cannot even define?

"The unexamined life is not worth living."

Socrates quizzing the shades in Hades

Is this not discouraging to the introductory students on their first day? Perhaps we will be a bit encouraged if we end the chapter with a famous passage from a philosopher who flourished twenty-five hundred years after Socrates, Lord BERTRAND RUSSELL (1872–1970):

LORD RUSSELL

Philosophy is to be studied not for the sake of any definite answers to its questions, since no definite answers can, as a rule, be known to be true, but rather for the sake of the questions themselves; because these questions enlarge our conception of what is possible, enrich our intellectual imagination and diminish the dogmatic assurance which closes the mind against speculation; but above all because, through the greatness of the universe which philosophy contemplates, the mind is also rendered great, and becomes capable of that union with the universe which constitutes its highest good. [8]

Conclusion

Plato claimed that philosophy begins in wonder, and Aristotle commenced one of his books with this line: "All men by nature desire to know." According to this ancient Greek view, we are all philosophers by nature. We are homo philosophicus. If that optimistic picture is true, then there is no need to justify an interest in philosophy. If someone sees you carrying your philosophy book and asks why you are studying philosophy, all you have to say is, "Because I am a human being."

And there is some truth to this ancient Greek view. A person's soul would have to be very shriveled indeed for him never to have asked himself some of the "big questions." Most people do not become professional philosophers, of course. (And there is something odd about the notion of a "professional philosopher." From the Greek point of view, that would be something like becoming a professional human being. Socrates would have been horrified!) Nor do most of us spend most of our time philosophizing. Furthermore, some are probably more naturally philosophical than others — there is such a thing as a philosophical temperament. What provokes us to philosophize? Sometimes the hormones. Sensitive adolescents spend much time agonizing over the meaning of Life, Death, Art (i.e., rock music), and Sociality; and many people seem to go through a classical "midlife crisis" in which the big issues are raised once again. But it doesn't have to be hormonal. Sometimes a most insignificant occurrence can plunge us into a philosophical meditation, as can a dramatic or traumatic event, such as the loss of a close relative, a friend, or a lover. We will be philosophers all of our lives, and I am partial to the Greek / Russellian view that philosophizing magnifies our humanity. I am guilty of holding the opinion that the person who never philosophizes is somehow less of a person.

A sensitive adolescent agonizing over the meaning of life while his father goes through midlife crisis.

So if one is necessarily going to philosophize, why not do it well? Why should we think that activities like eating, driving, and earning money should be done well, but thinking about the big questions can be done sloppily with impunity? Let's have a little _aretê_ here too. Therefore, I recommend that you give yourself over to the "professionals," if only for this one semester. For many of you, this will be the only philosophy course you take in your lifetime — a bunch of philosophy courses is not everyone's cup of tea, and there are many pressures on one's college planning. This is even more reason to take this one course seriously.

Philosophers and philosophical theories can be read like great novels. The great novelists (Cervantes, Flaubert, Dostoyevsky, Proust, Joyce, Mann, etc.) hand you a pair of magical spectacles and invite you to look through them. It is as if they said, "If you look at the world through these glasses, you will see things you have never seen before, and having once seen them, they will be yours to possess forever." So it is with really good philosophy. Philosophical concepts offer themselves as possible interpretations of the world. The world is very complex, and the more possible interpretations of it make themselves available to us, the more free and more effective we will be in the world. Philosophical concepts are like tools. The bigger our repertoire of tools, the more effective our work.

In this vein, the twentieth-century Austrian philosopher LUDWIG WITTGENSTEIN (_much_ more about him in Chapter 11) made great use of a figure now usually referred to as "Wittgenstein's duck/rabbit." Is this a duck or a rabbit? Of course, it can be read either way. The question "What is it _really_?" does not apply here. The suggestion I am making is that the world is much more like Wittgenstein's figure than we first realize. Creative solutions

The duck/rabbit

to the problems with which life presents us require the ability to make multifarious interpretations of the world. Philosophy gives us some tools for such creative interpretation. Often the world is much more varied than to allow only two interpretations (duck or rabbit?). It is more like this figure, suggested by Virgil Aldrich, who says, "...look at this figure under these five titles: (1) square suspended in a frame, (2) lampshade seen from above, (3) lampshade seen from below, (4) looking into a tunnel, and (5) aerial view of a truncated pyramid."⁹

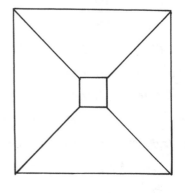

And if, after having inspected some of these philosophical tools, we choose never to use them as viable interpretations of the world, we still come away with an advantage, for they will have served as critical analyses of our ordinary beliefs. If we conclude that our ordinary beliefs have withstood philosophical scrutiny, so much the better. To paraphrase Aristotle (taking some liberties in doing so), in terms of getting you a job, philosophy may be the most useless of all studies, but it is nevertheless the best.

Notes

1. Robert Pirsig, _Zen and the Art of Motorcycle Maintenance_ (New York: Bantam Books, 1975), pp. 315-316.

2. William H. Capitan, _Philosophy of Religion: An Introduction_ (New York: Pegasus, 1972), p. 1.

3. Stuart Hampshire, _The Age of Reason_ (New York: New American Library, 1961), p. 12.

4. Craig Channell, "The Advocacy Method: A Reply," _Teaching Philosophy_, Vol. 1, No. 1 (Summer, 1975), p. 41.

5. Wilfrid Sellars, quoted in Richard Rorty, "The Fate of Philosophy," _New Republic_ (Oct. 18, 1982), p. 28.

6. Ludwig Wittgenstein, _Philosophical Investigations_ (New York: Macmillan, 1964), p. 32.

7. Robert Paul Wolff, _About Philosophy_, 4th ed. (Englewood Cliffs, New Jersey: Prentice-Hall, 1989), p. 14.

8. Bertrand Russell, _The Problems of Philosophy_ (New York: Oxford University Press, 1975), p. 161.

9. Virgil C. Aldrich, _Philosophy of Art_ (Englewood Cliffs, New Jersey: Prentice-Hall, 1963), p. 20.

Chapter 2

Truth Is Beauty, Beauty Is Truth

Rationalist Epistemology

Epistemology is theory of knowledge. These are the big questions in epistemology: what is knowledge? What is the difference between opinion and knowledge? Does knowledge require certainty? What are the limits of knowledge? Is knowledge in fact possible?

The word "knowledge" seems perhaps a bit highfalutin; still, we are all familiar with it, and we certainly use the verb "to know" a score of times throughout any day.

- Do you know what time it is?

- I used to know that word in French, but I've forgotten it.

- She knew all the material on the test.

- We didn't know he would arrive today.

In ordinary discourse, what do we mean by "know" when we say things like this? I take it that when we say someone knows something, we mean more or less that he or she could come up with a right answer on demand. But, justifiably or unjustifiably, philosophers have not been satisfied with this account of the meaning of

44

"knowledge." In fact, this dissatisfaction began early in the history of philosophy. We have already seen that in the fifth century B.C., Socrates insisted on a more rigorous notion of knowledge than that provided by common sense. His demand came to fruition in the epistemology of PLATO (427-347 B.C.).

The Philosophy of Plato

Plato's analysis of the concept of knowledge can be set forth in the following manner. Take the sentence, "P knows X" (where "P" is any person, and "X" is any fact). What must be the case before such a sentence could be true? First, it must be true that "P believes X." You can't claim that you _know_ something if you also claim that you don't believe it. (I can think of only one kind of case to the contrary. If someone knocks on your door and you open it to discover a friend with whom you've been out of touch for fifteen years, you may exclaim, "Joe Smith, I don't believe it!" But, of course, you _do_ believe it. Otherwise you would simply shut the door and go back to watching T.V.) Then _belief_ is a necessary part of knowledge, but it is certainly

45

Believing something very
very strongly

not the _whole_ of knowledge. (Just because I believe something strongly doesn't mean I _know_ it, ... not even if I believe it, very, very strongly.) Then what more besides belief is needed? Truth is required. X must be the case. No one has ever known that the earth is flat for the simple reason that the earth is _not_ flat. Even if thousands of people once claimed to know that the

earth was flat, _we_ know that all of them were wrong. (C. S. Lewis once suggested that, before Columbus, people did _not_ think that the earth was flat; not because they thought it was round, but because they didn't think about it at all.) So now we have this:

    P knows X .

entails (a) P believes X.,
and   (b) X is the case.

Knowing that the earth is flat

(a) and (b) are necessary parts of knowledge. But are they sufficient? That is, does _true belief_ constitute knowledge? Plato denied it, more or less for the following kind of reason. Suppose you ask me if I know that the earth is round, and I say I do. Do I believe that it is round? Yes. Is it round? Yes. (I am purposely ignoring here the fact that in truth the earth is slightly pear shaped. [Well, you would be pear shaped too if you were spinning at a thousand miles an hour.]) So why doesn't this constitute

Knowledge ? Suppose you ask me _how_ I know that the earth is round, and I say, "Take a look at the bottom of your feet. Do you see how they are arched? Now I ask you, would God give us rounded feet if the earth were flat?" Suddenly you would realize that I didn't know at all that the earth was round. I had just made a lucky guess!

Being pear shaped while spinning at 1000 miles per hour

Proof that the world is round — direct method

So if true belief is not sufficient for knowledge, what would be?

P knows X.

(a) P believes X.

(b) X is true.

(c) P can give the LOGOS for X. The Greek word "_logos_" is the source of our word "logic," as well as the source of all those terms ending in "....logy" (biology - the theory or study of living things, sociology — the theory or study of society, etc.). So to give the _logos_ for X is to be able to give the theory, or the result of a study, that explains X. _Logos_ also means "word" in Greek; one has to be able to _SAY_ what that theory is. If someone told Plato or Socrates that she knew the answer to a question but just couldn't _SAY_ it, Socrates and Plato would charge that precisely what was proved is that that person did _not_ know the answer.

For Plato, to give the _logos_ of X is to justify your belief in

X, and for him, knowledge is justified belief. This seems pretty sound, but the idea of justification is quite technical in Plato, as we have already seen. In fact, it is even more technical than the foregoing analysis revealed, as you will discover when we turn to Plato's famous "Simile of the Line," which is the centerpiece of his most important work, <u>The Republic</u>.

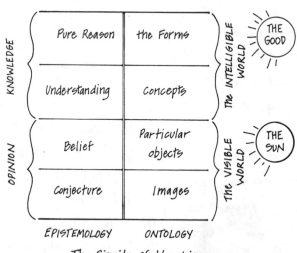

The Simile of the Line

What we get here is Plato's whole metaphysical scheme. The right side of the line is his ONTOLOGY (his theory of being). The left side is his EPISTEMOLOGY (his theory of knowledge). There is also implicit here an ETHICS and an AESTHETICS. We will concentrate on the left side of the line because it corresponds with the topic of this chapter, but in order to do so, a few words must be said about the ontological side of the line as well.

The <u>visible world</u> (i.e., the physical world) is composed of two strata: sensible objects and images.

Images

Shadows and reflections are the examples Plato offers us of images.

They are dependent on the sensible objects of which they are images. The shadow of a tree is for Plato _less real_ than the tree, both because the tree lasts longer than the shadow and because the tree can exist without the shadow, but the shadow can't exist without the tree. Now switch to the left side of the line. On this side, we have not _things_ (like shadows or trees), but _mental states_ — states of awareness. If the object of your state of awareness is an image, you are in a state of imagination. (There's a lot of trouble translating the Greek word _eikasia_. Other translations are "conjecture" and "guessing.") The implication in the _Republic_ is that this state is one of deception. The person in this state confuses an image with a thing. (Have

you ever been attracted to the _photo_ of someone, or yelled "Go 'Niners!" during a televised football game? No? It's never happened to _me_ either — but then, _we_ are philosophy students!)

Isolde mistaking the shadow of a tree trunk for Tristan

Sensible Objects

These are the individual things in the physical world: trees, books, cats. They are more real than images, but they are not absolutely real, both because they are not permanent (trees and cats grow old and die; books fall apart or are burned) and because they are dependent. They are dependent first of all on the _sun_. (If

the sun were closer
everything would burn up;
if it were farther away,
everything would freeze;
if it did not exist, there
would be no trees, books,
or cats and no images
of them either.) And
as we will see shortly,
sensible objects are
also dependent on the
forms.

Trees and cats grow old; books fall apart.
(The center does not hold.)

Back to the left
side of the line. If the
object of your awareness
is a sensible object, you
are in a state of <u>belief.</u>
Imagine seing an
animal in a field and
asking a local farmer
what the creature is.
He says, "It's a horse."

Cats and shadows are dependent on the sun.

you ask him how he knows it's a horse, and he says (impatiently,
no doubt), "It's a horse! Take a look. A horse is a horse!" OK. The
farmer <u>believes</u> it's a horse (belief); it is a horse (truth); so
why does Plato say that the farmer doesn't <u>know</u> it's a horse?
Because the farmer hasn't given the <u>logos.</u> What would that be like?
Well, perhaps something like this: you ask the farmer....

This man knows. He was able to raise the individual perception to the conceptual level. (There are lots of problems here, of course, including the problem of _elitism_ — on this account, of all the millions of people who have dealt with horses, only a select few have actually known what one is [and Plato wasn't one of them!]. Furthermore, it's hard to see how _you_ could know what a horse is without performing a biopsy and understanding biology and chemistry. Indeed, it's beginning to look as though one would have to know _everything_ in order to know _anything._ Some interpreters believe that this is exactly what Plato had in mind. It would at least make sense of Socrates' claim to be ignorant.)

Concepts

So we've seen that one leaves belief for understanding (and thereby opinion for knowledge) by raising the perception to the conceptual level, that is, by subsuming the particular under the general. One does this by placing it in the context of _logos_, of a _theory_ or a _science_. Let's illustrate this. Imagine three different episodes: (1) Your pen rolls from the desk and falls to the floor. (2) A meteorite falls into the earth's atmosphere, splashing silver sparks into the night sky. (3) In the sixth round of a heavyweight boxing match, the champion receives a body-jolting uppercut on the chin and falls to the canvas like a load of bricks. In each of these cases, the imagery would be described very differently (this is the level of perception), but to understand the three events, we would need a theory, the very theory discovered by Sir Isaac Newton: given any two masses, these masses mutually attract each other in direct proportion to their mass and in indirect proportion to their distance. This is knowledge. But apparently for Plato it is not the highest kind of knowledge. There is still pure reason to be dealt with.

Gravity at work

Forms

According to Plato, the concepts with which we have been dealing here (horse, gravity) are not mere abstractions from concrete cases. They are <u>images</u> of higher truths, and he called these higher truths the <u>Forms</u>. These Forms are the archetypes of everything existing in the visible world. They exist outside time and space. They are not physical, but they aren't mental either. Because they are not physical, they cannot be grasped by the senses; and even though they are not mental, they can be grasped only by the intellect, which has transcended the senses. These Forms are real in the sense that they are uncreated, indestructible, unchanging, and therefore eternal. Notice that they are not _absolutely_ real because they are still dependent — upon something Plato calls "the Good" — dependent in the same way that sensible things are dependent on the sun. The Good seems to be a kind of Super-Form, the Form of all Forms, which is an absolute value that grounds all reality and bestows worth on it, very much the way God would later do in the ontology of the medieval period. (Drop one letter, "o," from "Good" [= God],

GOOD

TRUTH

BEAUTY

JUSTICE

VIRTUE

GENERAL NICENESS

The heaven of Forms

and change the "u" in "Sun" to "o" [= Son], and you have a crude version of medieval Christian Platonism.)

Now, how can the mind grasp the Forms? Only by _totally_ transcending the senses, which are somehow committed to the world of Becoming, hence naturally hostile to the world of Being. Concepts, though definitely part of the intelligible sphere, are still image-bound and hence, somehow still _contaminated_. (Notice the anti-body bias that enters into Western philosophy

Transcending the five senses

here with Plato. It is very uncharacteristic of the Greeks.) Earlier, when you were presented with Newton's definition of gravity ("Given any two masses..., etc."), you saw two masses in your mind's eye. However, the mind grasps the Form and not merely the Concept when it frees itself from that visual imagery. This it does by mathematizing its object. It is as if, for person P, the move from the definition ("Given any two masses. ...") to the formula ($F = \frac{Gm_1m_2}{d^2}$) liberates the truth from the flux of the world, and grasping the ultimate

intelligible order of the universe is to grasp it purely formally, i.e., mathematically. If this interpretation of Plato is correct (and there certainly are other interpretations), then Plato believed that there existed not only a correct formula for Horse and Gravity but for Love and Beauty as well.

Many of us today are prepared to grant the former, but we resist the latter. We point to the notorious relativity of taste of

A punk beauty arguing with a Ubangi beauty about beauty

54

different individuals and cultures to refute Plato. (Parisians and Ubangis do not agree as to what beauty is.) But for Plato, if both the Parisian fashion model and the Ubangi princess are truly beautiful, there must be a common denominator. Perhaps it has to do with a mathematical account of "order" involving grace, balance, and "eros." Perhaps someday Beauty's Sir Isaac Newton will come along and finish this equation: "$B = \_\_\_\_\_.$"

Finally, concerning Plato, let's ask about the process of learning in his theory. The dialogue that deals with this process is the <u>Meno</u>. There, Meno and Socrates have been discussing "virtue," and whether it can be taught. Socrates has forced Meno to admit that he doesn't know what virtue is, hence that he doesn't know whether it can be taught. (That is, Socrates has brought the dialogue to the end of the "second phase" referred to in Chapter 1.) Both Socrates and Meno admit that they are ignorant, and Socrates says that he is willing to pursue the issue seriously if Meno is willing. Here Meno states what has come to be called "Meno's paradox":

MENO: And how will you try to find out something, Socrates, when you have no notion at all what it is? Will you lay out before us a thing you don't know, and then try to find it? Or, if at best you meet it by chance, how will you know this is that which you did not know?

SOCRATES: I understand what you wish to say, Meno. ... as if a man cannot try to find either what he knows or what he does not know. Of course, he would never try to find what he knows, because he knows it, and in that case he needs no trying to find; or what he does not know, because he does not know what he will try to find.

MENO: Then don't you think that is a good argument, Socrates?

SOCRATES: Not I. [1]

In the dialogue, Socrates seems not to take Meno's paradox very seriously.

This (false) impression is fortified
by the fact that Socrates responds
to Meno not with a philo-
sophical argument
but with a
story he
had heard
from
priests
and
poets:

How do you recognize the truth when you see it?

They say
that the
soul of
man is
immortal,
and sometimes it comes to an end — which they call death ~ and
sometimes it is born again, but it is never destroyed; ... Then,
since the soul is immortal and often born, having seen what is on
earth and what is in the house of Hades, and everything, there is
nothing it has not learnt; so there is no wonder about virtue
and other things, because it knew about these before.[2]

But the seriousness with which Socrates takes both Meno's paradox
and the poetic rejoinder to it is seen in the episode that occurs immediately after in the dialogue. Meno and Socrates are strolling in
a garden, and they come across the gardener, an untutored slave boy.
Socrates asks him to solve a fairly complicated geometrical problem
— that of doubling the square. The boy objects that he hasn't
studied mathematics, but Socrates, undeterred, begins to ask him
a series of questions: Should we solve the problem by using arcs
or straight lines? (Try straight lines.) Should we put the straight
lines inside or outside the square? (First outside, then, when
that fails, inside.) After a long series of questions that the boy can

answer with a "yes" or a "no," the boy eventually produces the correct answer — a diagram like this: ↘

The slave boy knows more than he knows that he knows.

So, according to Socrates, the unschooled slave boy was able to answer a difficult mathematical question without being given any information he did not already possess. You and I may feel that Socrates' method in this case involved some intellectual sleight of hand, but Plato's conclusion is that the slave boy already knew the answer to the question, but he did not <u>know</u> that he knew it. The truth, according to Plato, existed in the slave boy's soul. It was a piece of unconscious knowledge, knowledge based on an INNATE IDEA, that is, an idea present at birth in the soul of the individual. On this account, all learning is truly remembering, and it answers "Meno's paradox" (how will we recognize something we don't know?) by

Innate knowledge

57

saying that in fact we do know what we don't know, and recognition is recollection. So Plato, like Freud and Proust (author of the seven-volume novel, _Remembrance of Things Past_) takes the phenomenon of memory absolutely seriously and makes it a central feature of his theory of knowledge.

Let's review some of the key features of Plato's epistemology. To know is to transcend the ever-changing flux of the physical world and to grasp a permanent rational order behind the flux, an order that will demonstrate the universal in the particular. This "grasping" is an intellectual act of the mind, which, in its purest manifestation, is exclusively formal (i.e., mathematical). Such an intellectual act can take place only if there are certain innate ideas upon which it can be based. Knowing, then, is an act of making the observable world intelligible by showing how it is related to an eternal order of intelligible truths. All of this is the program of rationalism, one of the two key epistemological poles in Western thought.

Platonic rationalism was immediately countered by Aristotelian empiricism (to be discussed in Chapter 3) but managed to dominate later Greek and Roman philosophy and all of the early Middle Ages, once again to be countered by a revival of Aristotelianism in the work of St. Thomas Aquinas in the thirteenth century.

René Descartes' Rationalism

Rationalism may have achieved its fullest maturity in the seventeenth century in the work of RENÉ DESCARTES (1596-1650). We will inspect his version of rationalism before looking at rationalism's alternatives.

Theories of knowledge are never created in a vacuum. There are always psychological, economic, social, and political conditions behind them, acting as motives for them. In a certain sense, perhaps, each epistemology, rather than describing and accounting for some autonomous thing called "knowledge," actually creates and validates its own "knowledge," which is circumscribed and limited by the intellectual, economic, social, and political forces that motivated the epistemology in the first place. The external circumstances that motivated Plato were very different from those

RENÉ DESCARTES (1596-1650)

that motivated Descartes. Plato, a man of noble ancestry, lived at a time when the old aristocratic system of governing was collapsing in the face of the emergence of a new commercial class and an incipient democracy. In the two-hundred-year period before Plato's time, social and intellectual conditions had conspired to undermine the moral authority of the old aristocratic values, whose canon was the myths of Homer and Hesiod.

I do not know.

Theories of knowledge are never created in a vacuum.

As the old values of honor, loyalty, courage, and the natural right of the nobility to govern deteriorated, they were being replaced with what to Plato were plebeian values that thinly disguised greed and the thirst for power. These values were taught in Socrates' and Plato's day by the professors of rhetoric known as "the Sophists." In order to counteract their corroding influence and to maintain some structure that justified rule by an elite, Plato not only had to attack the Sophists, but also had to oppose

The old aristocratic values collapsing under the onslaught of the new rabble (Plato's view)

the authority of Homer and replace it with the authority of Pure Reason. The works of Homer had embodied the aristocratic values that Plato wished to support, but Homer had offered no defense of those values except an appeal to the emotions through his poetic discourse. If Plato was to defend values rationally, he had to replace the power of poetry (as manifested in Greek myth and drama) with that of philosophy, the spokeswoman for reason.

The poetry / philosophy opposition is _not_ the one that faced René Descartes in the seventeenth century; rather, he was

The contest between philosophy and poetry

60

confronted by the opposition religion/science. Descartes lived during the period that saw the birth of the new sciences. Copernicus had been dead only forty years when Descartes was born. Descartes was a contemporary of Galileo and Kepler. Newton was eight years old when Descartes died. In fact, Descartes himself had made a major contribution to the history of science while still in his twenties by discovering analytical geometry.

Now the ever-increasing power of the new science was beginning to challenge the waning authority of the Church, which, though having dominated for a thousand years, had suffered several important setbacks in the two hundred years before Descartes' birth (a series of internal schisms, defeats at the hands of secular rulers, and the creation of the Protestant reformation). The Church was fighting to retain not only what political power it still had, but also its custody over the human <u>moral</u> self-image. It was in this sphere that the new sciences seemed to be most directly challenging religious authority, and the confrontation came to a head in 1632, when the Inquisition arrested Galileo, tried him, and found him guilty of impiety. The specific event that provoked Galileo's arrest was the publication of an essay reporting his discovery that there were three moons orbiting the planet Jupiter. Now, it may not be obvious to you why the religious authorities would be threatened by such a claim. The traditional view of what was at stake in the Galileo

affair is this:[3] For a thousand years, the concept of human dignity was closely bound to the idea that God had created the Garden of Eden in the very center of the universe and that the rest of the cosmos was formed as a series of concentric circles radiating out of Eden, the belly button of reality. This meant that the human drama was the _key_ drama in the cosmos and that every other being in the universe was simply placed here as a witness to the human drama. This had the effect of imbuing every act with _meaning_. Even if one's life was filled with misery (and there was plenty of misery in the medieval world), at least that misery had _significance_; hence there was a certain dignity in even the most miserable human existence.

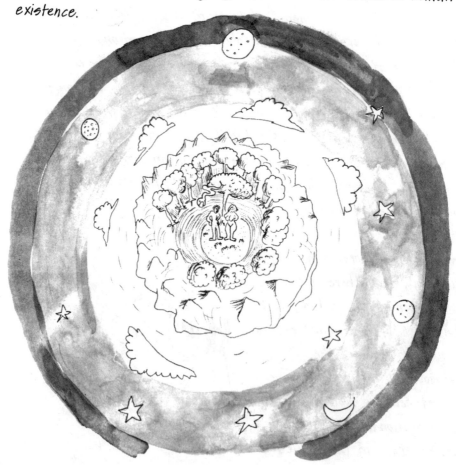

Now this heroic conception of human life was suddenly threatened by the Copernican theory that the earth was not the center of the universe — that the earth and the other planets actually orbited the sun (that is, that the heliocentric and not the geocentric theory was correct). If the earth is just hurtling through space with no more and no less meaning than that of any other body in the universe, what would this mean for the concept of human dignity? (Freud once said that human dignity has suffered three mortal blows: first, Copernicus' discovery that the human is not at the center of the universe; second, Darwin's discovery that the human is an animal; and third, Freud's discovery that the animal is sick.) But there was one scientific fact

I don't think I can take any more revelations, Doc.

that prevented the Copernican radicals from winning the day. It is the undisputed fact that the earth's moon orbits the earth. If the heliocentric theory were true, why would the moon orbit the earth? Why wouldn't it travel around the sun the same way the earth was supposed to do? Now you see the significance of Galileo's discovery. If Jupiter's moons orbit Jupiter, then that proves that moons can orbit planets which are <u>not</u> the center of the universe; and that proof kicked the last strut out from under the geocentric theory.

Descartes found himself in an awkward situation. He was a dedicated Catholic who did not look forward to a confrontation with the ecclesiastical authorities; yet he had just finished a manuscript on physics (_The World_), many sections of which he knew would agree with the views of Galileo. So rather than publish his manuscript, he decided to write a book of philosophy that would create an intellectual climate of reconciliation between science and religion. He wanted to show that the idea of being a "Catholic scientist" was not self-contradictory. Indeed, he wanted to show that the possibility of science itself presupposed certain theological assumptions. This book was called _Meditations on First Philosophy_ and was dedicated to "the Most Wise and Illustrious Men: The Dean and Doctors of the Sacred Faculty of Theology in Paris." To them he said,

> [E]veryone indeed believes that it is not possible to discover elsewhere more perspicacity and solidity, or more integrity

and wisdom in pronouncing judgment. For this reason, I have no doubt that if you deign to take the trouble in the first place of correcting this work, ... and then, after adding to it these things that are lacking to it, completing those which are imperfect, and yourselves taking the trouble to give a more ample explanation of those things which have need of it, ... when this is done, and when finally the reasonings by which I prove that there is a God, and that the human soul differs from the body, ... I do not doubt, I say, that henceforward all the errors and false opinions which have ever existed regarding these two questions will soon be effaced from the minds of men. [4]

The collision course between religion and science

Descartes' self-denigrating, humble deference to the theologians of the Sorbonne is moving, but to his friend, Father Mersenne, he wrote in a very different tone: "... and I want to say, just between us, that these six _Meditations_ contain all the fundamental ideas of my physics. But please keep this quiet, because if they knew it, the Aristotelians would be very reluctant to accept my views." [5]

In my own opinion, Descartes was succesful in his undertaking. As far as I can determine, Catholicism never again had a head-on confrontation with science. Descartes had demonstrated that such a collision course was not necessary. It seems to me that today most religious opposition to scientific theories comes from certain Protestant camps (e.g., opposition to the teaching of Darwin's theory of evolution). Perhaps the Protestants are still waiting for their Descartes.

Well then, let us turn to Descartes' epistemology as he developed it in the _Meditations_. In the first paragraph of that book, Descartes announces his grandiose proposal: " I must once for all seriously undertake to rid myself of all the opinions which I had formerly accepted, and commence to build anew from the foundation, if I wanted to establish any firm and permanent structure in the sciences (p. 165).

Notice that there is a key metaphor in this passage, one taken from carpentry. Knowledge is seen as a building in which all the superstructure is resting on a foundation, and the building is only as strong as the foundation. (You will observe as you proceed that philosophers often develop their ideas around a key metaphor. For instance, think of the role played in Plato's thought by the

notions of light and darkness.) Descartes continues:

I shall at last seriously and freely address myself to the general upheaval of all my former opinions.
Now for this object it is not necessary that I should show that all of these are false — I shall perhaps never arrive at this end. But inasmuch as reason already persuades me that I ought no less carefully to withhold my assent from matters which are not entirely certain and indubitable than from those which appear to me manifestly to be false, if I am able to find in each one some reason to doubt, this will suffice to justify my rejecting the whole (p 166).

Here we see Descartes' technique, which has come to be known as "methodological doubt." It has a motto, " De omnibus dubitandum est" (everything is to be doubted), and it requires Descartes to doubt any proposition whatsoever if he can find the slightest reason to do so. Notice that, unlike courts of law, methodological doubt does not require that the doubt be _reasonable_; rather, any possible doubt will be sufficient to put the proposition out of commission. And the point of all this doubting is to attempt to find something that cannot be doubted, something indubitable, absolutely certain. That absolute certainty, if it exists, will be the foundation of the house of knowledge.

> I shall proceed by setting aside all that in which the least doubt could be supposed to exist, just as if I had discovered that it was absolutely false; and I shall ever follow in this road until I have met with something which is certain, or at least, if I can do nothing else, until I have learned for certain that there is nothing in the world that is certain (p. 170).

A word more needs to be said about "methodological doubt," lest it be confused with _real_ doubt and Descartes be taken for a madman. Suppose I've got a girlfriend who tells me that she would prefer not to go out with me tonight. She'd like to relax by herself at her apartment. About 9:30 P.M. I give her a phone call, and no one answers. A half-hour later I call again. Still no answer. Then I call every ten minutes, with the same negative results. About 2 A.M. she answers and asks why I've called so late. I inform her that I called a bit earlier, and she stammers, "Oh yes, I ... I ... ran out of eggs, so I went down to the convenience shop to get some." I know that it doesn't take five hours to get eggs. A

Five hours to buy a dozen eggs?

Skepticism

67

doubt develops in my mind. It is a _real_ doubt and a reasonable one. I doubt that she is telling me the truth.

OK, now change the example. I am at a restaurant with my girlfriend. She excuses herself to go to the powder room. I time her. It takes her seventy-two seconds. When she returns, I demand, "What did you do there?!" Taken aback, she responds, "What does one do in a powder room? I powdered!" I say, "How do I know you didn't meet a man there? It is _possible_ to meet a man in seventy-two seconds. It's happened before!" _This_ doubt, which is surely a _paranoid_ doubt, is much more like Descartes' doubt than is the first one. If you confuse Descartes' methodological doubt with real doubt,

Paranoia?

Descartes will seem like a paranoid to you. He is not a paranoid; he is a philosopher (though it is true, as we've already mentioned, that some-times it's not easy to tell madness and philosophy apart).

Descartes' rule, "Every-thing is to be doubted," is not recommended as a way of life. It is part of a philosophical game, but a _serious_ game. The point of the game is to discover the foundations of knowledge, if there is such a thing to be discovered. And if there is no foundation to discover, then the game will be abandoned, and one will return to real life. But one will return with much more cynicism than one had before the game because one will "know" that there is no such thing as knowledge; only opinions, hearsay, prej-udices, and passions exist. The "house of knowledge" is built on shifting sands.

Let us return to the project of the <u>Meditations</u>. Descartes continues:

> All that up to the present time I have accepted as most true and certain I have learned either from the senses or through the senses; but it is sometimes proved to me that these senses are deceptive, and it is wiser not to trust entirely to anything by which we have once been deceived (p. 166).

Here we see that Descartes' dismantling of the rotten timbers from the house of knowl-
edge is done more with a bulldozer than a crowbar. Because the senses are known deceivers, they will be doubted away, which means that all beliefs based on the senses (and that is <u>most</u>

René Descartes - heavy equipment operator

of them, after all) will be jettisoned. But suddenly Descartes himself suspects that perhaps his house bashing is moving too fast. He says:

> But it may be that although the senses sometimes deceive us concerning things which are hardly perceptible, or very far away, there are yet many others to be met with as to which we cannot reasonably have any doubt, although we recognize them by their means. For example, there is the fact that I am here, seated by the fire, attired in a dressing gown, having this paper in my hands and other similar matters. And how should I deny that these hands and this body are mine, were it not perhaps that I compare myself to certain persons, devoid of sense, whose cerebella are so troubled and clouded by the

violent vapours of black bile, that they constantly assure us that they think they are kings when they are really quite poor, or that they are clothed in purple when they are really without covering, or who imagine that they have an earthenware head or are nothing but pumpkins or are made of glass. But they are mad, and I should not be any the less insane were I to follow examples so extravagant (p. 166).

So there is René Descartes, sitting in his PJs alone at his desk in front of his fireplace. (Quite a different stage from that of old Socrates, who philosophized in the streets of Athens, seeing philosophy as essentially a _social_ activity! It is clear that the notion of thinking has undergone a dramatic change since the Greek period.) He stares at his hand and thinks, "This is my hand." How could he possibly be wrong? Only a madman could stare at his hand and wonder if it is his hand. If, after leaving your classroom, you see someone sitting on the campus lawn staring at his hand, and the person says to you, "I'm not sure this is my hand," you won't say to yourself, "A philosopher!" Rather, you'll say, "A lunatic!" Descartes knows this perfectly well; yet, following the strictures of radical doubt, he does indeed question whether what he is looking at is his hand.

70

(By the way, did you notice the marvelous baroque description of madness? "... cerebella ... troubled and clouded by the violent vapours of black bile....") Descartes continues :

> At the same time I must remember that... I am in the habit of sleeping, and in my dreams representing to myself the same things or sometimes even less probable things, than do those who are insane in their waking moments. How often has it happened to me that in the night I dreamt that I found my-self in this particular place, that I was dressed and seated near the fire, whilst in reality I was lying undressed in bed! .... I remind myself that on many occasions I have in sleep been deceived by similar illusions, and in dwelling carefully on this reflection I see so manifestly that there are no certain indications by which we may clearly distinguish wake-fulness from sleep that I am lost in astonishment (pp. 166-167).

Do you get Descartes' point? Can you refute him? Can you <u>think of a test that will prove you are not dreaming now</u>? Obviously, pinching yourself (as they do in the comics) won't work because it is quite possible to dream that you are pinching yourself. For the same reason, you can't just ask your neighbor, "Am I dreaming?" It is possible to dream whatever answer she gives. In fact, it seems that Descartes has us over a barrel be-cause the only way to refute him would be to think of a test that

Philosophy student dreaming about dreams

can't be dreamed. But any test you can <u>think</u> of, you can dream. (A student of mine once suggested that one can't dream that one is dead. This may be true, but I think that killing yourself to refute Descartes would be a rather extreme measure. And, of course, even such a philosophical martyrdom would fail because you would never know whether it had worked.)

Philosophical martyrdom

Descartes' conclusion is not that one should keep wondering whether one is dreaming, but that there is no philosophical proof that at any given moment one is not dreaming. Therefore, the senses and the commonsense picture of the world based on the senses cannot be the foundation of knowledge.

Let's start diagramming some of this:

```
┌─────────────────────────────────┐
│   The commonsense picture       │
│   of the world, based on the    │
│         SENSES.                 │
├─────────────────────────────────┤
│   Argument from                 │
│      ILLUSIONS.                 │
├─────────────────────────────────┤
│   Argument from                 │
│      DREAMS.                    │
└─────────────────────────────────┘
```

⎰ The candidacy of this for
⎱ "foundation of knowledge"
  is attacked
by
these.

Can there be another candidate? What about mathematics? Descartes says: "For whether I am awake or asleep, two and three together always form five, and the square can never have more than four sides, and it does not seem possible that truths so clear and apparent can be suspected of any falsity or uncertainty" (p. 168). Descartes' point here as he states it seems wrong. If I can make a mathematical error when I'm awake, I can jolly well make one when I'm dreaming!

But the real point Descartes is trying to make here is worth pausing over. It requires learning two technical philosophical terms that are of some value, _a priori_ and _a posteriori_. An _a priori_ claim is a claim whose truth or falsity can be known independently of observation. An _a posteriori_ claim is one whose truth or falsity can be known only by appealing to observation. Now, Descartes' point can be put this way: the "argument from illusion" and the "argument from dreams" can attack only _a posteriori_ claims. But mathematics is _a priori_; hence it should escape both of these skeptical arguments. One does not prove that 3 + 2 = 5 by taking a field trip or doing an experiment. Putting three pieces of chalk next to two pieces of chalk and counting them is no proof that 3 + 2 = 5, any more than finding five white swans is proof that all swans are white. (The way you prove that 3 + 2 = 5 is by demonstrating that that proposition is a version of the proposition, A = A, then demonstrating that any denial that A = A leads to a self-

73

One plus one...

Mathematical experiment

contradiction. This kind of proof is not an act of perception but is what Plato would call an act of "pure reason.")

So what Descartes is asking is whether the _a priori_ truths of mathematics might not serve as the absolutely certain foundations of knowledge. Descartes was a mathematician, after all, so no doubt he would have loved to answer that question affirmatively, but the rigors of methodological doubt forced him to answer in the negative, as we will see:

> Nevertheless I have long had fixed in my mind the belief that an all-powerful God existed by whom I have been created such as I am. But how do I know that He has not brought it to pass that there is no earth, no heaven, no extended body, no magnitude, no place, and that nevertheless I possess the perceptions of all these things and that they seem to me to exist just exactly as I now see them? And besides, as I sometimes imagine that others deceive themselves in the things which they think they know best, how do I know that I am not deceived every time that I add two and three, or count the sides of a square or judge of things yet simpler, if anything simpler can be imagined? (p. 168)

This is the introduction to one of the most curious chapters in the history of philosophy: Descartes' "evil genius" hypothesis. Descartes asks himself, How do I know that the universe was not created by a malevolent demon whose only goal is to deceive, so that even when I make the most basic mathematical judgments, such as the judgment that 2+3=5, I err; yet I

74

Descartes and the Evil Genius

never know that I am erring? Much to Descartes' chagrin, he realizes that he <u>cannot</u> disprove that such a "god" exists. Therefore,
even if it is not very <u>likely</u> that such a demon exists, it is logically
<u>possible</u> that it does, and from this it follows that mathematics is
not absolutely certain. (Imagine a math teacher who tells his students,
"Two plus three is five, ... unless there is an evil genius, in which case
two plus three may not be five." If one has to add that qualification
to math, then math is not unqualifiably true, and it cannot be the
foundation of knowledge.)

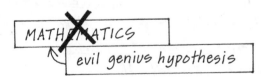

So, Descartes is stuck in the following state (which would surely be taken as the paradigm case of paranoia if methodological doubt were confused with real doubt):

> I shall then suppose, not that God who is supremely good and the fountain of truth, but some evil genius not less powerful than deceitful, has employed his whole energies in deceiving me; I shall consider that the heavens, the earth, colours, figures, sound, and all other external things are nought but the illusions and dreams of which this genius has availed himself in order to lay traps for my credulity; I shall consider myself as having no hands, no eyes, no flesh, no blood, nor any senses, yet falsely believing myself to possess all these things (pp. 169-170).

Well then, is there a truth so certain that it can be known indubitably even if the senses deceive Descartes, even if he is dreaming, and even if there is an evil genius?

> I myself, am I not at least something? But I already denied that I had senses and body. Yet I hesitate, for what follows from that? Am I so dependent on body and senses that I cannot exist without these? But I was persuaded that there was nothing in all the world, that there was no heaven, no earth, that there were no minds, nor any bodies: was I not then likewise persuaded that I did not exist? Not at all; ... without doubt I exist also if [the evil genius] deceives me, and let him deceive me as much as he will, he can never cause me to be nothing so long as I think that I am something. So that after having reflected well and carefully examined all things, we must come to the definite conclusion that this proposition: I am, I exist, is necessarily true each time that I pronounce it, or that I mentally conceive it (p. 171).

This, then, is the absolutely certain foundation of all knowledge. In the _Meditations_, the version is, "I am." In another work, the _Discourse_ on _Method_, it is, "I think, therefore I am" (_Cogito ergo sum_). This truth is certain under any possible conditions. Every time I make the assertion "I am," I am _right_. Not even an evil genius or madness can falsify this.

Now the nature of this foundation must be clarified.

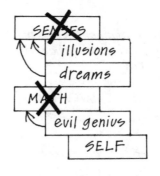

    I am, I exist, that is
certain. But how often?
Just when I think; for it
might possibly be the case
if I ceased entirely to
think, that I should like-
wise cease altogether to
exist. I do not now admit anything which is not necessarily true:
to speak accurately I am not more than a thing which thinks,
that is to say a mind or a soul, or an understanding, or a
reason, ... I am, however, a real thing and really exist; but
what thing? I have answered: a thing which thinks (p. 173).

So the essence of the selfhood of which Descartes is so certain is
thought or consciousness (which, as you see, Descartes conveniently
equates with "soul." Perhaps his hidden religious agenda is sticking out
a bit here).

    This is the beginning of Descartes' notorious mind / body dualism.
The self is defined as mind or soul (a "thing which thinks"), and the
body is not an essential part of the self. In order to see Descartes'
argument that leads to this strange conclusion (strange because
most of us have always assumed that our bodies are rather essential aspects of our selves and not baggage we take along with us
when we go out), take a look at a couple of sentences:

1. "I doubt that I have a body." Now this is an odd doubt, and if
you ever heard anyone express it, you would think that person to
be odd (either odd or a philosopher!). But it is only odd. It is not
an impossible doubt. So Descartes' method requires this doubt.

2. "I doubt that I have a mind." This is not only an odd doubt; it
is an impossible doubt. To doubt that one has a mind is to establish
that one has a mind because doubting is an activity of the mind.
To Descartes, this proves that there is a necessary relation between
self and mind

      (I) DOUBT THAT I HAVE A (MIND).

and only a contingent (i.e., non-necessary) relation between self and body.

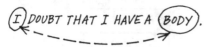 (I) DOUBT THAT I HAVE A (BODY).

This is a difficult argument to evaluate, but let's let it slip by just to see what Descartes does with it. "But what then am I? A thing which thinks. What is a thing which thinks? It is a thing which doubts, understands, conceives, affirms, denies, wills,

refuses, which also images and feels" (p.174). Here Descartes is defining the mind in terms of its capacity to perform certain mental acts: to doubt, to understand, etc. To say that anything has a mind is to say that that thing can perform these acts. For Descartes this seems to be a "package deal." If you can do any one of these, you can do them all. If there is any one of them you can't do, then you can't do any of them. It was for this reason that Descartes concluded that animals do not have minds. Dogs do not affirm or deny anything, so (appearances to the contrary notwithstanding) they

78

YAP YAP BOW WOW
AROOOOO
ARF·ARF

must not will anything either. (Perhaps there was a religious motive here as well. To admit that dogs have minds is to admit that they have <u>souls</u>. Now, do we really want dogs barking in heaven? Isn't it enough that they keep us awake and befoul our lawns here on earth?)

Divine barking

There is another feature of the mind that Descartes wanted to reveal. It comes out in the famous "wax example."

Let us begin by considering the commonest of matters, those which we believe to be the most distinctly comprehended, to wit, the bodies which we touch and see; ... Let us take, for example, this piece of wax: it has been taken quite freshly from the hive, and it has not yet lost the sweetness of the honey which it contains; it still retains somewhat of the odour of the flowers from which it has been culled; its colour, its figure, its size are apparent; it is hard, cold, easily handled, and if you strike it with the finger, it will emit a sound. Finally all the things which are requisite to cause us distinctly to recognize a body, are met with in it. But notice that while I speak and approach the fire what remains of the taste is exhaled, the smell evaporates, the colour alters, the figure is destroyed, the size increases, it becomes liquid, it heats. Scarcely can one handle it, and when one strikes it, no sound is emitted. Does the same wax remain after this change? We must confess that it remains; none would judge otherwise. What then did I know so distinctly in this piece of wax? It could certainly be nothing of all that the senses brought to my notice, since all these things which fall under taste, smell, sight, touch, and hearing, are found to be changed, and yet the same wax remains.
    ... We must then grant that I could not even understand through the imagination what this piece of wax is, and that it is my mind alone which perceives it (pp. 175-176).

This example constitutes another attack on the claim that the senses are the source of real knowledge (the view called "empiricism," which will be inspected in the next chapter), and Descartes has selected a brilliant example indeed. He goes through the five senses, cataloguing the information about the wax that the senses provide. Then, when he holds the wax to the fire, _every one_ of those characteristics changes. Yet we _know_, he says, that it is the same wax. How can we know this if the senses tell us the opposite? Where do we get the concept of "sameness"?

René Descartes inspecting his hands, which suddenly seem to be covered with melted wax

Clearly not from the senses, because their data are in constant flux (like Plato's "Becoming"). Descartes' answer is very Platonic. According to him, the concept of "sameness," i.e., the concept of identity, must be an _innate idea_ because it cannot be derived from observation. We are all born with the (apparently unconscious) knowledge of the "principle of identity," "A = A." This absolutely necessary and _a priori_ truth is presupposed by any other knowledge whatsoever. If we did not know this truth, we could not know any truth.

The wax example also generates the innate idea of "_substance_" (i.e., of substantiality, of "thingness") and particularly of _material substance_ (i.e., the idea of a physical body). According to Descartes, this idea _cannot_ be derived from the senses alone. In order to understand Descartes' point, consider it this way. Imagine that we build a computerized robot. We install five sensors in it, one for tactile data, one for visual data, one for olfactory data, another for tastes, and one for sounds; and we teach it a language to name the data of each of the sensors. Then we program it to record all the sensory data it receives, and we send it out into the world. Now the robot will send back reports like these: →

Blue, cylindrical, hard, cold, here now.

What the robot could <u>not</u> say is, "There is a blue pen on the table," and that's because it would be lacking the two key concepts, "identity" and "thingness." If we pre-programmed them into our robot, these concepts would organize the sensorial data into a coherent picture of the world.

So far, then, much of this is reminiscent of Plato, but Descartes' theory has the advantage of keeping the number of innate ideas down to a manageable handful. (Up to this point, we have only "self," "identity," and "substance.") For Plato, there seemed to be as many innate ideas as there were words, and that view is a bit implausible. But remember, in Descartes' system, before any innate idea can be accepted as true, it will have to be established that it was not placed there by the evil genius.

Now we are going to proceed with the construction of Descartes' house of knowledge, but we are going to speed things up quite a bit.   One reason we are going to do so is that this chapter is about the rationalistic conception of knowledge, and we have already discovered its essence in our discussion of Plato's simile of the line and of Descartes' quest for the foundation of knowledge. The other reason is that it is generally thought that Descartes' upward building is not as tight as his argument leading down to his foundation.

So Descartes knows that he is still operating in the shadow of the evil genius and that before he can progress, he must dispose of the demon. There is only one way this can be done, according to Descartes, and that is by proving the existence of God. This is because the concept of God as an all-powerful, all-knowing, all-good creator of the universe is logically incompatible with the concept of an evil genius. Either <u>one</u> of them could exist, but not both. So if Descartes can prove

Operating in the shadow of the Evil Genius

God's existence, he will have disproved the existence of the evil genius. Descartes' proof will have to be strictly <u>a priori</u> because no observation can be trusted. It will have to be absolutely certain and rest firmly on the foundation of the "cogito." Perhaps the simplest version of Descartes' first argument (he has a number of them) is this:

[R]eflecting on the fact that I doubted, and that consequently my existence was not quite perfect (for I saw clearly that it was a greater perfection to know than to doubt), I resolved to inquire whence I had learnt to think of anything more perfect than I myself was; and I recognized very clearly that this conception must proceed from some nature which was really more perfect. ... [B]ecause it is no less contradictory to say of the more perfect that it is what results from and depends on the less perfect, than to say that there is something which proceeds from nothing, it was equally impossible that I should hold [the idea of a perfect Being] from myself. In this way it could but follow that it had been placed in me by a nature which was really more perfect than mine could be, and which even had within itself all the perfections of which I could form any idea — that is to say, to put it in a word, which was God (pp. 128-129).

Let's formalize this argument:

1. A being that doubts is an imperfect being (because a perfect being would have full knowledge, hence no room for doubt).

2. I doubt; therefore I am an imperfect being.

3. Yet I could know that I am imperfect only by having the concept of perfection; therefore I do have the concept of perfection.

4. I could not have received the concept of perfection from something imperfect; therefore my concept was not derived from myself.

5. Therefore my concept of perfection was derived from something that is in fact perfect.

6. Only God is in fact perfect, so I derived my concept of perfection from him, and therefore he exists.

Do you find this argument convincing? (If not, perhaps you would be more convinced by Descartes' second argument, to be discussed in Chapter 5. You

Variation on a Cartesian theme

may want to jump ahead and look at it.) Here Descartes' "proof" will not be criticized. We will let it stand to see what Descartes does with it.

If Descartes really has proved the existence of God, then he has, by his reckoning, eliminated the evil genius. If he has eliminated the evil genius, then mathematics is valid (because the only argument against math was derived from the possibility of the evil genius). Also, Descartes now knows that his innate ideas were not placed in him by the evil genius, so they _may_ be true as well. Still, at this point, Descartes remains in a nearly solipsistic universe. That is, with the exception of his knowledge of God, Descartes does not know if anything other than his own mind exists. He does not even know if he has a body. So his next task will be to determine whether an external world exists, and his final epistemological task will be to determine what knowledge we can have of such a world.

Descartes in his solipsistic universe

First, Descartes notes that we have two sources for our idea of material objects. One source is a mathematical idea (i.e., one involving measurable objects). This idea is of something extended in three dimensions, having size, shape, part, and location. These are the objects of geometry. The other source, coming from the senses rather than from the innate ideas of corporeality and math in which geometry is grounded, is perhaps a naive idea of a world populated by physical things such as tables, rocks, and trees (and one's own body). But even if this idea is naive (i.e., not philosophically sophisticated), it is nevertheless _compelling_. It can be doubted "methodologically," but not _really_. Now, _could_ I be wrong about these ideas? In spite of the compelling nature of my idea of the existence of an external world, is it possible that there is in fact nothing "out there"? Descartes writes:

The idea that one has a body is a _compelling_ idea.

But since God is no deceiver, it is very manifest that He does not communicate these ideas [of material objects] immediately and by Himself, nor yet by the intervention of some creature in which their reality [is falsely] contained. For since he has given me no faculty to recognize that this is the case, but on the other hand, a very great inclination to believe ... that they are conveyed to me by corporeal objects, I do not see how He could be defended from the accusation of deceit if these ideas were produced by causes other than corporeal objects. Hence we must allow that corporeal things exist (p. 215).

So we _know_ there is a physical world because if there is not, God is a deceiver, which is impossible. Descartes' system now looks like this :

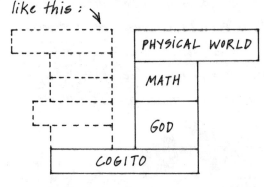

But what is the nature of these corporeal objects that make up the physical world ? According to Descartes :

> ... corporeal things exist. However, they are perhaps not exactly what we perceive by the senses, since this comprehension by the senses is in many instances very obscure and confused; but we must at least admit that all things which I conceive in them clearly and distinctly, that is to say, all things which, speaking generally, are comprehended in the object of pure mathematics, are truly to be recognized as in the objects.
>
> As to other things, however, ... for example, that the sun is of such and such a figure, etc., or which are less clearly and distinctly conceived, such as light, sound, pain and the like, ... they are very dubious and uncertain ... it may easily happen that these judgments contain some error. Take, for example, the opinion which I hold ... that in a body which is warm there is something entirely similar to the idea of heat which is in me; that in a white or green body there is the same whiteness or greenness that I perceive; that in a bitter or sweet body there is the same taste, and so on in other instances; that the stars, the towers, and all other distant bodies are of the same figure and size as they appear from far off to our eyes, etc. (pp. 215-217).

The upshot of all this is the following: The physical world that we know as philosopher-scientists is not the world of appearance, the world presented to us by the senses. It is the world as known by mathematical physics. It is, after all, the world as revealed to us by the new sciences — the world of Galileo. The senses continue to be permanent deceivers. They tell us that bodies contain colors, sounds, odors, tastes, and sensations of heat and cold. But in fact what exists "out there" is whatever math can measure: extension, size, shape, part, location, and moveability — mass in motion, conglomerations of atoms, light waves, and sound waves, but _no_ colors, sounds, and tastes. _These_ exist only in our sensations as subjective states, and not as objective reality.

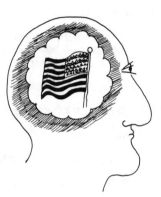

The flag's colors exist in here.

The flag's molecular structure exists out here.

So the world we lost is not the world we regained. But at

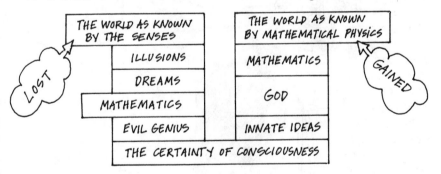

LOST	THE WORLD AS KNOWN BY THE SENSES	THE WORLD AS KNOWN BY MATHEMATICAL PHYSICS	GAINED
	ILLUSIONS	MATHEMATICS	
	DREAMS	GOD	
	MATHEMATICS		
	EVIL GENIUS	INNATE IDEAS	
	THE CERTAINTY OF CONSCIOUSNESS		

least there _is_ certain knowledge, and the world has been made manageable again. The center, which seemed to wobble, now holds.

We will speak more about the nature of the Cartesian world in Chapter 4. Here we will only take note of Descartes' success in creating a philosophical / theological compromise. We get both Galileo and God in this system. Not only are Galileo's world and God both _Knowable_, but both are _necessary_. In fact, science rests on a godly foundation. However, the soul (i.e., the self) is not the subject of science, because science can know only that which can be measured, and the soul cannot be measured. But it can be known immediately to itself. In truth, the self knows itself before it knows the world. So Descartes leaves our souls to ourselves (perhaps to be shepherded by the Church), and he leaves the physical world (Jupiter's moons included) to the scientists.

In spite of their historical differences, the epistemologies of Plato and Descartes are similar. Both repudiate the senses as sources of true knowledge. Both find that there is an intelligible order behind the flux of appearance. Both conclude that true knowledge must be _a priori_. Both use mathematics as their model

CE NE SONO TRE!

of knowledge. Both derive knowledge of the world from knowledge of a higher reality (the Good for Plato, God for Descartes). Both find the source of all knowledge in innate ideas located in the soul. This is the epistemological program of rationalism. It represents one of the two major polarities in theory of knowledge. We will now turn to the second one — empiricism.

Notes

1. Plato, "Meno," in *Great Dialogues of Plato*, Eric H. Warmington and Philip G. Rouse, eds., W.H.D. Rouse, trans. (New York: New American Library, 1956), p. 41.

2. Plato, "Meno," p. 42.

3. A recent book challenges the traditional interpretation somewhat. See Pietro Redondi, *Galileo Heretic*, Raymond Rosenthal, trans. (Princeton, New Jersey: Princeton University Press, 1988).

4. René Descartes, *Meditations on First Philosophy*, in *The Essential Descartes*, Margaret D. Wilson, ed., Elizabeth S. Haldane and G.R.T. Ross, trans. (New York: New American Library, 1969), pp. 157-158. Unless otherwise stated, all subsequent quotes from Descartes in this chapter are from this source.

5. René Descartes, *Essential Works of Descartes*, Lowell Blair, trans. (New York: Bantam Books, 1966), p. X.

Chapter 3

What You See Is What You Get

Empiricist Epistemology

The opposite extreme of rationalism is empiricism. According to it, the true foundations of knowledge are found not in "reason", but in observation.

The Empiricism of John Locke

Some people trace empiricism clear back to Aristotle's criticism of Plato, but its first modern expression appears in the work of the English physician, JOHN LOCKE (1632-1704).

Locke's main thesis is set forth in the following passage:

> Let us suppose the mind to be, as we say, a blank slate (*tabula rasa*) of white paper, void of all characters, without any ideas; how comes it to be furnished? Whence comes it by that vast store, which the busy and boundless fancy of man has painted on it with almost endless variety? Whence has it all the materials of reason and knowledge? To this I answer in one word, from

JOHN LOCKE (1632-1704)

<u>experience</u>: in that all our knowledge is founded, and from that it ultimately derives itself.[1]

Locke had read Descartes' work, and he knew that in order to establish the theory of the mind as a "blank slate," he would have to refute the rationalists' contention that knowledge is based on innate ideas. About this Locke says:

> <u>The way shown how we come by any knowledge, sufficient to prove it not innate.</u> — It is an established opinion among some men, that there are in the understanding certain innate principles; some primary notions, ... characters, as it were, stamped upon the mind of man which the soul receives in its very first being; and brings into the world with it. It would be sufficient to convince unprejudiced readers of the falseness of this supposition, if I should only show (as I hope I shall in the following parts of this discourse) how men, barely by the use of their natural faculties, may attain to all the knowledge they have, without the help of any innate impressions, and may arrive at certainty, without any such original notions or principles (bk. I, chap. II, sec. 1).

Locke is here appealing to a principle that would become dear to empiricism, what is known as OCKHAM'S RAZOR. William of Ockham (or Occam), a fourteenth-century philosopher, had set forth as a principle of economy the following thesis: "What can be done with fewer [terms] is done in vain with more." This simple principle sounds like something your English instructor might write in the margin of your essay, but William meant it as more than just a stylistic recommendation. (And indeed, William's principle got him into trouble with the ecclesiastical authorities, who suspected that Ockham was trying to shave off the Doctrine of the Trinity on the grounds that <u>one</u> divine entity is more simple than <u>three</u>.) William's point has been restated in modern terms in the following way: "Do not multiply entities beyond necessity." That is to say, given two theories both of which are compatible with all the observable data and both of which purport to explain the same phenomena, the <u>preferable</u> theory is the one with the fewer theoretical entities.

Let's consider a historical example. When telescopes were first trained on the sky, it was noticed that certain heavenly bodies seemed not simply to be travelling in a consistent orbit, but to stop suddenly, back up, and then lurch forward. This discovery was startling, and even embarrassing, because people were used to thinking of the movements of the heavenly bodies as exemplars of God's geometrical genius. Some scientific account was needed to "save the appearances." It came about in the theory of epicycles. According to this hypothesis, some heavenly bodies moved around the earth like this.→ In that case, from the perspective of the earth, these bodies would ap-

Ockham wielding razor

pear to be stopping, moving backward, then moving ahead. So, indeed, the appearances had been saved, along with God's geometrical genius. (Now the heaven's architect was still a mathematical wizard — even though his tastes did run a bit to the baroque.) But then, as telescopes got better, a new embarrassment came to light. Not only did these epicycling bodies seem to stop, move backward, then start

forward again, but they appeared to stop, _wiggle_ backward, then _wiggle_
forward again. This
problem was solved by
putting epicycles on the
epicycles. Now the Great
Architect had become positively
rococo. Appearances had been saved,
but at what cost? This whole structure

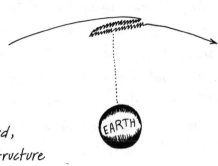

had now become so top-heavy
that it was obvious that it
would soon come crashing down.
It was crying out for Ockham's
razor to come along and shave
off the extra weight.

The razor appeared in the
form of Johann Kepler's
theory of planetary motion.
Kepler asked, what if the
heliocentric theory is true:
the earth travels around
the sun; but not in a circle,
rather in an ellipse, and in
such a way that "equal
areas are swept in equal
times"? Then the _apparent_

The system of epicycles comes
crashing down.

retrograde motion of some heavenly bodies would be explained by the speeding up and slowing down of the earth in its elliptical orbit. And what if the little wiggly movements are the result of the aberration caused by looking back through our own atmosphere? So much for the epicycles and for epicycles on the epicycles. Kepler's theory is simpler. It has fewer entities. It represents a triumph of Ockham's razor.

Now perhaps you can see what Locke hoped to accomplish. He hoped to do to "innate ideas" what Kepler had done to epicycles. He also wanted to do the same to Platonic "Forms." A theory in which <u>only particulars exist</u> would be simpler than one in which there existed particulars <u>and</u> abstractions. Locke believed that with the simple image of the "blank slate," he could account for all possible knowledge. He began with several sets of distinctions, one between simple and complex ideas, one between particular and general ideas, and one between primary and secondary qualities.

Simple and Complex Ideas

Simple ideas are those that cannot be further analyzed into simpler components, e.g., the idea of "solidity" (if someone doesn't understand this idea, you take her by the wrist and press her hand against a wall) or the idea of "yellow" (the person who doesn't understand this idea must be shown a ripe banana or a canary). These ideas usually come in through one sense, though some of them, such as the idea of "motion," can be derived either from the sense of touch or the sense of sight.

Complex ideas are (1) compounds of simple ideas (e.g., "beauty, gratitude, a man, an army, the universe"), (2) ideas of relations (larger than, smaller than) created by setting two ideas next to each other and comparing or contrasting them, or (3) abstractions, wherein the mind separates out a feature of an idea and generalizes it (e.g., blueness).

Particular and General Ideas

General ideas are the result of abstraction (hence this category over-laps that of complex ideas). Locke wrote:

> How general Words are made. — The next thing to be considered is, how general words come to be made. For, since all things that exist are only particulars, how come we by general terms, or where find we those general natures they are supposed to stand for? Words become general by being made the signs of general ideas; and ideas become general by separating from them the circumstances of time, and place, and any other ideas that may determine them to this or that particular existence. By this way of abstraction they are made capable of representing more individuals than one; each of which, having in it a conformity to that abstract idea, is (as we call it) of that sort (bk. III, chap. III, sec. 6).

General ideas, then, are formed when we recognize a certain charac-teristic that a group of objects has in common. That characteristic is assigned a name, which is a symbol for that characteristic. This theory has traditionally been called CONCEPTUALISM. Locke's view is that the rationalists had confused these "abstract general ideas" with actual existing entities (Platonic Forms) or with innate ideas. (For their part, the rationalists were quick to charge Locke with pre-supposing the truth of the very thing he thought he was refuting. They asked how the mind can recognize a characteristic that a number of objects have in common unless the mind already has the concept of "sameness.")

95

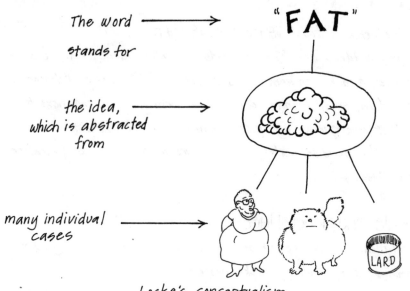

The word ⟶ "FAT"
stands for

the idea, ⟶
which is abstracted
from

many individual ⟶
cases

Locke's conceptualism

Primary and Secondary Qualities

Locke's distinction between primary and secondary qualities had been popularized by both Descartes and Galileo. Primary qualities were said to be characteristics that necessarily inhered in material bodies. They comprised "solidity, extension, figure, motion or rest, and number." Secondary qualities were defined as "such qualities, which in truth are nothing in the objects themselves but powers to produce various sensations in us by their primary qualities, i.e., by the bulk, figure, texture, and motion of their insensible parts, as colours, sounds, tastes, etc." (bk. II, chap. VIII, sec. 10).

Now, our _ideas_ of primary qualities are, according to Locke, _correct_ ideas. That is, these ideas are caused in our minds by those qualities, and these ideas correctly represent those qualities. On the other hand, the ideas we have of secondary qualities do not correctly represent the world. Locke says: "... the ideas of primary qualities of bodies are resemblances of them, and their patterns do really exist in the bodies themselves; but the ideas produced in us by these secondary qualities have no resemblance of them at all. There is nothing like our ideas existing in the bodies themselves" (bk. II, chap. VIII, sec. 15). This epistemological view is now known

SECONDARY QUALITIES
(colors, sounds, tastes, odors tactile sensations)
EXIST IN HERE.

PRIMARY QUALITIES
(extension, size, shape, location, motion/rest)
EXIST OUT HERE.

as REPRESENTATIVE REALISM. It is a version of _realism_ because it holds that there really is a real world "out there." It is _representative_ realism because, according to it, the mind does not give us direct access to reality; rather, it represents reality, much in the way that a photograph does. And just as some characteristics of a photo correctly represent the world (e.g., number, shape, relative size, etc.), so do some features of the mind correctly represent the world (these are our ideas of primary qualities). And just as some characteristics of a photo are purely features of the photo (e.g., its black and white presentation, its

This is a picture of you!

But I'm not flat, glossy, black and white, three inches tall with a white border around my head!!

two-dimensionality, its glossiness and portableness, etc.), so do some features of the mind pertain only to the mind and not to the world (these are our ideas of secondary qualities).

Substance

Now, with these tools in hand, Locke believed he had refuted Descartes because he thought he had given a complete account of knowledge using a theory simpler than that of Descartes. But perhaps things aren't that simple, as we see when we turn to Locke's account of the key philosophical category, SUBSTANCE.

<u>Our</u> <u>Obscure</u> <u>Idea</u> <u>of</u> <u>Substance</u> <u>in</u> <u>general</u>. — So that if anyone will examine himself concerning his notion of pure substance in general, he will find he has no other idea of it at all, but only a supposition of he knows not what support of such qualities which are capable of producing simple ideas in us.... If anyone should be asked, "what is the subject wherein colour or weight inheres?" he would have nothing to say but, "The solid extended parts." And if he were demanded "What is it that solidity and extension inhere in?" he would not be in much better case than the Indian ..., who, saying that the world was supported by a great elephant, was asked what the elephant rested on? to which his answer was, "A great tortoise"; but being again pressed to know what gave support to the broad-backed tortoise, replied — something he knew not what (bk. II, chap. XXIII, sec. 2).

Locke's rather cavalier account of substance is devastating to his own project, though he didn't seem to realize it. Once you buy into the metaphysics of substance, as both he and Descartes had done (viz., once you accept the view that, given anything in the world, it is either a substance or a characteristic of a substance), then you'd better be prepared to render a coherent account of _substance._ Remember in the wax example it was precisely Descartes' inability to come up with an _empirical_ account of "substance" and "identity" that allowed him to posit innate ideas. Now, Locke has claimed he can get rid of innate ideas by using Ockham's razor; yet when he turns to that key ontological category, substance, he says it is a "something I know not what." This could be the beginning of the end either of empiricism or of the metaphysics of substance. We shall soon see that it is the latter.

The beginning of the end of substance

Berkeley's Correction of Locke

Locke's empiricist successor, GEORGE BERKELEY (1685–1753), saw Locke's errors clearly and thought they could be corrected simply by a more rigorous application of Ockham's razor — this time, to the notion of material substance itself. Locke had written: "Since the mind, in all its thoughts and reasonings, hath no other immediate object but its own ideas, which it alone does or can contemplate, it is evident that our knowledge is only conversant about them" (bk. IV, chap. I, sec. 1). Berkeley immediately realized that if this statement was literally true, then it is impossible to know something that is not an idea.

But Locke, perhaps contra-
dicting himself, had claimed
that we _know_ that many
of these ideas are caused
by real things in the
physical world (material
substances), and par-
ticularly by their
primary qualities,
which have powers to
produce the ideas of
both primary and
secondary qualities
in our minds.

GEORGE BERKELEY (1685–1753)

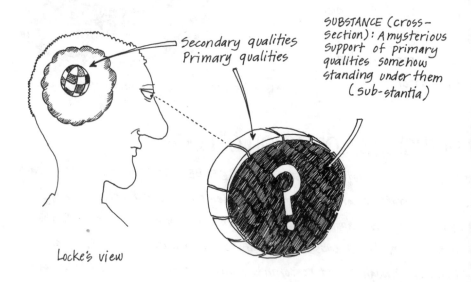

Secondary qualities
Primary qualities

SUBSTANCE (cross-
section): A mysterious
support of primary
qualities somehow
standing under them
(sub-stantia)

Locke's view

Sense-Data

One of Berkeley's first tasks would be to demonstrate Locke's self-
contradiction by undoing the primary / secondary quality distinction.

In his _A Treatise Concerning the Principles of Human Knowledge,_
Berkeley wrote:

> Some there are who make a distinction betwixt _primary_ and _secondary_ qualities. . . . They who assert that figure, motion, and the rest of the primary or original qualities do exist without the mind, in unthinking substances, do at the same time acknowledge that colours, sounds, heat, cold, and such like secondary qualities, do not; which they tell us are sensations existing in the mind alone, that depend on and are occasioned by the different size, texture, and motion of the minute particles of matter. This they take for an undoubted truth, which they can demonstrate beyond all exception. Now, if it be certain, that those _original_ qualities are inseparably united with the other sensible qualities, and not, even in thought, capable of being abstracted from them, it plainly follows that _they_ exist only in the mind. But I desire anyone to reflect and try whether he can, by any abstraction of thought, conceive the extension and motion of a body without all other sensible qualities. For my own part, I see evidently that it is not in my power to frame an idea of a body extended and moving but I must withal give it some colour or other sensible quality which is acknowledged to exist only in the mind. In short, extension, figure, and motion, abstracted from all other qualities, are inconceivable. Where therefore the other sensible qualities are, there must these be also, to wit, in the mind and nowhere else. [2]

Berkeley's point seems good here. If we admit that secondary qualities exist only in the mind (or, to use Berkeley's language, that their "_esse_ is _percipi_" – their "_being_ is to be _perceived_"), then we are forced to admit that the _esse_ of primary qualities is also _percipi_. This is because primary qualities and secondary qualities really are the same

The collapsing of the primary/secondary quality distinction

thing. How do I establish the size and shape of a table except by looking at it or feeling it? The first act produces the secondary qualities of color, and the second act produces the secondary qualities of tactile sensation (hard, smooth, etc.). In other words, our ideas of primary qualities are really nothing but _interpretations_ of secondary qualities. In fact, for Berkeley, all of our ideas (except for our idea of "self," which is known in a Cartesian manner, and, as we shall see, our idea of "God") are nothing but our ideas of secondary qualities or interpretations of them. Berkeley says:

It is evident to anyone who takes a survey of the _objects of human knowledge_, that they are either _ideas_ actually imprinted on the senses, or else such as are perceived by attending to the passions and operations of the mind; or lastly, _ideas_ formed by help of memory and imagination, either compounding, dividing, or barely representing those originally perceived in the aforesaid ways. By sight I have the ideas of light and colours with their several degrees and variations. By touch I perceive hard and soft, heat and cold, motion and resistance.... Smelling furnishes me with odours; the palate with tastes; and hearing conveys sounds to the mind in all their variety of tone and composition. And as several of these are observed to accompany each other, they come to be marked by one name, and so to be reputed as one _thing_. Thus, for example, a certain colour, taste, smell, figure, and consistence having been observed to go together, are accounted one distinct thing, signified by the name "apple"; other collections of ideas constitute a stone, a tree, a book, and the like sensible things; which, as they are pleasing or disagreeable, excite the passions of love, hatred, joy grief, and so forth   (part I, sec. I).

Almost the whole of Berkeley's theory is encapsulated in this remarkable passage. Let's summarize that theory: Like Descartes, Berkeley wants to start with what is certain, with what we can call "the given," and for him, "the given" is what earlier philosophers designated as "ideas of secondary qualities" and what he simply calls "ideas" or "sensations." (We will call them SENSE-DATA from now on.) Babies come into the world and they are "given" sense-data:

colors, sounds, tastes, odors, and "feelies" (tactile sensations). These data do not constitute a world for the baby; rather, they comprise a chaos of fluctuating sensations. (Actually, they constitute <u>five</u> chaotic worlds.) But slowly the child learns to "read" these data, very much the way we learn to read script as children. She does this by beginning to notice patterns in

The newborn infant confronts "the given."

the appearance of these data (the rationalist, of course, asks how the baby <u>recognizes</u> these patterns without knowing the principle of identity), and by having parents teach her a language ("... a certain colour, taste, smell, figure, and consistence having been observed to go together, are accounted one distinct thing, signified by the name 'apple,'...").

Notice that there are two features here in Berkeley's account of how we interpret our sense-data, transforming them into a picture of a <u>world</u>. First, there is the objective fact that sense-data appear in recognizable <u>patterns</u> ("... having been observed to go together..."). This is <u>nature's</u> role in making interpretation possible because these are

103

natural patterns — bright red, yellow, and orange flamelike sense-data are associated with heat and pain. Second, there is the fact that language is used to unify these ideas in our minds ("... signified by the name 'apple'..."). This is _convention's_ role in making interpretation possible.

Snow? No. There's no snow here.
Tiqsiq we've got, and _Tuva_, or _Pukajaq_, or _Piqsirpoq_, or _Gana_ or _Aput_. But snow there isn't any of. Lots of _Qimuqsuq!_

What makes Berkeley's theory so modern is the large part he assigns to language in his epistemology. Doing so allows him to account for a fact that modernity had discovered and traditional rationalism could not explain, namely that different peoples cut up the world so differently (all those stories that you've learned in your anthropology classes). If human conventions — primarily linguistic conventions — can determine which ideas are associated with each other, then this can explain quite nicely why Eskimos have no word for "snow" in their language but have a number of nouns designating different substances, all of which look like "snow" to us and to the Caucasian Yukon neighbors of the Eskimos and why Spanish speakers think that there are two kinds of "being" ("ser" and "estar"), although Americans find only one kind. If Descartes' theories of substance and of innate ideas were true, we should all see the world identically.

Furthermore, language plays a big role in Berkeley's epistemology as a bridge of intersubjectivity. This can be seen in the following consideration: no two people have exactly the same sense-data because no two people can share exactly the same geometrical perspective on any

object. If thirty people in a room look at a book on a table, each has a slightly different datum in consciousness. In fact, it is logically possible that no two people have the same experience when they use such basic terms as the word "red."

No two people see exactly the same thing.

But none of this matters practically because even if I see what you call "green" when I look at something "red," we both describe it as being red because we were taught to associate that particular noise ("rěd") with that particular experience. So the upshot is that each of us dwells in his or her little solipsistic world of sensorial consciousness, but language allows us to build bridges between those solitary islands.

Language forms the bridge of intersubjectivity.

The Source of Sense-Data

Now, a typical objection to Berkeley's theory at this point will be: if there exist only sense-data (ideas, sensations), where do these sense-data come from? Normally (or at least in the Cartesian-Lockean picture of normality), we would say that they come from material things "out there." But Berkeley has eliminated those "things" with Ockham's razor, so where _do_ these sense-data come from? Before we make Berkeley answer that question, let's ask Descartes and Locke where _material substances_ come from. Sense-data are caused by substance, but what causes substance? Both Descartes and Locke answer "from God." (In fact, the only other obvious answer would seem to be that it comes "from an infinite series of causes"— the table comes from atoms, the atoms come from the "atomic bake" that took place in the "Big Bang." But where does the stuff that was baked into atoms by the "Big Bang" come from? Presumably, from something yet earlier, and so on to infinity.) Now

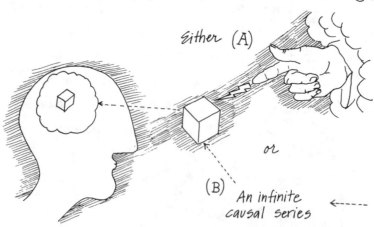

Either (A)

or

(B) An infinite causal series

Locke's version of causality

back to Berkeley. By eliminating material substance from this chain of events, he has simply eliminated "the middle person" (formerly "the middleman"). Consequently, he can give exactly the same answer to the question "Where do sense-data come from?" that everybody else

gives to the
question of
where matter
comes from:
either from
God or from
an infinite
causal series.

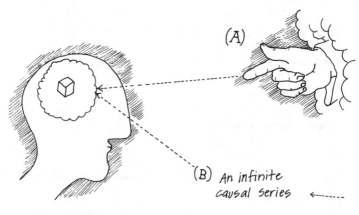

(A)

(B) An infinite
causal series ←-------

Berkeley's version of causality

Berkeley
preferred
the first alternative, of course. He was a bishop, after all. In fact,
God plays a key role in Berkeley's theory, just as it did in Descartes'.
God is the guarantor of the orderliness of the universe (i.e., the orderliness of sense-data). He is the "eternal perceiver" who guarantees by

his perpetual vigilance
that the room we are in
does not flash out of existence when we all leave it.
(And if it did flash out of
existence, who knows if it
would flash back on?)
Ronald Knox wrote a lovely
little limerick to express
this point:

There was a young man who said, "God
Must think it exceedingly odd,
If he finds that this tree
Continues to be
When there's no one about
          in the Quad."

Dear Sir:
Your astonishment's odd.
I am always about in the
 Quad.
And that's why the tree
Will continue to be
Since observed by me.
 Yours faithfully,
 GOD

There does seem to be a big problem here, however. How can a god exist in a system whose main claim is that <u>esse</u> is <u>percipi</u>? In such a system, it would seem that either God can be

perceived (which he can't), or he doesn't exist. Berkeley was obviously troubled by this dilemma and hoped he could escape it by calling our thought of God a "notion" rather than an "idea." But very few critics have accepted Berkeley's semantical solution.

Phenomenalism

Not only did Berkeley's philosophy contain this fundamental flaw, but it also seemed to go tremendously against the grain of common sense. Doctor Johnson thought that he could refute Berkeley by simply kicking a stone. This act of Johnson's shows a failure to understand Berkeley's theory, but unfortunately it does represent a fairly typical response to it. Furthermore, Berkeley's theory was eclipsed in the next generation by the radical and skeptical turn that empiricism took in the work of David Hume (1711-1776), a turn we shall not follow here. But Berkeley's brand of empiricism had a revival in the twentieth century under the title of PHENOMENALISM, where it had some rather distinguished defenders, including Sir Alfred Jules Ayer and, at one point in his career, Lord Bertrand Russell.

Talk about *percipi*! Cheez!

AAAYY

Dr. Johnson refutes Bishop Berkeley.

Precepts of Phenomenalism

Phenomenalism can be defined as "Berkeleianism without God." It follows a strict empiricist program by trying to give a complete account of all human knowledge in terms of either (1) reception and interpretations of sense-data (what Russell called, respectively, "knowledge by acquaintance" and "knowledge by description") or (2) linguistic tautologies. This latter idea, introduced by Hume, tried to account for the fact (heretofore embarrassing to the empiricists) that arithmetic, logic, and dictionary definitions are _a priori_ and not _a posteriori_. (Reminder: a claim is _a posteriori_ if its truth or falsity can be established only by observation

Sir Alfred Jules Ayer (1910-1989)

and experimentation. A claim is _a priori_ if its truth can be established independent of observation. The assertions of math [e.g., "3+2=5"], logic [e.g., "A=A"], and dictionaries [e.g., "A sister is a female sibling"] are all _a priori_, that is, no observation can confirm or refute their truth.) The

rationalists had viewed _a priori_ truths as the <u>deepest</u> kind of truth about reality, but Hume and the phenomenalists claimed that _a priori_ truths were merely tautologies — that is to say, redundancies or repetitions. The phenomenalists, taking a cue from Berkeley, decided that so-called "_a priori_" truths were truths derived from

This is my sister. She's a female sibling!

I'm not so sure.

certain features of linguistic conventionality, not from some eternal facts about the world. All knowledge of facts in the world would have to be based on observation, which is to say, on sense-data. So there are only two kinds of true statements: those traceable to sense-data and those true by definition (statements whose negation leads to a self-contradiction). According to this hard-nosed version of empiricism, all other sentences are nonsense (literally non-sense).[3]

   This device automatically eliminated Berkeley's God because the sentence "God exists" cannot be either confirmed or denied by appealing to observation, and the sentence is not true by definition. (The sentence "God does not exist" is not a self-contradiction. [See Chapter 5 for an argument to the contrary.]) But then how do phenomenalists respond to the problem of the world that flashes on and off, if God, Berkeley's solution to that problem, has just been eliminated? Ironically, they solve it using a passage from Berkeley, whose implications he himself may or may not have understood. Berkeley wrote: "The table I write on, I say, exists; that is, I see it and feel it: and if I were out of my study I should say it existed; meaning thereby that if I was in my study I might perceive it, or that some other spirit actually does perceive it" (part I, sec. 3). According to this schema, all declarative sentences are actually hypotheses about future sense-data. The sentence "There is a table in room 506" means "IF you went into room 506, THEN you would have the following sense-data: brown, rectangular, resistant, etc., etc." By claiming that the meaning of a declarative sentence can be correctly analyzed by translating it into an if/then hypothesis, where the _if_ clause contains an operation and the _then_ clause contains a prediction of sense-data, the phenomenalists totally bypass the problem of the table that flashes on and off. A table just is, to use the phrase of John Stuart Mill, "a permanent possibility of sensation."

The twentieth-century phenomenalists have had great difficulty with Berkeley's idealism. For Berkeley, what exist are selves and the sense-data perceived by these selves, and both selves and sense-data are spiritual or mental. The phenomenalists believed that this idealistic stance was both too metaphysical and not scientific enough. Their solution was to adopt a version of _neutral monism_, the view that reality (in this case, sense-data) is neither mental nor physical; rather, it is some third kind of unanalyzable, neutral "stuff." According to the phenomenalists, the categories "mental" and "physical" are simply LOGICAL CONSTRUCTS that are interpretations of sense-data from different perspectives. We call "material" those sense-data that we can categorize in terms of concepts like dimensionality, size, and shape; and we call "mental" those that somehow escape those categories. If the empirical facts about sense-data were slightly different, perhaps we would draw the boundaries of these categories differently. For example if every time people

entered room 506 they immediately got a headache, we might talk about headaches differently, warning folks to avoid that room because it contained a headache. We would thereby be placing

Oh Oh! There's a headache in room 506.

headaches in the category of the physical instead of the mental. So headaches, tables, mountains, rainbows, sandstorms, and acts of revenge are "logical constructs," that is, they are conceptual organizations of sense-data in ways that allow for objective analysis of them and communication about them. This view is not _so_ far from Berkeley's, after all, but it robs him of both his idealism and his theism.

Another problem with Berkeley's epistemology was that, like that of Descartes, it never solved the problem of solipsism. Berkeley can say "_esse_ is _percipi_ or _percipere_" (_to be_ is _to be perceived_ or _to perceive_), but how does he know that anyone besides himself perceives? All that I can be sure of is that I am the subject of my act of perceiving and that my sense-data are the object of

that act, but
I have no
access to
anyone else's
acts of per-
ceiving or to
anyone else's
sense-data.
Berkeley him-
self never
addressed
this problem

Does Berkeley know that
anyone besides himself truly exists?

head-on. As a theist, he probably made the Cartesian assumption
that God would not deceive him into thinking that there were other
"spirits" if there was in fact none. But the phenomenalists did not
have this option open to them because they had gotten rid of Berkeley's
God with Ockham's razor. So they took the heroic step of declaring that other people are also merely "logical constructs." In other
words, _you_ are my sense-data. (Sounds like the title of a phenom-
enalistic country and western song, though perhaps not a very
romantic one.) Or at least you are constructed out of my sense-data.
In other words, the phenomenalists became radical behaviorists
about everyone but themselves, and they even attempted a behavioristic account of themselves, that is, of the self in the first person.
In doing so, they took their cue from the notorious passage in
David Hume's _Treatise of Human Nature_ (1735), in which the Scottish
empiricist had written:

> There are some philosophers who imagine we are every moment in-
> timately conscious of what we call our _self_; that we feel its exis-
> tence and its continuance in existence; and are certain, beyond
> the evidence of a demonstration, both of its perfect identity and

113

simplicity. ... For my part, when I enter most intimately into what I call _myself_, I always stumble on some particular perception or other, of heat or cold, light or shade, love or hatred, pain or pleasure. I never can catch _myself_ at any time without a perception, and never can observe anything but the perception .... But setting aside some metaphysicians of this kind, I may venture to affirm of the rest of mankind that they are nothing but a bundle or collection of

Sung to the tune of "You Are My Sunshine"

Hume discovers the self — such as it is.

different perceptions, which succeed each other with an inconceivable rapidity, and are in a perpetual flux and movement. Our eyes cannot turn in their sockets without varying our perceptions. Our thought is still more variable than our sight; and all our other senses and faculties contribute to this change; nor is there any single power of the soul which remains unalterably the same, perhaps for one moment. [4]

Hume himself in the eighteenth century had found his skeptical analysis of the self to be very

114

disturbing, but the twentieth-century phenomenalists were inspired by it and concluded from it that the self is just another "logical construct." Where Descartes had said "I think, therefore I am," Hume and the phenomenalists could say, "I think, therefore there are sense-data." If there was to be any "self," it would have to be constructed out of these sense-data. There could be no substantiality to this self and no continuity because there were no sense-data justifying either notion.

This sacrifice of the self to logical rigor was just another radical application of Ockham's razor on the part of the empiricists. Locke had shaved away Descartes' innate ideas; Berkeley had shaved off Descartes' and Locke's notion of material substance; the phenomenalists trimmed away Descartes', Locke's, and Berkeley's notion of mental substance.

Finally, the phenomenalists introduced a category called THEORETICAL ENTITIES. This notion was meant to account for such items as atoms and electrons, whose _esse_ is clearly not _percipi_ because they can't be perceived at all. Theoretical entities are entities that are neither sense-data nor logical constructs composed of sense-data. Rather, they exist solely as entities in _theories_, and these entities are included in theories in order to facilitate more precise predictions of sense-data. For example, consider the notion of "the average American housewife." Obviously, it would be a big mistake to suppose that she actually exists, and it would be ludicrous to imagine trying to find her (perhaps in Akron, Ohio?) to interview her. The mistake becomes obvious once we remember that she has 1.78 children! Nevertheless, the notion of the average American housewife can be very useful in fields such as economics and sociology because it allows us to articulate information about consumer habits and demography in America and make accurate predictions concerning them. Now, the phenomenalists were forced to treat

The average American housewife
has 1.78 children.

atoms and electrons in the same way as they treated the average American housewife. These entities did not exist except in theories whose function it was to articulate information about sense-data and make accurate predictions about them. (Philosophers and scientists who were not phenomenalists did not find this to be a very convincing bit of theorizing; but they did have to admit that whatever status electrons, photons, and the like had, they did not exist in the same way that tables and chairs do. So any theory about their status probably would seem a bit odd.) So this is yet another radical application of Ockham's notorious razor. One begins to get the feeling that it is perhaps an _abuse_ of that razor, and one is reminded of Einstein's felicitous version of that principle: "Say everything as simply as possible, but not more so."

William of Ockham and Albert Einstein

Attacks on Phenomenalism

In spite of the flourish of interest in radical empiricism among philosophers from Britain, America, and Austria in the 1930s and 1940s, it has fallen on hard times in recent years. There have been a number of attacks on it from a variety of camps. A common denominator in these attacks (whether they come from Gestalt psychology, linguistic philosophy, structuralism, or poststructuralist positions such as deconstruction) is one that goes right for the jugular vein of classical empiricism — a denial of the existence of such a thing as a sense-datum (or an "idea" in Locke's and Berkeley's sense of the term). Phenomenalism (and with it, most empiricism) stands or falls with "psychological atomism" — the view that our knowledge of the world is built up from discrete sensorial impressions such as "yellow," "sharp," and "hot." According to this hypothesis, we construct the whole from the assemblage of parts. But recent developments in philosophical theory and psychological investigation have brought this hypothesis into doubt. The "Gestalt" psychologists, for example, claim that we move in the other direction, from whole to part, and that what creates the "whole" is not the bricks of ineffable, absolutely certain sensation (raw feels, sense-data) but a complicated and probably inextricably fused combination of neurological and social facts about perception. The neurological facts — expressed psychologically — have to do with the discovery that perception always takes place in a _field_ where a foreground is contrasted with a background. A sensation becomes a perception in a field of _meaning_, in which that sensation is given a specific meaning by being distinguished from its background, which also has a meaning, though perhaps a vaguer more inarticulate meaning than the "something" in the foreground that upstages it. The _social_ fact (i.e., conventional fact) here is the fact that what bestows meaning on the "field" is

117

a combination of knowledge and expectation that can be traced ultimately to a specific social structure.

This is a difficult point. Let me illustrate it with an example from my own experience. I was once sitting at my breakfast table, awaiting the arrival of a colleague who would drive me to work. I kept lifting my eyes from the morning paper, looking through the window down to the street in anticipation of the appearance of his bright red Volkswagen "bug," then finally I heard that unmistakable whining of a VW engine. Once again I looked to the road, where I saw, through the shrubs in the front garden, my friend's red car stationed in the driveway. I gulped down my coffee, grabbed my briefcase, and ran down the stairs to the road. Once in the driveway I was surprised to see nothing there. Puzzled, I waited a moment, thinking that my colleague might have driven up the street to turn around. After several minutes, I returned sheepishly to the house and sat down again at the table. I looked down at the driveway and suddenly realized that what I had taken to be the bright red paint of my friend's VW was in fact the dull orange of some poison oak

The case of the missing Volkswagen

leaves in the shrubbery between me and the driveway. My anticipation of his arrival, my knowledge of the color of his car, and the recognition of the sound of a Volkswagen automobile (which had probably driven past my house) conspired to create a "sense-datum" of bright red. My picture of the world at that moment had moved (fallaciously, in this case) from whole to part, not the other way around, as "psychological atomism" would have it.

Let me relate one more episode whose "moral" also undermines psychological atomism. I was sitting at that same kitchen table, reading and drinking a dark ale. My ten-year-old son was sitting across the table from me having a cola drink. Without moving my eyes from the page of my book, I reached for my ale and mistakenly grabbed his glass of cola. I took a big swig of what I expected to be ale and immediately suffered the shock of what psychologists call "cognitive dissonance." I knew that the taste was not that of ale, but for a brief moment, I had no idea what taste it was. It

Cognitive dissonance

was only once I had realized my mistake that the distinctive taste of cola came flooding into my consciousness. Again, the part had been created by the whole, by the "Gestalt," and the "whole" was composed not just of purely perceptual facts, but of anticipations and expectations drawn from my personal psychological history and from the history of my culture.

There is yet another major flaw in the empiricist program, according to contemporary wisdom. It has to do with the role of language in empiricism. Because of his Lockean suspicion about innate ideas, Berkeley ingeniously displaced the role of innate ideas (particularly the role of generating our concepts of "identity" and "thingness") onto language. For that move to work, however, it would have to be demonstrated that a consistent empiricistic theory of language is possible, one compatible with the "blank slate" hypothesis. This task was taken up in our own time by the behavioristic psychologist (or "behavioral engineer," as he preferred to be called) B.F. SKINNER. In his book, characteristically named

<u>Verbal Behavior</u>, using his notion of "operant conditioning" (involving the repetition of noises, reinforced or discouraged by a system of rewards and punishments), Skinner tried to show how we learn the language we speak. His idea has a certain natural plausibility. We've all watched the linguistic exchange when a parent teaches a small child the

Skinnerian linguistics

"color words" or the parts of the body. But Skinner's book was soundly trounced in a review of it by NOAM CHOMSKY, then a relatively unknown young linguist, now perhaps the best known living linguist in the world. Chomsky demonstrated that if all that were involved in language learning were the "blank slate" and operant conditioning, no one would ever learn a language. Among other things, Chomsky pointed out that Skinner's theory could not account for the linguistic novelty of which any competent native speaker is capable. Any such speaker can produce a completely new sentence that every other competent speaker can understand even though none of them has heard it

NOAM CHOMSKY
(b. 1928)

Hold the olive!

Uncle Elmo's martini

before. In fact, I shall produce such a sentence now: "It is not a good idea to freeze small wooly mammoths into tinted ice cubes that will be served in the dry martini of Uncle Elmo (whose grandmother fought in the Crimean War)." I am reasonably certain that no one has ever uttered just that sentence before (and for good reason!). Yet, according to Chomsky, Skinner cannot account for the fact that all of us understand it perfectly well.

Furthermore, Chomsky reminded us of the kinds of grammatical mistakes children make. The little boy comes crying to his mother, saying, "Johnny hitted me!" This is, of course, incorrect; yet it is incorrect in an interesting way. What the little boy had to "know" in order to make that error is that the way to make the preterite in English is to add "ed" to the infinitive. It's not _his_ fault that this particular verb is irregular. Where did he learn to say "hitted"? Not from imitating his parents or even from other kids, according to Chomsky, but from his _native_ ability to generate rules. This ability, which Chomsky calls the capacity for "deep grammar," is a result of the structuring of the human brain. It is something we bring to the phonetic system we learn, and not something we derive from it. All this sounds very suspiciously like the function of Descartes' _innate ideas_, and indeed, Chomsky has no qualms against making the connection between himself and the classical rationalists. He went so far as to title one of his books _Cartesian Linguistics_, and he has this to say:

Chomskian linguistics
(followed by a Skinnerian attempt
at negative conditioning)

On the basis of the best information now available, it seems reasonable to suppose that a child cannot help constructing a particular kind of transformational grammar to account for the data presented to him, any more than he can control his perception of solid objects or his attention to line and angle. Thus it may well be that the general features of language structure reflect, not so much the course of one's experience, but rather the general character of one's capacity to acquire knowledge — in the traditional sense, one's innate ideas and innate principles. [5]

Conclusion

So where does all this leave us? In the last two chapters, we have seen strengths in both the rationalists' camp and the empiricists' camp, but we have also seen weaknesses. If we accept the rationalists' notion of innate ideas, we will be able to explain how the human mind makes the translation from the reception of discrete physical data into a picture of a world of objects more or less independent of each other, and the rationalists also thereby manage to give a satisfactory account of mathematical knowledge. But rationalism does not fare well against Ockham's razor, and the notion of (God-given?) innate ideas is still somehow mysterious and easily abused. (E.g., imagine someone saying, "It is well known that women are inferior to men, and if there is no empirical evidence of this fact, that just goes to show that this knowledge is derived from an innate idea.") On the other hand, the empiricists do fare well with Ockham's razor, and there are few mysterious entities in their theories because everything is open to observation. Their ingenious move to make language carry the burden of the rationalists' "innate ideas" almost works because language is more open to investigation than are innate ideas and because such a move accounts for epistemological variation from culture to culture in a way not open to Descartes' kind of "nativism." However, as we've seen, apparently no viable empiricist theory of language has been forthcoming, and the latest data from the field of psychology indicate that "psychological atomism," the backbone of empiricism, is in deep trouble.

Skirmishes, and sometimes full-fledged wars, between the rationalists and the empiricists have been recorded for two thousand years. The first serious compromise between the two camps came at the hands of IMMANUEL KANT (1724 - 1804), whose <u>Critique of Pure Reason</u> was written as a direct response to David Hume's radical empiricism. Kant rejected the empiricists' "blank slate" hypothesis on the grounds that the mind was not simply a passive receptacle of neutral sense-data. However, Kant also rejected the rationalistic notion of "innate ideas" on the grounds that claiming that babies are born with ideas is just too farfetched. He replaced

124

these innate ideas with innate structures, which he called "categories of the understanding." These were formal and active features of the mind that imposed a kind of order on the raw data of the senses. Kant detected as innate structures of the mind a spatial / temporal perceptual gridwork (space and time) and twelve categories of the understanding, including the following:

IMMANUEL KANT
(1724 - 1804)

unity

plurality

totality

relations of substance and characteristics of substance

relations of cause and effect

relations of reciprocity

Again, these categories are not derived passively by the mind from sensorial data, but rather are actively brought by the mind to the world and imposed upon the raw data. But raw data themselves are never perceived; we perceive only data that have already been "processed" by the categories of the understanding and the spatiotemporal gridwork. This is the meaning of Kant's famous dictum: "thoughts without content are empty, intuitions without concepts are blind." This grants to the empiricists that there can be no knowledge in the absence of sensorial contribution and grants to the rationalists that sense-data alone cannot provide knowledge. It also squares with the Gestaltist insight about the relation between part and whole in our understanding of the world.

Kant's view, though definitely a compromise between rationalism and empiricism, sides more with the former than with the latter. As such, it still suffers from a few of the old Cartesian problems. Like Descartes' doctrine of innate ideas, it is still incapable of explaining why some cultures conceive differently than others such categories as space, time, unity, plurality, thingness, and causality. To bring Kant up to date, we might make Berkeley's move of supposing that these categories are more related to conventionality than Kant realized, particularly to language. But then we could preserve some rationalism by asserting Chomsky's thesis that these categories may be culturally relative because they are partially bound to "surface grammar," but that this surface grammar itself is bound to "deep grammar," which is derived from innate neurological facts.

Recent developments in philosophy may persuade us to make other adjustments as well. We may have to consider abandoning the search, shared by both rationalists and empiricists, for the foundations of knowledge. Descartes and all his epistemological followers as well as his detractors latched onto the architectural metaphor of "a house of knowledge," believing that knowledge could exist only if it were based on something absolutely certain. For the rationalists, this certainty was to be found in the _a priori_ truths derived from innate ideas. For the empiricists, it was derived from the privileged experience of sense-data. But it is beginning to look as though there is something wrong with the metaphor. Perhaps (as the contemporary American philosophers W.V.O. Quine and Richard Rorty suggest) rather than being like a house, knowledge is more like a net or a spiderweb. If some segments prove to be weak or worn-out, we repair them while hanging on to the relatively stable parts, which still offer support.

OH OH!

Is our system of knowledge more like a spiderweb than a house?

Besides objecting to the knowledge / house metaphor, Rorty suspects that the main error in epistemology was that of accepting Plato's simile that _Knowing_ is like a kind of _mental seeing_, in which case knowledge is always a relationship between a belief and its object. In Rorty's influential book, <u>Philosophy</u> <u>and</u> <u>the</u> <u>Mirror</u> <u>of</u> <u>Nature</u>, he accepts the Platonic view that knowledge is justified belief, but he tries to show that "justification" is not constituted by establishing a relation between a belief and an object of belief, but between a belief and <u>arguments</u>. He says, "If... we think of 'rational certainty' as a matter of victory in argument rather than of relation to an object known, ... we shall be looking for an airtight case rather than an unshakeable foundation." [6] We will then realize that there is no natural end to justification. Rather, the defense <u>could</u> go on forever. Perhaps, as in a court of law, the defense is usually terminated somewhat arbitrarily. Certainly, no claim to knowledge is ever immune to revision. Furthermore, according to Rorty, we have to realize that justification is a <u>social</u>, hence a historical, phenomenon. (Not every form of argument will be convincing at all historical moments.) Rorty holds that traditional epistemology is an attempt to escape from history by claiming to establish the extrahistorical and extrasocial criteria of rationality

127

and objectivity. Rorty distinguishes between "normal discourse" (any form of discourse – whether scientific, moral, theological, or political – governed by agreed-upon criteria for reaching consensus) and "abnormal discourse" (any form of discourse that lacks such criteria). And he claims that traditional epistemology has been "a self-deceptive effort to eternalize the normal discourse of the day."[7] Nevertheless, innovation has always been the result of struggles between "normal" and "abnormal" discourse. There is something exciting about this relativistic, pragmatic message, but also something slightly disconcerting because Rorty admits that his view brings us back to the position of the Greek Sophists.

Notes

1. John Locke, _An Essay Concerning Human Understanding_, A.C. Fraser, ed. (Oxford: Clarendon Press, 1894), bk. II, chap. I, sec. 2.

Unless otherwise stated, all subsequent quotes from Locke in this chapter are from this source.

2. George Berkeley, _A Treatise Concerning the Principles of Human Knowledge_, G. J. Warnock, ed. (Cleveland: World Publishing, 1963), part I, sec. 9. Unless otherwise stated, all subsequent quotes from Berkeley in this chapter are from this source.

3. Phenomenalism was an epistemology popular with some members of the influential philosophical school known as LOGICAL POSITIVISM or LOGICAL EMPIRICISM, which flourished between the two world wars. All the members of this school shared the theory of meaning here attributed to the phenomenalists.

4. David Hume, _A Treatise of Human Nature_, D.G.C. Macnabb, ed. (Cleveland: World Publishing, 1962), bk. I, part IV, sec. 6.

5. Noam Chomsky, _Aspects of the Theory of Syntax_ (Cambridge, Massachusetts: M.I.T. Press, 1965), p. 59.

6. Richard Rorty, _Philosophy and the Mirror of Nature_ (Princeton, New Jersey: Princeton University Press, 1980), pp. 156-157.

7. Rorty, _Philosophy_, p. 11.

Chapter 4

Who's on First, What's on Second?

Ontology

Ontology is theory of reality or theory of being. The big questions in ontology are these:

- What is real and what is merely appearance?

- Can there be a <u>theory</u> that draws the distinction between reality and appearance and accounts for everything that exists, or must these distinctions always remain contextual, <u>ad hoc</u>, and informal?

What is real and what is merely appearance?

The historical framework for ontological discussions has been in terms of the following categories:

MONISM: the view that there is only one reality or only one kind of thing that is real

DUALISM: the view that there are two forms of reality or two kinds of real things

PLURALISM: the view that reality is composed of many different kinds of real things

NIHILISM: the view that nothing is real (or sometimes, as a moral doctrine, that nothing _deserves_ to exist)

We have already inadvertently witnessed quite a bit of ontological discussion in Chapters 1-3 because most of the traditional epistemologists defined knowledge in terms of its _object_, which was always some real entity (e.g., Forms for Plato and sense-data for Berkeley). We have seen that Plato, Descartes, and Locke should all be categorized as dualists. Berkeley's idealism is a form of monism.

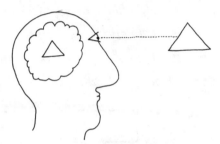

Knowledge defined in terms of its _object_ — which is some real thing

Dualism

Descartes' version is the most radical form of dualism, and even though it is an extreme version, its very exaggeration throws light on the problems of dualism in general. We saw in Chapter 2 that Descartes circumscribed two distinct spheres of being: the mental (mind, or as Descartes sometimes calls it, "spiritual substance") and the physical (body, or "material substance"). The subtitle of Descartes' _Meditations_ _on_ _First_ _Philosophy_ includes this line, "... in which ... the Distinction Between Mind and Body [is] Demonstrated." (In fact, in his first draft, the subtitle had been

"... in which the Immortality of the Soul Is Demonstrated," but when a critic pointed out that Descartes had nowhere even _mentioned_ the immortality of the soul, much less proved its existence, Descartes changed the wording of the subtitle to refer to the absolute distinction between mind and body, which to Descartes' way of thinking at least made _possible_ the immortality of the soul.) According to Descartes, a body is "an extended thing" (_res extensa_) whose characteristics are these: extension, size, shape, location, divisibility, motion, and rest. At the other extreme is mind (or soul or self), which is "a thing which thinks" (_res cogitans_). Descartes asks, "What is a thing which thinks? It is a thing which doubts, understands, conceives, affirms, denies, wills, refuses, which also imagines and feels."[1] These two "things" are completely different from each other and can exist independently of each other.

substance	MIND	BODY
essence	Thought	Extension
modes	affirmation	size
	denial	shape
	doubt	location
	volition	part
	hope	mobility
	...	
	...	

Descartes' ontology of finite things

Descartes says:

> I rightly conclude that my essence consists solely in the fact that I am a thinking thing (or a substance whose whole essence or nature is to think). And although possibly (or rather certainly, as I shall say in a moment) I possess a body

132

with which I am very intimately conjoined, yet because, on the one side, I have a clear and distinct idea of myself inasmuch as

I am only a thinking and unextended thing, and as, on the other, I possess a distinct idea of body, inasmuch as it is only an extended and unthinking thing, it is certain that this I (that is to say, my soul by which I am what I am), is entirely and absolutely distinct from my body, and can exist without it ("Meditation IV," pp. 213-214).

"I am absolutely distinct from my body and can exist without it."

Well and good! Descartes has established that, given his definitions of mind and body, they can exist without each other. But the real question is how they can exist _with_ each other. How can a nonextended spiritual substance located _nowhere_ have any effect on something so different from itself as inert matter? How can the human being be some strange combination of mind and body? (This is what the British philosopher Gilbert Ryle called the problem of "the ghost in the machine.") Now, we know that there _is_ interaction between mind and body. (If I stomp on your foot, you will be conscious

The ghost in the machine

of a sensation of pain [body influencing mind], and if you remember that you left your car lights on, you will rush to the parking lot to extinguish them [mind influencing body].) The question is, on Descartes' account, how is this possible? Descartes addressed the issue in the following way:

> ... I am not only lodged in my body as a pilot in a vessel, but ... I am very closely united to it, and so to speak so intermingled with it that I seem to compose with it one whole. For if that were not the case, when my body is hurt, I, who am merely a thinking thing, should not feel pain, for I should perceive this wound by understanding only, just as the sailor perceives by sight when something is damaged in his vessel; ... ("Meditation VI," p. 216).

This is good! Imagine a ship's pilot on his bridge trying to ma- neuver his vessel between two rocky promentories. It is a narrow passage- way, but he thinks he can make it. He keeps looking from left to right. As he is looking port side, suddenly there is a sickening "cruuunch" on his right. He looks starboard side and sees that he has scraped the rock. There is a yawning tear in the hull of the ship. "Oh criminey," he says. "Now I'm in trouble!" What if our relation to our body were like that of the captain to his ship? You are standing in the kitchen talking to a friend, resting your hand on the stove. After a while you smell the odor of burning flesh. You look to the stove and

The smell of burnt flesh

see that your skin is smoking. You pull your burning hand from the stove and say, "Oh criminey, _now_ I'm in trouble!" Or what if you were walking along, heard a sharp "snap", felt a loss of support, looked down, and _noticed_ that you'd broken your leg. Descartes is right. This is _not_ the relation that exists between our mind and our body. We do not observe that our

body is damaged, then deduce that we are in pain. As Descartes says, our consciousness and our body are "so intermingled" as to "compose... one whole." Yet once again, on his account, how is this possible? This is what Descartes has to say about this problem when he addresses it specifically:

> I had clearly ascertained that the part of the body in which the soul exercises its functions immediately is in nowise the heart, nor the whole of the brain, but merely the most inward of all its parts, to wit, a certain very small gland which is situated in the middle of its substance and so suspended above the duct whereby the animal spirits in its anterior cavities have communication with those in the posterior, that the slightest movements which take place in it may alter very greatly the course of these spirits; and reciprocally that the smallest changes which occur in the course of the spirits may do much to change the movements of this gland. [2]

Descartes has selected what is now called _the pineal gland_ as the locus of interaction between body and soul. Perhaps his logic was this: it doesn't seem to do anything else —

probably it does this! Using this logic, he could have as easily decided in favor of the tonsils or the appendix. (Besides, although there is still some debate about the function of the pineal gland, apparently it is now known that it has something to do with controlling the size of the gonads. If this is so, it makes Descartes much more of a Freudian than he'd like to be.) But the

Copy of a seventeenth century wood engraving demonstrating Descartes' theory of the pineal gland

real problem with selecting the pineal gland as the place where mind and body meet is that in doing so, he has located mind, and, as you will recall, "location" is a characteristic of body, not of mind. If Descartes locates the mind anywhere, he thereby transforms it into body, and therewith he becomes a

Herr Professor Doktor Freud and Monsieur Descartes

materialist. This conclusion, of course, would be exactly the opposite of the one Descartes set out to prove, and his whole ontology seems to unravel right here. At this point, Descartes conveniently died of the common cold and left the paradox to be sorted out by later generations.

Materialistic Monism

Materialism

Descartes had made the relation between mind and body so mysterious that it is no surprise to find later philosophers turning away from his dualism to monism. We have seen how Berkeley tried to apply Ockham's razor to dualism by eliminating the whole material side of it. But idealism has never been very popular in the West. Berkeley and Hegel (the other famous European idealist) each had followers, but even they tried to rewrite their mentors' works to avoid their idealistic conclusions. A much more popular form of monism in the West is that of MATERIALISM. This has been particularly true in the twentieth century because many people, both philosophers and nonphilosophers, feel that the authority of modern science is on the side of materialism. We will look at two different versions of this doctrine, BEHAVIORISM and the MIND-BRAIN IDENTITY THEORY.

Behaviorism

Though this doctrine is primarily promulgated by psychologists, it has philosophical import and philosophical disciples. It is the creature of the American psychologist JOHN WATSON (1878-1958), and its most articulate contemporary spokesman was B.F. SKINNER, whom we've already run into. One reason that this doctrine is a bit difficult to get a hold of is that there seem to be several variations of it, and sometimes its defenders slide from one version to another (perhaps so as not to get cornered). We will try to reduce these variations to a manageable handful, namely, to what we will call "hard behaviorism," "soft behaviorism," and "logical behaviorism."

"Hard behaviorism" is the view that there are no such things as minds or mental events, mental states, or mental processes. There are only bodies in motion (and these motions are "behaviors"). "Soft behaviorism" is the view that there _may_ be minds and mental events, mental states, and mental processes, but that _methodologically_, scientists can provide adequate explanations and predictions of activity in general, human or otherwise, without ever referring to anything mental.

You see? What'd I tell you? No mind.

This second view is not really a philosophical (i.e., ontological) one, and it is much less controversial than the first — though

138

not without difficulties of its own. The problem is that behaviorists who seem to be asserting the "hard" version sometimes slip into the "soft" version when cornered. When left alone again, they return to the "hard" position.

What behaviorists assert is something like this: all statements about human activity, including statements about people's so-called mental life, can be translated into statements about observable "behaviors" and, if not, can be shown to be either false or nonsense. So if I say, "Mary thinks it's going to rain," I should be able to show that saying this is really shorthand for a whole bunch of other assertions like:

"Mary utters the sentence 'I think it's going to rain'."

"Mary has worn her raincoat and taken her umbrella."

"Mary is wearing her boots, not her sandals."

"Mary cancelled her reservation at the outdoor restaurant."

If I say, "Bill is angry at Sam," I should be able to show that some or all of the following assertions are true:
"Bill utters the sentence 'I am angry at Sam.'"

"Bill raises his voice — he says rude things whenever Sam's name is mentioned."

"Bill's face is red; his knuckles are white."

All of this has some plausibility. After all, in a certain sense, we all _are_ behaviorists vis-à-vis other people. Whatever

I know it doesn't seem like it, but they are absolutely furious with each other.

139

you know about anybody, including your best friends, you know by virtue of observing their _behavior_ (which includes listening to what they have to say, of course). None of us has an antenna to pick up the thoughts of others. The only access to other people's mind is in fact through observation of those people's activity, which I suppose is in some sense observation of their bodies. Furthermore, behaviorism becomes philosophically plausible because we were led to it due to certain problems with dualism. It was, after all, Descartes who unwittingly opened the floodgates for behaviorism, first by failing to show how mind/body interaction was possible, second, by never dealing satisfactorily with "the problem of other minds." (How do I know that anyone besides myself has a mind?) Shortly after discussing the famous "wax example," Descartes addressed this problem, writing:

> ... when looking from a window and saying I see men who pass in the street, I really do not see them, but infer that what I see is men, ... And yet what do I see from the window but hats and coats which may cover automatic machines? Yet I judge these to be men. And similarly, solely by the faculty of judgment which rests in my mind, I comprehend that which I believed I saw with my eyes. ("Meditation II," p. 177)

Hats, coats, and automatic machines

Most critics find this very unsatisfactory. Descartes may have proved that _he_ has a mind (or, as he says, that he _is_ a mind), but he certainly hasn't proved that anyone else does. The observable data are quite compatible with the view that "everyone else" is really just a complicated robot (perhaps a _meaty_ robot, but a robot just the same). Furthermore, the mind that Descartes proved to exist — i.e., his _own_ mind — is _not_ _located_; that is, it is nowhere. The behaviorist asks how much better is a mind that's nowhere than no mind at all.

All these problems with dualism support the behaviorist's claims. But there are nevertheless problems for the behaviorist, and some of these problems are quite Cartesian in nature. For example, it may well be that I know that _you_ have a stomach ache because I see you grimace, hold your tummy, go to the medicine cabinet and prepare yourself a "fizzy." But that is certainly not the way that I discover that _I_ have a stomachache. I find out that I have a stomach ache just the way Descartes says I do — I am immediately _conscious_ of my pain. The soft behaviorist (but not the hard behaviorist) can retort that the scientist doesn't study himself; rather, he is studying others. Even so, a theory that is true for everyone but oneself is an odd one. (what if Newton had claimed that bodies on the earth's surface fall at thirty-two feet per second squared ... except for his own body, which was exempt from that law!)

I am popping aspirin; therefore I am in pain.

141

The second objection to behaviorism is also Cartesian in nature. Descartes had claimed that no account of human existence could be given without allowing a key role to a vocabulary designating mental acts: to affirm, to deny, to conceive, to know, to hope, to expect, to will, etc. Now, this is the very kind of list that

Sir Isaac Newton discovers the law of gravity, which applies to everything but himself.

Skinner wishes to get rid of on the grounds that these terms are names of mental events that in fact do not exist. Yet his own publications are rampant with these very verbs. Perhaps he thinks (thinks !?) that he is justified in using this "pre-scientific" language because he has to convert an unsophisticated public to his cause, and doing so requires speaking street language with them (in Berkeley's phrase, to speak with the vulgar but think with the refined). And every now and then Skinner catches himself using the hated vocabulary and offsets it by putting the questionable terms within quotation marks. (E.g., "Science ... has extended our 'understanding' [whatever that may be]...")[3] Whenever Skinner does this, the implication is that if he wanted to, he <u>could</u> translate these offending terms into truly scientific categories (i.e., into descriptions of behaviors brought about by conditioning).

But _is_ it really possible to do this? And would there really be an advance in scientific clarity if we were able to do so? I have a colleague who is a behaviorist, and when he was asked at a symposium on love whether he loved his wife, he responded saying, "I react positively to her behavioral configurations, and she to mine." (!!!) Once when describing panicked people at the scene of a fire, this same chap said, "They jumped from the windows and engaged in fleeing behavior" instead of saying, "They ran away." I suppose people _can_ learn to talk this way, but why would they want to?

The view called LOGICAL BEHAVIORISM

Some people engaged in fleeing behavior, others running away

143

is an important philosophical theory, but in one sense perhaps a treatment of it doesn't belong precisely at this point of our discussion. This is because logical behaviorists are not necessarily materialists — some are and some aren't. We will inspect the version of logical behaviorism set forth by GILBERT RYLE (1900-1976), the British "ordinary language philosopher," who in fact did not consider himself a materialist but a pluralist. Indeed, Ryle never even used the term "logical behaviorism" to describe his own view. But because Ryle's theory came to be the most widely discussed version of logical behaviorism, we will include it here in this section, even if it fits in a little awkwardly.

Ryle's influential book of 1949, _The Concept of Mind_, constitutes a sustained attack upon Cartesian dualism (though it also provides a critique of Skinner's hard behaviorism, which will be discussed shortly). In the first chapter of his book, Ryle wrote:

> The official doctrine, which hails chiefly from Descartes, is something like this. With the doubtful exceptions of idiots and infants in arms every human being has both a body and a mind. Some would prefer to say that every human being is both a body and a mind. His body and his mind are ordinarily harnessed together, but after the death of the body his mind may continue to exist and function.
>
> Human bodies are in space and are subject to the mechanical laws which govern all other bodies in space. Bodily processes and states can be inspected by external observers. So a man's bodily life is as much a public affair as are the lives of animals and reptiles and even as the careers of trees, crystals and planets.
>
> But minds are not in space, nor are their operations subject to mechanical laws. The workings of one mind are not witnessable by other observers; its career is private. Only I can take direct cognizance of the states and processes of my own mind. A person therefore lives through two collateral histories, one consisting of what happens in and to his body, the other consisting of what happens in and to his mind. The first is public, the second private. The events in the first history are events in the physical world, those in the

second are events in the mental world.

. . . .

Underlying this partly metaphorical representation of the bi-furcation of a person's two lives there is a seemingly more pro-found and philosophical assumption. It is assumed that there are two different kinds of existence or status. What exists or happens may have the status of physical existence, or it may have the status of mental existence. Somewhat as the faces of coins are either heads or tails, or somewhat as living creatures are either male or female, so, it is supposed, some existing is physical ex-isting, other existing is mental existing.

. . . .

Such in outline is the official theory. I shall often speak of it, with deliberate abusiveness, as "the dogma of the Ghost in the Machine." I hope to prove that it is entirely false, and false not in detail but in principle. It is not merely an assem-blage of particular mistakes. It is one big mistake and a mistake of a particular kind. It is, namely, a category-mistake. It represents the facts of mental life as if they belonged to one logical type or category (or range of types or categories) when they actually belong to another. [4]

A "category-mistake," according to Ryle, is the mistake of taking a term or phrase that belongs in one logical or gram-matical category and erroneously placing it in another cate-gory, then drawing absurd conclusions from that miscategorization.

In fact, the whole of Lewis Carroll's books _Alice in Wonderland_ and _Through the Looking Glass_ are great repositories of category-mistakes. Consider the discussion between Alice and the White King. The king is concerned about two messengers he is await-ing and says to Alice:

"Just look along the road, and tell me if you can see either of them."

"I see nobody on the road," said Alice.

"I only wish _I_ had such eyes," the King remarked in a fretful tone. "To be able to see Nobody! And at that dis-tance too! Why, it's as much as _I_ can do to see real people, by this light!" [5]

The source of the joke here is obvious. The sentences, "I see

145

I only wish I had such eyes!

(After Sir John Tenniel)

someone" and "I see no one" look similar. Grammatically, they each have a subject, a verb, and an object. But the "category-mistake" is that of believing that therefore the terms "someone" and "no one" are both names of existing entities.

Ryle, of course, gives us a couple of his own examples of category-mistakes. His first example is of a foreigner who visits a university. He is shown the library, the classrooms, the quad, the students, the professors, sport fields, and administrative offices. Thanking his guide, he then says, "But where is the university?" He fails to see that the university is not something else besides all those things — it just is the totality of those items.

Ryle's second example is of another foreigner visiting his first cricket game. Having been shown all the features of the playing field and explained all the functions of the players, he says, "But there is no one left on the field to contribute to the famous element of team spirit. I see who does the bowling, the batting, and the wicket-keeping; but I do not see whose role it is to exercise esprit de corps."

This second example is especially instructive. Let's change the sport in the example from cricket to baseball because, if you're like me, you _are_ a foreigner at a cricket game. Imagine that you are attending a baseball game with an interested but ignorant visitor from another culture who, after having been pointed out the bats, mitts, pitcher's mound, bleachers, pitchers, infielders, outfielders, base runners, umpire, base hits, home runs, and balls, now asks,

TEAM SPIRIT

"Where is the team spirit?" Obviously, you are not going to respond by saying, "Oh, terribly sorry to have left it out. It's right there between second base and third base." It's

not a _thing_ you could point out at all. What _would_ you say? Let's suppose you were René Descartes. In that case, you might say something like this: ⟶

Team spirit (like _all_ spirit) is a mental phenomenon, hence not a physical one. It is not located at all, and cannot be shown. It can only be experienced. Therefore, strictly speaking, there is nothing to see - period.

Now let's suppose you were B.F. Skinner. You might say something like this: →

Neither of these answers would be very satisfactory

"Team spirit" is supposed to be the name of some mysterious spiritual entity. In fact, there are no such things as spiritual entities, hence no such thing as "team spirit." Frankly, we'd be better off abandoning the term and replacing it with a description of what's really there — namely, behaviors!

to the foreigner, and, according to Ryle, they would both be based on a category-mistake, and the same category-mistake in each case — that of thinking that terms like "team spirit" are names of ghostly episodes, then deducing the absurd conclusions that either (1) they can only be experienced in the first person (Descartes' view) or (2) they don't exist at all (Skinner's view). In fact, to say that ball-players have "team spirit" is to refer to a certain way of playing. (They hustle; they "talk it up" [say "hey babe!" a lot]; they pat each other on the rear end; they throw the ball from player to player between plays; they run rapidly on and off the field at inning changes.)

when team spirit departs

Now, what Ryle would say about "team spirit" (which he thinks is what you and I would say about it in our non-"philosophical" moments [and this is why he is called an "ordinary language philosopher"]) is approximately what he says about other mentalistic terms like "intelligent," "stupid," "thoughtful," "hopeful," and "intentional." That is that these terms are _not_ names of ghostly events that may or may not exist; rather, they are references to ways people do things. To clarify this view, imagine the following scenario: I am your philosophy teacher. I am lecturing to you about Descartes. Suddenly the classroom door flies open, and in strides a young man with a particularly intense look on his face. Before I can prevent it, he reaches into his pocket, pulls out a bottle of ink, un- caps it, and pours it on my head. With a malicious grin on his face, he turns to you and says, "Palmer flunked me last semester." Then he strides out. I yell, "He did that on purpose!" Naturally, I sue! You are my witnesses

An intentional act

at the trial. In the state of California, in order to find a person guilty of a criminal act, in the first degree, it must be established that he had _mens rea_, criminal intent. Suppose the young man's lawyer is Descartes. He addresses the jury say- ing: "My client is accused of intentionally injuring Professor Palmer, but in fact no one can know anyone's intentions except his own because intentions are purely private phenomena. Therefore, in the absence of a confession by my client, there can be no evidence whatsoever that he had such an intention. Therefore, he must be found 'not guilty.'"

Or suppose the young man's lawyer is Skinner, who might say, "My client is accused of intentionally injuring Professor Palmer. But what in fact _is_ an intention? Can it be observed? Weighed? Passed around? Measured? Can samples be taken from it? No! There

Ladies and gentlemen of the jury, ...

are no such things as intentions; therefore my client could not possibly have done anything 'intentionally'; hence he must be found to be innocent."

Neither of these defenses would stand up in court for a minute. In order to establish that the act was done intentionally, all the prosecuting attorney would have to do is call you as witnesses, and you would describe the _manner_ in which he performed his act. According to Ryle, in saying that someone did something intention-ally, all we mean is that he did it in a certain manner. _What_ man-ner? What is the function of saying that someone did something intentionally? It is to distinguish that act from something done _ac-cidentally_. There is a big difference between running down the stairs to get the mail (intentionally), and falling down the stairs because of stepping on your son's skateboard (accidentally). Skinner's attempt to get rid of intentions has the consequence of abolishing that important distinction. Would this really be a scientific advance? It's difficult to think so.

The upshot of all this is that Ryle falls somewhere between Descartes and Skinner. He is in agreement with Descartes that it not only makes sense to use mentalistic terminology to describe human activity, but is absolutely necessary. He says:

Just going downstairs to check the mail

I am not ... denying that there occur mental processes. Doing long division is a mental process and so is making a joke. But I am saying that the phrase "there occur mental processes" does not mean the same sort of thing as "there occur physical processes," and, therefore, that it makes no sense to conjoin or disjoin the two.

If my argument is successful, there will follow some interesting consequences. First, the hallowed contrast between Mind and Matter will be dissipated, but dissipated not by either of the equally hallowed absorptions of Mind by Matter or of Matter by Mind, but in quite a different way.... It will also follow that both Idealism and Materialism are answers to an improper question. The "reduction" of the material world to mental states and processes, as well as the "reduction" of mental states and processes to physical states and processes, presupposes the legitimacy of the disjunction "Either there exist minds or there exist bodies (but not both)." It would be like saying, "Either she bought a left-hand and a right-hand glove or she bought a pair of gloves (but not both)."

It is perfectly proper to say, in one logical tone of voice, that there exist minds and to say, in another logical tone of voice, that there exist bodies. But these expressions do not in-dicate two different species of existence, ... [6]

In spite of his agreement with Descartes that mental terms are appropriate for describing features of human activity, Ryle is still closer to Skinner's behaviorism than to Descartes' dualism be-cause Ryle thinks that the meaning of mental terms must ulti-mately be linked up to observable behavior. To say that Peter inten-tionally poured ink on Don is to describe _a way of doing something_; it is _not_ to describe a ghostly event. This is why Ryle is called a "logical behaviorist." The _logic_ of a term like "intentional" must link that term up with some ob-servable behavior.

A ghostly event

I think it would be fair to say that Ryle has gone a long way toward dispelling the myth of the "ghost in the machine." Yet there still remain problems. Ryle thinks that mental terms generally refer to _dispositions to behave_ in certain ways. ("John is courageous." — He is disposed to stand his ground. "John knows long division." — He is disposed to be able to solve certain kinds of problems. "John is thoughtful." — He is disposed to pause in efficacious ways and not act precipitously.) So far, so good. But it is certainly possible to be generally courageous, yet unchar-acteristically do a cowardly thing. And it is certainly possible to think deeply about long division without being disposed to _do_ anything. In spite of Ryle's efforts, the ghost in the machine has not been completely exorcized. It still haunts us in philosophy.

Either some one-eyed, striped, paranoid cannibal anteaters are diaphanous, or they are not....

Oooo...

Not all thoughts can be acted upon.

The Mind-Brain Identity Theory

This version of materialism does not deny the existence of mental events (as does hard behaviorism) or claim that mental terminology is really a reference to ways of doing things (as does logical behaviorism). Rather, as the name indicates, it claims that mental terms do name real entities, but what they name are in fact neurological events. This theory has the advantage over all forms of behaviorism of not needing to deny the Cartesian and commonsensical claim that there exist mental states that are experienced as essentially private. (Only I can experience my thought, my headache.) Yet it avoids all the pitfalls of dualism and seems to have the authority of science behind it. In an influential article of 1959, the Australian philosopher, J.J.C. SMART, wrote:

It seems to me that science is increasingly giving us a viewpoint whereby organisms are able to be seen as psychochemical mechanisms: it seems that even the behavior of man himself will one day be explicable in mechanistic terms. There does seem to be, so far as science is concerned, nothing in the world but increasingly complex arrangements of physical constituents. All except for one place: in consciousness.... So sensations, states of consciousness, do seem to be the one sort of thing left outside the physicalist picture, and for various reasons I just cannot believe that this can be so. That everything should be explicable in terms of physics (together of course with descriptions of the ways in which the parts are put together - roughly, biology is to physics as radio-engineering is to electro-magnetism) except the occurrence of sensations seems to me to be frankly unbelievable. [7]

Smart's thesis is simply that "sensations are nothing over and above brain processes." He admits that his thesis cannot be <u>proven</u> to be true today, but he expects that someday it will be proven, and he is trying to pave the way for that development by establishing that there are no <u>a priori</u> (i.e., conceptual) objections to it. That is to say, he is trying to establish that there is nothing incoherent in the idea (as its critics claim). Smart thinks that the forthcoming discovery that mental states and processes are just brain

states and processes will be very much like the earlier discoveries that:

- Lightning is an electrical discharge from cloud to cloud or cloud to surface.

- Water is H_2O.

- The morning star is the evening star.

It is important to see that Smart is not claiming that the terms on the left side of the verb "is" _mean_ the same things as the terms on the right side. People used the words "lightning" and "water" long before the physical composition of lightning and water were discovered. So Smart's equation is not just a linguistic one, but a scientific one. It can't be proved by looking at words, but by looking at facts.

But a number of philosophers (including Jerome Shaffer, Norman Malcolm, and Richard Taylor) have registered objections to the identity theory's claim to be scientific by asking exactly _what_ facts would have to be discovered to prove the identity theory true.[8] Keep in mind the nature of a _strict identity_ of the type that holds between the morning star and the evening star (and between mental events and brain events, according to Smart). In terms of spatial and temporal features, everything that is true of the one side of the equation must be true of the other. If the morning star is the evening star, and if the morning star is X miles from the sun at time T', then the evening star must also be X miles from the sun at time T'. If the evening star has a mass of Y, then the morning star must have a mass of Y. If there is any difference in these characteristics, then the morning star is _not_ the evening star. What about thoughts and brain events? Do they have the same spatial and temporal features? But here's the rub. Does it make any sense at all to attribute spatial features to thoughts? Shaffer says:

> However, so far as thoughts are concerned, it makes no sense to talk about a thought's being located in some place or places in the body. If I report having suddenly thought something, the question _where_ in my body that thought occurred would be utterly senseless. It would be as absurd to wonder whether that thought might have been cubical or a micron in diameter. [9]

Shaffer's point is not that it is impossible to prove that thoughts have location, nor that the view that they are located may turn out to be false, but that that view is

We seem to have a rapidly fading, erratic, incoherent, possibly psychotic neuron firing here.

absurd. There are all sorts of things you can say about the physical properties of neurons —

you can talk about their size, their shape, their color, their weight. But what sense would there be in asking whether the realization that you left your lunch at home was a triangular or tubular realization, a yellow or a gray one, a light or a heavy one? According to Shaffer, if there are things that make perfect sense to say about brain states but are nonsense when said about mental states, then mental states are not brain states, and the identity theory is false (in the same way that if there were things that made perfect sense when said about the morning star but that were nonsense when said about the evening star, then the morning star could not be the evening star). In other words, Shaffer is accusing Smart of committing a category-mistake.

That's the morning star. It guides sailors across the wine-dark sea.

That's the evening star. Its slithy toves do gyre and gimble in the wabe.

Talking nonsense about the evening star

It is difficult to evaluate Shaffer's view. His argument has some weight because it certainly does seem odd to talk about thoughts, feelings, hopes, expectations, beliefs, and intentions using the vocabulary of three-dimensional physical objects. Yet perhaps Shaffer is open to the criticism that his argument "begs the question" (i.e., presupposes to be true the very thing it ought to prove to be true). Is it really impossible that someday linguistic

157

conventions will develop that will allow the association of mental phenomena with physical models? Probably it would have once seemed absurd to associate the experience of warmth or cold with a numerical value, but after the invention of the thermometer, we find that association perfectly normal. Who's to say that a future scientific discovery or an invention won't result in the normalization of sentences like "My C-fibers, section M12-0332, just fired at intensity n," instead of "I just realized I left my lunch at home."? (!) But even so, Shaffer would ask how could C-fibers firing be _false_ or _misleading_ in the way that thoughts and sensations can be?

However this may be, there is another argument against the "identity theory" that is easier to understand and evaluate. This criticism does not intend to show the identity theory to be nonsense but to demonstrate it as nonempirical, as not scientific. Suppose that neurophysiology advances so far that someday a kind of brain scanner will exist that will be able to show that every time any conscious activity takes place (thoughts, sensations, emotions) certain neurological activities are identified with exactitude. Every time Mary reports that she realizes she left her lunch at home, the scanner demonstrates that her C-fibers, section M12-0332, fired at intensity n, and vice versa. Would this prove that mental states _are_ brain states? No. The most it would prove is that mental states are _correlated_ with brain states, that is, that every time the one happens, the other happens simultaneously. But correlation — even strict correlation — is not identity. Even with the most advanced technological equipment, it would be impossible to establish that just because thoughts are always correlated with events in the brain, they are identical with those events. Therefore even if the mind-brain identity theory were true, it could never be _known_ to be true. It could not, as the philosophers of science say, be "falsified." That is, no evidence could possibly exist that would tend to establish its truth or falsity. This fact certainly detracts from the identity theory's claim to be scientific.

Some materialists have come to the conclusion that these arguments against the identity theory are cogent, so they have modified the theory to what is called ELIMINATIVE MATERIALISM. According to this version, the identity "Mental events are brain events" should no longer be thought of as being like "The morning star is the evening star," but more like the following:

Ben is about to learn something important.

"'Zeus' thunderbolts' are discharges of static electricity."

"'Demonical possession' is a form of hallucinatory psychosis."

"The 'quantity of caloric fluid' is the mean kinetic energy of molecules."

"'Unicorn horns' are narwhals' horns." [10]

In other words, the correct formula is no longer "X=Y." Rather, it is "What people used to call X is now known to be Y." Richard Rorty suggests that future scientific discoveries may so upstage our currently ordinary way of talking about "mental phenomena" that we may someday say, "My C-fibers are stimulated" instead of "I am in pain." Rorty is not actually claiming that a sentence like "I am in pain" is <u>false</u>, but that there might someday prove to be a better way of making this report. (By "better," he means better in terms of explanation and predictability.) In fact, Rorty seems loath to say that even sentences like 'Zeus' thunderbolts are lighting up the evening sky" or "Dora is possessed by demons" are false. (This is because he apparently thinks that terms get their meaning and their truth value

from being part of a theoretical or quasi-theoretical system, and not from some permanent and ahistorical thing called "meaning.") It is just that we have now eliminated these "language games" for "better" ones.

Nevertheless, Rorty admits that the claim that there might

turn out to be no such things as sensations of pain (in the way that there turned out to be no such things as demons) seems scanda- lous, but he thinks that the scandal alone does not constitute a refutation of his theory.

Not surprisingly, a goodly number of phi- losophers do think that the scandal is enough to refute eliminative materialism. The sentence "Dora is possessed by demons" is a _theoretical_ sentence. It is based on a _theory_ of demons. Not every culture has shared that

theory, and some that have held that theory during stages of their history have abandoned it at later stages. But "I am in pain" is not a _theoretical_ statement at all. One could know that one was in pain whether or not one believed any theory about pain. No doubt members of every culture have had such ex- periences as pain and have had linguistic ways of reporting those experiences that were independent of any theory and therefore incapable of being upstaged by a later theory. Phi- losophers like Richard Bernstein think that this fact alone is enough to show that what "eliminative materialism" wants to eliminate (viz., references to mental phenomena) cannot be eliminated."

Pluralism

There is another alternative besides dualism and materialistic monism, and that is pluralism. Ontological pluralism is the view that there is a plurality of real things and that this plurality cannot be reduced either to a duality or to a oneness. Historically, ARISTOTLE (384-322 B.C.) is the most famous defender of this view. He believed that reality was composed of individual "substances," which to him were, in almost all cases, material objects with an essence. The essence (or "form," as he called it, borrowing Plato's term but deflating its otherworldliness) is the thing's "whatness," and its materiality is its "thisness." That is,

ARISTOTLE
(384-322 B.C.)

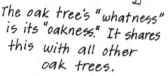

The oak tree's "whatness" is its "oakness." It shares this with all other oak trees.

Its "thisness" is what is unique about it — what distinguishes it from all other oak trees.

an oak tree's "whatness," its "essence" or "form," is the combination of characteristics that make it an oak tree rather than, say, a pussy cat; and its "thisness" is its individuality — what distinguishes _this_ oak tree from all other oak trees (especially its spatial materiality — the fact that this oak tree is here, now, and none other is). Aristotle would have disagreed with the contemporary scientific view that "oakness" itself could be further analyzed into chemical, then molecular, then atomic, then subatomic combinations; so anyone who chose Aristotle's pluralism today would have to rewrite and update it.

Something like a revision of Aristotle's views took place during the twenty-year period after World War II at the hands of a group of British philosophers to whom we have already referred as "ordinary language philosophers." Under the impact of Cambridge philosopher G.E. MOORE's (1873-1958) influential paper, "A Defense of Common Sense," and the philosophy of Ludwig Wittgenstein (see more about him in Chapter II), these philosophers defended a version of "naive realism" according to which reality is pretty much what it seems to be. Neither the categories of dualism or monism nor Kant's "categories of the understanding," but the categories of ordinary language correctly account for the real world. Members of this school, such as Gilbert Ryle (whose "logical behaviorism" we just inspected) ask why we should accept the dualist's

What you see is what you get.

Naive realism

Speech bubbles: "Everything goes in this box!" "No! Some things go in this box, some in this one."

The argument between the Monist and the Dualist

claim that everything in the world must fit in either of two boxes (mind or matter) or the materialists' view that everything must fit in <u>one</u> box. There are hundreds of boxes. There are humans, rocks, clouds, newts, prime numbers, plans, leopards, carrots, square roots, political parties, corporations, marriages, and birthday parties (just for starters). There are also symphonies. Take Beethoven's Fifth. Is it physical, is it mental, or is it a combination of a

Thought bubble: "Maybe this one will be mental and the Ninth physical..."

Ludwig Van Beethoven contemplating the Fifth Symphony, trying to decide whether it is a mental or a physical thing.

physical thing and a mental thing? Nobody (but a philosopher) would ever ask such a question. Very little of interest can be said about Beethoven's Fifth in terms of these categories, and those people who do have interesting things to say about it hardly ever deliver that information in terms of its being a physical thing or a mental thing.

What's true of Beethoven's Fifth is true of the U.S. Constitution. Is it a physical thing? No. Even if the parchment in Washington, D.C., burned, we would still have a Constitution. Nor does it make much sense to say that it is a mental thing (in which case, if for a moment everyone stopped thinking about it, would it cease to exist?). If it is a thing at all, it is a _social_ thing, which is not at all the same as being a physical and a mental thing. And what about the square root of nine?

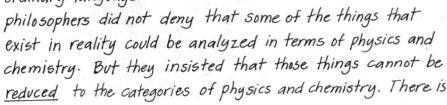

Well, that's it! Now nothing is illegal.

Ryle and the ordinary language philosophers did not deny that some of the things that exist in reality could be analyzed in terms of physics and chemistry. But they insisted that those things cannot be _reduced_ to the categories of physics and chemistry. There is a fallacy involved in saying that because a table can be analyzed in terms of its molecular structure, therefore the table itself

The table is not solid!

is unreal (or even less real than the molecules). A colleague of mine, a physics professor, tells his students that tables are not really solid. Then he explains that this is so because there is more space taken up by the distance between the atoms in the table than by the atoms themselves. As Ryle would say, this argument is absurd (another category-mistake). Here the scientist is wrong, and ordinary language is right. Tables are solid (or at least _good_ tables are solid) even though the space between the atoms is greater than the space taken up by the atoms. As Ryle points out, the so-called "world

This is definitely as real as it gets.

Definitely.

of science" is not a more _real_ world than the world of tables and chairs, any more than "the poultry world" (the name of a magazine for chicken farmers) is a more real world than the everyday world.

Conclusion

What conclusion should we draw from the various ontological alternatives presented and the welter of arguments for and against them? First, it seems to me that there is no good reason to believe radical dualism and lots of reasons to disbelieve it. The claim that there are two kinds of substances, a physical one and a spiritual one, has very little, if any, scientific evidence to back it up; and the philosophical problems generated by this view are so great as to overshadow any advantage the theory may have.

What about materialism? My own view is that in _some_ sense, materialism must be true. That is, it must be true that our small corner of the universe is composed of the same "stuff" that the rest of the universe is composed of, and at this point in the history of science, this means that it looks as though it is composed of subatomic

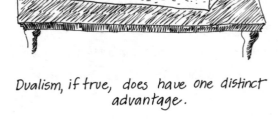

Dualism, if true, does have one distinct advantage.

particles that are themselves comprised of bundles or quanta of energy. But the sense in which materialism is true may turn out to be fairly trivial because I don't think there's much reason to expect that the accounts of human activity given by anthropologists, sociologists, psychologists, and by ourselves as ordinary individuals describing our own and other people's thoughts, actions, hopes, fears, and suspicions will ever be given in a more accurate form in terms of molecules, atoms, electrons, and quanta of energy. As the important American philosopher Saul Kripke puts it:

> Materialism, I think, must hold that a physical description of the world is a _complete_ description of it, that any mental facts are "ontologically dependent" on physical facts in the straightforward sense of following from them by necessity. No identity theorist seems to me to have made a convincing argument against the intuitive view that this is not the case. [12]

It isn't just with "mental facts" that materialism seems inadequate, but perhaps even more so with "institutional facts." Consider three examples. The first one is "Bill sees Mary." Is it possible that someday there may exist a purely physical description — a description in terms of the laws and entities of physics and chemistry — that logically entails this statement? I'm not sure what that would look like, but I think it is plausibly the case so we'll concede victory to the materialist here.

The second example is "Bill loves Mary." Is it possible that someday there may exist a purely physical description — a description in terms of the laws and entities of physics and chemistry — that logically entails the second statement? Can we imagine some kind of brain scanner, biopsy, or blood test that would definitively answer the question "Does Bill love Mary?" I don't think this is likely, but it may be possible, so I'll grant this possibility to the materialist too.

The third example is "Bill is married to Mary." Can we anticipate a purely physical description that replaces this? I think not. There will be no brain scanner, biopsy, or blood test that can determine that the third statement is

true or false for the simple reason that being married is not a *physical* state at all; nor is it merely an emotional or mental state. It is a *legal* state, a social state. If Bill is an unmarried, eligible male, and he stands before an ordained clergyman alongside Mary, who is an unmarried, eligible female, and if they

both respond to certain questions posed to them by the clergy-man by saying, "I will," then they are married, and no brain scanner, biopsy, blood or urine test will be pertinent to determine or refute that fact. Of course, it must be true that in _some_ sense all of Bill's and Mary's molecules had to be in a certain condition for all this to be the case, but this is the trivial sense in which materialism is true.

Sociology and anthropology are the sciences of human conventions, and there is no reason to expect that their descriptions of those conventions, along with our ordinary discourse about them, will someday be replaced by descriptions of molecules. The error of materialism is that of accepting J.J.C. Smart's claim, "... everything should be explicable in terms of physics." Why _should_ everything be explicable in terms of physics? Why, for example, should a description of the historical significance of Velazquez' painting The Surrender of Breda and of its aesthetic qualities be "explicable in terms of physics"? There are, as Ludwig Wittgenstein said, _many_ forms of life, and it is a philosophical error to assume that there must be _one_ model to account for all of them.

So in rejecting dualism and in rejecting materialism in any

170

but a trivial sense, I seem to be making a pitch for a Rylean kind of pluralism, and in some ways, I am. I find some loose combination of the categories of discourse of ordinary language, philosophy, literature, and the physical and social sciences to be adequate, or at least very helpful, in trying to make my way about

Look it up in the chapter on Spanish art.

BASIC PHYSICS

in the world. But what about myself as an _ontologist_? Remember the big questions we asked at the beginning of this chapter: what is real and what is merely appearance? Can there be a _theory_ that draws the distinction between reality and appearance and accounts for everything that exists, or must these distinctions always remain contextual, _ad hoc_, and informal? I think at this point in our intellectual development the latter option seems to be the correct one. But what does this mean for ontology? Can there not be a _theory of reality_? Maybe not. John Austin (1911-1960), perhaps the best practitioner of ordinary language philosophy, had this to say about the word "real":

> [... the word "real" is] highly exceptional; exceptional in this respect that, unlike "yellow" or "horse" or "walk," it does not have one single, specifiable, always-the-same _meaning_. (Even Aristotle saw through this idea.) _Nor_ does it have a large number of different meanings — it is not _ambiguous_,

even "systematically." Now, words of this sort have been responsible for a great deal of perplexity.... Consider, for instance,
a case which at first sight one might think was pretty straightforward — the case of "real colour." What is meant by the
"real" colour of a thing? Well, one may say with some confidence,
that's easy enough: the _real_ colour of the thing is the colour
that it looks to a normal observer in conditions of normal
or standard illumination; and to find out what a thing's real
colour is, we just need to be normal and to observe it in those
conditions.

But suppose ... that I remark to you of a third party,
"That isn't the real colour of her hair." Do I mean by this
that, if you were to observe her in conditions of standard
illumination, you would find that her hair did not look that colour?
Plainly not — the conditions of illumination may be standard
already. I mean, of course, that her hair has been _dyed_,
and normal illumination just doesn't come into it at all.

. . . .

Compare: "What is the real taste of saccharine?" ...
"What is the real colour of the sky? Of the sun? Of the moon?
Of a chameleon?" We say that the sun in the evening some-
times looks red — well, what colour is it _really_?

. . . .

Contrast this with cases in which we _do_ know how to proceed: "Are those real diamonds?" "Is that a real duck?" Items
of jewellery that more or less closely resemble diamonds may
not be real diamonds because they are paste or glass; that
may not be a real duck because it is a decoy, or a toy duck,
or a species
of goose
closely re-
sembling a
duck, or
because I
am having
a hallucina-
tion. These
are all of
course quite
different
cases. And
notice in
particular
(a) that, in

most of them "observation by a normal observer in standard conditions" is completely irrelevant; (b) that something which is not a real duck is not a <u>non-existent</u> duck, or indeed a non-existent anything; and (c) that something existent, e.g. a toy, may perfectly well not be real, e.g. not a real duck.

. . . .

But with "real"... it is the negative use that wears the trousers. That is, a definite sense attaches to the assertion that something is real, a real such-and-such, only in the light of a specific way in which it might be, or might have been, <u>not</u> real. "A real duck" differs from the simple "a duck" only in that it is used to exclude various ways of being not a real duck — but a dummy, a toy, a picture, a decoy, etc.; and moreover I don't know <u>just</u> how to take the assertion that it's a real duck unless I know <u>just</u> what, on that particular occasion, the speaker has it in mind to exclude.

. . . .

It should be quite clear, then, that there are no criteria to be laid down <u>in general</u> for distinguishing the real from the not real. How <u>this</u> is to be done must depend on <u>what</u> it is with respect to which the problem arises in particular cases.[13]

What if Austin is right, and there is no such <u>thing</u> as "reality," hence no such study as "the study of reality"? Does that mean that we have nothing to do as ontologists? No. We can still philosophically scrutinize the various "forms of life" (political, religious, artistic, moral, scientific, etc.) and try to see how they hang together, if in fact they do hang together. And we must be vigilant for new breakthroughs in some of these areas, for new "paradigm shifts" as they are now called, because a major shift in science, art, or politics may well call for a shift in both our "ordinary" way of looking at the world and in the content of our philosophy. So the ontological task, like most philosophical tasks, is an ongoing one.

Notes

1. René Descartes, _Meditations on First Philosophy_, in _The Essential Descartes_, Margaret D. Wilson, ed., Elizabeth S. Haldane and G.R. T. Ross, trans. (New York: New American Library, 1969),"Meditation II," p. 174. Unless otherwise stated, all subsequent quotes from Descartes in this chapter are from this source.

2. René Descartes, _The Passions of the Soul_, in Wilson, ed., _The Essential Descartes_, p. 362.

3. Carl Rogers and B.F. Skinner, "Some Issues Concerning the Control of Human Behavior: A Symposium," _Science_, Vol. 124 (Nov. 30, 1956), pp. 1057-1066.

4. Gilbert Ryle, _The Concept of Mind_ (New York: Barnes and Noble, 1962), pp. 11-13, 15-16.

5. Lewis Carroll, _Alice in Wonderland_ and _Through the Looking Glass_ (New York: New American Library, 1960), p. 194.

6. Ryle, _The Concept_, pp. 22-23.

7. J.J.C. Smart, "Sensations and Brain Processes," _Philosophical Review_, Vol. 68 (1959), pp. 141-156.

8. See Norman Malcolm, _Problems of Mind_: _Descartes to Wittgenstein_ (New York: Harper and Row, 1971); Jerome Shaffer, "Recent Work on the Mind-Body Problem," _American Philosophical Quarterly_, Vol. 2, No. 2 (1965), pp. 81-104; Richard Taylor, _Metaphysics_, 2nd ed. (Englewood Cliffs, New Jersey: Prentice-Hall, 1974).

9. Malcolm, _Problems of Mind_, pp. 68-69.

10. All these examples are from Richard Rorty, "Mind-Body Identity, Privacy and Categories," _The Review of Metaphysics_, Vol. 19, No. 1 (Sept., 1965), pp. 24-54. Other "eliminative materialists" are W.V.O. Quine and Paul Feyerabend.

11. Richard Bernstein, "The Challenge of Scientific Materialism," _International Philosophical Quarterly_, Vol. 8, No. 2 (June, 1968), pp. 252-275.

12. Saul Kripke, quoted in _The New York Times Magazine_ (Aug. 14, 1977), sec. 6., p. 14.

13. J.L. Austin, _Sense and Sensibilia_, G.J. Warnock, ed. (New York: Oxford University Press, 1964), pp. 64-76.

Chapter 5

Mount Olympus, Mount Moriah, and Other Godly Places

Philosophy of Religion

The big questions here are: Are there any good reasons for believing in God's existence or nonexistence? What kind of God exists or does not exist? What are the implications of God's existence or non-existence for us humans?

It looks as though every culture that has ever flourished has

what are the implications of God's existence ...

or of his nonexistence?

had some concept of divinity. Of course, it doesn't follow from that fact that therefore there _is_ a divinity (anymore than the fact that every culture believes itself to be superior to its neighbors means that every culture _is_ superior to its neighbors). Still, the mere cultural

Every culture has had a conception of divinity.

universality of religious belief is an impressive fact. The question "Why do so many people believe in gods?" is a very complicated one because it entangles us in a thicket of psychological, sociological, anthropological, and philosophical issues, not to mention purely religious issues. In this chapter, we shall be primarily interested in the philosophical issues, which means that we will attend to the kinds of _arguments_ that should be considered when asking whether there are any good reasons to believe or disbelieve in the existence of god(s).

Putting it this way, however, may make us sound unduly rational, as if on issues like this we all start with Locke's famous "blank slate," then fill it with different arguments for different positions, then choose the most reasonable one and discard the others. But this is not likely. On the issue of religious belief, very few of us are this antiseptically objective. Bertrand Russell was perhaps an exception. In his autobiography, he tells us that he became an atheist at eighteen when he decided that the "first cause" argument was invalid. But he became a theist again in his fourth year at Cambridge when he concluded that an alternative proof of God's existence was valid. Russell wrote:

> I had gone out to buy a tin of tobacco, and was going back with it along Trinity Lane, when suddenly I threw it up in the air and exclaimed: "Great God in boots! — the ontological argument is sound!" [1]

The young Bertrand Russell discovers that God exists.

Later, however, he discovered what he took to be a flaw in the argument and reverted to atheism.

I suspect that most of us have views on God's existence that are less obviously determined by the mere validity of arguments than Russell claimed to be the case with himself. (Keep in mind, however, that this is the man who wrote about his sixteenth year, "There was a footpath leading across the fields to New Southgate, and I used to go there alone to watch the sunset and contemplate suicide. I did not, however, commit suicide, because I wished to know more of mathematics.")[2] Then perhaps those of us who are not as dispassionate

I _was_ going to commit suicide, but I haven't finished my homework.

about religion are merely rationalizing when we give our "reasons" for believing or disbelieving in God (rationalizing in the pejorative sense, the sense of using reason and logic illegitimately to support biases and opinions that we dearly _want_ to believe)? Not necessarily. There probably is no such thing as the pure and blind pursuit of reason. Russell himself once said that the way the mind works on these things is like this. First you decide where you want to go. (This is where will, passion, bias, and wishful thinking are a legitimate part of the process of rationality.) Then you must ask

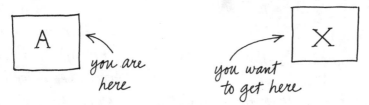

you are here

you want to get here

yourself, "What arguments will I need to get me from $\boxed{A}$ to $\boxed{X}$?"

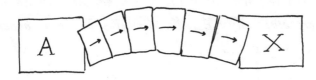

Next you need to ask, "Can such arguments be constructed, and are these _good_ arguments?" (Here is where we need to be most vigilant against rationalization, wishful thinking, and other forms of self-deception.) If the arguments withstand criticism and link up well with each other, then you have good reason to hold belief X. If not, then you should abandon X.

Theism

Well, what kinds of arguments have been set forth to get us to X, where X is a belief in the existence of God? The best ones in the Western tradition stem from the late medieval period, a time that has been called "God-intoxicated." This was a period in which, astonishingly, there does not seem to have been any atheism (though there was much heresy). If this is true, then it isn't quite accurate to say that the "proofs" of the Middle Ages provided reasons for believing in God because apparently there was no alternative. Rather, it's as if the medievals were giving an account to themselves of the rational status of their belief — or their knowledge — of God.

God-intoxicated

The Ontological Proof

Such an attitude is reflected in the curious introduction to one of the most famous of the medieval arguments and in the fact that this argument proving God's existence is not addressed to the atheist, but to God himself! It's hard to believe that God needed proof of his own existence, but its author, ANSELM OF CANTERBURY (1033-1109), was probably offering his meditation as a form of worship or a gift that could not possibly add anything to God's store (nothing could!), but one that nevertheless would be pleasing in God's sight. This is Anselm's introduction: "I do not seek to understand that I may believe, but I believe in order to understand. For this also I believe, that unless I believed, I should not understand."

Anselm goes on to refer to the "fool" of Psalms 53:1, who "says in his heart, 'There is no God.'" Even this fool

> is convinced that something exists in the understanding, at least, than which nothing greater can be conceived. For when he hears of this he understands it. And whatever is understood exists in the understanding. And assuredly that than which nothing greater can be conceived, cannot exist in the

There is no God.

Psalms 53:1

understanding alone. For suppose it exists in the understanding alone: then it can be conceived to exist in reality, which is greater.

There fore, if that than which nothing greater can be conceived, exists in the understanding alone, the very being than which nothing greater can be conceived, is one than which a greater can be conceived. But obviously this is impossible. Hence, there is no doubt that there exists a being than which nothing greater can be conceived, and it exists both in the understanding and in reality.

And it assuredly exists so truly that it cannot be conceived not to exist. For it is possible to conceive of a being which cannot be conceived not to exist. Hence, if that than which nothing greater can be conceived, can be conceived not to exist, it is not that than which nothing greater can be conceived. But this is an irreconcilable contradiction. There is, then, so truly a being than which nothing greater can be conceived to exist, that it cannot even be conceived not to exist; and this being thou art, O Lord our God. [3]

Let's try to simplify this argument a bit.

1. It is possible to conceive of a being "than which nothing greater can be conceived." (By "greatest," Anselm does not mean "biggest," but "most perfect.")

2. If that being than which nothing greater can be conceived exists only in the mind, then it is <u>not</u> the greatest being that can be conceived (because it is always possible to conceive of a <u>greater</u> one, viz., one that exists not only in the mind, but outside the mind as well).

3. Therefore the possibility of conceiving a being than which nothing greater can be conceived entails the logical necessity of the real existence of such a being.

4. This being than which nothing greater can be conceived is the being we call God.

One that exists only here is less perfect than one ...

that exists out here.

This argument looks suspicious. It appears as though it should be pretty easy to knock it over, but it is a slippery argument and more resistant to criticism than you might think. Maybe we can get a little clearer about the structure of the argument if we paraphrase a simpler version of it, one expounded by René Descartes some five hundred years after Anselm's version. It goes something like this:

1. God, by definition, is that being that is absolutely perfect.

2. It is more perfect to exist than not to exist.

3. Therefore, to conceive of God (i.e., to conceive of a being that is absolutely perfect) is necessarily to conceive of him as existing (because to conceive of God as not existing is self-cancelling).

4. Therefore, to say "God does not exist" is to contradict oneself.

5. Therefore, the sentence "God exists" is necessarily true.

If Descartes' or Anselm's version of this argument (which has come to be known as "the ontological proof") bothers you, it is probably because you think there is some illegitimate move in it from a mere _definition_ (an _a priori_ claim) to a statement of _fact_ (an _a posteriori_ claim). In that case, you might want to challenge Descartes' version of the argument, perhaps at step 2, saying that the assertion "It is more perfect to exist than not to exist" is a debatable value judgment, not a necessary truth of logic. But Descartes

It is more perfect to exist than not to exist.
(a hamburger that is perfect in every respect except that it does not exist)

could retort that if it is a value judgment, it is one _you_ obviously accept because if you had thought that nonexistence was better

Refuting Descartes (again)

than existence, you would have shot yourself this morning. The fact that you are here proves that you accept the value of existence. So you can only reject step 2 hypocritically. Furthermore, Descartes might offer an example like this: Suppose you ordered a truckload of bricks from the local brickyard, and the truck driver came to deliver your order, saying, "These are excellent bricks in most respects, but they have one little flaw, namely, they don't exist." If he tried to charge you for these nonexistent bricks, you would certainly refuse to pay – or perhaps you would pay with an equally "flawed" check (one that doesn't exist). "All this shows that you agree with me" (Descartes might say) "that existence is more perfect (i.e., better) than nonexistence."

(You might ask Descartes, what if instead of bricks, the driver were delivering an unsolicited load of horse manure. Then [because you don't want any manure], nonexistent manure is better than existent manure. But wouldn't Descartes be right to say that in terms of manure, real manure is always better manure than unreal manure?)

It's very *good* horse manure.

But I don't *want* any horse manure!

In spite of this defense, one may well feel that there is some sleight of hand involved in the ontological argument. Indeed, even Thomas Aquinas, that most religious of philosophers, thought the argument was invalid. One of the most famous critiques of the proof was written by David Hume. The following passage is taken from his posthumously published _Dialogues Concerning Natural Religion_:

> I shall begin with observing that there is an evident absurdity in pretending to demonstrate a matter of fact, or to prove it by any arguments _a priori_. Nothing is demonstrable unless the contrary implies a contradiction. Nothing that is distinctly

conceivable implies a contradiction. Whatever we conceive as existent, we can also conceive as non-existent. There is no being, therefore, whose non-existence implies a contradiction. Consequently there is no being whose existence is demonstrable. I propose this argument as entirely decisive, and am willing to rest the whole controversy upon it. [4]

Hume's point boils down to this. It is always illegitimate to move from a pure definition to a statement of fact about reality. Definitions are only about the relation between meanings and as such are purely representations of logic and of linguistic conventions. Statements of fact about reality are always based on observation. Because Anselm's proof moves from the purely ideational sphere to the factual sphere without any reference to observation, its argument must be invalid.

Hume is certainly correct in thinking that if there is a problem with the proof, it has to do with the illegitimate transition from the realm of pure ideas to the realm of factual reality. But is Hume correct in saying that we can never move from the realm of definition to statements about existence? Consider the definition of a "square circle" (four-sided equilateral figure any point of which is

equidistant from its center). We can deduce the following: "no square circles exist." [5] If even once we can go from a definition to a statement of fact about reality, then Hume's argument loses much of its

The hunt for the elusive square circle

force.

Hume's criticism implied that there must be something wrong with the _logic_ of Anselm's argument. Another well-known and more modern criticism is that there is something wrong with its _grammar_. Look at this famous passage from the _Critique of Pure Reason_ by Immanuel Kant :

> Being is evidently not a real predicate, or a concept of something that can be added to the concept of a thing. It is merely the admission of a thing, and of certain determinations in it. Logically, it is merely the copula of a judgment. The proposition, _God is almighty_, contains two concepts, each having its object, namely, God and almightiness. The small word _is_, is not an additional predicate, but only serves to put the predicate _in relation_ to the subject. If, then, I take the subject (God) with all its predicates (including that of almightiness), and say, _God is_, or there is a God, I do not ascribe a new predicate to the concept of God, but I only posit the subject by itself, with all its predicates, in relation to my concept, as its object. Both must contain exactly the same kind of thing, and nothing can have been added to the concept, which expresses possibility only, by my thinking its object as simply given and saying, it is. And thus the real does not contain more than the possible. A hundred real dollars do not contain a penny more than a hundred possible dollars. [6]

The central points of Kant's criticism are contained in the first line and the last line of the passage: "Being [existence] is evidently not a real predicate." and "A hundred real dollars do not contain a penny more than a hundred possible dollars."

These points can be clarified by returning to Descartes' version of the argument. Descartes saw "perfection" as a predicate of God in exactly the way that he saw "three-sidedness" as a predicate (or attribute or characteristic) of any triangle. Then he saw "existence" as following from perfection, so "existence" becomes a predicate of God. Now, Kant's claim that existence is not a predicate _at all_, hence not a predicate of God, might be demonstrated by imagining the following game, called "Guess the Predicate." Suppose I take something from my pocket and hide it in my hand behind my back and allow you to ask questions concerning its characteristics, to which I will answer "yes" or "no." You may ask, "Is it green?," "Is it round?," "Is it heavy?," etc. But could the question "Does it exist?" be a move in <u>this</u> game? The rules of the game already presuppose the

See if you can guess what I have behind my back.

The predicate game

existence of the object. If the object does not exist (i.e., if I have nothing in my hand), then I am not playing the game at all. I am simply deceiving you. Or try another game. This one is called "Imagine the Rose." First imagine a rose. Now imagine a <u>yellow</u> rose. Now imagine a yellow rose <u>with thorns</u>. Now imagine a yellow rose with thorns and <u>dew on the petals</u>. Now imagine a yellow, thorned rose

Oooh. They're all thorny and covered with dew!

Imagine they're not.

with dew on the petals, <u>which exists</u>. Notice the point. Nothing was added to the concept in the last instance. To imagine a rose and to imagine a rose that exists is to imagine the same thing. In the cases of the yellow color, the dew, and the thorns, we added something to the concept, so those were examples of real predicates. But in the case of existence, nothing was added, so existence "is not a real predicate."

Kant's criticism certainly does seem to have identified a linguistic weakness, if not a logical error, in the ontological proof. Is that the end of the story? Probably not. I mentioned earlier the fact that Anselm's argument has proved to be tremendously versatile and elastic, being able to bounce back from apparently deadly assaults. For example, the contemporary American philosopher Norman Malcolm has claimed to have discovered in Anselm's writings a version of the ontological proof that is immune to Kant's criticism. This argument, paraphrased, runs something like this:

1. If God does not exist, his existence is logically impossible (because by definition God is eternal and independent, so he cannot come into being or be caused to come into being).

2. If God does exist, his existence is logically necessary (because he cannot have come into existence [for the reasons given above] or cease to exist, for if he did, he would be limited, and by definition God is unlimited).

3. Hence, either God's existence is logically impossible or it is logically necessary.

4. If God's existence is logically impossible, the concept of God is self-contradictory.

5. The concept of God is not self-contradictory.

6. Therefore, God's existence is logically necessary.

7. Therefore, God exists. [7]

Here we will not try to analyze Malcolm's argument (though it has attracted a number of critics). [8] Rather, we will attend to the somewhat amazing conclusion that Malcolm draws from this argument:

What is the relation of Anselm's ontological argument to religious belief? This is a difficult question. I can imagine an atheist going through the argument, becoming convinced of its validity, acutely defending it against objections, yet remaining an atheist. The only effect it could have on the fool of the Psalm would be that he stopped saying in his heart "There is no God," because he would now realize that this is something he cannot meaningfully say or think. It is hardly to be expected that a demonstrative argument should, in addition, produce in him a living faith. Surely there is a level at which one can view the argument as a piece of logic, following the deductive moves but not being touched religiously? I think so. But even at this level the argument may not be without religious value, for it may help to remove some philosophical scruples that stand in the way of faith. ... It would be unreasonable to require that the recognition of Anselm's demonstration as valid must produce a conversion. 9

Atheist muzzled

It was Immanuel Kant who gave the name "ontological proof" to the kind of argument invented by St. Anselm. As we've seen, "ontological" means "having to do with the study of Being," and Kant noticed that Anselm's argument was derived purely from the logical analysis of the concept of a "most real Being" or a "most perfect Being," hence the name " the ontological argument." Notice that, unlike the argument we shall now examine, Anselm's argument is a very Platonic one. It is derived from "pure reason." In it, "most perfect" and "most real" turn out to be identical (as on the top of Plato's "Line"). And it is an exclusively _a priori_ argument. Nowhere did Anselm or Descartes ask you to _look_ anyplace or _touch_ anything or perform any physical experiments. All they asked you to do was to _think_. Anselm derived God's existence from pure thought. (That fact is probably what, in the final analysis, is wrong with the ontological proof, but one must also admit that the genius of the argument is its purely _a priori_ nature.)

The Cosmological Proof

There is another kind of argument for God's existence, which Kant called "cosmological." This is because the first premise of such an argument makes reference to some observable fact in the world ("cosmos") and is therefore an argument with an _a posteriori_ first premise. Surely the most famous examples of cosmological arguments were created by THOMAS AQUINAS (1225-1274), whose thought has inspired most Catholic philosophy ever since his time.

Take a look at one of the arguments from Thomas' _Summa Theologica_:

In the world of sense we find there is an order of efficient causes. There is no case known (neither is it, indeed, possible) in which a thing is found to be the efficient cause of itself; for so it would be prior to itself, which is impossible. Now in efficient causes it is not possible to go on to infinity,

THOMAS AQUINAS
(1225-1274)

because in all efficient causes following in order, the first is the cause of the intermediate cause, and the intermediate is the cause of the ultimate cause, whether the intermediate cause be several, or one only. Now, to take away the cause is to take away the effect. Therefore, if there be no first cause among efficient causes, there will be no ultimate, nor any intermediate cause. But if in efficient causes it is possible to go on to infinity, there will be no first efficient cause, neither will there be an ultimate effect, nor any intermediate efficient causes; all of which is plainly false. Therefore it is necessary to admit a first efficient cause to which everyone gives the name of God.[10]

The term "efficient cause" is one St. Thomas borrowed from Aristotle, and it is roughly equivalent to what we mean today by the word "cause." Therefore, Thomas' argument seems to boil down to this:

THE BUCK STOPS HERE

1. Every event in the world is caused by some event prior to it.

2. Either (a) the series of causes is infinite, or (b) the series of causes goes back to a first cause, which is itself uncaused.

3. But an infinite series of causes is impossible.

4. Therefore, a first cause, which is God, exists.

Hume's Criticism of the Cosmological Proof

Those philosophers like Hume and Kant who rejected this argument attacked the first and third premises and also questioned the conclusion. Hume is probably most famous for his critical analysis of

the concept of "causality." We would be led too far afield if we followed the details of Hume's controversial analysis. Suffice it to say that
Hume asserts that there is no good reason at all to claim to know the
first premise because it cannot be proven _a priori_ that every event
is caused, and no set of observations can establish it _a posteriori_
either. Also, Hume thought that the third premise was false. Why is
an infinite series of causes impossible? Unlike Thomas, Hume believed that nothing in the concept of a series of causes required that
there be a beginning, other than the need arbitrarily imposed by the
human mind. Hume thought that no matter what event you imagine, you
can always imagine an earlier event preceding it, regardless of how
far back into time the imagination goes, just as an infinite series
of numbers is possible in mathematics. Therefore, there is no _logical_

contradiction in the
notion of an "infinite
series of causes." And
because there are no
observable data with
which to prove the
third premise, Hume
concluded that we
must at least remain
skeptical concerning
its claim.

In the
beginning...

The need of the human mind to impose
a "beginning" on things

Finally, even if
the argument were
valid from steps 1 through 3, would it prove the existence of
the Christian God in whom St. Thomas believed? Aristotle
himself, from whom Thomas borrowed elements of his cosmological proof, believed in a narcissistic God who was so "into himself"

Narcissus

that he did not even know that human beings existed. Surely Thomas would not have wanted to prove the existence of _that_ God.

Lest we think that Hume has soundly refuted the cosmological argument once and for all, we should mention that recent Thomistic scholars have warned that Thomas' argument is more complicated than it appears, involving both a horizontal system of causes (in which an infinite series of causes cannot be ruled out) and a hierarchical system of dependencies (which, according to Thomas, cannot admit of an infinite regress).[11] This version of the argument, with its "hierarchy of dependencies," is

Absolute terminus here

Infinity this way (maybe)

much more Platonic than the earlier one, reminding us as it does of Plato's "simile of the line." A refutation of this interpretation of the proof would involve a rejection of Platonic metaphysics.

194

The Teleological Proof

A third kind of argument for God's existence goes by several names, the "teleological proof," the "argument from design," and the "argument from analogy." Though this proof was particularly popular in the eighteenth century, we find a thirteenth-century version of it once again in the _Summa Theologica_ of Thomas Aquinas:

> The fifth way is taken from the governance of the world. We see that things which lack intelligence, such as natural bodies, act for an end, and this is evident from their acting always, or nearly always, in the same way, so as to obtain the best result. Hence it is plain that not fortuitously, but designedly, do they achieve their end. Now whatever lacks intelligence cannot move toward an end, unless it be directed by some being endowed with knowledge and intelligence; as the arrow is shot to its mark by the archer. Therefore some intelligent being exists by whom all natural things are directed to their end; and this being we call God. [12]

A "teleological explanation" is one in terms of goals, purposes, and intentions (from the Greek _telos_, "goal" or "end"). We are familiar with teleological explanations because we use them every day to explain our own actions and those of people surrounding us: "Why did John go to the other room?" "In order to phone Jill." This explanation of John's behavior in terms of his purposes and goals makes his behavior intelligible to us.

Notice how different this teleological explanation of John's behavior is from a strictly causal explanation of the type we often employ to make intelligible to us the behavior of natural nonhuman objects: "Why did the tree fall?" "The roots were shallow and could not support the tree's weight in last night's wind storm."

We also use causal, nonteleological accounts in the case of _accidental_ human events: "What's John doing on the floor?" "He

tripped on his shoelace." Notice that here there were no references to goals, inten-
tions, or purposes, so these explanations were not teleological. Now it might seem that the employment of the two distinct forms of explanation is very clear; we use teleological accounts for

certain kinds of human behavior (i.e., purposeful as opposed to accidental) and causal explanations for natural phenomena. But consider such exchanges as these:

"Why do ospreys have such good eyesight?"
"In order to see fish from high in the air."

"Why does that moth have brown spots on its wings?"
"In order to blend in with its environment to protect itself from natural enemies."

Myopic osprey

"Why do we faint when not enough blood gets to the brain?"
"So that the heart can pump blood horizontally."

Each of these explanations is teleological. They explain in terms of goals and purposes. It may turn out that there is something wrong with these accounts, as Darwin would claim, but it can't be denied that people (usually parents talking to their children) say things like this all the time. To many people, these kinds of explanations seem perfectly natural. Now it is precisely the "naturalness" of these accounts from which the teleological proof gets its mileage. That proof says that natural phenomena are such that they demand a teleological explanation, or at least that the totality of natural phenomena taken as a system demands such an explanation; no other kind proves satisfactory.

A common version of the argument runs like this. If you found a watch on a mountain path, you would deduce from the functioning of the watch that it was designed to serve a purpose and that there had to be an intelligent watchmaker who created the artifact. It would be unreasonable to explain the watch in terms of natural accidents and coincidences. But nature is even more marvelous in the intricacies of its workings than is a watch. The human heart pumps blood at exactly the right pressure to sustain human life; the planets move in their orbits with absolute mathematical precision; each plant is in nearly perfect harmony with its environment. In summary, the world is such an intricate system of balanced mechanisms that it can be explained only in terms of the purposes and intentions of an intelligent creator, as

The not-so-intelligent watchmaker

in the case of the watch. In the case of the world, that intelligent creator is God.

197

Darwin's and Hume's Criticisms of the Teleological Proof

The most famous critics of this argument are Charles Darwin and (again) David Hume. Darwin's criticism, stated simply, runs like this: There is a difference between the concept of "design" and the concept of "order." It is true that whatever has been designed must have been designed by <u>somebody</u>, but not everything that exhibits order was designed. Take the example of a gravel beach. There we find a distinct order. The smallest grains of sand compose the top layers of the beach, the grains 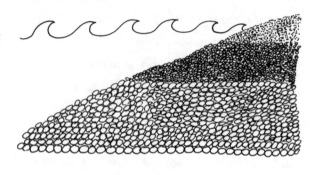 of the second layer are a bit larger, and the largest pebbles compose the bottom layer. But there is no "designer" needed to explain this order; much less is there any mystery. It is perfectly obvious why the larger pebbles are on the bottom. They are the heaviest, hence were deposited by the surf first. The smallest are the lightest and were deposited last.

Similarly, the order throughout nature, though often more complex than this, can be explained in the same kind of naturalistic terms. The perfect harmony between the heart and body is explained by the fact that the heart could sustain only a body that could survive with exactly as much blood pressure as that size heart could produce. All other bodies would not survive (and indeed did not survive). The coincidental combination of that particular heart size and this particularly structured body produced the organism that would survive (and did survive). The heart does not pump X pounds of blood pressure <u>in order</u> to sustain the body; rather, the body flourishes because the heart does pump X pounds of blood pressure. Similarly, ospreys do not have excellent vision in order to spy fish; rather, they spy fish because they have excellent vision. The moth does not have spots in order to avoid its enemies; it avoids its enemies because it has spots, etc.,

Evolutionary future of the human

etc. If Darwin's argument is successful, it shows that the teleological terminology ("in order to") can be replaced with purely causal terminology, thereby destroying the force of the teleological proof.

David Hume, in his <u>Dialogues Concerning Natural Religion</u>, had at least a pair of arguments against the teleological proof. First, he challenged the validity of the analogy, "watch is to watchmaker as world is to world creator." Hume claimed that the relation between the watch and the watchmaker that allows us to infer the existence of the latter when we find the former is an <u>empirical</u> relation. We are able to infer the existence of the watchmaker from the existence of the watch because we have <u>seen</u> watchmakers make watches. Any successful analogy based on the relationship between a watch and a watchmaker will also have to contain the empirical element of that relationship. But because the purported relation between the world and the world creator is not and <u>cannot</u> be empirical, the analogy fails. Besides, says Hume, the aspect of the world that excites the need for a theological explanation is very often the <u>organic</u> aspect of the world. The organic world is

more like a plant than a watch. Because we know (empirically) where plants come from, Hume states rather mischievously that the argument from analogy should lead us to conclude that the world creator is more like a kind of superturnip than like a watchmaker!

Another of Hume's criticisms of the argument from design can be stated in terms of these diagrams. Notice how orderly are the three dots in fig. 1.

Superturnip

Fig. 1   Fig. 2   Fig. 3   Fig. 4   Fig. 5

They form a perfect triangle. Fig. 2 contains even more order. The addition of only three dots created four triangles within the triangle, and an even more complex system of order appears in figs. 3 and 4. Then we get to fig. 5, and we realize that what we are actually looking at is a pile of sand, hardly what we think of as an orderly system, rather a purely random kind of haphazardness. Hume is suggesting that order is in the eye of the beholder. The human mind imposes order on the chaos of nature, then infers a divine orderer to account for it. Notice that Hume's point is much more radical than Darwin's. Darwin questioned the notion of "design in nature" but

There is a sandpile; therefore God exists.

never doubted whether there was "order" in nature. Hume questions the very notion of order.

Certainly this has not been a complete catalogue of the philosophical attempts to prove God's existence, and it does not even pretend to have exhausted the richness or variations of the three arguments we've inspected. But it is a fair sampling of this kind of attempt to demonstrate that there are rational arguments that give us good reasons to believe that God exists.

Atheism

We have seen that each of the arguments for God's existence is problematic, but surely no more so than the arguments attempting to prove that God does _not_ exist. Such proofs are arguments for atheism. Here we will catalogue a few such arguments, but we will not delay long to inspect them. These kinds of discussions could go on forever. (Indeed, after several hundred years of debate during the medieval period, it began to seem as if they _would_ go on forever.) In my opinion, neither they nor their refutations are very compelling. Like some of the arguments _for_ God's existence, these negative arguments seem to have the air of a word game about them. Here are truncated versions of a few of them.

1. God's omniscience is incompatible with the freedom he gave his creatures. (If God is omniscient, he knows the future. If God knows what humans will do in the future, then they _must_ do what God knows they will do [or else God is wrong]. If God does not know what they will do, then he is not omniscient.

2. God's omnipotence, omniscience, omnibenevolence, and

omni creativity are not compatible with the presence of evil in the world. (There is evil in the world — natural disasters, disease, crime, starvation, phlegm. If God did not create them, then he is not the creator of the universe. If he could not prevent them in his creation, then he is not all powerful. If he didn't foresee them, he is not all knowing. On the other hand, if he did willfully create them, then he is not all good.)

3. God is defined as omnipotent, but nothing can be defined as omnipotent because the concept of omnipotence is incoherent. (Can God create a rock that is too large for him to move? If he cannot, then he is not all powerful. If he can, then he is not all powerful.)

4. God's omnibenevolence is incompatible with his creation of the devil and of eternal punishment. (If God is all good, how can he loose a potent evil force like Satan to tempt such weak creatures as are humans and then punish with the horrors of eternal damnation those poor souls who succumb, even momentarily, to the devil's superior wiles?)

Notice that some of

these arguments are kinds of reverse ontological proofs, trying to show that the very concept of God as Western culture has conceived it is self-contradictory. Others of these arguments are kinds of reverse cosmological proofs, trying to show that certain facts in the world are incompatible with the concept of God. Most of these arguments already appeared in the medieval world, not as real attempts to raise doubts about God's existence — atheism was never a serious threat in the Middle Ages — but as a pretext for theologians to flex their philosophical muscles while clarifying to themselves their understanding of God's nature.

After a thousand years, the medieval period did come to an end; and when it did, the totalizing obsession with God ended. There are many historical reasons for the loosening of the viselike grip that religion had on the Western mind during the medieval period, and most of these reasons are historical and sociological rather than purely philosophical (for example, the great schisms in Christianity that detracted from the appearance of uniformity and universality of religious persuasion; the revelations of corruption within certain religious institutions, which detracted from the moral authority of religion; and the advent of scientific discoveries that seemed to contradict biblical explanations of the world). Since the eighteenth century, most philosophical arguments for atheism have not taken the form of a proof of the incoherence of the concept of God, of the incompatibility between that concept and the empirical facts. Rather, these arguments have had as their goal the undermining of religious faith by claiming to reveal that our motives for religious belief are fallacious and illusory. Typical of such arguments in the nineteenth century are those of LUDWIG FEUERBACH (1804-1872) and his erstwhile disciple, KARL MARX (1818-1883).

Feuerbach's "Religion of Man"

In his book, _The Essence of Christianity_ (1841), Feuerbach tried to show that religious beliefs were basically the result of confusion about human potentiality and that this confusion and the resultant beliefs prevented any serious solution of human problems. Feuerbach's theory went something like this: The human being is fundamentally good and as a species has certain legitimate aspirations that have been present more or less from the beginning of the race. These aspirations are the will to achieve love, truth, beauty, happiness, wisdom, purity, and strength, among others. That is, every human community has aspired, consciously or unconsciously, to

We want love, truth, beauty, happiness, wisdom, purity...

WISDOM, PURITY....

I am love, truth, beauty, happiness, wisdom, purity, + strength!

Fig. 1   Fig. 2   Fig. 3

achieve and express these values (fig.1) (shades of Plato!). But life was hard, individually and collectively, and these ideals were not realized. Natural disasters, wars, social chaos, and plagues resulted in these ideals receding, as it were, through the clouds and into the sky (fig. 2). Then suddenly a strange thing happened. (Unfortunately, Feuerbach does not give us much detail on _how_ it was supposed to have happened.) The clouds opened up, and those same ideals returned in a new, powerful form, as the voice of God (fig.3). And the great dialectical irony of history is that those same beautiful ideals that were expressions of true human nature now returned to

And if **I** am all these things, then you are nothing! (and don't you ever forget it!)

fig. 4

earth in the form of religion and crushed the human being to the ground (fig. 4). According to Feuerbach, the "And don't you ever forget it" line is "the essence of Christianity" and, in fact, the essence of all organized religion. He believed that religious history and religious scriptures are replete with illustrations of this thesis. Consider specifically the Old Testament story of Job from Feuerbach's point of view.

In a discussion with Satan and other angels, God points out his servant Job, complimenting him before the devil for being such a perfect, upright man. Satan retorts that Job is perfect only because God has protected him and blessed him. However, should God allow evil to befall Job, Satan wagers that Job would curse God. In order to prove the devil wrong, God delivers Job to Satan, giving him a free rein to torment Job, though the devil may not kill Job. ("Behold, he is in thine hand; but save his life" [Job 2 : 6].) The first day of the torment begins with a slave running to tell him that all his oxen and asses have been stolen and all his herdsmen murdered. Before the first slave is done relating his story, a second comes to inform Job that a fire has fallen from heaven and burned all his sheep and shepherds. Before this servant finishes his tale, a third runs up and announces that the Chaldeans have stolen all Job's camels and killed the cameleers. While Job is reeling from this news, yet another slave approaches, telling Job that a great wind has toppled the home of his eldest son, killing all ten of Job's children. Job rends his robe, shaves his head, and mourns, only to awaken on the second day of the torment to find himself smitten with painful boils from the soles of his feet to the crown of his head. Job's wife, seeing Job sitting among the ashes with his shaven head, his running sores, and his misery, says to Job, "Curse God and die"

Behold, my servant, Job.

OH OH

(Job 2:9). Though Job does not curse God, he does curse the day he was born, and he talks bitterly of the impossibility of fathoming God's ways. He says to God, "Show me wherefore thou contendest with me"; "Thou knowest that I am not wicked." (This is a version of the question "Why me?," which seems like a perfectly reasonable question under the circumstances.) When God, speaking from the whirlwind, does answer Job, he asks a series of intimidating questions: "Who is this that darkeneth counsel by words without knowledge?" (It's only Job.) "Where wast thou when I laid the foundations of the earth?" (Job doesn't know.) "Hast thou an arm like God?" (Job doesn't.) "Canst thou thunder with a voice like him?" (Job can't.) Finally Job understands. One does not question the ways of God. In God's case, might is right. When Job understands, then he recovers all that

207

was lost and more — new livestock, new lands, new slaves, and new children.

You can see how I have told this story in a Feuerbachian light (though of course there are many other possible interpretations as well).[13] One must be resigned to the misery inflicted upon one, never questioning the system that perpetrated it and never fighting it. Again, if God is everything, the human is nothing.

Feuerbach, like Marx after him, was a socialist; and he believed that a truly human society (i.e., a socialist society) would in fact finally be able to achieve those ideals of love, truth, beauty, happiness, wisdom, purity, and strength that are our legitimate aspirations. It seems as though Feuerbach, recognizing the tremendously important role religion has played in the history of human culture, thought that the only thing standing in the way of such an ideal human world was religion. If humans could only see that they had alienated their subjective essence, objectifying it in a foreign, artificial being, "God," then they could reclaim that essence and build a heaven on earth. It is as though Feuerbach believed that, upon perusing _The Essence of Christianity_, the reader would suddenly see that human alienation was in fact religious alienation. One would strike oneself on the forehead and exclaim, "Of course! Now I see it!" and at that point be delivered from religious

A moment of Feuerbachian illumination

alienation and dedicate oneself to the new "Religion of Man" and the building of the new Jerusalem.

Marx's Response to Feuerbach

Karl Marx was tremendously impressed by Feuerbach's book, and at one point early in his career, Marx claimed that the only correct way to philosophize was to "pass through the fiery brook." (In German, "Feuerbach" means "fiery brook.") But he soon began to turn against his mentor, basically on the grounds that Feuerbach was a crypto- (or "hidden") idealist, in spite of the fact that Feuerbach thought of himself as a materialist. (The nastiest thing that Feuerbach and Marx could call someone was "idealist.") Inspect these passages on religion written by Marx against Feuerbach:

Karl Marx crosses the fiery brook.

Feuerbach starts out from the fact of religious self-alienation, the duplication of the world into a religious, imaginary world and a real one. His work consists in the dissolution of the religious world into its secular basis. He overlooks the fact that after completing this work, the chief thing still remains to be done. For the fact that the secular foundation detaches itself from itself and establishes itself in the clouds as an independent realm is really to be explained only by the self-cleavage and self-contradictoriness of this secular basis. The latter must itself, therefore, first be understood in its contradiction and then, by removal of the contradiction, revolutionized

209

in practice. Thus, for instance, once the earthly family is discovered to be the secret of the holy family, the former must then itself be criticized in theory and revolutionized in practice.

. . . .

Religious distress is at the same time the expression of real distress and the protest against real distress. Religion is the sigh of the oppressed creature, the heart of a heartless world, just as it is the spirit of an unspiritual situation. It is the opium of the people.[14]

The language in which Marx writes in these passages is a bit difficult, but it is fairly easy to see Marx's objection to Feuerbach's theory. According to Marx, Feuerbach correctly sees that religion is a form of alienation but falsely believes that the solution to the problem is the critique of religion. Marx claims that religion is not the cause of the disease; rather it is the symptom. The disease is one of the social organization of the world. When Marx says that the earthly family must be "criticized in theory and revolutionized in practice," he means that the holy family (Mary, Jesus, and Joseph) is an inverted projection into the skies of a real problem on earth. Marx claimed that marriage in contemporary European society was a form of legalized forced prostitution and that the role of the father as "head of the family" was a form of violent tyranny over the mother and child. All this, he thought, gets dialectically reversed in the religious view of the holy family. There is no use in outlawing religion. When the tyranny, prostitution, and exploitation in the real family are abolished, religion will simply disappear. This is a controversial claim, to say the least, but it ought to be obvious that if Marx's theory is true, then Feuerbach's critique of religion is inadequate.

Notice that one of the ironies in the theories of both Feuerbach and Marx is that there is a significant sense in which religion contains the truth — a spiritual truth that should become a

social truth. This was seen to be so in Marx even more clearly than in Feuerbach. Remember that, for Marx, religion is "the sigh of the oppressed creature, the heart of a heartless world, ... the spirit of an unspiritual situation. It is the _opium_ of the people." This is hardly an absolute indictment of religion. Usually that last line is quoted in isolation from its context, in which case one thinks of opium as a soporific that lulls one into a grinning, drooling, undignified stupor. But Marx had in mind opium's medicinal powers. It kills the pain. And for Marx, the pain is real, so at least religion is addressing the correct issue, viz., human misery. This has been understood very well by the twentieth-century Marxian philosopher Herbert Marcuse, who wrote in his book, _Eros and Civilization_:

> Where religion still preserves the uncompromised aspirations for peace and happiness, its "illusions" still have a higher truth value than science which works for their elimination. The repressed and transfigured content of religion cannot be liberated by surrendering it to the scientific attitude.[15]

Sigmund Freud: The Psychoanalysis of Religion

In spite of their belief in the hidden truth value of religion, both Feuerbach and Marx were atheists who thought religion was ultimately an illusion. One of the most famous atheists of

the twentieth century was SIGMUND FREUD (1856-1939). He too
thought of religious belief as a kind of illusion, and his book on
- religion is called The Future of an Illusion. His theory of religion
is deeply entwined in the rest of his psychoanalytic theory of the
mind, however. Thankfully, we do not have to recount the whole
of Freud's psychology, but only a few of its essentials, in order to
get at the heart of his claim about religion. According to Freud,
the human mind preserves all of its earlier stages alongside its

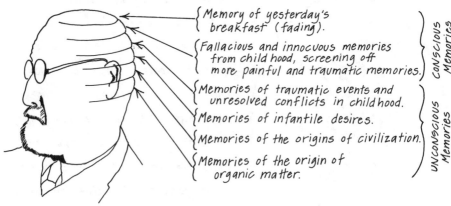

{ Memory of yesterday's
  breakfast (fading).

{ Fallacious and innocuous memories
  from child hood, screening off
  more painful and traumatic memories. } CONSCIOUS Memories

{ Memories of traumatic events and
  unresolved conflicts in childhood.

{ Memories of infantile desires.

{ Memories of the origins of civilization.

{ Memories of the origin of
  organic matter. } UNCONSCIOUS Memories

The human mind preserves all of its earlier stages.

final form. This is true both
ontogenetically and phyloge-
netically (i.e., true of the history
of the individual and true of
the history of the human race).
Unlike a city, in which some
parts must be destroyed in order
for newer parts to be constructed,
in the mind, the earliest stages
and the latest are contemporaneous.
However, the earlier ones are to

The bulk of the mind is
submerged.

a great extent submerged or even repressed into the unconscious. Therefore, from the point of view of consciousness, the structures and content of the earlier stages seem to have been forgotten forever, but in fact they are present and in some ways active as motives for behavior, as are our conscious thoughts. Now, concerning religion, Freud says:

> The derivation of religious needs
> from the infant's helplessness and
> the longing for the father aroused
> by it seems to me incontrovertible,
> especially since the feeling is not
> simply prolonged from childhood
> days, but is permanently sustained
> by a fear of the superior power
> of Fate. I cannot think of any
> need in childhood as strong as the
> need for the father's protection.[16]

The infant comes into the world in some way believing itself to be omnipotent. The slightest or greatest of its needs is attended to upon the simple registering of a complaint. It does not take long, however, for the horrible realization to dawn upon the infant that she is not only not all powerful and in command of reality, but that she is completely vulnerable and de-pendent. This discovery (from which she will never recover) produces both fear and resentment. The infant reluctantly recognizes her utter need of a protector to

The infant comes into the world thinking it is omnipotent.

213

shelter her from the many sources of pain and unhappiness in the world. She comes to see this protector in the guise of the father. This fearful discovery of her vulnerability and dependence on the father, along with the emotional luggage that accompanies this discovery — fear, need, love, resentment — remain active forces in the unconscious of the adult. As adults,

> each one of us behaves in some one respect like a paranoic, corrects some aspect of the world which is unbearable to him by the construction of a wish and introduces this delusion into reality. A special importance attaches to the case in which this attempt to procure a certainty of happiness and protection against suffering through a delusional remoulding of reality is made by a considerable number of people in common. The religions of mankind must be classed among the mass-delusions of this kind. No one, needless to say, who shares a delusion ever recognizes it as such.... [Religion's] technique consists in depressing the value of life and distorting the picture of the real world in a delusional manner — which presupposes an intimidation of the intelligence. At this price, by forcibly fixing them in a state of psychical infantilism and by drawing them into a mass-delusion, religion succeeds in sparing many people an individual neurosis (pp. 30-31, 34).

Although Freud does realize that religion can spare people a neurosis, he nevertheless seems to have contempt for it. He says, "The whole thing is so patently infantile, so foreign to reality, that to anyone with a friendly attitude to humanity it is painful to think that the great majority of mortals will never be able to rise above this view of life." (p. 49).

So according to Freud, religion is for weaklings, for people who need delusions to accompany them into the harshness of the world. In _Civilization and Its Discontents_, Freud deals with alcohol and drugs in the same paragraph in which he deals with religion. For him, too, religion truly is "the opium of the people." Religion can be escaped only by those who can

"Young man, you must choose: science, religion, or art."

"How about scientific religious art?"

"With a centerfold"

develop the courage to face the harshness of life without delusions and substitute them with scientific truth or by those who can create a different kind of paranoic-like illusion in the production of art. (See Chapter 11 for a development of this idea.)

Volitional Justifications of Religious Belief

Earlier we looked at a number of arguments claiming to demonstrate the rationality of a belief in God's existence. These arguments stressed reason and evidence. There have been other kinds of arguments for God's existence appealing not so much to the rational and intellectual side of our nature as to its passional side. (There have also been "passional" arguments _against_ God's existence. Nietzsche's probably takes the cake. "If there were gods, how could I

"You mean I'm not God? I can't stand it!"

"You win. Here's the cake."

Friedrich Nietzsche makes an important discovery.

stand not being one? Therefore there are no gods.") One of the most famous of such passional arguments for God's existence is that of the American Pragmatist, WILLIAM JAMES (1842-1910).

First, a bit about pragmatism. The term was coined by another American philosopher, CHARLES PEIRCE (1839-1914), and for him, it was essentially the name of a <u>method</u> whose goal was to clarify our thought processes by tracing out the practical consequences of beliefs in various ideas. James' version of pragmatism (which so repelled Peirce that he changed the name of his own view from "pragmatism" to "pragmaticism" — a name he said was "ugly enough to be safe from kidnappers") ultimately became a justification of a certain kind of religious belief. Before developing that justification, we must distinguish between the pragmatic theory of <u>meaning</u> and its theory of <u>truth</u>. Concerning the former, James wrote:

Ugly enough to be safe from kidnappers

Is the world one or many? — fated or free? — material or spiritual? — here are notions either of which may or may not hold good of the world; and disputes over such notions are unending. The pragmatic method in such cases is to try to interpret each notion by tracing its respective practical consequences. What difference would it practically make to any one if this notion rather than that notion were true? If no practical difference whatever can be traced, then the alternatives mean practically the same thing, and all dispute is idle.[17]

In other words, a sentence is _meaningful_ only if believing it would make a practical difference in your life, as opposed to believing some alternative to it. For example, take the sentence, "There is a table in the middle of this room." If you wanted to travel from one end of the room to the other, then believing that sentence to be true (as op-

posed to believing its opposite) would make a practical difference because your path across the room would be different in the one case as opposed to the other. Now consider a slightly more complicated case: "Jupiter has three moons." Whether you believe that sentence or an alternative (such as "Jupiter has no moons"), it probably won't make much difference in your life either way unless you are an astronomer or an astronaut. But if you _were_ an astronomer or an astronaut, we could certainly imagine conditions in which believing the one alternative as opposed to the other would have definite practical consequences. (You won't try to land a rocket on Jupiter's third moon unless you believe that Jupiter _has_ a third moon.)

So the examples about tables and moons that we have considered are meaningful because believing any of them could make a difference. Contrast those examples with this: "There are many

diaphanous, unknow-
able, invisible, in-
tangible beings
floating around
certain items such
as daisies and
hamburgers." Be-
lieving this sentence
or believing its
opposite will produce
exactly the same practice;
hence each belief is <u>practically</u> identical.

There's just <u>something</u> about this hamburger...

Hey Dad, check out this flower!

Now what about <u>truth</u>? First of all, notice that only meaningful sentences can be either true or false. (From this it seems
to follow rather curiously that our last example about diaphanous beings is neither true nor false.) James had this to say about truth: "ideas (which themselves are but parts of our experience) become true just in-sofar as they help us to get into satisfactory rela-tions with other

Yes, but <u>was</u> it brillig? ... And <u>do</u> the slithy toves gyre and gimble in the wabe? I mean, do they <u>truly</u>?

Only meaningful sentences can be true or false.

218

parts of our experience, ... truth in our ideas means their power to 'work'" (p.49). So the key notion here is that of an idea "working," which James defines as "help[ing] us to get into satisfactory relations with other parts of our experience." James also calls this the "cash value" of ideas. Now, if believing that

there is a table in the middle of the room pre-vents you from bruising your legs and making a fool out of yourself, then that belief <u>works</u>. That is, it is true.

Let us finally turn to the pragmatists' thoughts about believing in God. James' discussion of this topic was a response to the scientistic view that we have no right to hold any beliefs for which we do not have adequate evidence. This view (held by Hume in the eighteenth century and Bertrand Russell in the twentieth) had been popularized in James' own time by the British mathematician, W.K. Clifford (1845-1879), who had said, "Belief is desecrated when given to unproved and unquestioned statements for the solace and private pleasure of the believer. . . . It is wrong always, everywhere, and for every-one, to believe anything upon insufficient evidence."[18] To this, James responded by saying:

> Our passional nature not only lawfully may, but must, decide an option between propositions, whenever it is a genuine option

that cannot by its nature be decided on intellectual grounds; for to say, under such circumstances, 'Do not decide, but leave the question open,' is itself a passional decision, — just like deciding yes or no, — and it is attended with the same risk of losing the truth. [19]

Now, for James, the issue of God's existence is one that the intellect by itself definitely cannot resolve. So if it is a "genuine option" (that is, a meaningful belief), it may be entertained on purely volitional grounds. Is the proposition "God exists" pragmatically meaningful? Does believing it make a practical difference in one's life? This is problematical. I take it that for some people it does, but for some people it doesn't. Some people would behave exactly the same whether they believed in God's existence or not. But others would behave very differently if

they believed in the existence of the God of the Judeo-Christian tradition from the way they would behave if they did _not_ believe in him. (If they believe, perhaps they will be nicer to their neighbor than if they do not believe.) But not everybody for whom a belief in God makes a difference would behave in exactly the same way. Some might become monks or nuns; in the case of others, the only difference their belief makes is that on Sundays, they dress up and go to church. This shows the _subjective_ side of James'

I am dressed up; therefore God exists.

A pragmatic proof of God's existence

theory of meaning because the meaning of a proposition is just the difference in behavior resulting from belief in the proposition. So for some, there is no _practical_ difference between the sentences "God exists" and "God does not exist." For others, belief, as opposed to nonbelief, would make a radical difference. For yet others, belief would result in very minor differences (e.g., putting on a dark suit on Sundays).

Now, what about the _truth_ of the claim "God exists"? According to James, a proposition is true if believing it _works_ — that is, if the belief puts the believer in a more satisfactory relationship with the rest of his or her experience. Concerning this, James says:

On pragmatistic principles, if the hypothesis of God works satisfactorily in the widest sense of the word, it is true. Now whatever its residual difficulties may be, experience shows that it certainly does work, and that the problem is to build it out and determine it so that it will combine satisfactorily with all the other working truths (p. 192).

So we see that for James, both meaning and truth are relative. To some people, the sentence "God exists" is true; for others, it is false. Most philosophers rejected James' solution to the problem of religious belief because they balked at his relativism concerning meaning and truth. Others felt that James left untouched the real question, which they took to be, regardless of the personal satisfaction or lack of it found in a belief in God's existence, does God _really_ exist?

Religious Existentialism

One of the most interesting antirationalistic religious stances
(I am loath to call it a _theory_) held by any philosopher is that
of the nineteenth-century Dane, SØREN KIERKEGAARD. Kierkegaard, whom I would call a
radical Christian, but who
never dared in his writings
to call himself a Christian
(he was busy attempting to
become a Christian), admired
Feuerbach's atheism and
loathed all attempts to
prove God's existence. Indeed, Kierkegaard took as
a personal affront all
efforts to demonstrate
God's being. ("Woe unto

SØREN KIERKEGAARD
(1813-1855)

all those unfaithful stewards who sat down and wrote false
proofs.") This is because he felt that for something to be a truly
religious belief, it had to be just that — a _belief_, something
that is not knowledge. Indeed, a religious belief would have
to be not only something that is not knowledge, but that can
not _be_ knowledge. Rather, it could be accounted for only in
terms of what Kierkegaard called "the category of the absurd"
— a category he felt Kant had left out of his twelve "categories
of the understanding." (This is reminiscent of the view of
the early Christian theologian Tertullian [169-220], whose

motto was "I believe that which is absurd.") According to Kierkegaard, knowledge must be something _objective_ — in the case of
mathematics (e.g., "3 × 3 = 9"), science (e.g., "f = ma"), history
(e.g., "Caesar crossed the Rubicon in 49 B.C."), or common sense
(e.g., "The cat is on the mat"), there are objective criteria for
establishing their truth value. But in the case of religious claims
(e.g., "God is love," "Whosoever believeth in him shall inherit
everlasting life"), there are only subjective criteria, which is to
say, _personal_ criteria.

Perhaps this notion can be best addressed by taking a look
at Kierkegaard's perplexing account of the biblical story of
Abraham and Isaac as it is related in his book, _Fear and
Trembling_ (1843), for it is there that we find his most sustained,
if convoluted, discussion of religious belief. (Our problem is
confounded by the fact that Kierkegaard wrote the book under
one of his many pseudonyms, that of "Johannes de Silentio"
[an intentional irony worthy of Kierkegaard's hero, Socrates —
John the Silent speaks!], and later claimed that he took no responsibility for any views held by his pseudonyms. The curious
relation between Kierkegaard and the volumes he wrote under

ficticious names has been the topic of more than one book, but here we will ignore Kierkegaard's disclaimer and attribute the views in _Fear and Trembling_ to Kierkegaard himself.)

Let us begin by reviewing the pertinent aspects of the biblical text as related in Genesis, chapters 11-22. Abraham was a hereditary tribal leader of the Hebrews. Late in life he married his half-sister, Sarah, who was barren. When Abraham was seventy-five years old, God commanded him to take his people and begin a journey to a land that God would show him. God made a covenant with Abraham and promised him that Sarah would become the mother of a son who would be the father of a great nation. The years passed and Sarah did not conceive. Then when Abraham was ninety-nine and Sarah ninety ("... and it ceased to be with Sarah after the manner of women" [Genesis 18:11]), God appeared to Abraham again and renewed the promise. Sarah conceived and gave birth to Isaac. The circumcision and weaning of the child were celebrated with great joy by Abraham, who loved his son. Then came that terrible night described in Genesis 22:1-2.

> And it came to pass ... that God did tempt Abraham, and said unto him, Abraham: and he said, Behold, here I am. And he said, take now thy son, Isaac, whom thou lovest; and get thee into the land of Moriah; and offer him there for a burnt offering upon one of the mountains which I will tell thee of.

Without hesitation and telling no one, Abraham took Isaac, travelled with him three days through that lonely desert, placed him on the appointed altar, lifted the sacrificial knife and was prepared to make the fatal thrust when the Angel of the Lord stopped him, saying that Abraham had passed the test and allowed him to sacrifice in Isaac's stead a ram that was conveniently caught in a nearby thicket. So Abraham got Isaac back, returned to his people, and lived in blessedness the rest of his days.

Now, this story provokes a state of deep perplexity in Johannes de Silentio, the pseudonymous author of <u>Fear</u> <u>and</u> <u>Trembling</u>. First of all, Johannes is perplexed

because he cannot understand the story; second, he is perplexed because everyone else seems to understand the story perfectly well. (Why else would all the others replace the Bible on the shelf after reading the account, comment "What a wonderful story of faith!," and then go along on their merry way without being the least bit affected by the story? Yet the story leaves Johannes

Johannes de Silentio reads before retiring.

sleepless in the night and inspires in him the fear and trembling of the book's title.) Johannes cannot understand the story because he cannot understand Abraham himself. He asks:

> Who gave strength to Abraham's arm? Who held his right hand up so that it did not fall limp at his side? He who gazes at this becomes paralyzed. Who gave strength to Abraham's soul, so that

his eyes did not grow dim, so that he saw neither Isaac nor the ram? He who gazes at this becomes blind.[20]

Johannes tries to conceive of Abraham as a real human being of flesh and blood, not as a fantastic personality from mythological literature. As an existing human, Abraham is incomprehensible. How could he be so resolute in the face of the horror of his task? "And if ... the individual was mistaken — what can save him? ... and if the individual had misunderstood the deity — what can save him? ... if this man is disordered in his mind, if he had made a mistake (pp. 71-72)!"

Furthermore, Johannes cannot be certain what it is that makes Abraham "the father of faith" and hence the father of us all. Many say that Abraham is great because he was willing to sacrifice to God the best thing he had. Johannes demonstrates the falsity of this view by way of an illustration. He imagines a clerical orator who eloquently presents his flock with just such a misleading interpretation of the story of Abraham. One of his parishioners, taken by the sermon, returns home and executes his son. When the preacher hears of this, he goes to the sinner and thunders down upon him in righteous indignation, "O abominable man, offscouring of society, what devil possessed thee to want to murder thy son?" The point, of course, is that this is precisely the attitude the preacher should have had toward Abraham. Johannes de Silentio asks:

> How is one to explain the contradiction illustrated by that orator? Is it because Abraham had a prescriptive right to be a great man, so that what he did is great, and when another does the same it is sin, a heinous sin? In that case I do not wish to participate in such thoughtless eulogy. If faith does not make it a holy act to be willing to murder one's son, then let the same condemnation be pronounced upon Abraham as upon every other man (p. 41).

Johannes' conclusion is that, "... either Abraham was every minute a murderer, or we are here confronted by a paradox which is higher than all mediation." This thought horrifies Johannes, who says, "... Abraham enjoys honor and glory as the father of faith, whereas he ought to be prosecuted and convicted of murder." But if Abraham is not to be condemned as a potential murderer (surely that cannot make him the father of faith), then he must be condemned as insane. "Humanly speaking, he is crazy and cannot make himself intelligible to anyone. And yet it is the mildest expression to say that he is crazy" (p. 86).

One of the most striking ideas to emerge from Kierkegaard's account of Abraham's madness (and one that is meant to evoke the fear and trembling of the book's title) is that granting the theological premise changes nothing. Abraham is mad whether or not God really did speak to him. If a law-abiding, moral man "hears the voice of God" and becomes so inspired as to become socially irresponsible, if he sacrifices his son, without criminal intent, in order to obey a secret order that God has communicated to him alone, then certainly from the medical-social point of view (i.e., "humanly speaking"), that man is mad.

Jean-Paul Sartre was particularly impressed with this aspect of Kierkegaard's analysis of the plight of Abraham, and he referred to it in order to elucidate his own theory of anguish. Sartre wrote:

> You know the story: an angel[21] has ordered Abraham to sacrifice his son; if it really were an angel who has come and said, "You are Abraham, you shall sacrifice your son," everything would be all right. But everyone must first wonder, "is it really an angel and am I really Abraham? What proof do I have?"
> There was a madwoman who had hallucinations; someone used to speak to her on the telephone and give her orders. Her

doctor asked her, who is it who talks to you?" She answered, "He says it's God." What proof did she really have it was God? If an angel comes to me, what proof is there that it's an angel? And if I hear voices, what proof is there that they come from heaven and not from hell, or from the subconscious, or a pathological condition? What proves that they are addressed to me? [22]

Abraham is mad not only in the sense referred to earlier (unable to communicate, prepared to perform an act that goes against his own moral standards and will horrify all), but in the following sense as well. He not only believes his son will die, but at the same moment, he believes his son will <u>not</u> die. (Abraham still has faith that God will keep the old covenant.) Abraham believed with certainty two mutually exclusive theses, and he acted on each of them in a single project. (It is as if Columbus believed both that the world was flat and that it was round, and he set out to prove both points by embarking on a single voyage.)

So either Abraham is a murderer, or he is mad, or the story of Abraham is rationally unintelligible. It will probably come as no surprise to you to discover that Kierkegaard (or at least, Johannes de Silentio) draws the latter conclusion. Faith, he says, is "a paradox which is capable of transforming a murder into a holy act well-pleasing to God." Abraham acted "by virtue of the absurd," and "by virtue of the absurd" he became the father of faith. "Abraham was greater than all, great by reason of his power whose strength is impotence, great by reason of his wisdom whose secret is foolishness, great by reason of his hope whose form is madness, great by reason of the love which is hatred of oneself" (p. 31). Adopting a term from Plato, Kierkegaard calls Abraham's condition "divine madness." For Kierkegaard, of course, the question was not whether Abraham was mad, but whether his madness was divinely or demonically inspired. Still, "humanly speaking," it does not matter. In either case, society has an asylum for such heroes.

Earlier it was mentioned that, for Kierkegaard, there could be no objective but only subjective, or personal, justification of religious belief. This idea can be clarified if one considers certain features of Kierkegaard's account of the story of Abraham. Notice that Abraham's act is not authorized or justified by God's command; rather, God's command is authorized by Abraham's decision to interpret it in a certain way. When Abraham was awakened on that horrible night by a voice commanding him to kill his child, he could have responded in a number of ways. He might have said, "This is not the voice of God, but of the devil. Only the devil tempts men to do evil deeds. Get thee hence, O Satan!" Or he might have said (especially if he had read Freud), "This is not the voice of God, but the voice of my own madness. I shall kill myself rather than perform this insane act!" Or he might have said, "This is the voice of God, who is testing me to see if I am willing to perform an immoral act for no good reason. I shall pass the test by refusing to perform the act!" Or he might have said, "If this is the voice of God, then he is not the God I thought he was; rather, he is an evil and cruel monster whose bidding I shall

229

Abraham reads Freud.

not do!" Or, ... he might have said any number of other things. Instead, he chose to accept the assignment, and in so choosing, he bestowed his own authority on God's command. Kierkegaard is suggesting that ultimately the individual is the source of all authority and is totally responsible for all his or her decisions and actions. (This is the beginning of the school of thought known in the twentieth century as EXISTENTIALISM, which puts the existence of the individual human being at the center of the philosophical stage. [See Chapter II for a more thorough discussion of existentialism.] Kierkegaard's views greatly influenced such members of that school as Jean-Paul Sartre, Martin Heidegger, Karl Jaspers, Albert Camus, Miguel de Unamuno, and Gabriel Marcel.)

Kierkegaard's complex demonstration of the irreducibility of faith to intellectual categories (and it is even more complex than it has been presented here) is indeed profound. Both the traditional proofs of God's existence and the traditional atheistic criticism of the irrationality of religious belief seem lifeless and shallow in the face of Kierkegaard's account. Especially weak vis-à-vis Kierkegaard's explosive treatment of faith are those rationalistic arguments like Freud's, which see religion as a crutch for the weak. Kierkegaard's religious discourse is meant to strengthen, not weaken, the soul. It is not "lemonade-twaddle" for the fainthearted (as he calls most sermonizing); rather, it is only for those who can stand the drama of striving with God and with oneself.

Yet, it must be obvious that this account raises tremendous philosophical problems, not the least of which is the problem of fanaticism (and our poor world has been plagued with plenty of <u>that</u> since Kierkegaard's day). Also, we may ask, <u>must</u> we accept Kierkegaard's implication that a truly religious conception of life is ultimately incompatible with a social conception of life? Must one become "divinely mad" to be considered authentically religious? Well, Kierkegaard could at least point to plenty of biblical evidence for his thesis, but it isn't surprising that, as William Barrett says, Kierkegaard's harshness has driven at least as many away from religion as it has into religion's embrace.[23]

Kierkegaard driving people from religion

231

Conclusion

What conclusion do we draw from all this? I must be very careful here, for in talking about religion, everything is controversial. No matter where you walk, you tread on someone's toes. Still, walk we must. Let it be a relatively gentle path!

Stepping on toes

First, concerning the various arguments meant to prove God's existence: it seems to me that no one of them is powerful enough to force rational assent. (The same is true concerning the arguments for atheism.) Yet, taken all together, it is possible to imagine the _combination_ as powerful enough to remove certain philosophical scruples one had against belief. And what is wrong with taking them all together? Usually people have more than _one_ reason for believing what they believe. Our systems of belief and justification are usually multilayered. If I asked you why you enrolled specifically in this class, you would probably answer with a number of reasons: "I needed three units of humanities credit." "This is a good hour for me; it frees my time up for work." "I

232

heard the professor was good." "I noticed that the course at-
tracts bright people, and I would like to be considered in that
category." "There are a number of attractive members of the
opposite sex in this class." "My parents said they would cut off
my finances if I didn't take some philosophy." Maybe no <u>one</u> of
these reasons is a sufficient explanation, but the group together
is quite compelling.

As I said, I can imagine someone finding all the arguments
for God's existence similarly compelling as a group. Frankly, I
do not find them to be so. (Nor do I find compelling all the
arguments for atheism together.) Perhaps more subtle versions
of the arguments than I have presented would do the trick, but
in their absence, I have to think that there are too many obvious problems with each of them as they stand. So I have to
conclude with a negative answer to the question, "Is there
any good reason for believing in God's existence?," if by
"reason" we mean "logical argument" or "compelling piece
of evidence." However, I have learned enough from Kierkegaard, James, and from the mystical poets (whom we did
not discuss here) to know that such a definition of "reason"
is too confining and that there are, as Pascal said, "reasons of
the heart." These are perplexing and, as are so many things
of the heart, very personal and difficult to evaluate, but one
scoffs at them at his own risk. Such a "reason" just may
sneak up upon one some fine day as a "thought that
wounds from behind" (Kierkegaard's phrase).

My own choice has been a kind of impressionable agnosticism, asserting a negative answer based on the "evidence"
presented so far but open to new evidence or new interpretations of old evidence. I say this knowing full well of the

disdain with which Kierkegaard would greet my response. He would be quick to point out that the word "agnostic" translates into Latin as "ignoramus." He was not surprised that there _were_ lots of ignoramuses. He was only surprised that they touted their ignorance as an important philosophical position — usually at cocktail parties.

Thoughts that wound
from behind

Well, I myself am
an ignoramus.

Touting an important philosophical position

Notes

1. Bertrand Russell, _The Autobiography of Bertrand Russell_ . _The Early Years_: _1872 - World War I_ (Boston : Bantam Books, 1969), p. 43.

2. Russell, _The Autobiography_, p. 45.

3. Anselm of Canterbury, _Proslogium_, in Anne Fremantle, _The Age of Belief_ (New York : New American Library, 1954), pp. 88 - 89.

4. David Hume, _Dialogues Concerning Natural Religion_ (New York : Hafner, 1960), p. 58.

5. The example is taken from Richard Taylor, "Introduction," in _The Ontological Argument_, Alvin Plantinga, ed. (Garden City, New York: Doubleday, 1965), p. XV.

6. Immanuel Kant, _Critique of Pure Reason_ (Garden City, New York: Doubleday, 1961), p. 358.

7. Norman Malcolm, " Anselm's Ontological Arguments," in Plantinga, ed., _The Ontological Argument_, pp. 141-147.

8. See Alvin Plantinga, "A Valid Ontological Argument?" and Paul Henle, " Uses of the Ontological Argument," in Plantinga, ed., _The Ontological Argument_, pp. 160-171, 172-180.

9. Malcolm, " Anselm's Ontological Arguments," p. 159.

10. Thomas Aquinas , _Summa Theologica_, in Fremantle, _The Age of Belief_, p. 153.

11. Frederick Copleston, _Aquinas_ (London : Penguin Books, 1955), pp. 110-122.

12. Aquinas, _Summa Theologica_, pp. 154-155.

13. For example, see Carl G. Jung, _Answer to Job_ (Princeton, New Jersey : Princeton University Press, 1973).

14. Karl Marx, *Marx and Engels : Basic Writings on Politics and Philosophy*, Lewis Feuer, ed. (Garden City, New York: Doubleday, 1959), pp. 244, 262-263.

15. Herbert Marcuse, *Eros and Civilization* (New York: Vintage, 1955), p. 66.

16. Sigmund Freud, *Civilization and Its Discontents* (New York: Norton, 1962), p. 19. Unless otherwise stated, all subsequent quotes from Freud in this chapter are from this source.

17. William James, *Pragmatism* (New York: World Publishing, 1961), p. 42. Unless otherwise stated, all subsequent quotes from James in this chapter are from this source.

18. Quoted in William James, "The Will to Believe," in *Pragmatism: The Classic Writings*, H.S. Thayer, ed. (New York: New American Library, 1970), p. 191.

19. William James, "The Will to Believe," in *Philosophy of Recent Times*, Vol. 2, James B. Hartman, ed. (New York: McGraw-Hill, 1967), p. 28.

20. Søren Kierkegaard, *Fear and Trembling*, Walter Lowrie, trans. (Garden City, New York: Doubleday, 1954), p. 36. Unless otherwise stated, all subsequent quotes from Kierkegaard in this chapter are from this source.

21. We know the story, indeed, but Sartre's biblical knowledge fails him here. It was not an angel who spoke to Abraham, but God himself.

22. Jean-Paul Sartre, *Existentialism and Human Emotions* (New York: Philosophical Library, 1957), p. 19.

23. William Barrett, *Irrational Man* (Garden City, New York: Doubleday, 1962), p. 262.

Chapter 6
The Largest Airline in the Free World
Philosophy of Freedom

A few years ago there was a TV commercial that caught my attention. "Blah-Blah Airlines is the largest airline in the Free World." What information was being communicated in that commercial, and what information was being suppressed? The latter question is easy to answer. The suppressed truth in the commercial is this: "The official Soviet airline, Aeroflot, is the largest airline in the world. Blah-Blah is only the second largest." (But don't expect to hear _that_ as a commercial.) Well, if we weren't supposed to think the hidden thought, what were we supposed to think? I take it that we were supposed to associate in our minds BLAH BLAH AIRLINES / BIGNESS / ANTITOTALITARIANISM / THE FREE WORLD (hence FREEDOM). These thoughts together were meant to loosen a few dollars from our pockets. Here is the problem. In our culture, freedom is, on the one hand, so cherished that we are taught that it is worth dying for ("Live free or die": motto on the New Hampshire license plate). Yet on the other hand, it has been co-opted by the ideologues and moneymakers to the extent that it has become a meaningless "buzz word." Yes, there is indeed a lot of talk in our society about freedom. We hear about it in TV commercials, in political speeches from the left, middle, and right, and not uncommonly see reference to it on bumper stickers.

Spend your money with us, and strike a blow for freedom!

When philosophers turn to the topic of freedom, they ask the following kinds of big questions:

- What do we mean by "freedom"?

- Does freedom exist, or is there only necessity?

- How is freedom possible in a world governed by natural laws?

- Can we ever know whether there is freedom?

- If there is freedom, is it an "either/or" proposition, or are there degrees of it? Can we do anything to maximize it or endanger it?

- Does any of this matter practically, or is all of it only of academic interest?

Determinism: Ancient Greek and Enlightenment Views

DETERMINISM is the thesis that everything that occurs happens of necessity. This thesis first appears in the history of philosophy in the theories of LEUCIPPUS (c. 460 - ? B.C.) and DEMOCRITUS (c. 460 - c. 370), who, as the culmination of a hundred years of speculation about the nature of reality (what we call "the pre-Socratic tradition"), concluded that every existing thing was composed of atoms in

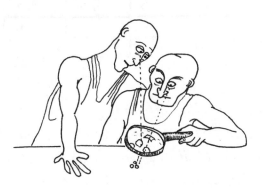

motion. These atoms moved inexorably along trajectories necessitated by the very nature of atoms and the nature of motion. The single fragment of Leucippus' book that remains to us today says, "Naught happens for nothing, but everything from a ground of necessity."

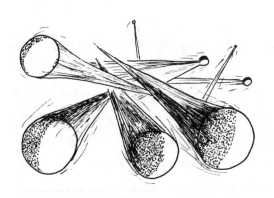

Imagine the following schema. Each letter in the diagram represents a movement in space. Each number represents a moment in time. Each dot represents an atom. The symbol "⊃" represents a relation of necessity between movements.

Let us arbitrarily say that the following relations hold:

	1	2	3	4	5	6	7
A							
B							
C							
D							
E							
F							

A ⊃ D
D ⊃ B
B ⊃ E
E ⊃ F
F ⊃ C
C ⊃ A

If we let the left-hand column represent the laws of nature, we can see that we could predict the trajectory of each atom in each moment of its career. Given any atom at "F," it _must_ move to "C," and any atom at "C" _must_ move to "A," etc. Of course, Leucippus and Democritus did not claim to know those laws, but they suspected that they existed, that therefore every-thing that happened did so of necessity, and that "free will" was an illusion.

Democritus' view did not become the dominant one in his day, mostly because he stood not at the end of the history of science, but on its threshold, and he could not appeal to any tradition of scientific authority to support his views. It would take another two thousand years before such a tradition could establish itself as authoritative. But when it did, Democritus' theory came to the fore with a vengeance. In the eighteenth century, armed with the prestige of the discoveries of Sir Isaac Newton, a number of Enlightenment figures put forth new versions of Democritus' old argument. Foremost among them were the Baron HENRI D'HOLBACH (1723-1789) and PIERRE-SIMON LAPLACE (1749-1827). D'Holbach argued that the same principles that applied

There is a drunken ladybug on this leaf now. Therefore on June 19, 2010, there will be a mudslide in Rangoon.

PIERRE - SIMON LAPLACE
(1749 - 1827)

to the physical world must necessarily apply to the human brain, which was as material in nature as were the moon and the stars. Therefore every thought of every brain followed necessarily from the brain states that preceded those thoughts. Laplace held a similar view and went so far as to say this:

If I knew all the laws of nature and had one complete description of the universe at any given moment, then I could predict all future events and retrodict all past events.

Hard Determinism: Modern Views

This view has come to be known as HARD DETERMINISM. It is called determinism because, according to it, every event is _determined_ by the state of the world preceding the event. (Let A, B, C, D represent all the states in the universe preceding event X. Then, whenever A, B, C, D happen, X _must_ happen, according to this view; and we can say that A, B, C, and D _cause X_.) This

241

I'll have a T-bone, rare.

Sorry. There's no free lunch.

But I need one.

True, they're <u>necessary</u>, but not <u>free</u>.

view is called HARD DETERMINISM because, according to it, determinism rules out freedom. If everything is necessary, then nothing is free.

B. F. Skinner

In the contemporary world, hard determinism is perhaps most clearly defended by B.F. Skinner (whom we have already met in Chapter 3). In his book with the telling title, <u>Beyond Freedom and Dignity</u>, Skinner says:

> [M]any anthropologists, sociologists, and psychologists have used their expert knowledge to prove that man is free, purposeful, and responsible.
>   This escape route is slowly closed as new evidences of the predictability of human behavior are discovered. Personal exemption from a complete determinism is revoked as a scientific analysis progresses, particularly in accounting for the behavior of the individual.'

(As an aside, I might point out what looks to me like a logical fallacy in Skinner's argument. He says, because behavior

Beyond Freedom and Dignity

242

is predictable, it must be determined. Now, it is certainly true that (A) if behavior is determined, then (B) it is in principle predictable [for Laplace's reasons]. But it isn't true that because a behavior is predictable, it is determined.

valid → [A implies B.
A.
Therefore B.]

[A implies B.
B.
Therefore A.] ← invalid

For the sake of argument, imagine that there is such a thing as freedom and that Pierre freely chooses to abide by Christian values. I think in such a case we could correctly predict that Pierre will attend church services and will offer help to his neighbor in distress. Does this mean that he <u>Could</u> <u>not</u> <u>do</u> <u>otherwise</u>? Of course not.)

Skinner correctly associates the concept of freedom with the teleological model of explanation. You will recall from Chapter 5 that a teleological model is one in terms of goals, purposes, plans, and intentions. Skinner, an empiricist and a materialist, is

Pierre attends church.
(He could not do otherwise.)

suspicious of nonphysical, unobservable entities, so he wants to get rid of the teleological model of explanation. He has this to say about it:

. Physics did not advance by looking more closely at the

jubilance of a falling body, or biology by looking at the nature of vital spirits, and we do not need to try to discover what ... plans, purposes, intentions, or the other prerequisites of autonomous man really are in order to get on with a scientific analysis of behavior. [2]

The Causal Model   The Teleological Model
(push from behind)   (pull from ahead)

What exactly is at stake here? Well, it's important to remember that normally our explanation of our own behavior is in terms of the teleological model. If you ask me why I am in such a hurry, I explain that I'm trying to arrive at the grocery store before it closes at 6 P.M. This is an <u>explanation</u> of my behavior (it renders it intelligible), and it is an explanation in terms of my <u>intentions</u> and <u>purposes</u>. Skinner wants to do away with such explanations.

Furthermore, it is important to note that in our moral and legal tradition, we hold people fully responsible only for their <u>intentional</u> acts. If your lawyer can convince the jury that your act was accidental rather than intentional (and we've already seen that the concept of an accident makes sense only against a backdrop of intentionality), the jury will find you not fully responsible for the act. (If you caused someone's death accidentally and not purposefully, you could be convicted of manslaughter due to negligence, but not of murder.) Similarly, we hold people responsible only for their _free_ acts, not for acts they cannot help (which is why we excuse the mentally ill from responsibility). So if Skinner does away with the teleological model, he also overturns our moral and legal institutions, such as courtrooms and prisons.

His theory is a radical one, and he is well aware of that fact.

Skinner wishes to replace the teleological model with a _causal_ one, namely, with a _stimulus/response_ model based on Pavlov's famous experiment with his

Free! Hallelujah, I am free at last!

Not really.

Implementation of Skinner's theories would empty the prisons.

drooling dog. When you feed a steak to a dog, the animal begins to salivate as soon as it sees or smells the meat. Now, if you repeatedly ring a bell just before you serve the steak, eventually the dog will begin to salivate at the sound of the bell. We

DING DING DING DING

SLOBBER SLOBBER SLOBBER

Pavlovian science

need no "dog psychology" to explain this fact, and no references to purposes, plans, intentions, and goals. It can be explained in purely mechanical terms. Skinner believed he could extend the Pavlovian model to the human sphere, thereby overturning the traditional teleological model and placing us "beyond freedom and dignity."

Sigmund Freud

An even more powerful version of hard determinism comes out of some interpretations of the psychoanalytical theories of Sigmund Freud, whom we have also already encountered in this book. The deterministic argument runs like this: An individual's personality has crystallized by the age of five years. One has no personal control over the formation of one's own personality; yet everything that happens to an individual after that age will be responded to by that already completed character structure. Furthermore, the bulk of one's motivational system is unconscious, structured by anti-social biological urges, painful childhood memories, unresolved emotional conflicts, fantastic desires, and fears, all of which have been repressed

What's the matter? Aren't you happy? It's your birthday!

No, I'm depressed.

Why?

I'm five years old. Everything important that will ever happen to me has already happened.

into the unconscious. The "ego" (more or less the conscious self) is
nothing more than a façade masking a ferocious struggle between
the "id" (the antisocial, animal self that "wants it all now") and
the "superego" (the irrational, nay-saying, guilt-spawning social
conscience). According to this deterministic reading of Freud, the
actions of the so-called
"normal person," as much
as those of the psychotic,
are unfree. And, as
was the case with
Skinner's deterministic
scheme, there is no such
thing as responsibility
here. John Hospers, a
philosopher who interprets
Freud as a hard deter-
minist, says:

The standoff between the id
and the superego

> But what is not wel-
> come news is that
> our very acts of
> volition, and the entire
> train of deliberations leading up to them, are but façades for
> the expression of unconscious wishes, or rather, unconscious com-
> promises and defenses
>
>   . . . .
>
> we may ... say that a man is free only to the extent that his be-
> havior is <u>not</u> unconsciously motivated at all. If this be our crite-
> rion, most of our behavior could not be called free: everything,
> including both impulses and volitions, having to do with our basic
> attitudes toward life, the general tenor of our tastes, whether we
> become philosophers or artists or business men, our whole affective
> life including our preferences for blondes or brunettes, active or
> passive, older or younger, has its inevitable basis in the unconscious.
> Only those comparatively vanilla-flavored aspects of life - such as
> our behavior toward people who don't really matter to us - are
> exempted from this rule.[3]

It should be noted that not every reader of Freud interprets him as a hard determinist. Consider the case of the woman who comes to the psychoanalyst trying to find out why every man she has ever been involved with brutalizes her. "Why do men want to beat me?" (This case may seem on its surface to be a typical example of Freudian sexism, of which there is plenty, but I think a careful scrutiny of it demonstrates that such is not the case here.) Investigation reveals an unconscious childhood memory on the part of the woman, a memory of having observed her father beating her mother. On the typical Freudian model, the woman has chosen her mother as her model of femininity and her father as her model of masculinity, so in choosing herself as a woman, she unconsciously chooses men who will beat her. Yet these are not true choices because she has no control over them. (So far, the model is one of hard determinism.) But what can Freud do for this woman? He cannot "cure" her. Perhaps she will always be in some way attracted to brutal men. But now that she is aware of the motivational forces that are operating on her, she can gain some control over her life. There are certain taverns she will know better than to frequent, and she certainly will **not** accept an invitation to the annual Hell's Angels picnic! Surely this new control restored

Déjeuner sur l'herbe sans Marie, Hell's Angels style
(with apologies to Edouard Manet)

to her by psychoanalysis is a kind of FREEDOM that is incompatible with the theory of hard determinism.

Furthermore, as the British philosopher Richard Peters has pointed out, it is rather farfetched to read Freud as claiming that every act is motivated by the unconscious. Suppose you and I are playing chess, and you see that my queen is unprotected. It's your turn, so you take my piece. We don't need to seek for an unconscious motive to explain your act. We don't need to know anything about your unhappy childhood or your repressed sexual fantasies. Some of these psychoanalytic topics might be pertinent to the question of why you like to play chess in the first place, but not to the question of why, while playing chess, you decide to take my unprotected queen. Your ordinary conscious reasons, combined with a knowledge of the rules of chess, are perfectly adequate to explain your action.

Why did you take my queen? Is there something unresolved from your childhood?

In another of Peters' examples, he says that if a person explains why he is crossing the road by asserting that he wants to buy tobacco, this is a perfectly sound explanation under certain circumstances. (The person smokes, he is out of cigarettes, there is a tobacco shop across the street.) No unconscious motive or any psychoanalytic theory is needed here (though an unconscious motive might be useful in explaining why the man smokes in the first place). On the other hand, if the man _rolls_ across the street and explains doing so by saying that he's going to get tobacco, _this_ explanation needs looking into. In such a case, a psychoanalytic account _might_ be needed precisely because our normal account has broken down. Concluding his nondeterministic interpretation of Freud, Peters says,

What are you doing?

Going to get tobacco.

Oh

> When Freud wants to describe goings-on of which it is appropriate to say that a man is acting, that he has a _reason_ for what he does, and so on, he talks about the Ego; when on the other hand, he wants to say that a person suffers something, or is made or driven to do something, he speaks of the Id. [4]

Soft Determinism

There have been philosophers who have affirmed the truth of determinism but who have denied that their deterministic views preclude the existence of freedom. Some of these philosophers have been motivated to prove the compatibility of freedom and determinism because they don't like the conclusion, reached by hard determinists like Skinner and (Hosper's) Freud, that no one is ever responsible for anything. Correctly seeing that there can be responsibility only when there is freedom, but also believing in the truth of determinism, they have been pressed to demonstrate that freedom can exist even in a world of necessity. This view is called SOFT DETERMINISM. It has been quite common among some philosophers in the twentieth century, but its roots go back to Roman times. The Stoics (first century A.D.), St. Augustine (fourth century), Thomas Hobbes (seventeenth century), and Baruch Spinoza (seventeenth century) all defended versions of it. Augustine's interpretation is fairly representative, even though his concern about determinism was different from those we've mentioned so far. (Modern determinists derive their conception of

A soft determinist

necessity from the laws of nature. Augustine derives his from his belief in God's omniscience. If God knows everything, he knows the future; and if he knows the future, the future must unfold in accordance with God's knowledge of it.)

251

What do we mean by "freedom"? Augustine and other soft determinists ask this not so much as philosophers, but as ordinary persons in everyday life. What we mean by freedom is the coincidence of will and capacity; that is, <u>we are free to the extent that we are able to do and get what we want</u>. If you ask me if I am free to go to the movies tonight, and I say that I am not, I am implying that I <u>want</u> to, but <u>am not able</u> <u>to</u>. This is the sense in which the prisoners at San Quentin are not free. They are not free to leave if they want to. However, they <u>are</u> free to write to their mothers. So, according to this common-sense definition, freedom is relative to context. One is both free and not free at the same

time. Nevertheless, <u>everyone</u> is free sometimes. (No one has ever been so miserable as <u>never</u> to have gotten what he wants.) Some are freer than others or more free at certain periods of their lives than at others. And when one wants to do X, and does X, then doing X is a free act, and one is responsible for that act.

Furthermore, in this definition, freedom is <u>compatible</u> with determinism. I sometimes do what I want to do even if my will was determined according to Freudian or Skinnerian principles. So both freedom and necessity can exist in the same world.

One of the most curious versions of soft determinism was put forward in the first century A.D. by the <u>Stoics</u>, named after the "stoa," or porch, from which their founder, Zeno of Cyprus (334-262 B.C.), preached. (A similar view was held by Spinoza in the seventeenth century.) Having accepted the claim that one is free to the extent that one gets what one wants,

the Stoics, such as SENECA and EPICTETUS, added that one is happy to the extent that one is free. Then, pointing out that we are all free and happy sometimes, they make the astonishing claim that it is possible to be totally free and totally happy <u>all the time</u>. How is this to be done? <u>Not</u> by trying to get what one wants, but by wanting what one gets — by identifying your will with the "world will," what Nietzsche called <u>amor fati</u>, love of one's fate.

Now, it is easy enough to parody this view ("Just what I wanted, etc."), but there is an interesting truth here that escapes our mockery,

Just what I wanted! To be robbed while fixing a flat in a rainstorm.

Don't try to get what you want. — Rather, want what you get.

namely, the truth that the unhappiness of many people comes from the fact that they want things they can't have — especially in our materialistic consumer culture, where we are constantly being bombarded by images of objects of pleasure and power that we absolutely <u>must</u> possess if we are to consider ourselves attractive, desirable, independent, smart, clever, and, mostly, "cool." So we spend most of our lives burning with frustrated desire for this and that. Happiness and freedom elude us. The stoic wisdom (and I think it is wisdom, of an almost oriental type) is that there is happiness in tranquility, and there is tranquility in "flowing with the river." But the stoics knew, as do the Asian philosophers, that such peace is not easy to acquire, and sometimes it takes a lifetime to achieve. Furthermore, its quest presupposed an

You can either flow with the river or swim against the current.

ideal of passivity, of inaction, of quietism, which for better or for worse, is not compatible with the mainstream Western ideal of the self. Hence, this stoic form of soft determinism is not a "live option" for most of us.

Indeterminism

The opposite of determinism is called INDETERMINISM. This is simply

254

the view that determinism is false. The indeterminist does not need to claim that _no_ event is caused, only that _not every_ event is caused (that is, that there exist some "uncaused events"). (An uncaused event would be a happening that is not a necessary happening, an event that does not follow necessarily from the events that precede it.) Indeterminism has been given a new respectability because of recent developments in physics. (This is somewhat ironic because the authority of determinism has usually been associated with its relationship to classical physics.)

Ever since the work of the Nobel Prize recipient, WERNER HEISENBERG, it has been suggested that, at the subatomic level of physical reality (that is, at the most basic level), the causal model does not work and must be replaced with a statistical model. Let's explain this by imagining a billiard ball in a classical Newtonian world. If the ball is propelled here, and we know the exact force applied to it by the

cue stick, the exact point of application of the force, and exactly the amount of friction provided by the felt tabletop, then in theory, we can predict with accuracy the trajectory of the billiard ball and its location at times t^1, t^2, t^3, and t^4. Now, if the Heisenbergian "principle of uncertainty" is true (and apparently most physicists think it is), then the same model will not work at the subatomic level. Imagine an electron instead of an eight ball. Even if we knew its mass, its location, its velocity, and its trajectory at times t^1, t^2, and t^3 (which we can't, by the way), we still could not predict with certainty the location of the electron at time t^4. It might end up at point Y or point X,

t^1 t^2 t^3 Point Y

t^4

Point X

even though there is a greater statistical probability of it ending up at X. And this failure to be able to predict the fate of the electron is not merely a weakness in our human ability to know, but is a fact about the nature of the subatomic world. It follows from all this that the movement of our electron from t^3 to t^4 would be an <u>uncaused</u> <u>event</u>. If there are such events (as most physicists believe to be the case), then, strictly speaking, determinism is false, and indeterminism is true.

Libertarianism

Heisenberg himself waxed philosophical at this point and tried to derive a libertarian position from his indeterminism.[5] LIBERTARIANISM (which has nothing to do with the political movement of the same name) is indeed a version of indeterminism. It is the view that determinism is false and that freedom does exist; that is, some acts are uncaused and free. Heisenberg hoped that the fact that some events in the brain are uncaused might be the scientific basis for a theory of freedom. But his critics pointed out that uncaused, subatomic events can hardly be called <u>free</u>. Rather, they are more correctly called <u>random</u> <u>events</u>. Similarly, a human act based on such an uncaused brain event would itself be a random event and not a free event. If I intend to walk to the window to open it for fresh air and if, upon arriving there, I have an uncaused brain event and throw myself through the window, we should not call this event a "free act." If a person walking through her living room cannot know whether

A free act?

she will get to the other side of it without kicking the dog or doing a back-flip, this will be the very opposite of freedom. Freedom may well be considered the opposite of necessity. Yet there are not just two components of this formula, but three.

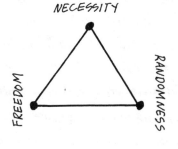

Well then, it seems that Heisenberg has not given us theo-retical freedom, but at least his principle of uncertainty has broken the backbone of classical determinism by removing the scien-tific stamp of approval from it. This should be worth something to the libertarians.

I shall now present what I take to be the mainstream libertar-ian argument, using ideas from two well-known articles, one by C.A. Campbell and another by Richard Taylor.[6] The first point to make (one that is perhaps a bit surprising) is that the libertar-ian sides with the "hard determinist" against the "soft determinist" on one important topic; viz., the libertarian and the hard deter-minist agree that if determinism is true, then there is no freedom. Recall that the soft determinist, while accepting determinism in general (the view that every event follows necessarily from its antecedent conditions), did not like the radical conclusions the hard determinists drew from this fact (namely, that there is no free-dom, hence no responsibility). The soft determinist, in attempting to salvage responsibility, pointed out that "freedom" means the coinci-dence of will and capacity ("I can"). Then the soft determinist claimed that, given such a definition of freedom, freedom certainly does exist, even in a deterministic universe. And if freedom exists, says the soft determinist, so does responsibility. Now, libertarians such as Campbell argue that the soft determinists' definition of freedom is only half the truth. Freedom entails not only the ability to achieve what one desires ("I can"), but also access to genuine alternatives, real choices ("I could have done otherwise"). That is, if I perform act X under conditions A, B, and C, X is a free act for which I could be held responsible only if under those iden-tical conditions I could have performed act Y instead of act X. But it is precisely this ability that determinism denies. So the soft determinists are wrong. Their theory does not generate a genuine concept of freedom; hence it does not generate a legi-timate concept of responsibility.

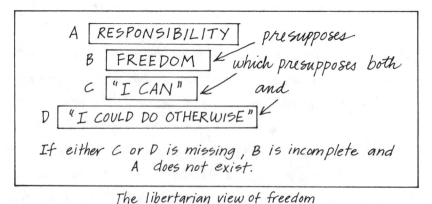

The libertarian view of freedom

Well then, is there such a thing as freedom as I have defined it ("I can" and "I could do otherwise")? Libertarians point out that if we appeal to actual experience, our own and that of other humans, we would have to answer that question in the affirmative. Our experience of ourselves in the world certainly seems to tell us that sometimes we are free. But is our experience shown to be illusory by the theory of determinism? The libertarian wants to stress that determinism _is_ a theory (that is, it is an intellectual construct); it is not a _better_ description of our experience than is ordinary language. In fact, it is not a description of our experience at all. What is the role of a _theory_ in general? Normally, a theory's function is to explain some feature of experience. (Newton's theory of gravity is meant to explain features of the physical world as we experience it. Freud's theory of the unconscious is meant to explain certain impulsive acts as we experience them.) But the puzzling feature of the theory of determinism is that, far from _explaining_ the data of our experience, this theory _denies_ them.

There are little invisible rubber bands connected to everything. That's why things go down.

SNAP

An alternative to Newton's theory of gravity

Given this curious fact about the theory of determinism, the libertarian thinks we should be very skeptical of it. I'll make this point concrete. Let's say that I hold my index finger out and I consider the possible ways I can move it. I can move it up (call this act A), down (B), to the left (C), or to the right (D). And let us say that at times t^1, t^2, and t^3, I have held out my finger but have not yet decided how to move it. Then at time t^4 I move my

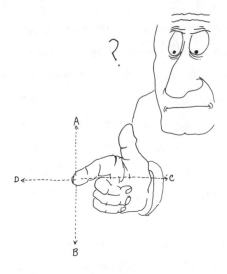

?

A

D ← - - - - - - - - - - - - - → C

B

Freedom in action

finger to the left (act C). Now, I experience this act (as trivial as it might be) as a _free_ act. I chose to do C, and I could have chosen to do A, B, or D instead. But determinism says that act C was a determined act — that it followed necessarily from the event that preceded it at t^1, t^2, and t^3. Libertarians such as Campbell point out that no one has ever established that such is the case. If determinists want to fly in the face of experience and claim that all acts, including act C, are necessary, then the onus is on them to prove that counterintuitional claim. And until they do, the rest of us have every good reason to believe determinism to be false.

Existential Freedom

The foregoing discussion of libertarianism defended a fairly moderate, commonsensical position — commonsensical in that it was based on our common experience of ourselves in normal circumstances and moderate in that it recognized that determinism _might_ be true in spite of our experience to the contrary and also moderate in the sense that it recognized that we are free in only some of our acts, not in all of them. There are, however, more radical versions of the libertarian view, and of them, the existentialist perspective of JEAN-PAUL SARTRE (1905-1980) is perhaps the most interesting.

JEAN-PAUL SARTRE (1905-1980)

We shall now look at a few technical terms that need to be defined here by way of introduction to Sartre's theory. First is BEING-FOR-ITSELF. This is Sartre's term for the human's experience of itself. It is _roughly_ the equivalent of "consciousness," but only roughly because it also includes our experience of our own bodies. (Therefore, it is not simply Descartes' COGITO, which was pure consciousness.) Second is BEING-IN-ITSELF. This is nonhuman reality as it exists prior to human intervention in it. Sartre says of being-in-itself, "Being is. Being is in-itself. Being is what it is." It is full; it is inert. It _is_. Nothing more can be said. Now, let the figure below represent the two forms of being.

This represents being-for-itself, and this represents being-in-itself.

The "for-itself" is open to being. But the in-itself is closed.

There are certain features of the in-itself about which we humans can do nothing, and those features Sartre calls _facticity_. Now, the "space" between the for-itself and the in-itself constitutes _the world_ for human experience. It includes such items as language, institutions, conventions, and theories. It is created by human interpretations of the in-itself and of responses to facticity. Sartre argues that these interpretations, though necessary (we _must_ interpret and respond to being; we have no choice about that), are radically _free_ at the same time. Let's explain this claim with a very Sartrean example. Imagine a group of people who set out on a day hike in the Alps. Their goal is to reach a certain mountain peak and return to their camp before dark. After hiking for a number of hours, they find their mountain path suddenly blocked by a large boulder that has recently crashed down upon the trail from above. The path is completely barricaded. There is no hope of getting past the rock. Its presence constitutes facticity.

Facticity

262

One hiker looks at the boulder and is swept with discouragement. He throws his backpack down in the grass and falls back on it, saying, "Well, that's it! The hike is over." He begins unpacking his lunch as a consolation for his disappointment. For Sartre, this man has chosen the boulder as an "insurmountable obstacle" and has chosen himself as "defeated." He sinks back into nature in what Sartre calls a "quasi-pantheistic synthesis of the totality of the in-itself with the for-itself."[7] But there might be another person who responds to this situation by saying, "No! We can get around this! There must be a way," and begins scurrying about looking for an undiscovered bypass. This person has interpreted the facticity of the boulder as "challenge" and has chosen herself romantically and heroically as "the challenged one." Yet another whips out his camera or water colors and

Sinking back into nature as a quasi-pantheistic synthesis of the totality of the in-itself with the for-itself

says, "Look how beautifully that boulder is framed by the pine trees on either side, and look at the mountain peak glistening behind it" (world as photo opportunity, self as artist). And another, examining the boulder closely, says, "Look at these interesting quartz crystals here. Notice that they aren't found in any of the other rocks around here. This boulder must have tumbled at least a thousand meters - probably from that outcropping up above there" (world as specimen; self as scientist).

Sartre argues that each of these hikers has created his or her own world and has chosen him or herself in that world. Of course, the determinist will argue that each reaction to the situation is the product, not of freedom, but of the past of each individual. But Sartre denies this strenuously. He says, "No factual state of affairs whatever it may be (the political and economic structure of society [attack on Marx's determinism], the psychological 'state' [attack on Skinner's and Freud's determinism], etc.) is capable by itself of motivating any act whatsoever" (p. 245). No matter what interpretation I give to being, I always _could_ give others. There is never a moment when I am robbed of alternative readings.

Sartre's point can be stated in its most radical form by saying that in the face of any apparent necessity, one could _always_ choose death. Of course, deciding to throw oneself off the cliff because of the boulder's presence would be a rather extreme and stupid response to the discovery that one's hike had been interrupted, but doing so _is_ an alternative, and as long as one pursues some other alternative in preference to suicide, one has _chosen_ that alternative and is responsible for it. If you didn't shoot yourself this morning, then you chose all of today's projects instead, and they are _your_ projects.

Sartre is not claiming that choosing an alternative would

A boulder? I can't stand it!

264

necessarily always be _easy_. He says, "I could have done otherwise. Agreed. But _at what price_?" (p. 255). What he means is this. the act of falling back into the grass in defeat is probably not an isolated action, but is rather a manifestation of a whole form of life. The person I described as "the defeated one" probably almost always chooses himself passively in the world, and for him, choosing to persevere despite the presence of the boulder would have been tantamount to what Sartre calls a "radical conversion," i.e., to choosing oneself as a different person. But it is precisely this of which we are all capable. Most people, however, prefer to deny this "existential truth," but according to Sartre, they do so in "bad faith."

BAD FAITH (which Sartre sometimes calls "inauthenticity") always takes the form of a flight from freedom, from responsibility, from subjectivity, from anguish (a flight from _anguish_ because, according to Sartre, ultimate recognition of one's freedom is experienced as anguish). However, Sartre's concept of "bad faith" is very subtle, as can be seen in this famous episode from Sartre's _Being and Nothingness_:

Take the example of a woman who has consented to go out with a particular man for the first time. She knows very well the intentions which the man who is speaking to her cherishes regarding her. She knows also that it will be necessary

Condemned to be free

265

sooner or later for her to make a decision. But she does not want to realize the urgency; she concerns herself only with what is respectful and discreet in the attitude of her companion. She does not apprehend this conduct as an attempt to achieve what we call "the first approach": that is, she does not want to see possibilities of temporal development which his conduct presents. She restricts this behavior to what is in the present; she does not wish to read in the phrases which he addresses to her anything other than their explicit meaning. If he says to her, "I find you so attractive!" she disarms this phrase of its sexual background; she attaches to the conversation and to the behavior of the speaker, the immediate meanings, which she imagines as objective qualities. The man who is speaking to her appears to her sincere and respectful as the table is round or square, as the wall coloring is blue or gray. The qualities thus attached to the person she is listening to are in this way fixed in a permanence like that of things, which is no other than the projection of the strict present of the qualities into the temporal flux. This is because she does not quite know what she wants. She is profoundly aware of the desire which she inspires, but the desire cruel and naked would humiliate and horrify her. Yet she would find no charm in a respect which would be only respect. In order to satisfy her, there must be a feeling which is addressed wholly to her _person-ality_ — i.e., to her full freedom — and which would be a recognition of her freedom. But at the same time this feeling must be wholly desire; that is, it must address itself to her body as object. This time then she refuses to apprehend the desire for what it is; she does not even give it a name; she recognizes it only to the extent that it transcends itself toward admiration, esteem, respect and that it is wholly absorbed in the more refined forms which it produces, to the extent of no longer figuring anymore as a sort of warmth and density. But then suppose he takes her hand. This act of her companion risks changing the situation by calling for an immediate decision. To leave the hand there is to consent in herself to flirt, to engage herself. To withdraw it is to break the troubled and unstable harmony which gives the hour its charm. The aim is to postpone the moment of decision as long as possible. We know what happens next; the young woman leaves her hand there, but she _does not notice_ that she is leaving it. She does not notice because it happens by chance that she is at this moment all intellect. She draws her companion up to the most lofty regions of sentimental speculation; she speaks of Life, of her life, she shows herself in her essential aspect — a personality, a consciousness. And during this time

266

the divorce of the body from the soul is accomplished ; the hand rests inert between the warm hands of her companion — neither consenting nor resisting — a thing.

We shall say that this woman is in bad faith (pp. 146 -148).

The plot thickens. He takes her hand.

What would this young woman have to do to be in good faith ? Has Sartre made good faith so difficult that no one can achieve it? He says that the woman's problem is that "she does not quite know what she wants." <u>Must</u> we always know exactly what we want? Sartre explains his objection very technically in the following abstruse paragraph :

> We have seen... the use which our young woman made of our being-in-the-midst-of-the-world — i.e., of our inert presence as a passive object among other objects — in order to relieve herself suddenly from the functions of her being-in-the-world — that is, from the being which makes there to be a world by projecting itself beyond the world toward its own possibilities (p. 150).

Sartre's point is this : we <u>are</u> bodies in the world. This fact is what he calls our "being-in-the-midst-of-the-world." But we also <u>create</u> the world we inhabit, and this is our "being-in-the-world." Choosing ourselves at any moment as exclusively being-in-the-midst-of-the-world, that is, as

passive, inert being, is bad faith. Good faith is choosing ourselves as what we are, as being-in-the-world, and accepting respon-sibility therefor. (It is still not particularly clear what the young

Choosing oneself as
being-in-the-midst-of-the-world

woman should have done to be in good faith.)

The extremes to which Sartre takes his claims about freedom can be seen here:

> Thus there are no <u>accidents</u> in a life; a community event which suddenly bursts forth and involves me in it does not come from the outside. If I am mobilized in a war, this war is <u>my</u> war; it is in my image and I deserve it. I deserve it first because I could always get out of it by suicide or by desertion; these ultimate possibles are those which must always be pre-sent for us when there is a question of envisaging a situation. For lack of getting out of it, I have <u>chosen</u> it. This can be due to inertia, to cowardice in the face of public opinion, or because I prefer certain other values to the value of the refusal to join in the war (the good opinion of my relatives, the honor of my family, etc.). Any way you look at it, it is a matter of choice. This choice will be repeated later on again and again without a break until the end of the war. Therefore we must agree with the statement by J. Romains, "In war there are no innocent victims." If therefore I have preferred war to death or to dishonor, everything takes place as if I bore the entire

This is your war, kid. You chose it.

responsibility for this war. Of course others have declared it, and one might be tempted perhaps to consider me as a simple accomplice. But this notion of complicity has only a juridical sense, and it does not hold here. For it depended on me that for me and by me this war should not exist, and I have decided that it does exist. There was no compulsion here, for the compulsion could have got no hold on a freedom. I did not have any excuse; for as we have said repeatedly in this book, the peculiar character of human-reality is that it is without excuse (pp. 278-279).

Now it seems to me that many people might be prepared to accept Sartre's claim that an adult human being of normal intelligence has options in almost all circumstances and therefore must accept responsibility proportional to the amount of freedom available. But Romain's line, of which Sartre approves ("there are no innocent victims in war") rings hollow when we recall the news photo of the naked little Vietnamese girl running in terror down a country road, her back covered with napalm burns. Perhaps Sartre needed to augment his theory with an account of how children and the mentally handicapped fit into his claim that everyone is always free and responsible for the worlds they create (although it seems that such a distinction would be very un-Sartrean).

Maybe the truth is that Sartre has not <u>described</u> an already preexisting human freedom, as he claimed he was doing, but that he opened up new aspects of freedom. Perhaps those who have the good fortune to read and understand Sartre's philosophy thereby acquire a new kind of awareness that is in fact tantamount to a new kind of freedom,

and those who haven't read him (and who have had no other intellectual experience of a similar nature) do not acquire this freedom. The trouble with this is that it makes freedom (or at least this <u>kind</u> of freedom) a sort of bourgeois luxury because the ability to study philosophy is in some sense just a luxury. (Sartre himself seems to have come to a similar conclusion in his last works.)

Perverse Freedom

Besides Sartre's existentialist theory, there is yet another radical theory of freedom in the literature, called "perverse freedom,"[8] this appears not in a philosophical treatise, but in a novel, FYODOR DOSTOYEVSKY's <u>Notes from the Underground</u>. (Apparently a more literal translation would be "Notes from Under the Floorboards," implying that the "underground man's" perspective on life is, like that of a rat, looking up at it through the cracks in the floor.) The novel begins with the following curious passage:

> I am a sick man.... I am a spiteful man. I am an unattractive man. I believe my liver is diseased. However, I know nothing at all about my disease, and do not know for certain what ails me. I don't consult a doctor for it, and never have, though I have a respect for medicine and doctors. Besides, I am extremely superstitious, sufficiently so to respect medicine, anyway (I am well-educated enough not to be superstitious, but I am superstitious). No, I refuse to consult a doctor from spite. That you probably will not understand. Well, I understand it though. Of course, I can't explain who it is precisely that I am mortifying in this case by my spite: I am perfectly well aware that I cannot "pay back" the doctors by not consulting them; I know better than anyone that by all this I am only injuring myself and no one else. But still, if I don't consult a doctor it is from spite. My liver is bad, well — let it get worse!" [9]

The man under the floorboards

As the "argument" of the novel develops, we discover that the underground man takes deep offense at all the restrictions imposed upon his freedom by society and by reality at large. He takes them as personal insults. He is offended by the demand that his acts be _prudent_. He is told that he is supposed to act in ways that are in his own best interest. If his liver is ailing, he is supposed to

See a physician. If the weather in Moscow is bad for him, he is supposed to move to St. Petersburg. If his food doesn't agree with him, he is supposed to change his diet. But in these cases, according to him, _prudence_ is a determining factor restricting his freedom. Therefore, he refuses to act for his own advantage, though he admits that there is one advantage, "the most advantageous advantage," on which he will act:

> One's own free unfettered choice, one's own caprice — however wild it may be, one's own fancy worked up at times to a frenzy — is that very "most advantageous advantage" which we have overlooked, which comes under no classification and against which all systems and theories are continually being shattered to atoms. And how do these wiseacres know that man wants a normal, a virtuous choice? What has made them conceive that man must want a rationally advantageous choice? What man wants is simply _independent_ choice, whatever that independence may cost and wherever it may lead. And choice, of course, the devil only knows what choice. . . . [10]

Furthermore, the underground man is offended by the demand that his actions be _reasonable_, that whenever he does anything, he is supposed to have a reason for doing it. In that case, he believes, reason delimits his freedom. The underground man seeks a mode of action that is _unmotivated_. He seeks to perform acts for which there are no reasons. He says he is a "spiteful man." That is, his acts are motivated by _spite_, not by reasons. The Russian word is _zlost_,

Encumbrances on freedom

272

and apparently it means more than "spite"; it also means "whim" and "fancy," "contrariness" and "caprice." If someone points out to the underground man that operating from whim, fancy, or spite is itself to operate with a <u>reason</u>, is still to have a <u>motive</u>, the underground man will not object because to him, in those cases, the motive for his action is pure freedom. Indeed, we know from experience that children often do things out of spite, and when they do so, they are often trying to establish their independence from their parents.

But it is not only children who operate out of spite. In his book, <u>On Being Free</u>, Frithjof Bergmann gives us an excellent example of this spiteful freedom.

> Still another parallel to the Underground man's extreme idea of freedom appears in a scene in the film made after the life of T.E. Lawrence. It occurs in the last third of the film when Lawrence is already in command of a small but formidable Arab army with a long string of brilliant exploits to its credit. After a temporary setback Lawrence is in the process of preparing a major and well-planned campaign that promises defeat to the Turks and glory and loot to his men. He needs troops, however, and the scene narrates his interview with a proud tribal leader. In its course Lawrence tries out reason after reason on the chieftain. "Your fame will spread far if you join me. There will be much money. This is your long-sought chance to get even with the Turks. Together we will lead your people out of their servility. We will lift them up out of their obeisance. You can be the father of a new, proud nation." The Arab sits unmoved and distant. Disdainfully he shakes his massive head to each of these reasons. But he knows full well what force they have, and he feels it. His gesture is a refusal, a fending off; really the sign of his determination not to surrender to their power. Eventually Lawrence's arsenal is exhausted. He has given every reason and all have been parried by the same shaking of the head. So both men sit through a silence, till Lawrence is just at the point of rising and taking his curt leave. Then at last the chief speaks: "I will join you," he says, "but not for fame, nor for money; not even for my people. Not for any of the reasons you have offered. I will do it, but only because it is my whim." [11]

273

As extreme as this version of freedom is, it does capture something of the aboriginal attraction of the idea of freedom. As Bergmann says, "The idea of being totally unbounded, of yielding to no authority whatever (not even to that of reason), of acting without any encumbrances — that image seems close to the root-experience of freedom, ... a distant memory of this expectation still glows behind all talk of liberation. ..."[12]

Conclusion

So what are we to believe? First, what about determinism? There are some good reasons for taking it seriously, after all. At the macrocosmic level, physical bodies do seem to behave according to laws and to be in principle predictable. And because human beings are physical bodies (I do not mean that they are _merely_ physical bodies), and because human behavior is to a great extent predictable, we might have a suspicion that determinism is true. Even Heisenberg's attack on determinism at the microcosmic level seems to replace determinism only with a randomness that may exist at the subatomic level but that leaves necessity unchallenged at the level of things the size of human bodies. (Not only that, but random human action might be worse than predetermined action.) Moreover, the belief in human freedom can seem a bit presumptuous, because it seems to entail the claim that in one otherwise insignificant minuscule corner of a cosmos so large as to overwhelm the

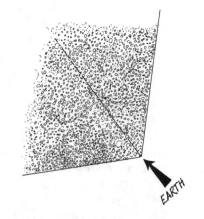

In one small corner of the universe, there is freedom.

understanding there exists a feature or quality (freedom) that may be nonexistent elsewhere in the cosmos.

Nevertheless, we do not _know_ that determinism is true, even if we do not know that it is false. It may well be that freedom is an emergent characteristic of certain physical systems (in the same way that consciousness might be such an emergent characteristic). By "emergent characteristic," I mean a feature of a _system_ that is not a feature of any of its _parts_, something in the way that "liquidity" is a feature of water, but not of either hydrogen or oxygen. Again, we do not _know_ that this, or any other, explanation of freedom is true, but there are some good reasons for believing in freedom nevertheless.

First, there is the experiential reason. As the Campbell/Taylor type argument indicated, we certainly do experience ourselves in the world as free, and we should reject this experience as illusionary only if we are given a very compelling reason to do so. In my opinion, such a reason has not been forthcoming.

Second, there is a practical reason for rejecting determinism. If determinism is true (especially if "hard determinism" is true), then no one is ever responsible for his or her actions and there is no moral reason for ever praising or blaming anyone for any act whatsoever. Indeed, in this case, all of our moral and juridical institutions and ideas are wrong and should be dismantled, as Skinner suggested. I would

I'm sorry I'm doing this to you, but I'm not responsible for my actions.

think that the determinist's argument would have to be tremendously convincing for us to be willing to accept such radical consequences.

Furthermore, there is the practical problem of consistency. Is it really possible to make a belief in determinism consistent with our thoughts and actions in the world? Our normal understanding of reality and our discourse about it are loaded with concepts that presuppose notions of freedom and responsibility. As we saw in Chapter 3, when a determinist like Skinner finds it convenient to use these concepts in his more popular works, he likes to put the words denoting them in quotation marks (e.g., he says that a person "can be made to 'choose'"). He seems to be implying that he <u>could</u> restate these concepts in more appropriate, scientific language if he wanted to. But <u>could</u> he, and with what consequences? Even if Skinner taught us to replace the term "chose" with the term "was reinforced by," would it really change our <u>understanding</u> of the situation (or as Skinner says, "our 'understanding' [whatever that may be]")? If we outlawed the word "cow" and replaced it with "hide-bound milk machine," would we really

have changed our conceptualization of cows? (Moreover, it should be pointed out that Skinner often fails to notice quickly enough his libertarian-laden concepts to put them in quotation marks. In describing his behavioristic utopia in <u>Walden Two</u>, he says it is a place

Hide-bound milk machines refueling

"where everyone chooses [<u>sic</u>] his own work." Elsewhere he says, "We

276

must decide [sic] how we are to use the knowledge which a science of human behavior is now making available." Finally, he says "... we shall, of course, be ready to resist any tyrannical use of science for [sic] immediate or selfish purposes [sic]."[13] If that isn't teleology, I don't know what is.)

All right then, if there are good reasons for rejecting the deterministic claim, can we accept a form of libertarianism? Let us run through a short list of the kinds of freedom that might exist. I will divide these rather arbitrarily into two groups, which I will call "metaphysical freedoms" (denoting their more philosophical nature) and "practical freedoms" (denoting their more pragmatic nature), and I will ask whether we can reasonably believe that any of these freedoms exist. Also, keeping in mind the example with which this chapter began, we will, as an aside, ask to what extent it makes sense to claim that we Americans are members of (nay, leaders of) the Free World.

I. Metaphysical Freedoms

A. Pure Volitional Freedom. We can conceive of something we might call by this name, wherein volition and creation are identical. If person P is the possessor of this kind of freedom, and if P wants X to happen, X happens automatically simply because P wants it to do so. This is clearly God's freedom (if there is a God). In the Bible, God says, "Let there be light," and there is light. You and I do not possess freedom in

Little boy playing God

277

this sense, nor can we. (In this sense of "free," we are clearly not members of the "Free World." In this sense, our world has at most one member.)

B. Restricted Volitional Freedom. If person P wants X, and by virtue of his or her desire and effort, <u>gets</u> X, then the act of obtaining X was a free act. This is the freedom of soft determinism. It definitely does exist. Some people have more of it than others, and it is quite possible that some societies create conditions that allow more of this freedom than do other societies. (In this sense, are we members of the Free World? That is, is the typical American citizen more likely to get what he or she wants than is the typical Soviet citizen? I really do not know. It is surely the case that there are more opportunities for self-fulfillment here than in the USSR, but it is also the case that modern capitalism creates more expectations [hence, more desires] than do other social systems. So the question we are posing here, though an empirical one, is nevertheless difficult to answer. I suspect that the

I wanted vodka. I got vodka. Therefore I am free. (And now I want some more vodka.)

answer is "yes," and I hope I am not simply being chauvinistic in saying so.)

C. Mental Freedom. This is the freedom to assent to or dissent from any assertion or demand. You can hold a sword to my chest and tell me that I <u>must</u> believe that the emperor is divine, and perhaps you can force me to _say_ that I believe so, but you can't actually make me _believe_ so. There's an old Spanish Civil War song, sung by the German contingent of the International Brigades, "Die Gedanken sind frei" (thoughts are free). This sense of freedom is what I'm calling "mental freedom," and

there is good reason to believe that it does exist universally. In that case, in this sense of freedom, there is no place in the world more free than another, though saying this overlooks the problem of "brainwashing," and the seriousness of that problem should qualify my earlier claim that "mental freedom" is universal. Then the question about the "Free World" would have to be posed like this: "Are citizens of our society less brainwashed than those of other societies, such as the Soviet Union prior to glasnost?" I don't know the answer to that question. (Determinists cannot say, "Everyone is always brainwashed," because without a significant opposite, the term brainwashing is meaningless.)

   D. Ontological Freedom. This is a "libertarian" freedom that in its more restricted version (Campbell/Taylor) says that there are _almost_ always alternative possibilities open to us. In its more radical version (Sartre), it says that no matter what course of action we

279

choose, there is always some alternative action we could have chosen. Now, there is probably no way of ever proving that such freedom exists. It is true that no matter what act we perform, we usually have a strong feeling that we "could have done otherwise," but in fact, it is possible that such a feeling is delusory, and that in exactly those circumstances, we could not have done otherwise than what we actually did do. That is, there is always the possibility that determinism is true. But I say that we should opt for the validity of the experience of freedom rather than for the mere possibility that the experience is deceptive. It is possible that my Aunt Minnie will grow antlers, but that possibility is no reason for me to expect her to do so.

However, experience does not bear out Sartre's claim that we always have alternatives. On rare occasions, we feel that we have no alternatives, that our acts are compelled. So if we appeal exclusively to experience here, we have to accept the modified thesis of ontological freedom. Some may believe that Sartre's more radical claim is true — that even when we feel that our acts are compelled, we still have alternatives. But to accept this view is, as in the case of accepting determinism, to go against, or at least beyond, normal experience and intuition. (In terms of this kind of freedom, no particular society can lay more of a claim to the title of "the

Aunt Minnie

280

Free World" than another. In fact, Sartre says, "We were never more free than under the German Occupation." [14] In other words, under conditions of political repression, the presence of our alternatives is clearer, and the need for decision is more obvious than under more standard conditions.)

E. Perverse Freedom. This is the freedom of Dostoyevsky's "underground man." It is based on the rejection of rationality and prudence and manifested in an action motivated solely by whim. Such freedom does exist. Of course, the determinist denies that "perverse freedom" is freedom, saying it is rather a symptom of a deranged mind. But I think that the case of perverse freedom must provoke great anxiety in the determinist. Here is the reason: human nature is such that it can perversely thwart every attempt to make it predictable. If I know that you are trying to predict my behavior, I can incorporate that knowledge into my motivation and behave in ways that will be nearly impossible for you to predict. There may be some deterministic _theory_ that purports to explain this phenomenon, but the fact is that this phenomenon destroys any deterministic program.

II. Practical Freedoms

A. Freedom to ....

1. Political Freedom. This term is meant to designate the type of freedom guaranteed by the U.S. Constitution and Bill of Rights (freedom to worship, freedom to associate with people of like interests, freedom to state one's opinions, etc.).

2. Economic Freedom. This term designates the right to buy and sell on the open market without unreasonable governmental interference — what we mean by "free enterprise."

Now, such freedoms as these do exist in certain societies and are often guaranteed by the laws of those societies. In both of

281

these categories, I think it is fair to say that we citizens of the Western liberal democracies live in "the Free World." I believe that we have many more of these freedoms than do, for example, the citizens of the Soviet Union.

B. Freedom Through . . . . This kind of freedom is the result of social agreement and laws of enablement. For example, our laws creating an educational system provide the freedom to learn; our laws creating a highway system provide the freedom to travel; our laws creating a postal service provide the freedom to communicate. (I suspect — but do not know — that we Americans are at least as free in this respect as are the Soviets, and probably more free.)

C. Freedom From . . . . This kind of freedom designates freedom from hunger, from medical burden, from unemployment, and from vulnerability in old age. These are relative freedoms, but we do find some societies more dedicated to guaranteeing these freedoms than do other societies. I am afraid that in this area (which is, after all, not an unimportant one) we do not have a special right to call ourselves "the Free World." Let me tell you a story that my friend Al told to me. Al and his wife flew to Moscow on a vacation. They arrived at the airport late at night and took a cab to their hotel. But before arriving at the hotel, the cab pulled under a dark bridge, the driver stopped, turned off the motor, and asked Al if he had any blue jeans to sell. My friend likes a good argument (even when he's jet-lagged under a bridge in Moscow at midnight, apparently); so he said to the cabby, "Now, this is marvelous. Here I am in the workers' paradise of the world, and you sneak off in the darkness at midnight to ask me to sell you a pair of clandestine jeans. Where I live, I can buy as many jeans as I want, probably twenty-four hours a day, so what kind of paradise _is_ this, anyway?" The cabby (who apparently also liked an argument) said,

"All right. You are correct. I can only buy blue jeans illegally on the black market. In that sense, you have more freedom than I do. But on the other hand, I never have to worry about a catastrophic illness ruining me financially, or about becoming homeless because of losing my job, or about where I will get my meals and lay my head when I'm old. And none of that is true of you. So I am more free than you."

Now, that cab driver was wrong on a number of scores. First, my friend Al has done very well for himself under the capitalist system and will never have to worry about any of the possible disasters mentioned by the cabby. Also, I have read that medical services have deteriorated greatly in the Soviet Union, that the quality of apartments is shameful, and that a job is guaranteed to you only if you are willing to "travel." This takes some of the sheen off the cabby's freedom. Nevertheless, I am embarrassed to say that there is still something to his argument. All in all, in the sense of freedom we are discussing here, there is a legitimate debate concerning what constitutes the "Free World."

So the result of all this is that there is good reason to believe in freedom, but that there is no <u>one</u> thing called

"freedom." There are a number of areas of human life where the concept of freedom correctly applies, but that concept is not always identical in each of those areas. Some of these conceptions of freedom are compatible with determinism; some are not. However, I think it's safe to say that you are free to reject determinism.

Notes

1. B.F. Skinner, *Beyond Freedom and Dignity* (New York: Knopf, 1971), pp. 20-21.

2. Skinner, *Beyond Freedom and Dignity*, pp. 12-13.

3. John Hospers, "Meaning and Free Will," *Philosophy and Phenomenological Research*, Vol. 10, No. 3 (March, 1950), pp. 316-330.

4. Richard S. Peters, *The Concept of Motivation* (New York: Humanities Press, 1969), p. 69.

5. Werner Heisenberg, *Physics and Philosophy: The Revolution in Modern Science* (New York: Harper & Row, 1962).

6. C.A. Campbell, *In Defence of Free Will, An Inaugural Lecture* (Glasgow: Jackson, Son and Co., 1938). Richard Taylor, "I Can," *Philosophical Review*, Vol. 69 (1960), pp. 78-89.

7. Jean-Paul Sartre, *Being and Nothingness*, in Robert Denoon Cumming, ed., *The Philosophy of Jean-Paul Sartre* (New York: Random House, 1972), p. 258. Unless otherwise stated, all subsequent quotes from Sartre in this chapter are from this source.

8. I have borrowed the notion of "'perverse freedom'" from Robert C. Solomon, *Introducing Philosophy*, 3rd ed. (New York: Harcourt, Brace, Jovanovich, 1985), p. 457.

9. Fyodor Dostoyevsky, *Notes from the Underground*, Constance Garnett, trans. (New York: Dell, 1960), p. 25.

10. Dostoyevsky, *Notes from the Underground*, p. 46.

11. Frithjof Bergmann, *On Being Free* (Notre Dame, Indiana: University of Notre Dame Press, 1977), pp. 21-22.

12. Bergmann, *On Being Free*, p. 18.

13. Carl Rogers and B.F. Skinner, "Some Issues Concerning the Control of Human Behavior: A Symposium," *Science*, Vol. 124 (Nov. 30, 1956), pp. 1057-1066

14. Jean-Paul Sartre, *Situations III*, in Cumming, *The Philosophy of Jean-Paul Sartre*, p. 233.

Chapter 7

Thou Shalt Become Perfected

Ethics

Ethics, or moral philosophy, asks the following kinds of "big questions": What is the Good? What is the good life? What ought we to do? Are there such things as moral duties and obligations? Are there absolute moral values, or are moral values relative to time, place, culture, and the individual? Is there any reason to be moral at all?

Ancient Greek Moral Philosophers

Like most traditional philosophical problems, those of moral philosophy began with the Greeks. This is true even though ethical concepts have evolved greatly since Greek times, and some modern moral concepts like "duty" do not seem to have had any direct counterpart in Greek thought. We will begin our discussion of ethics where so many philosophical discussions do begin — in Athens during the fourth century B.C.

Justice/Morality

Plato's major work, and one of the masterpieces of world literature, The Republic, opens with a discussion of dikaiosyne, which is an umbrella term for all those conventions that command respect for the interests of other people. This concept covers much of what we mean in English by the term "morality," though the word dikaiosyne is usually translated as "justice." Unfortunately, the term "justice" designates a much narrower concept than does the original Greek. So when the question is raised in The Republic, "Why should I be just?", the ensuing conversation probably makes more sense to us today if we read it as asking, "Why should I be moral?" Knowing what you already know about Socrates and Plato, you will not be surprised to find out that they thought this question could not be answered until we knew what dikaiosyne was. (Once again, the question "What is X?" is the key theme of the Platonic dialogue.)

Justice!

Early in the first chapter of The Republic, we are shocked by the bald assertion of the Sophist, Thrasymachus, one of the protagonists of that dialogue, who informs us that "Justice is the advantage of the stronger." Thrasymachus explains his claim in the following passage:

> Don't you know then ... that some states are under despots, and some are governed by a democracy, and some by an aristocracy? ... Is not the strong power in each the ruling

power? And each power lays down the laws so as to suit itself, a democracy, democratic laws, and a despotism, despotic laws, and so with the rest; and in laying them down, they make it clear that this is a just thing for their subjects, I mean their own advantage; one who transgresses these they chastise as a breaker of laws and a doer of injustice. Then this is what I mean, my good friend: that the same thing is just in all states, the advantage of the established government. This I suppose has the power, so if you reason correctly, it follows that everywhere the same thing is just, the advantage of the stronger.[1]

So according to Thrasymachus, "morality" is nothing but a concatenation of rules and conventions imposed upon a gullible community by those who command political power, and these rules and conventions are always such as to be of advantage to the rulers. So the institutions that enjoin us to behave in ways that are truthful, honest, fair, equitable, open, helpful, and merciful are manipulated by those in power for their own use.

But Socrates gets Thrasymachus to admit that sometimes morality does _not_ benefit those in power, and that therefore morality cannot be _defined_ in terms of benefit to the strong. In spite of his concession, Thrasymachus nevertheless insists that being moral is a great disadvantage to the individual. Thrasymachus says:

You must consider, my most simple Socrates, that a just man comes off worse than an unjust man everywhere. First of all in contracts with

Agent Reginald Smith, Internal Revenue Agency. We're levying a 2000% tax on income. How much did you earn today? (And remember, it would be immoral to lie about it!)

288

one another, wherever two are in such partnership, and the partner-ship is dissolved, you would never find the just man getting the better of the unjust, but he always gets the worst of it. Secondly, in public affairs, when there are taxes and contribu-tions, the just man pays more and the unjust less from an equal estate; when there are distributions the one gains nothing and the other much. Again, when these two hold public office, the just man gets his private affairs, by neglecting them, into a bad state, if he has no other loss, and he has no profit from the treasury because he is just; besides, he is unpopular with friends and acquain-tances if he will not serve them contrary to justice; but it is quite the opposite with the unjust man (pp. 142-143).

HAPPINESS
THROUGH
IMMORALITY
unabridged
illustrated

Thrasymachus' best-seller

So, for Thrasymachus, being im-moral "is to one's profit and ad-vantage." Socrates must prove the opposite — that being moral is profitable and advantageous, and being immoral is unprofitable and disadvantageous. This will be dif-ficult to do in the face of Thrasy-machus' examples. The truth of some of those examples grates on us. We all know cases of people who, because of their manipulative life-style and shady business practices,

drive the cars we would like to drive, maintain great bank ac-counts, seem attractive to people of the opposite sex, travel exten-sively, and in general lead a life we could easily envy. We would like Socrates to be able to prove that, in spite of appear-ances to the contrary, these people are in fact miserable because of their immorality; but it is hard to imagine what kind of argument could demonstrate a priori that this class of people must be unhappy.

Actually, he's abysmally miserable. He just doesn't know it.

At the end of Book I of <u>The Republic</u>, Socrates, employing some very questionable rhetorical strategies, manages to befuddle Thrasymachus, who leaves the scene angrily. But the problem Thrasymachus posed does not leave and in fact is continued and intensified in Book II. The second book begins with a discussion of three kinds of good:

1. Good in itself (e.g., harmless small pleasures)

2. Good for its consequences (e.g., taking medicine)

3. Combination of #1 and #2 (e.g., being healthy)

Thrasymachus leaving angrily

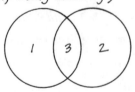

Socrates says that morality ought to be a #3, but most people take it to be a #2. We engage in moral behavior because we fear the consequences of <u>not</u> doing so. Glaucon, one of Socrates' companions, paraphrases what he takes to be the general view of people concerning justice:

> They say, then, that to be unjust is good, and to suffer injustice is bad, and the excess of evil in suffering injustice is greater than the excess of good in being unjust; so that when people do and suffer injustice in dealing with one another, and taste both, those who cannot both escape the one and take the other think it profitable to make an agreement neither to do nor to suffer injustice; from this they begin to make laws and compacts among themselves, and they name the injunction of the law lawful and just. This, they say, is the origin and nature of justice, which is something between the best, namely to do wrong and not to pay for it, and the worst, to suffer wrong and not to be able to get vengeance. Justice, they say, is between these two, and they are content with it not as a good, but as honoured in the weakness of injustice; since one who was able to do injustice, if he were truly a man, would never make an agreement neither to wrong nor to be wronged — he would be mad to do so. Then this ... is the nature of justice, Socrates, and such is its origin, as they say (p. 156).

Glaucon illustrates his point with the story of the magic ring of Gyges. In the story, the man who possesses the ring is able to become invisible and avoid the normal consequences of his actions. He seduces the queen, kills the king, and takes

Gyges and his magic ring

over the Kingdom. The implication of the story is that anybody would do the same and would be a fool not to. If we condemn Gyges, it's because we are envious or don't want to be thought badly of.

At this point, another companion, Adeimantus, chimes in agreeing with Glaucon. Morality is definitely a #2. People praise it for the rewards it brings. But the _appearance_ of morality gets these rewards as well as does morality, so the prudent person will be concerned with _reputation_, not morality. (This view was later defended by Machiavelli in _The Prince_. It is not necessary for the Prince to have piety, faith, honesty, humanity, and integrity. But it is necessary for him to _seem_ to have them.) At this point, Socrates apparently recognizes that he is facing some heavy artillery, and he responds the way many of us do in such situations; he changes the subject... or so it seems.

City/Soul

In fact, Socrates concludes that the problem has become so complex and the details so unclear that it can be resolved only by holding a magnifying glass up to it. This metaphor becomes the pretext for Socrates to present a curious theory that will go on to occupy a large part of _The Republic_ and will even give the book its title. The theory comes in two parts: first, that the problem of morality can be resolved only by coming to an understanding of the human soul, and, second, that such an understanding can best be achieved by studying the nature of the City (the Polis, the Republic) because, ideally at least, the City is the soul writ large. The study of the ideal City will reveal to us the ideal soul, and from that picture, we can deduce the nature of justice and an answer to the question of why one should be moral.

Socrates' analysis leads him to the following conclusion (summarized rather cursorily here). The ideal City contains three distinct classes. First are the rulers who know philosophy; hence they have beheld the "Platonic" essence of citizenship and, as a class, have the virtue of <u>wisdom</u>. Second, there is a military caste called the guardians whose job it is to protect the City from enemies, internal and external. The members of this class know

The City is the soul magnified.

<u>some</u> philosophical principles (otherwise they would not know the difference between friends and enemies of the City). The guardians can eventually be promoted to the ruling class if they prove their philosophical mettle. The collective virtue of this class is <u>courage.</u> Finally, there is the class of artisans. This class comprises the numerical majority of the City, but it is incapable of self-governance because it is incapable of philosophy.

The guardian must know the difference between friends and enemies of the city.

It must submit to the rule of reason imposed upon it by the ruling class. When it does so, its collective virtue is that of _moderation_.

Because the City is the magnification of the soul, it follows that the soul, though a unity in fact, can be analyzed into three components— reason, spirit, and appetite. The rational component, reason, finds itself constantly opposed to the appetitive component, which is what we might call the animal part of the psyche. This lower part of the soul contains all the primitive lusts and irrational desires, which must be constrained if psychic peace is to be achieved. It is very much like the Freudian "id," and this is surely no mere coincidence because Freud was greatly influenced by Platonic philosophy. In fact, there is one passage in which Plato describes (in a most "Freudianly" graphic way) the desires of the appetitive soul as manifesting themselves in dreams. Discussing "lawless desires" as "those which are aroused in sleep," he says:

> ... whenever the rest of the soul, all the reasonable, gentle and ruling part, is asleep, ... the bestial and savage, replete with food or wine, skips about, and, throwing off sleep, tries to go and fulfill its own instincts. You know there is nothing it will not dare to do, thus freed and rid of all shame and reason; it shrinks not from attempting in fancy to lie with a mother, or with any other man or god or beast, shrinks from no bloodshed, refrains from no food — in a word, leaves no folly or shamelessness untried (p. 370).

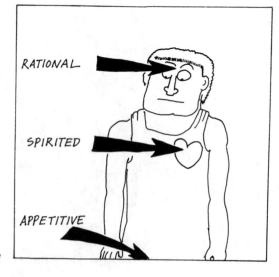

RATIONAL

SPIRITED

APPETITIVE

Perhaps not surprisingly, Plato metaphorically

locates the appetitive soul "below the midriff" and the rational soul in the head. The spirited soul Plato locates in the heart. We can view the battle of the psyche as the struggle between reason and lust for the allegiance of the spirit because spirit is the source of action. If the appetites persuade spirit to join them, then the individual will become lustful and unruly. If reason persuades spirit to side with it, then the individual becomes rational. Each of the components of the soul has its own virtue (_arete_), which manifests itself in the actions of the individual when each component is operating under optimal conditions. The virtue of reason is _wisdom_. The virtue of spirit is _courage_. The virtue of appetite is _moderation_. When the three parts of the soul operate under the law of reason, the result is _justice_ (_dikaiosyne_), and it would be clear to anybody whose soul was in order why he or she should behave in a just (i.e., moral) manner. Why is this so? Because the opposite of justice, injustice, is _confusion_, with that part that naturally should be a slave trying to rebel against rational rule. Confusion is incompatible with _arete_. The expression of human excellence is possible only where justice triumphs, that is to say, only where the individual takes into consideration the interests of other human beings and not only his own private interests. In other words, the individual

Confusion in the psyche

discovers that it is in his interest to take others' interests seriously.

Plato has Glaucon say, "Virtue [arete] then, it seems, would be a kind of health and beauty and fine fitness of the soul; vice is disease and ugliness and weakness." What about Thrasymachus' question of whether it is more profitable to be just than unjust? Glaucon says, "The inquiry seems to me to become from now absurd." Why? Because Socrates has shown that the question "Why should I be just?" is identical to the question "Why should I be healthy?" This is an absurd question, and anyone who asks it does not understand it. (With the possible exception of Dostoyevsky's "underground man.")

Let us turn once more to Plato's formula, "City equals soul magnified." We saw that each of the three classes in the City has its virtue, and when each class sought its virtue, the result was justice in the City. Both in the City and the soul, justice follows from certain rational principles that must be obeyed. The individual human behaves morally when he or she grasps these rational principles, se- duces the heart to follow its rule,

So what's the big deal about being healthy? — cough sputter wheeze —

and, with the help of the heart, imposes a regimen on the passions. But there is a grating paradox when this model is ap- plied to the City. Most people in Plato's good City are __bad__. That is, most of its inhabitants are congenitally incapable of discovering the rule of reason for themselves and of applying it to their

296

Most people are bad.

own behavior, so it must be dictatorially imposed upon them. Ethics must be grounded in _reason_, but reason itself is not a _force_ — it has no binding power, and it must be en-forced. As the contemporary British philosopher Bernard Williams puts it, "For Plato, the political problem of making the ethical into a force was the problem of making society embody the rational justification, and that problem could only have an authoritarian solution."[2]

I suppose that today the majority of us in our most negative moments suspect that Plato is right — many people will not behave morally unless coerced to do so. But most people cannot accept Platonism as their own moral doctrine, not only because they don't agree with his elitism and its totalitarian implications, but because they are much less certain than he that there is an _absolute Good_ and that the only sin is ignorance of it.

Egoism

Plato argued that being moral was in the interest of the individual (though he thought that, unfortunately, most people were too benighted to understand that truth). Plato believed that no one would ever knowingly operate in a way that ran counter to her own interests, and if we ever saw someone who was operating in that manner, that would simply be proof that she was _ignorant_ of her best interests. We can call this the _egoistic_ assumption in Plato's thought.

The assumption is that _every act is motivated by self-interest_. (Notice that the appropriate term is EGOISM and not "egoTism." If I call you an "egotist," I am intentionally insulting you; I am calling you a name. If I call you an "egoist," I am ascribing to you a view about motivation: "ego" — the Latin word for "I.") Plato never actually formulated this principle in _The Republic_, but it's there; and it is interesting to note that in this important respect, the Socrates of _The Republic_ and his antagonist, Thrasymachus, share the same view. The difference is that Thrasymachus thought that it is _not_ in in one's best interest to act morally, but Socrates thought that it is. Thrasymachus' egoism, then, creates an opposition between the individual and society (society's interests are not _my_ interests), but Socrates' egoism does not. Socrates (like Karl Marx after him) tried to show that the interests

I would be glad to help you, but as far as I can determine, there's nothing in it for me. Make me an offer.

We're all in this together!

And you're for Communism, too?

Yes, but only for the elite. The workers are too stupid to get the point.

Karl Marx and Socrates agree (sort of).

of the individual are identical to the interests of the community.

The philosopher who is most famous for his direct commitment to egoism is THOMAS HOBBES (1588-1679). In his book, The Leviathan, Hobbes wrote: "of the voluntary acts of every man, the object is some good to himself." [3] Notice what is at stake here. Hobbes is ruling out the possibility of altruism (ego = I , alter = other; "I-ism" vs. "otherism"). Altruism is the view that morality sometimes enjoins us to sacrifice our own interests in the name of the interests of others. Altruism, which would be very foreign to the ancient Greek mentality, is a view we often associate with Christianity (though perhaps not correctly, because Jesus tells us "Love thy neighbor as thyself" and "Do unto others as you would have them do unto you" [emphases added]. On the other hand,

Love thy neighbor as thyself.

Jesus also said, "If any man cometh unto me and hateth not... his own life, ... he cannot be my disciple" [Luke 14:26]). If altruism is impossible, then surely it cannot be a moral duty. (As David Hume said, "Ought" implies "can.") Well then, is altruism impossible? Is it ever possible to sacrifice one's own interests in order to act in the interest of another? Hobbes says this is

299

possible <u>only</u> <u>if one</u> <u>perceives</u> <u>it</u> <u>to be</u> <u>in</u> his <u>interest</u> <u>to</u> <u>sacrifice</u> his <u>interests</u>. Certainly most of us are surprised by Hobbes' claim because we tend to draw certain distinctions that he rejects. For example, in the case of a person who, at great risk to his own life, saves a drowning child from the surf, consider the kinds of explanations he might give after the fact:

I saved her because ...

A. I saw that she would drown if I didn't go in after her. (Somebody had to do it!) (responsibility)

B. her father helped me once when I was down and out. (debt)

C. I know that family, and I love that little girl. (love)

D. I recognized that it was my duty to try and save her. (duty)

E. only an animal would have stood by and let her drown. (responsibility)

F. ... well, I don't know why I did it. I'm as surprised as you are. (?)

G. my conscience would have plagued me for the rest of my life if I hadn't tried. (guilt)

H. I didn't want people to say that I was a coward. (reputation)

I. I hoped I would get some recognition out of all this. (reputation)

J. I wanted to satisfy a need I have to help others. (self-aggrandizement [perhaps out of guilt or feelings of inferiority])

K. I wanted to achieve a benefit for myself. (?)

L. I wanted a pleasant sensation. (hedonism)

Hobbes says that reasons A through J are really versions of K, and indeed that K is a version of L, because he defines "benefit" in terms of pleasure. ("<u>Pleasure</u>, ... or <u>delight</u>, is the appearance

You risked your life to save her. Why?

Funzies!

or sense of good, and molestation or displeasure, the appearance, or sense of evil." This means that Hobbes' egoism is a form of HEDONISM. More about hedonism shortly.)[4]

How does Hobbes know that human action is always motivated by self-interest? Surely this claim purports to be an empirical one — one that ought to be the result of a scientific investigation. Yet Hobbes has not only failed to conduct a scientific investigation; he has in fact subverted the possibility of any such investigation. That is because truly scientific theories must always be open to possible refutation if new disconfirming data are discovered. This fact is embodied in what has come to be known as "the principle of falsifiability" (associated with the British-Austrian philosopher of science, Sir Karl Popper). In other words, for a thesis to be a truly scientific view, its defender must be able to state the conditions under which it would be admitted that the hypothesis had been refuted. For example, obviously, Isaac Newton would admit that his theory of gravity was false if, all other things being equal, repeated instances were reported and confirmed of heavier-than-air objects hovering, floating, or rising. Precisely what makes Newton's theory so convincing is the fact that no such events have been confirmed, but what makes his theory scientific is that we know what

301

it would be like for it to be
false.

Now, in the face of the
principle of falsifiability,
what is the status of
Hobbes' thesis? What kind
of data, if discovered,
would refute Hobbes' view?
I think the answer to
this is: <u>none</u>. No matter
what possible counterevi-
dence could be imagined,
Hobbes would claim that

Things going up

his theory can account for it. For example, let's try to imagine
an event that we believe to be paradigmatic of altruism. What
about the case of the young soldier who throws himself on the
grenade, thereby saving the lives of his comrades at the cost of
his own life? Such heroic events are possible (in fact, they
have happened). Are
these possibilities not
evidence of altruism,
hence evidence
against Hobbes'
egoism? Not at all,
Hobbes would say. If
the soldier sacrificed
his life, it was be-
cause (whether fool-
ishly or not) he con-
strued it as being

Wow! A chance to
earn a medal!

in his interest to do so. ("He knew he would be dead either way, and preferred to be remembered as a hero," "He was raised in such a way that his concept of self-esteem was intimately tied up with the performance of heroic acts," or "He thought people would like him...," etc.) Hobbes probably believed that it was to his theory's credit that it could be applied to any possible contingency, but we see that the opposite is the truth. Any theory that accounts for every possible case in effect accounts for no case. Or, to put it slightly differently, any "theory" that is compatible with every possible state of affairs is no theory at all because real theories must exclude some possibilities. Confucius is supposed to have said, "If the mind is _too_ open, everything falls out." The same goes for theories.

If Hobbes had stated his proposition differently, we might have more sympathy with it. What if Hobbes had said, "There is more self-interest in most motivation than is usually admitted. One should be generally suspicious when estimating an agent's intentions. One should ask, 'What's in it for the agent?'" Then Hobbes would be admitting the possibility, though not the likelihood, of altruistic acts, and the question concerning which acts are egoistic and which altruistic would be an _empirical_ one (i.e., one to be determined by _evidence_). As it stands, however, it is hard to take Hobbes' thesis totally seriously when

Mommy! Flower for you.

Thanks, dear. (What's the hidden agenda here?)

trying to construct a moral picture for oneself.

Hedonism

It was mentioned that Hobbes' egoism is a form of hedonism, which is the view either that human action _is_ motivated by the pursuit of pleasure or that it _ought_ to be. The first view, which is Hobbes' view, is called _psychological hedonism_ because it is a theory of _motivation._ The second is called _moral hedonism_ because it is a theory about how we ought to live. Notice that, strictly speaking, psychological hedonism cannot be a form of moral hedonism because the latter, in asserting that one _ought_ to pursue one's own pleasure, presupposes that it is possible _not_ to do so, but that _not_ doing so is unwise. There would be no sense in writing moral tracts advocating acts that in fact were the only show in town. Because psychological hedonism claims that hedonism _is_ the only possibility, psychological hedonism cannot be a thoroughgoing _moral_ view. The most it could do as a moral theory would be to advocate certain kinds of acts as being more wise than others (i.e., as bringing more pleasure than others). Moral hedonism, on the other hand, is logically committed to admit that it is possible to act

December 12 ought to precede December 13! We must struggle to bring this about!

??? Right on!

SOAP

304

motivated by interests other than one's own pleasure, but it claims that doing so is a bad idea, indeed, that it is somehow immoral to do so. This distinction, however, has not been drawn by some of the most prominent hedonists, including hedonism's most famous ancient defender, EPICURUS (341-270 B.C.). But this is probably because the ancients did not always conceive of ethics the way we do. They were on a Platonic-like quest, looking for "the good." Epicurus thought that this good was _pleasure_. He wrote, "For it is to obtain this end that we always act, namely, to avoid pain and fear. ... And for this cause we call pleasure the beginning and end of the blessed life."[5] According to Epicurus, no act should be undertaken except for the pleasure in which it results, and no act should be rejected except for the pain it produces. This provoked Epicurus to analyze the different kinds of pleasure. There are two kinds of desires, hence two kinds of pleasure as a result of gratifying those desires: _natural desire_ (which has two subclasses), and _vain desire._

1. Natural desire
   A. Necessary (e.g., desire for food and sleep)
   B. Unnecessary (e.g., desire for sex)

2. Vain desire (e.g., the desire for decorative clothing or exotic food)

Natural necessary desires _must_ be satisfied and are easy to satisfy. They result in a good deal of pleasure and in very few painful consequences. Vain desires do

The pursuit of vain pleasure

not need to be satisfied and are not easy to satisfy. Because there are no natural limits to them, they tend to become obsessive and lead to very painful consequences.

The desire for sex is natural but usually can be overcome. When it can be, it should be because satisfaction of the sexual drive gives intense pleasure but involves one in relationships that are usually ultimately more painful than pleasant and are often extremely painful.

Epicurus actually subscribed to the most traditional Greek values (he advocated the pursuit of beauty, prudence, honor, justice, courage, and honesty), but only because he believed that holding them led to more pleasure than pain. He wrote, "Beauty and virtue and the like are to be honoured, if they give pleasure, but if they do not give pleasure, we must bid them farewell." But he added, "It is not possible to live pleasantly without living prudently and honourably and justly."[6] Apparently, Epicurus thought that rejecting these values would result in tense, hence unpleasant, relations with other people and also in a guilty conscience. Epicurus would probably be right about the majority of us, but isn't it possible to imagine a cynical sociopath who, operating on Adeimantus' and Machiavelli's advice, is motivated not by a desire for virtue, but by the advantages of the _appearance_ of virtue and who has no guilty conscience whatsoever? Or what about sadists

and masochists?
Are they _necessarily_
more unhappy than
the virtuous? And
if they are not
more unhappy, are
they really under
a kind of moral
obligation to
pursue the unvir-
tuous acts that
give them pleasure?

Epicurus was wrong.
I'm allergic to beauty
and virtue. I'm into
ugliness and vice.

We will notice that Epicurus' definition of pleasure is _nega-tive_, that is, pleasure is the absence of pain. This negative definition prevents Epicurus from falling into crass sensualism. The trouble with this definition is that, taken to its logical extremity, the _absence_ of life is better than any life at all (as Freud discovered in his _Beyond the Pleasure Principle_, where he claimed that behind the "pleasure principle" is THANATOS, the death instinct). This is a bit ironic because Epicurus himself had claimed that his philos-

Beyond the Pleasure Principle

ophy dispelled the fear of death. Epicurus' materialism led him to believe that death was merely the absence of sensation and consciousness; therefore, there could be no sensation or consciousness of death to fear. "Where death is, we are not. Where we are, death is not."

Some of Epicurus' Roman followers interpreted "pleasure"

quite differently, defining it as positive titillation. It is because of
these extremists that today Epicureanism is often associated with sen-
sualistic hedonism. Sickly Epicurus, swinging in his hammock, would
have disapproved (though not too harshly, because polemics cause agita-
tion, which is painful). Epicurus' theory never constituted a major
philosophical movement, but he had disciples in both Greece and Rome
for a number of centuries. His most famous follower was the Roman
LUCRETIUS, who, in the first century B.C. wrote a long poem "On the
Nature of Things," expounding the philosophy of his master. It is
through Lucretius' poem that many have been introduced to the
thought of Epicurus.

Utilitarianism

There is a historical connection between Epicurus' hedonism and a
very influential contemporary moral theory called UTILITARIANISM.
This view was first put forth in the nineteenth century by the British
philosopher JEREMY BENTHAM (1748-1832). Then it was criticized and revised by his somewhat wayward disciple, JOHN STUART
MILL (1808-1873). The essential difference between Greek hedonism
and utilitarianism is that the former was egoistic in nature, but the
latter is social.

The Calculus of Felicity

Bentham, who may not have been one of the deepest philosophers in
the Western tradition, was certainly one of the most practically
oriented and most influential. He had an active hand in the reformation of the British legal system of his day. Agreeing with
Hobbes, Bentham began his philosophy with the assumption
that, like it or not, we humans are all governed by the desire for

pleasure and the aversion to pain. Unlike Hobbes, however, he did not conclude that therefore altruism was either impossible or unwise. Again like Hobbes, he believed we are endowed with reason and that therefore it was possible to give moral advice on how one should pursue the goal of "the pleasure principle" (Freud's term).

Bentham's advice was articulated in what he called "the calculus of felicity." According to it, there are seven categories into which pleasure can be catalogued, and this catalogue provides a rational analysis of pleasure. The seven categories are:

1. Intensity – how intense?

2. Duration – how long?

3. Certainty – how sure?

4. Propinquity – how soon?

5. Fecundity – how many more?

6. Purity – how free from pain?

7. Extent – how many people are affected?

On a scale of one to ten, this is about a "ten" in all categories.

According to Bentham, whenever you consider performing any action, you can analyze its value in terms of these categories and contrast it with its alternatives. For example, say you need to study for tomorrow's chemistry examination, but it turns out that today promises to be the most glorious day of the year. The beach positively beckons. Try out the "calculus of felicity" on a decision such as that between studying for a chemistry midterm and going to the beach with some friends. Obviously, the beach party will be strong in some categories (#1, #3, #4, #6) and weaker in others (#2, #5). Studying will be weak in most categories but strong in a few (#2, and #5, and #7 also, if other persons have an interest in your succeeding in college). Are the assets of studying strong enough to overcome its deficits in the face of the fun enticing you to the beach? (Of course, the guilt you would experience at the beach has to be taken into consideration too.)

We can imagine that if Bentham had lived in today's world of inexpensive calculators, he would have invented a pocket "calculator of felicity." There is something silly about the image of someone punching the values of various acts into his calculator, but Bentham thought that his

Beach guilt

calculus of felicity was actually the schematization of something we do semiconsciously (hence often poorly) anyway, and that once we became experienced in manipulating these figures, we would be able to do it intuitively.

Looking back at the calculus of felicity, take note of category 7, "extent." It is this category that makes utilitarianism a form of social hedonism. One must consider the pleasures and pains of others, and not only one's own. In fact, what Bentham and Mill call "the principle of utility" stresses precisely this aspect, which allows for the possibility of altruism in utilitarianism—

"the greatest amount of happiness for the greatest number of people."
If an act I am about to perform will bring about a great amount of
happiness for a large number of people, then I should perform it even if it
brings mostly misery to me.

Besides this social aspect of utilitarianism, there is also a democratic bias built into it — especially in the case of Bentham. When it comes
to evaluating acts in terms of the pleasure they will produce, Bentham
firmly believed in the "one person, one vote" principle. Each person's
judgment is as important as every other's. No one — be he your parent
or the state — has the right
to _inform_ you that you are
or are not having fun. According to Bentham, "Preju-
dice apart, the game of
push-pin is of equal value
with the arts and sciences
of music and poetry. If the
game of push-pin furnishes
more pleasure, it is more
valuable than either."[7]

You are now enjoying yourselves! This is an official proclamation!

Fascistic hedonism

The Quality of Pleasure

John Stuart Mill thought of
himself as a disciple of Bentham, but he was clearly concerned about
the implications of some of Bentham's formulations of utilitarianism.
One of the things that Mill feared was that an adherent of the calculus of felicity might conclude that push-pin (or watching football
on TV) _is_ better than the arts and sciences, and Mill knew in his
heart that this is simply not the case. Utilitarianism would have
to be rewritten in such a way as to be able to demonstrate that

the reading of Shakespear-
ian sonnets is _better_ than
some of its alternatives.
Part of the problem is that
"the calculus" generates a
purely quantitative an-
alysis, and Mill was con-
vinced that _quality_ in
pleasure was even more
important than quantity.
Furthermore, he feared
that a literal application
of the calculus of felicity
would, over a number of
generations, completely
erode culture. What if
you offered the following
proposition to the elector-

Shakespeare or the NFL?

ate of a particular state: "It has been determined that the teaching
of Shakespeare in the schools of this state costs each taxpayer $25
each five years. Now, the state would like to know if you taxpayers
would prefer to continue paying $25 a person for the next five years
of instruction of Shakespeare, or would you prefer a rebate of $25
in the form of two cases of beer per voter?" Mill was afraid that,
given the tenuous foothold that culture has among the masses and
given Bentham's "one person, one vote" principle, Shakespeare would
lose out. In a number of generations, no one would even remember
who Shakespeare was. (In fact, a proposition something like
this was presented to the voters of California in 1978. It was called "Proposition 13." The voters went for the beer.)

In order to counteract the possibility of this "leveling down" of culture, Mill insisted on the fact that it was part of our human heritage to have desires higher than those that lent themselves to analysis in terms of the calculus of felicity. He wrote:

> Few human creatures would consent to be changed into any of the lower animals for a promise of the fullest allowance of a beast's pleasures; no intelligent human being would consent to be a fool, no instructed person would be an ignoramus, no person of feeling and conscience would be selfish and base, even though they should be persuaded that the fool, the dunce, or the rascal is better satisfied with his lot than they are with theirs. [8]

Tough Benthamite decisions

Apparently, Mill felt that the "lower" desires (those of animals and perhaps the most biologically basic human desires) could be adequately dealt with in terms of the quantitative analysis provided by the calculus of felicity but that the "higher desires" could be talked about only in terms of <u>quality</u>, something no calculus could evaluate. According to Mill:

> It is quite compatible with the principle of utility to recognize the fact that some kinds of pleasure are more desirable and more valuable than others. It would be absurd that, while in estimating all other things quality is considered as well as quantity, the estimation of pleasure should be supposed to depend on quantity alone.
>   If I am asked what I mean by difference of quality in pleasures, or what makes one pleasure more valuable than

another, merely as a pleasure, except its being greater in amount, there is but one possible answer. Of two pleasures, if there be one to which all or almost all who have experience of both give a decided preference, irrespective of any feeling of moral obligation to prefer it, that is the more desirable pleasure. If one of the two is, by those who are competently acquainted with both, placed so far above the other that they prefer it, even though knowing it to be attended with a greater amount of discontent, and would not resign it for any quantity of the other pleasure which their nature is capable of, we are justified in ascribing to the preferred enjoyment a superiority in quality so far outweighing quantity as to render it, in comparison, of small account. [9]

Mill's objection is perhaps summed up in this famous line: "The uncultivated cannot be competent judges of cultivation."

One can certainly be sympathetic to Mill's concerns. Bentham's "calculus" does seem to be a bit crass, and in a democracy there is always the danger of every standard falling to the lowest common denominator. But Mill's solution to these problems brings about

The uncultivated cannot be competent judges of cultivation.

problems of its own. Mill can be accused of abandoning democracy for elitism and of abandoning hedonism altogether. The basis of the charge of elitism must be obvious. If one must demonstrate "competence" before one is granted a vote, then on many issues, only a small minority will have the right to express an opinion. This minority will probably tend to be the best educated, the wealthiest, and most powerful segment of society. (In the United States, we have accepted a compromise version of Mill's solution. We are not a "participatory

POLLING PLACE
(only the competent
will be allowed
to vote*)

* Sheriff
Billy Joe Bob
will
determine
competency

democracy" but a "representative democracy." Not everybody votes on all issues; rather, we elect representatives who in theory are, by virtue of their excellent education and their paid staff of assistants, competent to decide certain issues concerning which we ourselves have no competence. However, we reserve the right, through the initiative process, to bypass those representatives on certain matters. This is how the system works in theory, though of course not always in practice.)

Let us now look at the charge that Mill has abandoned hedonism. In itself, this charge is perhaps not so devastating, though Mill himself would have been displeased by it. Mill accepts the basic principle of hedonism — the sole criterion of value is pleasure — but he also claims that some pleasures are _better_ (more valuable) than others. We must ask, more valuable according to what criterion? It can't be just "pleasure" because some pleasures are _better_, and "better" here no longer means "more intense, purer, more lengthy, more certain, more immanent," etc. Rather, it means "has more quality." But what is this elusive thing called "quality" that only the "competent" can recognize? In an odd way, we seem to have returned to the Platonic doctrine of _aretē_ because one of the English translations of that word is "quality." But perhaps this isn't so bad after all. In fact, most contemporary utilitarians feel no need to defend hedonistic principles. Rather than talking about "pleasure," they prefer to stick to the broader terms like "happiness," "interests," "well-being," and "human flourishing," without trying to "cash them out" in terms of specific ingredients.

Utilitarianism's Problems

There seems to me to be something very plausible about utilitarianism on the face of it. It does appear that morality must essentially have something to do with promoting happiness and well-being and with minimizing unhappiness and misery. It would be very odd to claim that some act was _good_ even though it brought nothing but unhappiness and misery to absolutely everybody. Therefore, there must be something right about the opposite view (viz., the view that an act is good if it brings happiness and well-being to everyone), and this just happens to be utilitarianism's view. Still, there are some serious problems with utilitarianism. One of them has to do with its "consequentialist" nature (to be dealt with shortly), and the other has to do with the notions of _justice_ and _meritoriousness_.

The problem of justice and meritoriousness can be revealed in a fictitious example. Suppose you had to go to court for failing to pay a few parking fines. You are alone in a small courtroom with the judge, the bailiff, and the court reporter. After the bailiff reads the charge ("failure to pay three fines for expired parking meters"), you respond ("Guilty, your Honor"), and he announces his judgment: "I find you guilty on all charges. The punishment will be that you shall suffer death at the hands of a firing squad." "What?!!" you scream. "Death for three lousy parking tickets??" The judge leans forward and whispers: "I know you don't deserve this punishment, but there has been a rash of murders in our com-munity, and a study has just been re-leased demonstrat-ing that immediately after an execution, the crime rate drops substantially. Unfor-tunately, we don't have any convicted murderers on our hands right now. But

we do have you, and there is every reason to believe that if we execute you, the public good will be served. Hence, even though my decision may seem unfair to you personally, it will certainly promote the great-est amount of happiness for the greatest number of people. So it is the only judgment I can reach in good conscience."

Take another example (one that appears in almost every critical discussion of utilitarianism and that even has a name — "the case of Sam"). Sam, a basically normal, rather nondescript, but "nice" human being, goes to the hospital to visit his only living relative, his

317

senile, sick aunt. His visit coincides with five medical emergencies at the hospital. One person needs a liver transplant, another a spleen transplant, another a lung transplant, another a new heart, and a fifth a new pineal gland. Each of the five patients is a tremendously important, much-loved person whose death would bring a great deal of grief and actual physical discomfort to a great number of people. Sam's death, on the other hand, would be mourned by no one (except possibly by his aunt in her lucid moments). The top members of the hospital administration, all strict utilitarians, lure Sam into an operating room, remove all his vital organs, and distribute them to the other needy patients, thereby operating (literally) in accordance with the principle of utility: the greatest amount of happiness for the greatest number of people.

Sam visiting his sick aunt

The reason these fictitious cases are so jarring is that they go so radically against our intuitive sense of justice and meritoriousness. Neither the parking meter violator nor Sam deserves the fate dished out by the executing judge and the hospital staff. Because these cases are compatible with utilitarianism, either there is something wrong with our intuitive sense of justice, or there is something wrong with utilitarianism. Most people are probably more likely to jettison a _theory_ than to go against their sense of justice.

Many contemporary utilitarians have recognized this and have tried to adjust utilitarian theory to correspond more with our intuitions. To this end a distinction has been drawn between <u>act utilitarianism</u> and <u>rule utilitarianism</u>. The term "act utilitarianism" designates the traditional form. According to it, one must perform the specific <u>act</u> that will produce the greatest amount of happiness for the greatest number of people. "Rule utilitarianism" says, to the contrary, that in contemplating one of two acts, a person should perform that act governed by a (hypothetical) rule whose general obeyance would produce the greatest amount of happiness. This means that even if a particular self-serving deceit or lie may go undetected, hence cause no one any unhappiness, nevertheless, I probably should not engage in them because <u>generally</u> lying and deceiving cause more unhappiness than happiness. It also means that the executing judge and the hospital administrators cannot proceed as they desire because the rule governing their acts would be something like this: "If the lives of a number of people (or even of a few exceptional people) can be saved by sacrificing an innocent bystander, the sacrifice should be performed." But members of a community who knew that they might be set upon by the authorities and arbitrarily killed or disemboweled would be members of a community of fear, one whose citizens would be loath to set foot on the streets in daylight.

A community of fear

A critic has argued that rule utilitarianism can lead to unpalatable consequences. He asks, What about the Dutch family during World War II who hid Jews in their attic? According to rule utilitarianism, would they be required to answer truthfully when the Gestapo comes to their house looking for Jews (on the grounds that lying _generally_ creates more unhappiness than does honesty and that therefore one may not lie)? But surely the rule utilitarian can operate according to the general rule: "Lying is wrong, except when directed to evildoers in order to save the lives of innocent people." The problem here is that one begins to suspect that the clever, self-serving rule utilitarian can think of a general rule to rationalize all sorts of questionable behavior. ("Shoplifting from large department stores is OK as long as one doesn't get caught and no one ever finds out.") This would surely be the beginning of the unraveling of rule utilitarianism.

So the modification of traditional utilitarianism (or "act" utilitarianism) to rule utilitarianism _may_ allow the utilitarian to meet the objection that utilitarianism does not square with our sense of justice and meritoriousness, but there was another related objection concerning utilitarianism's "consequentialist" nature. Notice that according to the view we are now studying, no act is good or bad in and of itself. Rather, an act is good or bad only in terms of its _consequences_. Acts that result in happiness, well-being,

YELP!!

Mama! Isn't that bad?

Depends on its consequences.

and flourishing are good; acts that result in the opposite are bad. Now, there is a certain *prima* *facie* plausibility to this view, but at some point it too runs up against the moral intuition of many people because a lot of us feel that certain acts, such as wanton cruelty, are bad in and of themselves regardless of their consequences, and that some acts — those performed out of moral duty — are right independent of their consequences. The philosopher who most clearly defended a moral doctrine based on this kind of reasoning was Immanuel Kant.

Consequentialism: The moral worth of act X depends on the consequences of X.

Nonconsequentialism: The moral worth of act X depends exclusively on act X.

Duty-Oriented Morality

Immanuel Kant, whose epistemology we inspected briefly in Chapter 3, took a strictly nonconsequentialistic view of ethics. For him, the empirical consequences or results of an act had nothing whatsoever to do with the moral worth of the act. In fact, according to him, any attempt to justify an act by appealing to its consequences immediately removes the act from the ethical sphere. In order to demonstrate this point, Kant distinguishes between two kinds of "oughts" or "shoulds" — a *moral* ought, which he calls a CATEGORICAL IMPERATIVE, and a merely *practical* ought, which he calls a HYPOTHETICAL IMPERATIVE. Let's illustrate this distinction. Suppose I say to you, "You know, you really ought not to come to class with your shoes untied, fly open, and eating ice cream that is melting down your arm and dripping off your elbow." You ask, "Why not?" I say, "Because you look like a fool when you do that!" You approach me and whisper in my ear, "That's exactly the impression I _want_ to give. Actually, I'm an undercover agent tailing a suspected Soviet spy who is in your class." I respond, "Oh! Well in _that_ case, you _ought_ to do just as you are doing because you appear to be a _perfect_ fool." This is an example of a hypothetical imperative. The "imperative" (ought) can be placed in the "then" clause of a hypothetical conditional sentence.

Undercover agent

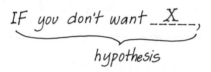

IF you don't want __X__,

hypothesis

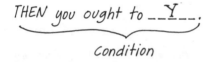

THEN you ought to __Y__;

Condition

In hypothetical imperatives, the "ought" can be defeated by rejecting the hypothesis ("Oh, but I _want_ to look like a fool...."). This analysis shows what's wrong with the following exchange:

Fran: "You ought not to steal my car."

Jan: "Why not?"

Fran: "Because they'll put you in jail."

Jan can always rejoin, "Oh, but I _want_ to go to jail. I've decided that I can't afford life on the outside. I'd like to have the state provide me with room and board, and it seems to me that the most certain way of achieving my goal is to steal your car." Fran now seems to be in the curious position of having to assert, "Oh, in that case, you _ought_ to steal my car."

According to Kant, a truly _moral_ ought cannot be conditional upon any individual's desires. It must be _absolute_, or as he calls it, "categorical." Are there  any such moral demands, and how would we demonstrate their existence? According to him, there are indeed such moral oughts, and once we have discovered them we can discern what our moral duty is. They are rooted in a certain fact about human nature, namely, the fact that we are _rational_ beings. (Notice that utilitarianism is rooted in the fact that we are _passionate_ beings — that we have desires. Kantianism is rooted in a very different fact about us — that we have reason. As in Plato, there is more than the subtle implication in Kantianism that reason should override desire.)

The principle behind the categorical imperative is a principle that every rational agent must accept. Refusing to do so would be tantamount to abandoning one's rationality, leading to "the obliteration of one's dignity as a human being." Let us state the categorical imperative: "Act only according to that maxim by which you can at the same time will that it should become a universal law." This means something like the following: it is possible to state the

323

general principle behind any act you may consider performing. Before engaging in an act (such as helping your neighbor fix her flat tire), you can ask, "What principle (maxim) governs this act?" In this case, it might be: "It is good to help one's fellow human in distress." Now, what we must do is ask this additional question: would a world governed by such a rule be a <u>consistent</u> world? If the answer is negative,

A world in which everyone is fixing flat tires

then the performance of the act is <u>wrong</u> on the grounds that it is unreasonable — indeed, illogical (in the same way that a game would be illogical if it were impossible to play by its rules without contradiction). If, on the contrary, the answer is affirmative (as it is in this case), then at least you know that your proposed action is not immoral. Kant thought that, as creatures of reason, we are duty-bound to obey such principles. Here, we will oversimplify this idea a bit to see what Kant was talking about.

Let's suppose that you owe a friend five dollars, and, to your annoyance, he pressures you to repay. So you say to yourself, "If I kill him, I won't have to repay the debt." But as a true Kantian, you first check to see if you could universalize the principle governing the proposed action. You ask yourself, what if everyone accomplished his goals by killing someone? Could there exist a universal law, "Everyone ought to kill someone"? This would be an impossible law because if everyone complied with it, there would be no one left to comply with it. Therefore we are duty-bound not to kill as a way of solving problems. OK, then what if you

lie to your friend, telling him that you already repaid the dept? Can the principle behind this proposal be universalized? Could there be a general law, "Everyone ought always to lie"? Obviously

not because it would be impossible even to state the law without breaking it. Therefore we are duty-bound not to lie. Well, what if you repay the five dollars, then steal them back?

Can the principle behind this act be universalized? Imagine a general law saying, "Everyone ought always to steal." But this too is an impossible law because the concept of stealing is parasitical upon the concept of property. If everyone always steals, there can be no property; there can be only temporary possession,

325

where theft is the law of the land

that is, stuff passing from person to person. So we are also duty-bound to refrain from stealing. (If you are a true Kantian, it's beginning to look as though you will have to pay your debt!)

Kant's Strengths and Weaknesses

There are some interesting things going on here. There is some genuine insight, and there are some serious problems, too. Let's talk first about the positive features. Kant's moral philosophy recognizes that an essential aspect of morality is the need to view the world, in-cluding one's own actions, from the point of view of others. We need to climb out of our own shoes and stand in the shoes of other people. (This view Kant shares with utilitarianism and with Jesus' "Golden Rule," though the latter two moral codes are based on the universaliz-ability of desire, and Kant's is based on the

standing in someone else's shoes

326

universalizability of reason.) Kant's principles are fine tools for revealing hypocrisy — that of others or of oneself. If it is wrong for
someone to take my property without my permission, then it is wrong
when I take the property of another person without permission. I
am a hypocrite if I claim that it is <u>theft</u> when you take my stereo
but that it is simply redistribution of wealth when I take your stereo.
Kant is correct. If it is wrong for you to take mine, then, in
circumstances that are identical in all relevant respects, it is
wrong for me to take yours.

But the problems with Kant's theory lie in the same area as do
its strengths. There is something too absolutistic about his view.
If a heavily armed madman, frothing at the mouth, asks me if
I know where Sue Smith is, and I realize that he intends to kill
her if he finds her, my moral intuition tells me that I <u>ought</u> to
lie — and in fact that it would be immoral to tell the truth. Yet
Kant says that I must tell the truth even to a murderous madman, on the grounds that the principle behind lying cannot
be universalized without con-
tradiction.

Critics of Kant have
pointed out something that
was mentioned in connection
with rule utilitarianism,
namely, that it is possible
to generate modified rules
that can be universalized,
such as this one: "One ought
to lie when doing so will save
the life of an innocent person."
Kant argued against such

I cannot tell a lie. She's over there.

327

modifications on the grounds that they destroy the universalizability of the rule by making it more context bound, but many critics find this argument unpersuasive and point out that Kant believed in capital punishment for capital crimes; hence Kant himself was modifying his injunction against killing. It does seem that only by accepting in principle the possibility of modifying Kant's general rules can we save his moral philosophy from absurdity.

Kant thought that acts whose principle cannot be universalized cannot in any way commit us to moral obligation. This seems correct for reasons mentioned previously. (Reminder: if an act is declared to be bad when _you_ perform it, then an act that is the same in all relevant respects must be bad when _I_ perform it, in exactly the same way that if this figure → △ is a triangle when _you_ draw it, then it must also be a triangle when _I_ draw it.) But from this principle, how can we generate the concept of _duty_, which is so close to Kant's heart? Surely we don't have a moral obligation to perform every act whose maxim can be generalized. (I like to smile when I see birds. The maxim behind that act might be: it is good to express joy in the presence of pretty things. This _can_ be generalized without contradiction, but it's hard to believe that therefore we all have a moral obligation to smile at birds, to whistle in the dark, or to clear our throat before scratching our nose.)

Kant agrees. What gives

The moral obligation to smile at birds

an act _moral_ worth is not simply the fact that it _can_ be universalized, but the fact that it was chosen as a moral act. Our duty is not that of performing any specific acts, but to choose only acts that can be universalized, and what makes them _moral_ is that we chose them in order to be performing our duty. In the first sentence of his _Foundations of the Metaphysics of Morality_ (1785), Kant says, "Nothing in the world — indeed nothing even beyond the world — can possibly be conceived which could be called good without qualification except a _good will_." What he means by "good will" is the _desire_ to do one's duty. (This rather subverts Kant's claim that his ethical system transcends desire.) The same act — let's again say the act of helping your neighbor fix her flat tire — may be either moral, morally neutral, or even immoral, depending on its motivation. (Here we see the big difference between utilitarianism, which is _consequentialist_ in nature, and Kant-

ianism, which is _nonconsequentialistic_. That is, for Kant, the act's moral worth is not determined by its _results_, but by its _intention_.) The act is immoral if my motivation is to deceive her into thinking that I'm a nice guy so she will bestow favors on me. It is morally neutral if the reason I helped her is because I felt sorry for her. (Mere _feelings_ can never be the basis of morality, according to Kant.) The act is moral only if my motive for performing it is the desire to do my duty. Kant is surely right to think that the agent's intention must be considered when assigning moral worth (an act motivated

Expectation of reward

Pity

Duty

Three different motives for
helping your neighbor
fix her flat

by pure greed is not _morally_ worthy even if it happens to benefit many). But there is something disturbing going on here. Kant thought that the "good Samaritan" who helped the wounded stranger because the Samaritan's heart went out to the suffering human being had not performed a moral act; yet he thought that a "good Samaritan" who _loathes_ people, including the man he helps, yet helps him nevertheless out of a sense of duty, is a _moral_ man. There is a coldness in the heart of this doctrine. Perhaps feelings cannot be the sole criterion of moral worth, but they certainly enter into the picture in a big way. A truly good person must have sympathy and empathy for his fellow human being.

A Kantian hero

Thank goodness this icy side of Kant's moral philosophy can be ignored without damaging his insights about universalizability.

Kant's Second Formulation

Kant presented his categorical imperative in two forms. His second formulation runs like this: "Act so that you treat humanity, whether in your own person or in that of another, always as an end and never as a means only." Apparently Kant thought that this formulation was simply another way of stating his first version, which itself was an expression of the principle of universalizability. Whether such an identity between the two versions exists is certainly debatable. Perhaps it is true that the principle of universalizability prohibits one from _using_ other people for one's own ends. At any rate, Kant is suggesting that anyone who is committed to rationality is also committed to treating other people as "ends in themselves," and not as pawns in one's own game of personal advantage. To see why this is so according to Kant, we will have to summarize in a very cursory manner a number of complicated arguments that he presents in his _Foundations of the Metaphysics of Morals_.

First of all, if there were no _persons_ in the world,

Using people as pawns

only _things_, there would be no _values_. Nothing would be worth anything more or less than anything else. There are values in the world only because there are persons — that is, individual entities that have not only desires (animals too have desires), but also rationality and freedom. Something is valuable only relative to a human goal. Then, as the source of values, humans have _dignity_, which Kant defines as something so valuable that nothing could transcend it in worth. Therefore, to claim one's status as a human — that is, to claim one's dignity — one must value above all else that which bestows dignity and humanness on one, viz., rationality, freedom, and autonomy. This means one must value absolutely the rationality, freedom, and autonomy of oneself, but also of individuals other than oneself. Or, in

Kant's words, one must treat them as ends in themselves.

There are some striking features of Kant's position here. In spite of his argument's highly abstract nature, its conclusion does square with the very widespread moral intuition that it is wrong to use (exploit) people for one's own purposes. Furthermore, if that conclusion is accepted, it can be the basis of taking positions on such morally loaded topics as euthanasia, abortion, racism, equal rights, and feminism. But, of course, there are some difficulties. First, it seems to me that the ecological crisis we humans have provoked must force us to realize that any adequate moral code today will have to be one that demonstrates some responsibility to the natural world. A doctrine like Kant's, which says that nature has value only as a means to human ends, must seem to us today to be not just a bit arrogant but perhaps ironically even dangerous – ironic because that doctrine is itself not conducive to human ends. Second, arguments as abstract as Kant's are hard to evaluate and are not always very compelling. (Pointing this out, of course, does <u>not</u> <u>refute</u> Kant's argument.) Third, the difference between using people as a means and treating them as ends-in-themselves is not always clear. For example, I must admit that one of my main motivations in teaching philosophy is to earn a living for myself. Does that prove that I am using my students as means to satisfy my own ends?

332

Fourth, real-life situations often present us with dilemmas in which no matter what we do, our act can be interpreted as using someone. For example, the existentialist philosopher Jean-Paul Sartre cites the case of one of his students who, during the German occupation of France, approached him for advice. The young man came to Sartre under the following circumstances:

> ... his father was on bad terms with his mother, and, moreover, was inclined to be a collaborationist; his older brother had been killed in the German offensive of 1940, and the young man, with somewhat immature but generous feelings, wanted to avenge him. His mother lived alone with him, very much upset by the half-treason of her husband and the death of her older son; the boy was her only consolation.
>
> The boy was faced with the choice of leaving for England and joining the Free French Forces — that is, leaving his mother behind — or remaining with his mother and helping her to carry on.... Who could help him choose? Christian doctrine? No. Christian doctrine says, "Be charitable, love your neighbor, take the more rugged path, etc., etc." But which is the more rugged path? Whom should he love as a brother? The fighting man or his mother? Which does the greater good, the vague act of fighting in a group, or the concrete one of helping a particular human being to go on living? Who can decide _a priori_? Nobody. No book of ethics can tell him. The Kantian ethics says, "Never treat any person as a means, but as an end." Very well, if I stay with my mother, I'll treat her as an end and not as a means; but by virtue of this very fact, I'm running the risk of treating the people around me who are fighting, as means; and, conversely, if I go to join those who are fighting, I'll be treating them as an end, and, by doing that, I run the risk of treating my mother as a means.... You will say, "At least, he did go to a teacher for advice." But if you seek advice from a priest, for example, you have chosen this priest; you already knew, more or less, just about what advice he was going to give you. In other words, choosing your adviser is involving yourself. The proof of this is that if you are Christian, you will say, "Consult a priest." But some priests are collaborating, some are just marking time, some are resisting. Which to choose? If the young man chooses a priest who is resisting or collaborating, he has already decided on the kind of advice he's going to get. Therefore, in coming to see me he knew the answer I was

going to give him, and I had only one answer to give: "You're free, choose, that is, invent." No general ethics can show you what is to be done; there are no omens in the world. [10]

From this story we see that, even accepting Kant's categorical imperative in both or either of its forms, we still might be confronted with real moral situations in which Kant's philosophy is of little help to us. In fact, Sartre himself accepted Kant's view that to claim our status as human beings, we must recognize ourselves and others as autonomous, free, and rational, but he obviously held that ultimately our freedom overrides our rationality. Ultimately, our freedom, not our rationality, generates values. Kant would surely see this Sartrean view as a form of subjective irrationalism (more on Sartre shortly).

Conclusion

We shall not attempt to reach any conclusion concerning ethical theory until we have examined some attacks on its foundations in the next chapter.

Notes

1. Plato, The Republic, in Great Dialogues of Plato, W. H. D. Rouse, trans. (New York: New American Library, 1956), p. 137. Unless otherwise stated, all subsequent quotes from The Republic in this chapter are from this edition.

2. Bernard Williams, Ethics and the Limits of Philosophy (Cambridge, Massachusetts: Harvard University Press, 1985), p. 27.

3. Thomas Hobbes, Leviathan: Or the Matter, Forme and Power of a Commonwealth Ecclesiasticall and Civil (New York: Collier Books, 1962), p. 105.

4. Hobbes, _Leviathan_, pp. 49-50.

5. Epicurus, _Epicurus: The Extant Remains_, C. Bailey, trans. (Oxford: Clarendon Press, 1926), p. 87.

6. Epicurus, _Epicurus_, p. 99.

7. Jeremy Bentham, _The Rationale of Reward_, in _The Works of Jeremy Bentham_ (Edinburgh: Tait, 1838-1843), Vol. II, Sec. i, p. 253.

8. John Stuart Mill, _Utilitarianism_ (New York: E.P. Dutton, 1951), p. 10.

9. Mill, _Utilitarianism_, p. 10.

10. Jean-Paul Sartre, _Existentialism and Human Emotions_ (New York: Philosophical Library, 1957), pp. 24-28.

Chapter 8

Different Strokes for Different Folks

Attempts to Undermine the Foundations of Morality

Existentialism

At the end of the previous chapter, we saw that in a certain sense, Jean-Paul Sartre's existentialism challenges the possibility of any moral code or system. This is in spite of the fact that at one level, Sartre accepts Kant's moral views, as we see in passages like these:

> ... I am responsible for myself and for everyone else. I am creating a certain image of man of my own choosing. In choosing myself, I choose man.... Certainly, many people believe that when they do something, they themselves are the only ones involved, and when someone says to them "What if everyone acted that way?" they shrug their shoulders and answer, "Everyone doesn't act that way." But really, one should always ask himself, "What would happen if everybody looked at things that way?" There is no escaping this disturbing thought except by a kind of double-dealing. A man who lies and makes excuses for himself by saying "not everybody does that," is someone with an uneasy conscience, because the act of lying implies that a universal value is conferred upon the lie.

This reference to the universalizability of acts is the Kantian side of Sartre's moral views. He goes on to say: "Therefore though the content of ethics is variable, a certain form of it is universal. Kant says that freedom desires both itself and the freedom of others. Granted."[1]

In spite of granting the Kantian premise, in the example of the young man who came to Sartre for advice, Sartre has demonstrated very convincingly that when moral values conflict, no moral formula can resolve the opposition. The young man simply had to invent, that is to say, choose. This is because Sartre has radicalized Kant's view that the source of value is always the human being, and he has prioritized freedom over rationality. If Sartre is right, then reason cannot compel anyone to behave in one way as opposed to another, because reason can be an authority only if one _chooses_ to authorize reason. Once I decide that reason has value, then reason can force me to behave

Reason tries to compel Sartre to do the right thing.

only in ways for which I can give cogent reasons. But what if rather than valuing reasons, I, like Dostoyevsky's "underground man" (see "Perverse Freedom" in Chapter 6), choose _unreason_ to guide me? Then I do not need to, nor can I, give _reasons_ for my choice. So we see that even though Sartre accepts many of the same facts about humans that Kant does (that humans are free and autonomous), he draws exactly the opposite conclusion from Kant's. Because we are free and autonomous, we cannot be _naturally_ rational. We are rational only by choice. Or, to put it another way, if we are free, then no moral code can be binding on us.

Hume and the Naturalistic Fallacy

Sartre was certainly not the first philosopher to challenge the foundations of morality. Already in the eighteenth century David Hume had exploded a bombshell whose reverberations are still heard up through our time. This explosive device had the form of a simple five-worded phrase: "No 'is' implies an 'ought.'" What Hume meant by this is that no moral claims whatsoever could be derived from any merely <u>factual</u> claims. Let's clarify this by choosing a moral principle with which almost everyone would agree: "It is morally wrong to torture innocent children just for the pleasure of doing so." Now, Hume's point is this. If someone challenges this claim and says, "How do you know this to be true?" what demonstration can we give him? The utilitarian will say that the act is wrong because it goes against the principle of utility ("the greatest amount of happiness for the greatest number of people"). But what if the utilitarian is asked why we should accept the principle of utility? Bentham answered that we

338

should do so because "Nature has placed mankind under the governance of two sovereign masters, _pain_ and _pleasure_. It is for them alone to point out what we ought to do...."[2]

But even if Bentham's factual claim is true and we are all motivated by the desire for pleasure, would it follow logically that we _ought_ to be? What if most people, or even all people, derived

I enjoy doing this. Therefore, I am morally obligated to continue.

Aii. Aii, more!

Faulty logic

great pleasure from cruelty? Would it follow in some moral sense that people _ought_ to be cruel? Of course not. So the utilitarians' claim that we _ought_ to adopt the principle of utility because we all _do_ desire happiness simply doesn't work. This leaves unanswered the question as to why we ought not to torture innocent children.

Kant would answer that we ought not do so because such behavior conflicts with the categorical imperative. But why should we follow that principle? Kant says we must do so because we are rational. But Hume's point is that even if we _are_ rational, it does not follow that we _ought_ to be. Hence, from his point of view, the question of why we ought not torture children is still un-answered.

In the twentieth century, Hume's moral skepticism influenced the important Cambridge moral philosopher GEORGE EDWARD MOORE (1873-1958), usually called G.E. Moore. Moore pointed out that the concept of good cannot be _defined_ in terms of any "nat-ural" quality, such as "pleasure," "happiness," or "survival value." (What Moore called a "natural quality" is more or less the same as Hume's "factual claims," his "is"). In a true definition, such as "a sister is a female sibling," it would be nonsense to question the predicate of the subject— to ask, for example, "Yes, but _is_ a sister a female sibling?" Of _course_ she is—that's what "sister" means. (Or try these: "_Is_ a bachelor an unmar-ried male?" "_Is_ a triangle a three-sided figure?")

Yet when we turn to attempted definitions of the word "good," curious things happen. For example, the hedonist tries to de-fine "good" in terms of _pleasure_. Yet the question "_Is_ pleasure good?" is not nonsense in the way that the question "_Is_ a square four-sided?" is nonsense. (For example, what about Hitler's pleasure? Is it necessarily good?) A similar result is obtained when social Darwinists try to define good in terms of survival value. The question "Yes, but _is_ survival always good?" is not non-sense. (Being willing to betray one's friends may have survival value in some situations, but that doesn't necessarily make treachery good.) The same thing is true of religious attempts to define "good" in terms of obedience to God's will. The question "But _is_ it always good to obey God?" at least makes sense, even if we don't know the answer. (Think of God's instruction to Abraham to kill his innocent son.) So the result of this is that all attempts to define "good" in terms of any existing facts whatever result in a fallacy.

340

Moore called it "the naturalistic fallacy." Pointing it out was his way of affirming Hume's dictum, "No _is_ implies an _ought_." (Moore's own view in his _Principia Ethica_ was that the good is some "nonnatural" simple quality that cannot be analyzed but that can be recognized. Hardly any moral philosophers have agreed with Moore's mysterious claim or even been able to make much sense out of it.) So the

There it is, right there. Don't you see it?

No

No

The good as a nonnatural, unanalyzable, simple quality

question remains: if we cannot derive our moral values from any facts in the world, from where can we derive them? This question threatens any attempt to ground morality in objectivity.

Logical Positivism

Another group of twentieth century philosophers who were influenced by Hume is called "the logical positivists." Their views are no longer fashionable, but in their day, they were tremendously influential, and ghosts of their ideas still abound. They are worth studying for this reason and also, more pertinent to the point of this chapter, because they mounted one of the most powerful attacks on the possibility of moral philosophy to be carried out by any group of philosophers.

The logical positivists were a bunch of hard-nosed, scientific-minded philosophers whose original position was formulated at the University of Vienna in the early 1920s. There a small group of philosophers calling themselves "the Vienna Circle" was led by

Professor Moritz Schlick. We have already run across them briefly in Chapter 4 because many of them accepted the ontological view we studied there known as "phenomenalism," inspired by Berkeley and Hume. Their attack on ethics derived from their theory of meaning, according to which there are only two kinds of genuine propositions: ANALYTIC and SYNTHETIC PROPOSITIONS. "Analytic propositions" are true by definition, mere tautologies, telling us nothing about reality, only something about how concepts are related (e.g., "All circles are round"). "Synthetic" (or "empirical") propositions can be confirmed or refuted only by some actual or possible observation. Only these propositions are truly about reality. Any putative proposition that is neither analytic nor synthetic is "cognitively empty," or _nonsense_. A sentence like "Torturing innocent children

The Three Possibilities		
ANALYTIC	SYNTHETIC	NONSENSE
True by definition	Established by observation	. . . . . .
"Unicorns have one horn."	"Pickles are sour."	"Twas brillig."
		"God loves you."

is immoral" is not analytic; that is, it is not true simply by virtue of the meaning of its words (as is proved by negating the sentence and seeing that the negation, "Torturing innocent children is _not_ immoral," is not a self-contradiction in the way that the sentence "A sister is not female." _is_ self-contradictory).

On the other hand, neither is our sentence empirical. That is, there is no observation, actual or possible, that could confirm or refute the sentence. If we watched a brute torturing a small child, we would feel horror, revulsion, and fury, but there would be nothing we could point at and say, "There it is! _That's_ the immoral

part" (in the way
that we <u>can</u> say,
"That's the yellow
part" or "that's the
heavy part"). So what
<u>is</u> the status of our
moral claim, ac-
cording to the positiv-
ists? Because it is
"cognitively empty,"
it is merely "express-
ive." The British
member of the school

Find the immoral part.

of logical positivism, A.J. Ayer (we've met him already in "Phenomenalism" in Chapter 3), claimed that moral language was simply a
disguised display of emotion, often coupled with "commands in a
misleading grammatical form." So the sentence "torturing is immoral" really means something like this →

Only the third part of this
division could have truth value;
therefore, the whole sen-
tence, "torturing is immoral,"
can be neither true nor false.
It expresses what Ayer
called "a pseudoconcept."

TORTURING!
DON'T DO IT!
I DON'T LIKE IT!!

Logical positivism inspired many in its day, and we still see its
influence here and there (e.g., in B.F. Skinner's conception of
science), but positivism's rather shocking views about morality need
not distress us too much. The general consensus today is that we

343

do not have to take logical positivism all that seriously. It offers some good tools for analysis, but it is fairly obvious that its theory of meaning is much too restrictive. Furthermore, it suffers from a deadly internal defect. If every proposition is analytic, synthetic, or nonsense, what is the status of the proposition that asserts that every proposition is analytic, synthetic, or nonsense? It is not analytic because its negation does not lead to a self-contradiction. It is not synthetic because no observation would tend to confirm it or refute it. What status is left for it except that of nonsense according to its own criterion? Perhaps Professor Jon Wheatley was writing an obituary when he said, "Logical positivism is one of the very few philosophical positions which can be easily shown to be dead wrong, and that is its principal claim to fame." [3]

So what impact, ultimately, do these various philosophical assaults on the foundations of morality have? Notice that, each in its own way, the Sartrean, Humean, and positivistic critiques are indeed just that — assaults on the foundations of morality. Sartre tries to show that the foundations of morality must be

The assault on the foundations of morality

344

subjective and unstable. Hume and the positivists try to show that morality cannot have its foundation in any true facts about the world. But what if talk about the <u>foundations</u> of morality turns out to be misconceived? At the end of Chapter 3, we saw that the attempt to discover the foundations of knowledge might have been completely wrong-headed. It was suggested there that knowledge may prove to be more like a net or a spiderweb than like a house. The same is true in ethics. As the influential British moral philosopher, Bernard Williams, says:

> ... the foundationalist enterprise, [that] of resting the structure of knowledge on some favored class of statements, has now generally been displaced in favor of a holistic type of model, in which some beliefs can be questioned, justified, or adjusted while others are kept constant, but there is no process by which they can all be questioned at once, or all justified in terms of (almost) nothing. In Neurath's famous image we repair the ship while we are on the sea. [4]

According to Williams, the same is true of ethics. "The aim of ethical thought," he says, "is to help us to construct a world that will be our world, one in which we have a social, cultural, and personal life." [5] Now, for <u>that</u> activity, no

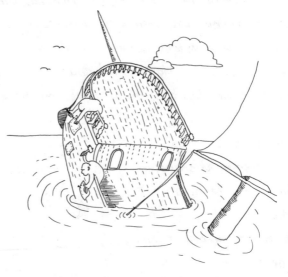

"foundation" is needed. By virtue of being human, we find ourselves engaged in it willy-nilly. That is why Williams prefers a version of Aristotle's moral question over that of Socrates. Williams takes it that Socrates' ethical question is,

"How should <u>one</u> live?" This is a theoretical question abstract in nature. It tends toward foundationalism. Aristotle's question is more concrete. He asks, "How should <u>we</u> live?" Socrates' question presupposes some abstract human nature in universal conditions; Aristotle's presupposes a concrete psychological and communal social situation in which <u>we</u> actually find ourselves engaged on a daily basis.

But before we can accept this pragmatic solution to the problem of ethics, we must address one more objection to morality, an objection that seems to threaten even a pragmatic solution, the problem of cultural relativism.

Cultural Relativism

Here we must talk about another kind of twentieth-century assault on the possibility of ethics, one that has come not from the field of philosophy, but from the social sciences. It has been associated with some important names in anthropology and psychology. It is called "cultural relativism," and it denies that there can be any absolute or objective moral values on the grounds that moral values are the products of individual cultures, which differ from one another in such a fashion that the values central to each society differ from one another. In a famous article of 1934, the anthropologist Ruth Benedict wrote:

Every society,

Anthropologists attacking moral philosopher

346

beginning with some slight inclination in one direction or another, carries its preference farther and farther, integrating itself more and more completely upon its chosen basis, and discarding those types of behavior that are uncongenial. Most of those organizations of personality that seem to us most incontrovertibly abnormal have been used by different civilizations in the very foundations of their institutional life. Conversely the most valued traits of our normal individuals have been looked on in differently organized cultures as aberrant. Normality, in short, within a very wide range, is culturally defined. It is primarily a term for the socially elaborated segment of human behavior in any culture; and abnormality, a term for the segment that that particular civilization does not use. The very eyes with which we see the problem are conditioned by the long traditional habits of our own society. . . . .

We recognize that morality differs in every society, and is a convenient term for socially approved habits. Mankind has always preferred to say, "It is morally good," rather than "It is habitual," and the fact of this preference is matter enough for a critical science of ethics. But historically the two phrases are synonymous.

The concept of the normal is properly a variant of the concept of the good. It is that which society has approved. A normal action is one which falls well within the limits of expected behavior for a particular society. . . . .

Each of these traits, in proportion as it reinforces the chosen behavior patterns of that culture, is for that culture normal. Those individuals to whom it is congenial either congenitally, or as the result of childhood sets, are accorded prestige in that culture, and are not visited with the social contempt or disapproval which their traits would call down upon them in a society that was differently organized. On the other hand, those individuals whose characteristics are not congenial to the selected type of human behavior in that community are the deviants, no matter how valued their personality traits may be in a contrasted civilization. [6]

Benedict's views were echoed a generation later by the psychologist B.F. Skinner, who said:

What a given group of people calls good is a fact: it is what members of the group find reinforcing as the result of their genetic endowment and the natural and social contingencies to which they have been exposed. Each culture has its own set of goods, and what is good in one culture may not be good in another. To recognize this is to take the position of "cultural relativism." What is good for the Trobriand Islander is good for the Trobriand Islander, and that is that. Anthropologists have often emphasized relativism as a tolerant alternative to missionary zeal in converting all cultures to a single set of ethical, governmental, religious, or economic values.[7]

The views of Benedict and Skinner resonate with ideas with which we have all become acquainted and that to many people (especially to many college students) seem quite correct — namely, that "good" must always mean "good for her" or "good for them" or "good for me," but never just _good_. What is good for one person or culture is not necessarily good for another, and therefore there can really never be any genuine moral _reasoning_, only "acknowledgment" of others' "good." ("I hear what you're saying.") And the data from the social sciences sometimes do seem to support such a relativism. (It is not "good" for me to worship cows, but it is "good" for Hindus to worship cows because cow manure provides both fertilizer and fuel for Hindu culture.) It cannot be denied that this kind of relativism is healthy

It is _wrong_ to take things that do not belong to you!

I acknowledge your space on that.

in struggling against puritanical "up-tightness" and dangerous ethnocentric arrogance. ("Our values are right, and we'll impose them on you if we have to kill you to do it!") But our relativism runs up against problems when we turn to questions like this: Must we withhold moral judgment about Nazi "brutalities" on the grounds that we are <u>not</u> members of a

A Texas cow worshipper

Nazi culture? Exterminating six million people is "good" for Hitler but not for me? This "different strokes for different folks" philosophy seems dangerously hollow here. So let's go back and take a closer look at what ethical relativism is saying. Under scrutiny, its thesis becomes less clear. Is the cultural relativist saying (1) "There are no universally held moral values" or (2) "No value or set of values can justifiably be recommended for all people"? These are very different claims. Let's look at each of them.

No Universally Held Moral Values

Notice that this first claim is an empirical one. In theory at least, it is capable of confirmation or refutation through scientific investigation. Now, there are several things to say about it. First, if it is meant to be interpreted <u>individually</u>, saying that there never

349

has been a moral value accepted by <u>absolutely</u> <u>everybody</u>, then, no doubt, the claim is true, but not very impressive. (Just because one person — Cronos perhaps — broke the law against eating one's children doesn't mean there is something wrong with the law.) Then what about interpreting the relativist's thesis culturally rather than individually? Certainly not <u>all</u> social scientists are in agreement concerning the truth of this version of the claim. For example, the eminent anthropologists Alfred Kroeber and Clyde Kluckhohn argued that there are certain universal values that have been accepted by all cultures : no culture tolerates indiscriminate lying, stealing, or violence within the in-group. The incest taboo is virtually universal. No culture places value on suffering as an

Cronos eating his children
(after Francisco Goya)

end in itself. Every culture ceremonializes death. "All cultures define as abnormal individuals who are permanently inaccessible to communication or who fail to maintain some degree of control over their impulsive life." [8] Kroeber and Kluckhohn do not deny that what <u>counts</u> as lying, stealing, or violence might be culturally defined, but they think that these values are universals behind the particulars.

   The social psychologist Solomon Asch holds a similar view. He claims that every society despises cowardice and honors bravery. In every society, modesty, courage, and hospitality are encouraged.

Even in cultures where acts that are horrible to us are routinely performed, it is often possible to find that the disagreement between their culture and ours is really more of a debate about apparently empirical facts than it is a debate over values. Ancient Chinese cultures commonly engaged in infanticide (leaving unwanted infants exposed to die in nature). But Asch

All cultures define as abnormal individuals who are permanently inaccessible to communication.

claims that in that culture, infants were not considered human until their first year. The ancient Chinese and we may actually be seen to agree on the value of human life, but to disagree on the facts concerning what constitutes a human being.

At least _those_ kinds of disagreements are not just disagreements of taste and hence are debatable and, in principle, resolvable — though perhaps not easily, as is seen in the amount of passion engendered by the debate over abortion. Again, to a great extent, this debate is not over the value of human life — both parties are probably more or less in agreement over that — but over the facts concerning what constitutes a human being. Still, I don't want to be seen as oversimplifying a complicated issue. The question "What is a human

351

being?" <u>looks</u> like a straightforward question that could be answered either with a dictionary-type definition or with some empirical research. But in fact, the concept "human being" probably is one involving a complex concatenation of facts and values and does not admit of a purely scientific determination. In an odd way, it is probably a socially negotiable concept, and we are in the midst of a rather painful, protracted debate right now. Perhaps we always have been. For example, it has not always been clear to all cultures whether to treat women, strangers, and minorities as fully human or whether to treat volcanoes and winds as if they were adversarial entrepreneurs.

So then, if the thesis of cultural relativism is that there are no values held by all or by most cultures, that thesis is probably false. What about cultural relativism's second formulation?

OK, OK. I'll tell you what. For six smokeless years and no lava, I'll offer you a firstborn infant, three oxen, and a dozen pastrami sandwiches.

Cutting a deal with a volcano

No Value or Set of Values Recommendable for All People

The thesis that no value or set of values can justifiably be recommended for all people cannot be the conclusion drawn from a legitimate scientific investigation. Even if, contrary to the implication of the foregoing discussion, it did turn out that no values are universally held, it wouldn't follow from that that no value is _worthy_ of adoption by all. (This is another version of the is/ought problem.) Even if we found out that all people enjoyed inflicting suffering on others, it wouldn't follow that they _ought_ to inflict

All people enjoy inflicting suffering on others.

suffering on others. In _this_ sense, anthropology has nothing to offer to moral philosophy. In _this_ sense, it doesn't matter what people from other cultures do. We can't deduce what they _ought_ to do from their current or past practices. But there _is_ a sense

in which anthropology is helpful to moral philosophy. We've already pointed out that the study of the values of other cultures can have a salutary humbling effect, cutting into our tendency to assume that the values of _our_ culture are somehow "natural," hence superior. But also if we accept Kroeber's and Kluckhohn's claim that the universals they listed obviously have survival value, that they are "necessary conditions to social life," _and_ if we accept as a moral principle the view that "human life should prevail and flourish," then anthropology, sociology, and social psychology can help us think clearly in our own moral reasoning.

It's natural to keep your lawn mowed at one inch. I keep *my* lawn mowed at one inch. You keep *yours* mowed at one inch, too.

Conclusion

My own conclusions concerning the topic of moral philosophy are cautiously skeptical. We cannot know what "the Good" is, not for Plato's reasons (that too much ignorance and too many obstacles exist), but because there is no such thing as "the Good" — in about the same sense as there is no such thing as "the Real," according to John Austin. Concerning the question "What is the good life?" we can perhaps be more positive, but only if we make some utilitarian-type assumptions about human desires and goals. If we do (and I see no reason not to), then I think that both Aristotle and the utilitarians can be very instructive for us. It should be possible to create a general theory of what is most likely to contribute to a life of happiness — a theory showing the approximate role in such a life of the pursuit of pleasure, of the development of potentialities, of creative expression, of commitment to other persons (including family, friends, and lovers), of commitment to causes and a professional life, of acceptance of social responsibilities and personal obligations, of respect for nature as well as of the "virtues" (courage, honesty, temperance, etc.) in one's life.

But it should be understood that though such a theory can be normative (i.e., can guide us in our decision making and in the forming of our habits), it cannot make anyone either good or happy. Socrates was wrong to think that if one <u>knew</u> the good, one would necessarily <u>become</u> good.

Unfortunately, it is possible to know what one ought to do (to know what one's obligations are), to know what would be a good thing or the right thing to do, yet to do the opposite. A moral theory can be part of an argument meant to motivate a certain kind of thinking and acting, but philosophy by itself cannot create right action. (In my view, Plato and Socrates were wrong about that, too.) If one's only reason for behaving in a certain way comes from a philosophical theory, one will probably not find oneself behaving in the desired way very often. And even if one is already motivated by extraphilosophical reasons to engage in a moral form of life, a moral theory can be a guide, but not a final source of judgment. Sartre is right to

You <u>will</u> be good!

Moral theory cannot make you good.

say that a theory never makes moral judgments, that only a human being does. He has also shown us that in real life, moral problems are often caused by "conflicts of ideals" (the name of an excellent book on this topic written by Luther Binkley) and not by questions like, "Should I be moral?" or "Why should I be moral?"[9] No ethical theory will be able to solve these real conflicts, and we should not expect one to do so.

The moral skeptics (Hume, the logical positivists, the cultural relativists, the existentialists) were right to say that it is impossible to discover the _foundations_ of morality, and those philosophers who claimed to do so (Plato, the hedonists, the utilitarians, Kant) were wrong to think that they had succeeded. But this admission is not so disastrous after all. It is true that a _house_ without foundations would be in a sorry state, but morality is not a house. Just as many philosophers today have concluded that foundationalism is wrong in epistemology (see "Conclusion," Chapter 3), so it is beginning to look as though it is wrong in moral philosophy. As Bernard Williams said, the role of philosophy in this region is not to discover the foundations of morality, but "to help us to construct a world that will be our world, one in which we have a social, cultural and personal life." In this quest, I believe (following the legal philosopher Christopher Stone) that a kind of moral pluralism is required.[10] We should not feel that this quest must be guided by only _one_ principle (e.g., a hedonistic one, a utilitarian one, a Kantian one, or one derived from the current ecological movement).[11] Rather, we should develop some system of "moral mapping." A Kantian principle of universalizability can be very useful vis-à-vis our relations to other humans yet be fairly useless, and even destructive, vis-à-vis the natural world. A kind of Spinozistic "deep ecology" principle may be needed to reveal the intrinsic value of the natural world, but

356

that same principle might seem perverse vis-à-vis my relations to other people. The decision as to when one moral map should be abandoned and another made to "kick in" would not itself be purely the function of a philosophical theory, though philosophical speculation can guide such a decision. So here, as elsewhere, if we do not expect *too* much of philosophy, she can be an excellent companion.

Notes

1. Jean-Paul Sartre, *Existentialism and Human Emotions* (New York: Philosophical Library, 1957), pp. 18-19, 47.

2. Jeremy Bentham, *An Introduction to the Principles of Morals and Legislation* (Darien, Connecticut: Hafner, 1970), p. 1.

3. Jon Wheatley, *Prolegomena to Philosophy* (Belmont, California: Wadsworth, 1970), p. 103.

4. Bernard Williams, *Ethics and the Limits of Philosophy* (Cambridge, Massachusetts: Harvard University Press, 1985), p. 113.

5. Williams, *Ethics and the Limits*, p. 111.

6. Ruth Benedict, "Anthropology and the Abnormal," *Journal of General Psychology*, Vol. 10 (1934), pp. 72-74.

7. B.F. Skinner, *Beyond Freedom and Dignity* (New York: Bantam Books, 1972), p. 122.

8. Alfred Louis Kroeber and Clyde Kluckhohn, "Values and Relativity," in *Culture, a Critical Review of Concepts and Definitions*, Papers of the Peabody Museum, Harvard University, Vol. 47, No. 1 (1952), pp. 174-179.

9. Luther Binkley, *Conflict of Ideals: Changing Values in Western Society* (New York: D. Van Nostrand, 1969).

10. Christopher D. Stone, _Earth and Other Ethics: The Case for Moral Pluralism_ (New York: Harper & Row, 1987).

11. Bill Devall and George Sessions, _Deep Ecology: Living as if Nature Mattered_ (Layton, Utah: Peregrine Smith Press, 1985).

Chapter 9

We, the People
Political Philosophy

In a famous passage, Jean-Jacques Rousseau once wrote, "Man is born free; and everywhere he is in chains." This is an appropriate idea with which to begin a discussion of political philosophy. There is a significant sense in which we, like the beasts of the field and the birds of the sky, are "born free." It was once believed that some people were born to be slaves to others or to be their natural servants,

Everywhere we are in chains.

but in our culture, we no longer believe that. We are not born with any natural masters (though it is possible, as we saw in Chapter 5, that we are born with a <u>supernatural</u> master — but even most of the theories that argue for a supernatural lord also hold that he created us

RULES

I. CLOTHING
  A. YOU MUST WEAR CLOTHES ON ALL SOCIAL OCCASIONS.
  B. SUCH CLOTHING MUST COVER ALL PRIVATE PARTS (AS DEFINED BELOW)
  C. CLOTHING MUST BE SUCH AS TO AVOID PROVOKING SHOCK OR OUTRAGE.

II. NOISE
  A. NOISE MAY BE MADE, BUT ONLY UNDER CERTAIN CONDITIONS
    1. IT IS SENSIBLE NOISE
    2. IT DOES NOT ANNOY GREAT NUMBERS OF PEOPLE.
    3. IT IS APPROPRIATE NOISE

III. SNEEZING

as free beings). Yet, Rousseau says, everywhere we are in chains. Well, that is surely a bit exaggerated, but look at it this way. In civilized society, there are rules governing almost every aspect of our behavior. There are rules telling us what we have to wear, how we must behave with other people, where we can and cannot go, how fast we must do it, and in what circumstances it is all right to say certain things but not others. Furthermore, all these rules are enforced by an implied threat of immediate violence and of eventual loss of your property, your freedom, and in some cases, even your life. Even breaking a fairly simple rule, such as that against jay-walking, can produce billy clubs, body searches, and handcuffs if you persist in breaking the rule numerous times in sequence contrary to the advice of a passing "peace officer." So in a sense, Rousseau is right. We perform all of our acts looking up the barrel of a gun. This raises one of the key questions in political philosophy—

Performing our acts looking up the barrel of a gun.

360

Why should we put up with it? This is just a rhetorical way of posing some of the big questions in this area, such as these:

• Are we naturally political, or is the political body a mere artifice? (If the latter, is it a necessary one, or could we do without it?)

• Is there a real distinction between legitimate and illegitimate authority? If so, how can we draw that distinction?

• Do political bodies necessarily produce injustice? Or is it possible to conceive of a good and just society?

Plato

We begin once more with Plato. We started with him in our discussions of epistemology, ontology, and morality; we saw his influence in philosophy of religion; we will begin with him again in Chapter 11, on art. This is because, for better or for worse, Plato determined the course of Western philosophy. In some respects it is true, as A. N. Whitehead said, that the history of Western philosophy is a series of footnotes to _The Republic_. Consciously or unconsciously, philosophers seem to have spent an inordinate amount of time either trying to achieve Plato's ideals or trying to escape from them. But precisely because so much has already been said here about Plato, we will not have

The history of philosophy as a series of footnotes to _The Republic_

to deal with him extensively now. We will give a cursory sketch of his political views, using them to set the stage for later developments in political philosophy.

Plato shared the typical Greek view that we are <u>naturally</u> social beings. But the "naturalness" of our sociality stems from a natural weakness on our parts as individuals. As individuals, we are not self-sufficient.

In <u>The Republic</u>, Plato has Socrates say,

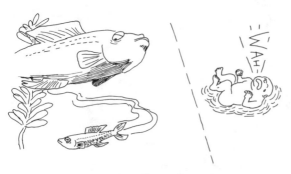

Guppies are self-sufficient at birth. Humans are not.

A city [<u>polis</u>, republic], I take it, comes into being because each of us is not self-sufficient but needs many things. Can you think any other beginning could found a city? ... one man gives a share of something to another or takes a share, if he gives or takes, because he thinks he will be better for it....[1]

As we saw in Chapter 6, from our necessary dependence on each other, Plato deduces a kind of natural division of labor along class lines, with skilled laborers and artisans forming one class, a military police caste forming another, and philosophers forming a third, the ruling class, which is created by promoting older members of the military caste. The lower class is incapable of philosophy (though there is no clear explanation in <u>The Republic</u> why some people are capable of it and others are not — it seems that these abilities and disabilities must be congenital). Those unfit from birth or habit for the rule of reason must be forced or tricked into submitting to it. The work and productivity of the laboring class is needed by society, and these workers must be rewarded for their output. Hence, they

are allowed to have families, are paid salaries, and are allowed to wear gold and silver decorations. The military caste is capable of philosophy, so its members are able to understand that their virtues of courage and determination are their own rewards. In a remarkable passage, Plato has Socrates describe to Glaucon the conditions in which the two upper classes will live.

"Then besides this education any sensible man would say that we must provide their lodgings and their other property such as will not prevent them from being themselves as good guardians as they can be, and such as will not excite them to do mischief among the other citizens."

"That will be quite true," said Glaucon.

"Look here, then," said I; "do you think some such manner of life and lodging as this will do, if they are to be as we describe? First of all, no one must have any private property whatsoever, except what is absolutely neces-

sary. Secondly, no one must have any lodging or storehouse at all which is not open to all comers. Then their provisions must be so much as is needed by athletes of war, temperate and brave men, and there must be fixed allowances for them to be supplied by the other citizens as wages for their guardianship, so much that there shall be plenty for the year but nothing over at the end. They must live in common, attending in messes as if they were in the field. As to gold and silver, we

Virtue is its own reward.

363

must tell them that they have these from the gods as a divine gift in their souls, and they want in addition no human silver or gold; they must not pollute this treasure by mixing it with a treasure of mortal gold, because many wicked things have been done about the common coinage, but theirs is undefiled. They alone of all in the city dare not have any dealings with gold and silver, or even touch them, or come under the same roof with them, or hang them upon their limbs, or drink from silver or gold. In this way ... whenever they get land of their own and houses and money, they will be householders and farmers instead of guardians, masters and enemies of the rest of the citizens instead of allies; so hating and hated, plotting and plotted against, they will spend all their lives fearing enemies within much more than without, running a course very near to destruction, they and the city together. For all these reasons," I said, "let us agree on this manner of providing our guardians with lodging and all the rest, and let us lay it down by law. What do you say?"
   "I agree wholly with you," said Glaucon (pp. 216-217).

Furthermore, we are told that for the "guardians" (the military and ruling castes), there will be no families as such: "... no one must have a private wife of his own, and the children must be common too, and the parents shall not know the child nor the child its parent" (p.255). So sexual relations will be by lottery — though there is a hint that the lottery is rigged and that the rulers know who is sleeping with whom. Hence, the upper classes will produce children according to eugenic principles.

   Plato prescribes a kind of absolute

Communism, but only for the upper classes. This will protect them from the greed that permeates the lower, more ignorant class; and, as we saw, greed is allowed to motivate the workers and the artisans but is always contained and controlled by the philosopher rulers and their military allies. Like Karl Marx some 2,250 years later, Plato saw society as <u>natural</u> but capable of being undermined by greed if not structured in such a way as to contain it. (The difference between Plato and Marx is also striking, of course. For the latter, the destiny of the human race is associated with the communism of the working class; for Plato, that class is so benighted that it [and only it] is incapable of communism.)

In <u>The Republic</u>, a character named Adeimantus points out that the ideal city Socrates is describing may, through its totalitarian practices, be immune to the dangers of <u>greed</u>, but it can still be corrupted by <u>envy</u>. The lower class will envy the upper classes because of their power and intelligence, and the upper classes will envy the lower class because life at that level just seems more fun. In order to answer this objection, Plato has

Greed and envy: Two forces that can undermine the Republic

Socrates make a very curious suggestion, one that plagues political science down to our day. (Indeed, Socrates admits that he is quite embarrassed to have to make the suggestion.) The suggestion is that all members of the City — including the rulers — be told a lie about

365

why they must accept the order of things. Plato calls it a "noble lie," and it is introduced in The Republic in the following manner:

"You remember a while since," I said, "we spoke of necessary lies. Is there any device by which we might tell one genuine lie worthy of the name, and persuade the rulers themselves that it is true, or at least persuade the rest of the city?"

Socrates trying to get people to believe the noble lie

"What may that be?"

. . . . .

"Here goes, then, although I don't know how I shall dare, or what words to use. Well, I will try first to convince the rulers themselves and the soldiers, then the rest of the city; and this is the story. The training and education we were giving them was all a dream, and they only imagined all this was happening to them and around them; but in truth they were being moulded and trained down inside the earth, where they and their arms and all their trappings were being fashioned. When they were completely made, the earth their mother delivered them from her womb; and now they must take thought for the land in which they live, as for their mother and nurse, must plan for her and protect her, if anyone attacks her, and they must think of the other citizens as brothers also born from the earth."

"I am not surprised," he said, "that you were shy of telling that lie!"

"There was good reason for it," I said, "but never mind, listen to the rest of the fable. 'So you are all brothers in the city,' we shall tell them in our fable, 'but while God moulded you, he mingled gold in the generation of some, and those are the ones fit to rule, who are therefore the most precious; he mingled silver in the assistants ; and iron and brass in farmers and the other craftsmen. Then because of being all akin you would beget your likes for the most part, but sometimes a silver child may be born from a golden or a golden from a silvern, and so with all the rest breeding amongst each other. The rulers are commanded by God first and foremost that they be good guardians of no person so much as of their own children, and to watch nothing else so carefully as which of these things is mingled in their souls. If any child of theirs has a touch of brass or iron, they will not be merciful to him on any account, but they will give him the value proper to his nature, and push him away among the craftsmen or the farmers; if again one of them has the gold or silver in his nature, they will honour him and lift him among the guardians or the assistants, since there is an oracle that the city will be destroyed when the brass or the iron shall guard it.' Now have you any device to make them believe this fable?"(pp. 214 - 215).

This is very curious and even quite discouraging. It is curious because, as has already been mentioned, part of the job of The Republic was to destroy the authority of myth in the Greek world and to replace it with the authority of reason (i.e., philosophy); yet here Plato is required to create a new myth to keep the City cohesive. And it is discouraging because Plato is admitting that reason itself is not strong enough a force to bind the City together. It is especially striking that even the rulers must be lied to, this in spite of the fact that we are supposed to be naturally social. Plato raises a specter that has haunted some thinkers even in our century : the idea that perhaps

Each culture must have its own myth.

a society can remain vibrant and vital only if it has a myth about itself that it can tell itself. And unfortunately, these myths are usually nationalistic and ethnocentric, hence often aggressive, arrogant, xeno-phobic, racist, and imperialistic. The great twentieth-century sociologist Emile Durkheim thought that when a society lost the capacity to tell it-self such a myth, "anomie" (a sense of loss of meaning and direction) set in. Anomie leads both to cultural and individual suicide, according to Durkheim.

Anomie

Thomas Hobbes

In the modern period, a number of important philosophers addressed the "big questions" of political philosophy. Thomas Hobbes' book, <u>Leviathan</u> (1651), had as one of its main goals the resolution of the problem of politics, and we shall turn to it now.

It will be recalled from Chapter 7 that Hobbes had a very distinctive view of human motivation, a view called "psychological egoism," according to which all human actions are motivated by self-interest. Hobbes' political views presuppose the truth of psychological egoism, and even though that theory was rather soundly criticized in our earlier discussion as an unsuccessful account of individual human actions, it must be said that it is probably more acceptable as a

368

political model, or perhaps a political metaphor. When we think not of individuals, but of foreign policies of various nations, it is difficult to believe that they are _not_ motivated by what their framers conceive as the interest of their nation; or when we think of negotiations between labor and management groups, it is hard to imagine them as motivated by pure altruism.

So perhaps Hobbes' psychological egoism is a little less offensive here than in a discussion of morality, though here too its harshness may taint Hobbes' political views, especially when we combine it with Hobbes' idea

> Please accept the $20 an hour raise.

> No, no, we really couldn't! You keep it. Spend it on yourselves.

Altruistic labor negotiations

POWER

Life according to Hobbes

that people are motivated not only by self-interest, but also by a desire for power. He says: "...I put for a general inclination of all mankind, a perpetual and restless desire of power after power, that ceaseth only in death."[2]

Like the authors of the American Declaration of Independence, Hobbes begins his essay with the assumption that all people are equal. But his reasons for this assumption are very different from those of the Founding Fathers, who believed that

369

our equality was a kind of moral state into which we were all created by our maker. Hobbes asserted the thesis of equality as a purely physical fact. Even the strongest or smartest among us is not <u>so</u> strong or <u>so</u> smart that two or three

weaker, dumber ones could not overcome him or her. One may have some slight advantage over another, but not enough to make a difference in the long run. We humans are, after all, more or less the same.

Now, given the fact that human nature is selfish, power-mongering, and equally distributed, Hobbes tries to imagine what human beings would be like in a "state of nature," that is, in a condition prior to any civil state, any rule by law. Concerning such a condition, Hobbes says:

> From this equality of ability, ariseth equality of hope in the attaining of our ends. And therefore if any two men desire the same thing, which nevertheless they cannot both enjoy, they become enemies; and in the way to their end, which is principally their own conservation, and sometimes their delectation only, endeavor to destroy, or subdue one another.
>
> . . . .
>
> Whatsoever therefore is consequent to a time of war, where every man is enemy to every man; the same is consequent to the time, wherein men live without other security, than what their own strength, and their own invention shall furnish them withal. In such condition, there is no place for industry; because the fruit thereof is uncertain: and consequently no culture of the earth; no navigation, nor use of the commodities that may be imported by sea; no commodious building; no instruments of moving, and removing, such things as require much force; no

knowledge of the face of the earth; no account of time; no arts;
no letters; no society; and which is worst of all, continual fear,
and danger of violent death; and the life of man, solitary, poor,
nasty, brutish, and short (pp. 98-99, 100).

Hobbes' five dwarves plus two

To this bleak and depressing picture, Hobbes now adds:

To this war of every man, against every man, this also is consequent; that nothing can be unjust. The notions of right and wrong,
justice and injustice have there no place. Where there is no common power, there is no law: where no law, no injustice. Force, and
fraud, are in war the two cardinal virtues. Justice, and injustice
are none of the faculties neither of the body, nor mind. If they
were, they might be in a man that were alone in the world, as well
as his senses, and passions. They are qualities, that relate to
men in society, not in solitude. It is consequent also to the same
condition, that there be no propriety, no dominion, no _mine_, and
thine distinct; but only that to be every man's, that he can get;
and for so long, as he can keep it. And thus much for the ill
condition, which man by mere nature is actually placed in;
though with a possibility to come out of it, consisting partly in
the passions, partly in his reason (pp. 101-102).

So Hobbes' view is this: Concepts like right and wrong, justice and
injustice, and "mine and thine" (property) are concepts generated
by _law_, hence dependent on law. In the absence of law, these
concepts cannot be meaningful. Furthermore, the concept of law is
itself dependent upon _power_. A law with no power behind it is not

371

authoritative because it cannot be enforced. This view is called "legal positivism," and according to it, justice is whatever legality _calls_ just, and what is legal has been established as legal by the powers that be and for just as long as

POWER
↓
Law
↓
justice / injustice
right / wrong
property / theft

they are able to enforce the law. According to this tradition (pretty much the tradition of Thrasymachus and Machiavelli), talk about "unjust laws" just doesn't make much sense. (In this tradition, calling a law _morally_ unjust doesn't carry any weight because the

Legal positivism

"moral sphere" is just a fantasy, the mental projection of an ideal legal system where the power of the rulers is replaced by the power of an imagined God.)

Notice at the end of the previous anxiously pessimistic passage there was one glimmer of hope. Hobbes said, "And thus much for the ill condition, which man by mere nature is actually placed in; though with a possibility to come out of it, consisting partly in the passions, partly in his reason."

The _passionate_ part of our self desperately desires to survive. (How

372

else could we acquire power and enjoy pleasure?) And there is a _natural right_ to attempt to do so. Hobbes writes:

> The RIGHT OF NATURE ... is the liberty each man hath, to use his own power, as he will himself, for the preservation of his own nature; that is to say, of his own life; and consequently, of doing anything, which in his own judgment, and reason, he shall conceive to be the aptest means thereunto (p. 103).

Notice that for Hobbes, there is only _one_ natural right, not a great group of them, as we find in our Bill of Rights, Declaration of Independence, and Constitution. However, it isn't perfectly clear how Hobbes arrives at even this _one_ right, given his system in which right and wrong can be established only by laws, which in turn can be established only by power. In other words, are there really _any_ rights in nature? (This is another version of the is/ought problem because a "right" is a _value_. Perhaps the best way to put this for Hobbes is that everyone naturally values his or her own survival. It is perhaps the only _natural_ value.)

Now, unfortunately for me, _you_ also have a natural right to try to preserve yourself, with the following consequences:

> And because the condition of man, ... is a condition of war of every one against every one; in which case every one is governed by his own reason; and there is nothing he can make use of, that may not be a help unto him, in preserving his life against his enemies; it followeth, that in such a condition, every man has a right to every thing; even to one another's body. And

Two people pursuing their natural right

therefore, as long as this natural right of every man to every thing endureth, there can be no security to any man, how strong or wise soever he be, of living out the time, which nature ordinarily alloweth men to live (p. 103).

Hobbes assumes that in a state of nature, there will be a general scarcity of goods. Because there are not enough goods for everyone's survival and flourishing in a state of nature, each becomes an enemy of all others. In this condition, even though I have a _right_ to try to survive, in fact, there isn't much likelihood of my lasting very long.

So, based on our passions alone, we would not survive long enough to enjoy the goal of the natural right. But this is where our _reason_ comes into play. It is associated with what Hobbes calls "natural law."

A LAW OF NATURE, ... is a precept or general rule, found out by reason, by which a man is forbidden to do that, which is destructive of his life, or taketh away the means of preserving the same; and to omit that, by which he thinketh it may be best preserved (p. 103).

Because none of us has much chance of survival if we each blindly pursue our own natural right, we must appeal to our reason and the "natural law" it discovers:

And consequently it is a precept, or general rule of reason, _that_ _every_ _man_, _ought_ _to_ _endeavor_ _peace_, _as_ _far_ _as_ _he_ _has_ _hope_ _of_ _obtaining_ _it_; _and_ _when_ _he_ _cannot_ _obtain_ _it_, _that_ _he_ _may_ _seek_, _and_ _use_, _all_ _helps_, _and_ _advantages_ _of_ _war_. The first branch of which rule, containeth the first, and fundamental law of nature; which is, _to_ _seek_ _peace_, _and_ _follow_ _it_. The second, the sum of the right of nature; which is, _by_ _all_ _means_ _we_ _can_, _to_ _defend_ _ourselves_.
From this fundamental law of nature, by which men are commanded to endeavor peace, is derived this second law; _that_ _a_ _man_ _be_ _willing_, _when_ _others_ _are_ _so_ _too_, _as_ _far_ _forth_, _as_ _for_ _peace_, _and_ _defence_ _of_ _himself_ _he_ _shall_ _think_ _it_ _necessary_, _to_ _lay_ _down_ _this_ _right_ _to_ _all_ _things_; _and_ _be_ _contented_ _with_ _so_ _much_ _liberty_ _against_ _other_ _men_, _as_ _he_ _would_ _allow_ _other_ _men_ _against_ _himself_. For as long as every man holdeth this right, of doing any thing he liketh; so long are all men in the condition

of war. But if other men will not lay down their right, as well as he; then there is no reason for anyone, to divest himself of his: for that were to expose himself to prey, which no man is bound to, rather than to dispose himself to peace (pp. 103-104).

So this is the foundation of Hobbes' <u>social</u> <u>contract</u>. My natural right justifies my use of violence against you if I perceive the use of such violence as being in the interest of my survival. Unfortunately for me, <u>your</u> use of violence against me is equally justified. So I agree to renounce my right to use violence against you if you agree to renounce your right to use violence against me. However, our contract is conditional because each of us will break it the moment we think the other is not going to hold to it. But this does not provide a very stable peace, especially if Hobbes is right to attribute to each of us

a selfish and power-mongering nature. If I see any advantage to myself in breaking the contract, I will do it. None of us can sleep very easily. In fact, none of us dares sleep at all in this tenuous peace.

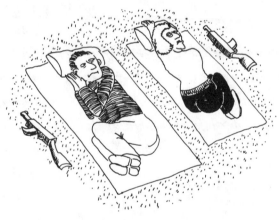

None of us can sleep very easily.

The solution to this dilemma requires another step in the contract. All of us must agree to transfer our right to violence and our right to sovereignty over ourselves to a mutually agreed-upon sovereign (a parliament or a monarch), who now has absolute political authority over us. In exchange for absolute power (including an army), this sovereign promises to pass laws that create a state of peace.

Basically, what this means is that the sovereign promises to restrain and punish anyone who breaks the initial part of the contract and uses violence against any other member of this newly created artificial body, the state.

The sovereign

Hobbes realizes that there are no guarantees that the sovereign won't abuse its absolute power. In fact, it's almost certain that the sovereign _will_ do so, given his, her, or their egoistic propensities. Nevertheless, even abused authority is better than no authority, according to Hobbes. Furthermore, it is hoped that the sovereign will use both its passion (the egoistic side) and its reason (the natural law) and realize that a peaceful state is beneficial to _it_ as well because otherwise the angry populace may revolt and kill the sovereign. Notice, however,

that in Hobbes' political system, revolt is never legitimate _unless it succeeds_, because only power legitimates for Hobbes. However, not even the legitimate absolute tyrant can pass a law that succeeds in taking away my natural right. This is because that right is inalienable. No law can remove my right to resist law if law tries to deprive me of my life.

So, returning to the "big questions" with which we began this chapter, we see that for Hobbes, the state is an artifice (a monster, a "Leviathan"), but a <u>necessary</u> one. Legitimate authority is empowered authority. Political bodies themselves determine what counts as just or unjust, so in one sense, they cannot be unjust. Yet even when they create a <u>sense</u> of injustice, they are almost always better than their alternative. This is the reason we accept the gun constantly aimed at us and

Leviathan –
The best show in town

the threat of state violence. No matter how brutal the state is, it is the best show in town. Its alternative is chaos, misery, and death, a condition wherein life is "solitary, poor, nasty, brutish, and short." <u>Any</u> state is better than no state.

John Locke

Locke, writing fifty years after Hobbes, used much of the same language as did Hobbes, but with very different meanings. For example, Locke too discusses a "state of nature," but for him, such a state is the <u>moral</u> state into which all of us are born by virtue of being God's creatures. Hobbes had obviously intentionally kept God out of political theory, not because Hobbes was an atheist (he may or may not have been), but because he thought God belonged no more in political science than he did in physics and because Hobbes was sick

of tyrants justifying their power by something called "divine right."
But though Locke too was against the so-called divine right of kings,
he had no such qualms against grounding his political theory in a
religious belief. For him,
God's power plays a role similar to that of secular power
in Hobbes' theory, so for
Locke, God created humans
and gave them basic rights,
the right to "life, health,
liberty, and possessions." Each
of us is born into a moral
"state of nature" in which
these rights are ours, along
with certain moral obligations,
which Locke calls the "law
of nature," which, as in
Hobbes, is a law of <u>reason.</u>

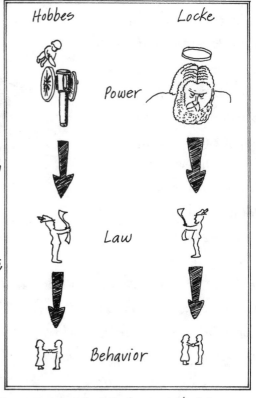

To understand political
power right, and derive
it from its original, we
must consider what state all men are naturally in, and that is a
state of perfect freedom to order their actions and dispose of their
possessions and persons as they think fit, within the bounds of
the law of nature, without asking leave or depending upon the
will of any other man....
   The state of nature has a law of nature to govern it which obliges
every one; and reason which is that law, teaches all mankind who
will but consult it that, being all equal and independent, no one
ought to harm another in his life, health, liberty, or possessions;
for men being all the workmanship of one omnipotent and in-
finitely wise Maker — all the servants of one sovereign master,
sent into the world by his order, and about his business —they
are his property whose workmanship they are, made to last during
his, not one another's, pleasure; and being furnished with like

faculties, sharing all in one community of nature, there cannot be supposed any such subordination among us that may authorize us to destroy another, as if we were made for one another's uses as the inferior ranks of creatures are for ours. [3]

Hobbes had made a particular point of claiming that there is no such thing as "natural property." Property itself could be created only by laws. In the state of nature, there were no laws. Hence, for Hobbes, property is, as Marx was later to call it, a "legal fiction." But, as we have seen, for Locke, God's law creates natural property. Let's look at this curious idea.

According to the biblical account, God created the earth and provided it with natural resources for the benefit of humankind. As was indicated earlier, Locke, like Hobbes, was anxious to counter monarchical claims of divine right to property, and he used the biblical account to do so, then added a philosophical touch of his own. In his Two Treatises on Government, he wrote, "... the earth and all that is therein ... belongs to mankind in common ... and ... nobody has originally a private dominion, exclusive of the rest of mankind"(p. 134). Now, the one uniquely natural piece of property we each have is our own body. The property right we have to our bodies can be extended to that which is created by our bodies' labor.

Though the earth and all inferior creatures be common to all men, yet every man has a property in his own person; this nobody has any right to but himself. The labour of his body and the work of his hands, we may say, are properly his. Whatsoever then he removes out of the state that nature hath provided and left it in, he hath mixed his labour with, and joined to it something that is his own, and thereby makes it his property. It being by him removed from the common state nature hath placed it in, it hath by this labour something annexed to it that excludes the common right of other men. For this labour being the unquestionable property of the labourer, no man but he can have a right to what that is once joined to, at least where there is enough and as good left in common for others....

It will perhaps be objected to this that "if gathering the acorns, or other fruits of the earth, etc., makes a right to them, then any one may engross as much as he will." To which I answer: not so. The same law of nature that does by this means give us property does also bound that property, too. "God has given us all things richly" (I Tim. vi. 17), is the voice of reason confirmed by inspiration. But how far has he given it us? To enjoy. As much as any one can make use of to any advantage of life before it spoils, so much he may by his labour fix a property in; whatever is beyond this is more than his share, and belongs to others. ...

I think it is plain that property in that, too, is acquired as the former. As much land as a man tills, plants, improves, cultivates, and can use the product of, so much is his property. ...

Nobody could think himself injured by the drinking of another man, though he took a good draught, who had a whole river of the same water left him to quench his thirst; and the case of land and water, where there is enough for both, is perfectly the same (pp. 134, 136, 137).

Then one may accumulate as much "natural property" as one can use without its spoiling, as long as one leaves enough for everyone else. This idea reveals a tremendous attitudinal difference between Locke and Hobbes. Hobbes' political philosophy presupposes a condition of scarcity. Locke's presupposes a condition of abundance. Locke's picture of human nature is much more generous than Hobbes'.

We might consider the possibility that Locke and Hobbes are both right. Under conditions of abundance, altruism, generosity, and magnanimity might be natural virtues; and under conditions of scarcity, stinginess and coldheartedness might be natural. When I was a boy

The state of nature
(According to Hobbes)

The state of nature
(According to Locke)

growing up in the fifties, there was a campaign to get people to build backyard A-bomb shelters. At that time, there was a lot of talk concerning a hypothetical post-nuclear attack scenario when social order had broken down and the food and water supply had been contaminated with radiation. The typical question was, would you have the right to shoot your neighbor who had foolishly failed to build a shelter for himself and was now trying to get into your already crowded shelter? The general consensus was that you would be justified in doing so. This was Hobbes' world, not Locke's. And I suppose that if your neighbor tried to get ahold of the gallon of uncontaminated water that would keep you and your children alive, you might well defend it with violence.

Protecting your backyard A-bomb shelter
from covetous neighbors

Back to Locke's

concept of "natural property." When he turns to his analysis of money, he says: "And thus came in the use of money — some lasting thing that men might keep without spoiling, and that, by mutual consent, men would take in exchange for the truly useful but perishable supports of life"(p.144). So there is nothing wrong with hoarding money, or

What are you complaining about? You have plenty for your meager needs.

passing it along to your sons and daughters, as long as you leave enough for others, because "gold and silver may be hoarded up without injury to anyone." This doctrine was very convenient for Locke and his well-to-do friends and somewhat counteracted the radicalness of his view that the land belongs to whoever tills it. But it failed to recognize that the excessive accumulation of wealth is a form of power that can be used to undermine that moral state of equality into which we were all supposed to be born. It is well known that Locke's political philosophy was one of the major blueprints for the American Founding Fathers. Some think that Locke's failure to combat the possibility of unjust accumulation of wealth infected our own political system. (Later we will talk again of economic justice in the "good society.")

Locke believed that his theory of our natural moral status (the state of nature) entailed a theory of justifiable punishment. He wrote:

And thus in the state of nature one man comes by a power over another; but yet no absolute or arbitrary power to use a criminal, when he has got him in his hands, according to the passionate heats or boundless extravagancy of his own will; but only to retribute to him, so far as calm reason and conscience dictate, what is proportionate to his transgression, which is so much as may serve for reparation and restraint; for these two are the only reasons why one man may lawfully do harm to another, which is that we call punishment. In transgressing the law of nature, the offender declares himself to live by another rule than that of reason and common equity, which is that measure God has set to the actions of men for their mutual security; and so he becomes dangerous to mankind, the tie which is to secure them from injury and violence being slighted and broken by him. Which being a trespass against the whole species and the peace and safety of it provided for by the law of nature . . . . _every_ _man_ _hath_ _a_ _right_ _to_ _punish_ _the_ _offender_ _and_ _be_ _executioner_ _of_ _the_ _law_ _of_ _nature_ (pp. 124 - 125).

So in the state of nature, each of us has the right to our "life, liberty, health, and property." If any person violates those rights, that person alienates himself from the state of nature and thereby forfeits his own natural rights. He has thus _earned_ a punishment, which ought to be meted out. On the principle that "the punishment must fit the crime"
(Gilbert and Sullivan), even capital punishment is possible in the state of nature:

By the same reason may a man in the state of nature punish the lesser breaches of that law. It will perhaps be demanded: with death? I answer: Each transgression may be punished to that degree and with

383

so much severity as will suffice to make it an ill bargain to the offender, give him cause to repent, and terrify others from doing the like. Every offence that can be committed in the state of nature may in the state of nature be also punished equally, and as far forth as it may in a commonwealth. . . . (p.126).

(Those who are against capital punishment today may find Locke's views too harsh, but keep in mind that he was very progressive for his time on this score because in the eighteenth century, there were dozens of crimes that could be punished with death. Locke has at least reduced capital punishment to apply to only one crime — murder.) We see here that Locke's theory of justice is _retributive_ (the criminal has earned the punishment with his acts and we owe it to him), and _preventative_ (he will be restrained from committing similar crimes). In terms of _distributive_ justice, Locke's state of nature is a meritocracy. That is, one may own only as much property as one merits by virtue of one's labor (or inherits from the labor of one's ancestors).

In Thomas Hobbes' political theory, the conditions under which the citizens would probably revolt were pretty predictable, but there could be no such thing as _legitimate_ revolt because legitimacy is determined by law, and the sovereign has been given the authority to create law by the social contract. In Locke, however, there is a very clear doctrine of legitimate revolution, once again grounded in our God-given moral condition, the state of nature. Locke wrote:

There is, therefore, secondly, another way whereby governments are dissolved, and that is when the legislative or the prince, either of them, act contrary to their trust.
... The legislative acts against the trust reposed in them when they endeavour to invade the property of the subject, and to make themselves or any part of the community masters or arbitrary disposers of the lives, liberties, or fortunes of the people.
... since it can never be supposed to be the will of the society that the legislative should have a power to destroy that which every one designs to secure by entering into society, and for which the people submitted themselves to legislators of their own making. Whenever

the legislators endeavour to take away and destroy the property of the people, or to reduce them to slavery under arbitrary power, they put themselves into a state of war with the people who are there-upon absolved from any further obedience (p. 233).

So the function of the political state is to guarantee our moral state. In this sense, the political state is potentially superior to the state of nature because the latter lacks impartial judges, precise laws, and sufficient power to uphold the moral law. The justification of the political state is the consent of its citizens. The citizens consent to submit to political authority only with the proviso that such political authority will do whatever is necessary to protect our natural rights. This is Locke's "social contract." But the citizen is bound to the contract only so long as the government upholds its end of the contract. Locke thought that the populace should not go lightly into a condition of revolt. Because of the seriousness of such a condition, all sorts of attempts should be made to correct the abuses of power before a revolution is declared. But if the state not only fails to uphold the citizens' rights to life, health, liberty, and possessions, but also becomes the violator of those rights, then revolution is justified. Locke was writing at a

What? The cost of postage stamps has gone up a penny? That's it! To the barricades!

Revolution should not be entered into lightly.

time when King James II tried to impose Catholicism in Britain, which provoked "the Glorious Revolution," a bloodless civil war that ended in a
parliamentary victory and the flight of the King. It is somewhat ironic that
the next use of Locke's doctrine of legitimate revolution was by the American
colonists revolting against the British government of King George III.
The Founding Fathers wrote in the American Declaration of Independence:

> We hold these truths to be self-evident, that all men are created equal;
> that they are endowed by their Creator with certain unalienable
> rights; that among these are life, liberty, and the pursuit of happi-
> ness. That, to secure these rights, governments are instituted among
> men, deriving their just powers from the consent of the governed;
> that, whenever any form of government becomes destructive of
> these ends, it is the right of the people to alter or to abolish it,
> and to institute a new government, laying its foundation on such
> principles, and organizing its powers in such form, as to them shall
> seem most likely to effect their safety and happiness.

As was mentioned before, the United States is sometimes thought of as
a giant Lockean experiment, containing all the best features of Locke's
political theory (government justified by consent of the citizens, basic
rights guaranteed by law, recognition of moral and legal equality, and

the recognition of the right to revolt if government abrogates its duties), but also suffering from some of the defects of his theory (the contradiction of separating religion and politics, yet grounding political rights in a theological conception of the human being, the lack of a theory of distributive justice based on anything other than merit or inheritance, the failure to recognize that the accumulation of power in the form of wealth can jeopardize the democratic foundations). Attempts have been made to address some of these problems through the passage of laws legalizing labor unions and creating a graduated income tax, among others.

Jean-Jacques Rousseau

Rousseau (1712-1778) stands approximately to the French Revolution as Locke stands to the American Revolution, though the United States probably continues today to be more of a Lockean experiment than France does a Rousseauvian one. (And the Soviet Union is probably even less of a Marxian experiment.)

Rousseau, like Locke, believed that all humans are born free and autonomous and that the only legitimate government is one that preserves and maximizes that condition. Again, like Locke, he believed that such legitimacy can come about only through consent to a social contract. However, he believed that such legitimacy in fact existed nowhere in his time and that even the English parliamentarians deceived themselves concerning their own freedom. In fact, we began this chapter with Rousseau's words, "Man is born free, and everywhere he is in chains." Indeed he thought that men were also born good but had been corrupted by society. Let's take a look at his diagnosis of the political situation of his time and his prescription for it.

Men are born good but are corrupted by society.

Rousseau too begins his analysis with an account of the "state of nature." Like Hobbes, and unlike Locke, Rousseau claims that in a condition outside of the social order, there would be no <u>morality</u> (no "ought," no "duty"). However, it is possible to talk about <u>virtues</u> in the state of nature. For example, Rousseau takes it that <u>self-love</u> (<u>amour de soi</u>) is a <u>natural</u> <u>virtue</u>, a natural good. Anyone who lacks it is in some sense perverted and is incapable of truly moral development. (Notice that Jesus' moral teaching — "Love thy neighbor as thy self" — also presupposes

Hiya big boy!

Amour de soi?

self-love as the necessary condition of morality.) Similarly, according to Rousseau, there is (contrary to Hobbes' claim) a natural pity or pain at the misfortune of others. Unfortunately, traditional societies pervert the first of these virtues (self-love) and invert the second (pity). Self-love is turned into <u>pride</u> (<u>amour propre</u>), and pity is transformed into its opposite – delight taken in others' misery. Pride results from anxious reflection about oneself and the need to feel superior. This need induces one to compare oneself forever with others, to the extent that one finds one's most exquisite pleasure in the misfortune or inferiority of others. Pride and envy are encouraged everywhere by traditional social organization, but in truth, they prevent one from developing into a full person.

Pleasure derived from the unhappiness of others

This speculation leads Rousseau to the view (in _Émile_) that a truly correct education of a child would require the child to be as far from society's corrupting influences as possible. The child should be reared in as nearly a "state of nature" as is possible (hence, the understandable but misleading attribution to Rousseau of the philosophy of "back to nature"). In this primary state, the child will be allowed to develop her own natural virtues. Such a child, left to her own devices, learns through <u>trial</u> <u>and</u> <u>error</u>, not theories, through <u>facts</u>, not words, through <u>sensations</u> <u>and</u> <u>feelings</u>, not abstractions. This child is freed from the necessity of holding "opinions" and lives a happy, self-sufficient, timeless existence unaware of artificial needs or worries about the future. The child will be taught to read, but the only book allowed in her education will be <u>Robinson</u> <u>Crusoe</u>!

Those who have read only _Émile_ sometimes think that Rousseau was calling for the abolition or minimalization of the state and demanding a "return to nature" for all. But they have failed to see that, for Rousseau, if one remained at the state of natural virtues, one would fail to develop fully one's humanity. This requires the development of the virtues into morality, and morality and politics go hand in hand. The

Child reading <u>Robinson Crusoe</u> (Classic Comics version)

move from natural virtuousness to morality involves the development of our social being. Only by filling out the social side of our nature (which was necessarily underdeveloped in childhood) can we find our fullest freedom. But if society is to be a <u>natural</u> extension of ourself, it must be consistent with our natural virtues and with our <u>free</u> and <u>rational</u> status. (A society founded on sheer force would be both unnatural and unjust.) The natural and just society will be constituted by the social contract, which Rousseau describes:

> The clauses of this contract are so determined by the nature of the act that the slightest modification would make them vain and ineffective; so that, although they have perhaps never been formally set forth, they are everywhere the same and everywhere tacitly admitted and recognized, until, on the violation of the social compact, each regains his original rights and resumes his natural liberty, while losing the conventional liberty in favor of which he renounced it.

These clauses, properly understood, may be reduced to one — the total alienation of each associate, together with all his rights, to the whole community; for, in the first place, as each gives himself absolutely, the conditions are the same for all; and, this being so, no one has any interest in making them burdensome to others.

Moreover, the alienation being without reserve, the union is as perfect as it can be, and no associate has anything more to demand: for, if the individuals retained certain rights, as there would be no common superior to decide between them and the public, each, being on one point his own judge, would ask to be so on all; the state of nature would thus continue, and the association would necessarily become inoperative or tyrannical.

Finally, each man, in giving himself to all, gives himself to nobody; and as there is no associate over which he does not acquire the same right as he yields others over himself, he gains an equivalent for everything he loses, and an increase of force for the preservation of what he has.

If then we discard from the social compact what is not of its essence, we shall find that it reduces itself to the following terms:

"Each of us puts his person and all his power in common under the supreme direction of the general will, and, in our corporate capacity, we receive each member as an indivisible part of the whole."

At once, in place of the individual personality of each contracting party, this act of association creates a corporate and collective body, composed of as many members as the assembly contains voters, and receiving from this act its unity, its common identity, its life, and its will. [4]

A number of problems leap out at us from this statement. First, notice that Rousseau completely rejects the notion of <u>representative democracy</u>. According to him, in a true democracy, all citizens must vote on all issues of public interest.

Sovereignty, for the same reason as makes it inalienable, cannot be represented; it lies essentially in the general will, and will does not admit of representation: it is either the same, or other; there is no intermediate possibility. The deputies of the people, therefore, are not and cannot be its representatives: they are merely its stewards, and can carry through no definitive acts. Every law the people has not ratified in person is null and void — is, in fact, not a law. The people of England regards itself as free; but it is grossly mistaken; it is free only during the election of members of parliament. As soon as they are elected, slavery overtakes it, and it is nothing. The use it makes of the short moments of liberty it enjoys shows indeed that it deserves to lose them (p. 240).

Notice that this means that a legitimate political body must be very limited in size because all its members must be capable of convening at regular intervals. Rousseau was from Switzerland, and his model is similar to the democracy of the local Swiss cantons (though they did not completely legalize voting on national issues for women

All in favor of giving women the vote say "AYE."

Nay!
Nay!
Nay!
Nay!
Nay!

The hills are alive with the sound of democracy.

until 1981, and as late as April 29, 1990, the male citizens of Appenzell denied the vote to women in local elections!) or of the town meetings of New England. A country as massive as the United States could not possibly be a true democracy for Rousseau — at least, not in his own day. Ironically, today, with our sophisticated technology, it would be at least theoretically possible to engage every American on every vote. Imagine that Monday evenings were set aside for politics. For three hours, the TV stations would be dedicated to debating the political issues, followed by a vote, in which each legal voter would punch his or her social security number into a computer and would vote on each issue. These would be instantly tallied and the results known immediately.

Another problem in Rousseau's political schema is the apparent contradiction between his claim that only in the political body does one find one's

And our fourteenth topic tonight: Should dogs weighing less than five pounds require collars?

SNORE

SNORE

Whatever happened to Monday night football?

Monday evening TV

true freedom and his assertion that one must transfer all of one's rights to the whole political body and accept as one's own will what he calls "the general will." Rousseau was aware of the problem. He wrote:

> When the State is instituted, residence constitutes consent; to dwell within its territory is to submit to the Sovereign.
>
> Apart from this primitive contract, the vote of the majority always binds all the rest. This follows from the contract itself. But it is asked how a man can be both free and forced to conform to wills that are not his own. How are the opponents at once free and subject to laws they have not agreed to?
>
> I retort that the question is wrongly put. The citizen gives his consent to all the laws, including those which are passed in spite of his opposition, and even those which punish him when he dares to break any of them. The constant will of all the members of the State is the general will; by virtue of it they are citizens and free. When in the popular assembly a law is proposed, what the people is asked is not exactly whether it approves or rejects the proposal, but whether it is in conformity with the general will, which is their will. Each man, in giving his vote, states his opinion on that point; and the general will is found by counting votes. When therefore the opinion that is contrary to my own prevails, this proves neither more nor less

than that I was mistaken, and that what I thought to be the general will was not so. If my particular opinion had carried the day I should have achieved the opposite of what was my will; and it is in that case that I should not have been free (p. 250).

In other words, in consenting to live in a state (and tacit consent is given by mere residency ["love it or leave it"]), one is not only consenting to abide by the will of the people, but one is recognizing that that will _is_ the state. Therefore, every vote is a vote for the general will, even if one's vote on any particular issue is overridden. So even if I vote "No" on Proposition P, and Proposition P wins the majority of the votes, then I have actually voted _for_ P in a general sense even though I voted against it in fact. Therefore, I can happily follow it as a law even if I thought it was a bad idea when it was first proposed. Or, to put it another way, all legitimate political activity must transcend individual opinion and selfish desire. The only non-despotic way of determining the general will is through a democratic act determined by majority rule. Therefore, I am not only bound by the outcome of such an act, but I recognize

The general will

that its outcome is my desire _qua_ social being.

Of course, Rousseau's readers must decide for themselves if this is a real insight or mere sophistry.

John Stuart Mill

We have just seen that according to J.J. Rousseau, individuals come into their full humanity precisely by alienating their individual wills to the general will (or by submitting it to the general will, thereby identifying their individual wills with the general will). John Stuart Mill (1806-1873), whose utilitarian moral philosophy has already been discussed, three-quarters of a century after Rousseau and on the other side of the Channel from him, had a political agenda that was exactly the opposite from that of Rousseau. Mill saw his goal as that of distinguishing between the public and the private. He believed there was a realm that was genuinely the concern of society (and hence of the body politic). But he believed there was also a realm that was genuinely the concern of the individual, and in that realm, politics had no business. Even if with 100 percent unanimity the "general will" conceived as its business interfering in the legitimately private

The private vs. the public

sphere, it would do so only by doing violence to the truly human charter. On this, Mill wrote:

> Let us suppose, therefore, that the government is entirely at one with the people, and never thinks of exerting any power of coercion unless in agreement with what it conceives to be their voice. But I deny the right of the people to exercise such coercion, either

by themselves or by their government. The power itself is illegitimate. The best government has no more title to it than the worst. It is as noxious, or more noxious, when exerted in accordance with public opinion, than when in opposition to it. If all mankind minus one, were of one opinion, and only one person were of the contrary opinion, mankind would be no more justified in silencing that one person, than he, if he had the power, would be justified in silencing mankind. [5]

In order to draw the distinction between the public and the private, Mill formulated a principle he called "the principle of liberty." Mill began his essay, On Liberty, with this assertion:

The object of this Essay is to assert one very simple principle, as entitled to govern absolutely the dealings of society with the individual in the way of compulsion and control, whether the means used be physical force in the form of legal penalties, or the moral coercion of public opinion. That principle is, that the sole end for which mankind are warranted, individually or collectively, in interfering with the liberty of action of any of their number, is self-protection. That the only purpose for which power can be rightfully exercised over any member of a civilized community, against his will, is to prevent harm to others. His own good, either physical or moral, is not a sufficient warrant. He cannot rightfully be compelled to do or forbear because it will be better for him to do so, because it will make him happier, because, in the opinions of others, to do so would be wise, or even right. These are good reasons for remonstrating with him, or reasoning with him, or persuading him, or entreating him, but not for compelling him, or visiting him with any evil in case he do otherwise. [6]

In other words, the body politic, the general will, or whatever one wants to call political authority can legitimately restrain the action of individual members of the society only if those actions harm other members of the society. What Mill is ruling out here is what is called "state paternalism." Or, to put it another way, he is ruling out "victimless crimes." That is, the state has no right to criminalize behavior it deems harmful to the agent but to no one else. This means that drunkenness or drug abuse in the privacy of one's home cannot be a crime, nor prostitution, nor the reading of pornography, nor the refusal to wear a helmet while riding one's motorcycle, among other activities.

Mill's principle strikes an intuitive cord with me. There are certain things I could do or say or think that I claim are nobody's business but my own and over which society has no legitimate authority. Nevertheless, there seem to me to be serious problems with Mill's principle. First, the social world has become much more complicated

state paternalism,
or government as daddy

since Mill's time. Social welfare schemes and tax schemes have become so entwined today that the motorcyclist who foolishly opts to forego a helmet in the name of "coolness" no longer involves just himself when he enters the hospital for brain surgery. Rather, the price of his surgery is charged partially to <u>me</u>, the taxpayer.

A drunken male prostitute riding his motorcycle
without a helmet in the privacy of his own home

397

This is also somewhat true concerning the abuse of alcohol and drugs. And some studies conclude that there is a significant connection between the pornography industry and violent crimes. If this is true, then the demarcation between the private and the public begins to deteriorate. Furthermore, there is a conceptual difficulty with Mill's notion of "harm to others" that emerges as soon as we try to define "harm." If we construe it as merely "physical harm," we shall have circumscribed it too narrowly because it will exclude theft, fraud, and, in rare cases, even rape. As the contemporary American philosopher Richard Taylor says:

> If we say, for example, that <u>harming</u> a man consists not merely of injury to his body, but to any of his deepest interests then of course we bring such things as theft and fraud within its meaning. Men do have a deep interest in the security of their property as well as of their persons. But unfortunately, men have <u>other</u> deep interests as well which no believer in freedom supposes for a minute should never be foiled.
>
> Thus, there are men who have a deep interest in such things as religion, patriotism, public manners, the preservation of wildlife, and so on, without end. Now if we say that no one shall be permitted to do anything that would foil, frustrate, or damage any such interest held by anyone, this will be about equivalent to saying that no one may do anything at all. The whole of the criminal law would be summed up in saying that all actions are

Officer, that man is parting his hair in the middle. That does irreparable harm to my sense of propriety. Arrest him!

prohibited. And a principle having that consequence can hardly be called a principle of liberty. [7]

The solution will have to be that it would fall to actual courts of law to determine exactly what constitutes harm, using the concept of criminal law to make the appropriate distinctions. The problem with that approach is that the principle of liberty was meant by Mill to determine criminal law, not the other way around, or the whole process becomes circular.

Mill extended his principle of liberty to encompass such areas as freedom of thought, freedom of expression, and freedom of assembly. No government, not even a pure democracy, can legitimately legislate against these, according to Mill. He would have approved of the American idea of a "Bill of Rights" that in fact if not in principle somehow transcends public opinion. It is clear that, for him, democracy was the best form of government. But it was not an end in itself; rather, it was the most likely means of guaranteeing the interests of both the public and the private domains. And these, contrary to Rousseau, not even democracy could override.

Majority rule

This is the doctrine of _laisser-faire_ or "hands off" (literally, "to let alone"). There are certain realms where government has no business, except to protect the existence of precisely those realms. Otherwise, government must "butt out" of them. Mill extended this doctrine of _laisser-faire_ throughout his social philosophy. Not only must there be no state interference in the inner life and harmless activities of the citizens, but in general "_Laisser-faire_ ... should be the general practice: every departure from it, unless required by some great good, is a certain evil." [8] Among other applications, this means that in most respects, the government ought to keep its hands off the marketplace, allowing a system of free enterprise unhampered by state controls. Mill wrote:

> We have observed that, as a general rule, the business of life is better performed when those who have an immediate interest in it are left to take their own course, uncontrolled either by the mandate of the law or by the meddling of any public functionary. The persons, or some of the persons, who do the work, are likely to be better judges than the government, of the means of attaining the particular end at which they aim (p. 952).

Even though John Stuart Mill is thought of as "the saint of liberalism," the doctrine of _laisser-faire_ today is usually associated with the economic policy of conservatism. Still, in spite of his enthusiasm for economic _laisser-faire_ policy, he thought that deviations from it were required:

> But if the workman is generally the best selector of means, can it be affirmed with the same universality, that the consumer, or person served, is the most competent judge of the end? Is the buyer always qualified to judge of the commodity? If not, the presumption in favor of the competition of the market does not apply to the case; and if the commodity be one, in the quality of which society has much at stake, the balance of advantages may be in favour of some mode and degree of intervention, by the authorized representatives of the collective interest of the state.
> Now, the proposition that the consumer is a competent judge

400

of the commodity, can be admitted only with numerous abatements and exceptions. He is generally the best judge (though even this is not true universally) of the material objects produced for his use. These are destined to supply some physical want, or gratify some taste or inclination, respecting which wants or inclinations there is no appeal from the person who feels them; or they are the means and appliances of some occupation, for the use of the persons engaged in it, who may be presumed to be judges of the things required in their own habitual employment. But there are other things of the worth of which the demand of the market is by no means a test; things of which the utility does not consist in ministering to inclinations, nor in serving the daily uses of life, and the want of which is least felt where the need is greatest. This is peculiarly true of those things which are chiefly useful as tending to raise the character of human beings (pp. 952-953).

Such a policy of legitimate state intervention not only justifies for Mill a governmental subsidy of the arts, but it could be used in today's world to protect citizens from the contamination of dangerous pesticides and to protect the environment from the competition of vicious profiteers who see their short-term profit as necessitating the destruction of the natural world. To quote Mill once more, "The uncultivated cannot be competent judges of cultivation"(p.953).

Conclusion

We began this chapter by noting the fact that much of our behavior is controlled by rules and laws enforced by a not-so-subtle threat of the use of force against violators. The question was posed, why do we put up with it? Well, I think at one level we can accept Hobbes' answer to this question: putting up with the regulation of our behavior by a threat of force is better than the radical alternative – anarchy. But this doesn't mean (as it seems to for Hobbes) that we should settle for just _any_ form of government. Exactly what we can reasonably expect from a government depends very much on whether the Hobbesian (and Freudian) picture of the self is true. Is the self essentially a selfish atom, naturally seeking only its own gratification and acting cooperatively only when forced to do so? Or is the self naturally social, cooperative, and sympathetic to the plight of others, as Locke and Marx would have us believe?

The self as a selfish atom

If the former picture is true, the political state *is* an artificial creation, and a culture without excessive repression (and also excessive guilt, in the Freudian account) is impossible. Furthermore, some kind of "noble lie" or myth will be required to keep the citizens in line. If the latter, more optimistic picture is true, and we are naturally social, then society is not artificial or *necessarily* excessively repressive; and reason, rather than myth, should be able to represent, explain, and justify social values to its citizens. But which picture is correct?

This is a tough question. One could spend

The noble lie keeping citizens in line

a lifetime pondering it and testing different hypotheses concerning it (though Freud thought the issue could be settled in twenty minutes of observing children's play in the sandbox). My own view is that no believable account of human nature corresponds to one or the other of these pictures. But in a situation of scarcity, Hobbes is more or less right, and in situations of abundance, Locke is more or less right.

Children at play

The British anthropologist Colin Turnbull in his book, The <u>Mountain</u> <u>People</u>, has described the effect of virulent scarcity on a particular culture, the Ik. These people seem to have no sympathy for each other, they are selfish and vicious, parents withhold food from their children, children steal from their parents and take advantage of the feebleness of their grandparents. Yet in his other book, The <u>Forest</u> <u>People</u>, Turnbull describes another culture, the BaMbuti, Pygmies of the Congolese rainforest, who have a fairly easy time filling their basic material needs and whose members are social, cooperative, and sympathetic. Turnbull's data don't <u>prove</u> anything, but they can give us hope that when our fundamental material needs are met, a more positive aspect of human nature can be activated. Turnbull's descriptions also lead us to fear that when those basic needs are not met, a more sinister side of human nature may be activated. And if <u>that</u> is true, then the governments

403

role cannot be simply that of protecting us from each other (following Hobbes), but must also be that of promoting a certain moral or spiritual state (following Locke). On my hypothesis — though not explicitly on Locke's — this means that the government must also promote a certain level of material well-being. But this cannot be done in an authoritarian mode. Hobbes, Locke, and Rousseau are right to say that the key concept of legitimacy is _consent_, though it is problematical exactly how this concept is to be understood. One of the primary features of political theory must be the development of a theory of consent.

All this leads us to the topic of _justice_, which is a key concept of social philosophy, to be dealt with in the next chapter.

Notes

1. Plato, _The Republic_, in _Great Dialogues of Plato_, W. H. D. Rouse, trans. (New York: New American Library, 1956), pp. 165-166. Unless otherwise stated, all subsequent quotes from _The Republic_ in this chapter are from this edition.

2. Thomas Hobbes, _Leviathan: Or the Matter, Forme and Power of a Commonwealth Ecclesiasticall and Civil_ (New York: Collier Books, 1962), p. 80. Unless otherwise stated, all subsequent quotes from Hobbes in this chapter are from this source.

3. John Locke, _The Second Treatise of Civil Government_, in _Two Treatises of Government_ (New York: Hafner, 1964), pp. 122-124. Unless otherwise stated, all subsequent quotes from Locke in this chapter are from this source.

4. Jean-Jacques Rousseau, _The Social Contract and Discourses_, G. D. H. Cole, trans. (London: J. M. Dent and Sons, 1982), pp. 174-175. Unless otherwise stated, all subsequent quotes from Rousseau in this chapter are from this source.

5. John Stuart Mill, _On Liberty_ (Chicago: Henry Regnery, 1955), pp. 23-24.

6. Mill, _On Liberty_, p. 13.

7. Richard Taylor, _Freedom, Anarchy, and the Law: An Introduction to Political Philosophy_ (Englewood Cliffs, New Jersey: Prentice-Hall, 1973), p. 58.

8. John Stuart Mill, _Principles of Political Economy_ (New York: Longmans, Green, 1929), p. 950. Unless otherwise stated, all subsequent quotes from Mill in this chapter are from this source.

Chapter 10

Let Them Eat Care

Social Philosophy

The distinction between political philosophy, the topic of the previous
chapter, and social philosophy is a fairly arbitrary one. In Chapter 9,
we treated the problem of the legitimacy of government as the key
issue in political philosophy. Here in our chapter on social philosophy,
we will deal with the problem of <u>justice</u>. This problem is usually
seen as having to do with
fairness and desert
(deservedness) in meeting
the claims of citizens
and in the distribution of
goods and services. The big
question here is, what is
the state's legitimate
role in these activities?
We will look at three
views concerning this
issue: the communist
solution, the minimal-state

We want
Justice!

I can't
really see
what I'm
doing.

solution, and liberalism. I will view liberalism as located between the other two positions, though I do not mean to imply that because communism and minimalism are extremes relative to liberalism therefore they could not be true. Indeed, these two "extreme" views are not the most extreme possible in any absolute sense. Such extremes would be these: On the one hand is a kind of statism that holds the state and only the state totally responsible for the fair distribution of goods and services to its citizens and says only it can determine the legitimacy of the citizens' claims. On the other hand is an anarchistic position, claiming that the state itself is illegitimate, hence can never play a role in fair distribution or in responding to legitimate claims of individuals.

Communism

The political philosophy of KARL MARX (1818-1885) was greatly influenced by his early contact with the metaphysics of G.W.F. HEGEL (1770-1831), whose theory of reality is distinctly organistic. (ORGANICISM is the opposite of atomism. Atomism says that reality is composed of individual, simple units — that the individuals are more real than the whole, which is somehow actually only an abstraction. organicism says that the whole is more real than the parts; the whole is an organic unity, and the parts depend

Hegel's spirit reigns supreme.

completely on the whole. Hence, the parts are somehow less real than the whole.) In Hegel's version of organicism, the so-called individuals are themselves just points of intersecting relations of power within the system, so in a certain sense, each individual is really a microcosmic mirror of the macrocosm — a reflection of the whole system. Hegel was, like Berkeley, an idealist, so for him the system and all of its parts were spiritual. In his pantheistic tendencies, he saw the whole system as the mind of God; or, to put it more baldly, because everything _is_

The individual as a point of intersecting relations of power

mind, the system _is_ God.

Marx's Materialism

Marx, who "stood Hegel on his head," was a materialist. He rejected not only Hegel's idealism, but also his grandiose metaphysical schema — The System. Still, he too tended toward organicism. He not only saw the human race as ecologically closely related to nature (he had written to Charles Darwin asking Darwin's permission to let Marx dedicate _Das Kapital_

Marx stands Hegel on his head.

to him, but Darwin declined the honor, saying that he had enough trouble based on his own theory without being blamed for Marx's theory as well), but Marx also saw the individual human as ecologically related to his or her society. Society was not merely the totality of individuals; rather, it was an organic whole that in certain ways created the individual. Therefore for Marx, there could be no question of individual rights that somehow superseded social rights. Everything that an individual does is a result of the efforts of many people, living and dead. Hence, all products were in that sense _social_ products and belonged to society.

Historical societies have been unjust, according to Marx, almost from the very beginning (even though the most ab-original social arrangements,

Every product is the result of the efforts of many people, living and dead.

hence the most natural ones, were forms of primitive communism). This is because a minority of individuals managed to wrest power and material wealth from the majority, thereby setting up systems of privilege and generating social institutions that would guarantee those privileges — protected at first by armed thugs called "police" or "army," eventually by social institutions and internalized guilt. (Marx thought that this grabbing of power and wealth was some-how "unnatural." Some of his Hobbesian critics claim it was all _too_ natural.) Nevertheless, the history of the social world has always been the history of the quest for material justice. This quest has taken on the guise of class antagonism and sometimes of class

The interests of the few versus the interests of the many, according to Karl Marx

warfare, where the interests of the majority (a dispossessed working class: slaves, serfs, laborers) is pitted against the interests of the privileged minority. Marx's optimistic teleological conception of history tells him that the interests of the majority _must_ finally triumph.

Marx's materialistic organicism, based as it is on categories from economics and sociology rather than physics, is such that the socioeconomic structure of society is a very powerful determinant of the individual in society. So the problem is not simply that unjust socioeconomic structures of power create unfair conditions for individuals; rather, they create _mutilated_ _individuals_. For example, Marx writes:

> The alienation of the worker in his object is expressed as follows in the laws of political economy: the more the worker produces the less he has to consume; the more value he creates the more worthless he becomes; the more refined his product the more crude and misshapen the worker; the more civilized the product the more barbarous the worker; the more powerful the work the more feeble the worker; the more the work manifests intelligence the more the worker declines in intelligence and becomes a slave of nature. Labor certainly produces marvels for the rich but it produces privation for the worker. It produces palaces, but hovels for the worker. It produces beauty, but deformity

for the worker. It replaces labor by machinery, but it casts some of the workers back into a barbarous kind of work and turns the others into machines. It produces intelligence, but also stupidity and cretinism for the workers.[1]

According to Marx's positive, optimistic conception of human nature, humans are naturally creative, productive, artistic, aesthetic beings who must express their being in their products. (Humans thus objectify their subjectivity.) Marx prefers the name <u>homo faber</u> (man the maker) over <u>homo sapiens</u> (man the knower) because, for him, all <u>knowing</u> follows upon <u>doing</u> and <u>making</u>. So another effect of unjust socioeconomic systems is that the individual's being is stolen from her. She does not produce as a natural outlet of her creative urge; rather, she is forced to sell her work to another person. Her work is stolen from her and becomes a part of an economic system that is hostile to her own interests. This is what Marx calls "alienated labor." He says this about it:

You are what you make.

> What constitutes the alienation of labor? First, that the work is <u>external</u> to the worker, that it is not part of his nature; and that, consequently, he does not fulfill himself in his work but denies himself, has a feeling of misery rather than well being, does not develop freely his mental and physical energies but is physically exhausted and mentally debased. The worker therefore feels himself at home only during his

leisure time, whereas at work he feels homeless. His work is not voluntary but imposed, _forced labor_. It is not the satisfaction of a need, but only a _means_ for satisfying other needs. Its alien character is clearly shown by the fact that as soon as there is no physical or other compulsion it is avoided like the plague. External labor, labor in which man alienates himself, is a labor of self-sacrifice, of mortification. Finally, the external character of work for the worker is shown by the fact that it is not his own work but work for someone else, that in work he does not belong to himself but to another person.[2]

Marx's Vision of Society

So what would a just society look like for Marx? (Or what _will_ it look like — he thought its advent was inevitable?) First, its social production must be addressed to what he calls _true needs_ rather than _false needs_.

True needs derive from our real nature as biological, social beings (e.g., the need for food, shelter, clothing, medical care, love, and education). False needs are any artificial needs of the privileged that are at the expense of the true needs of the majority, any exaggeration of true needs that

Mama! Me **need** green cereal!!

FLAKEY FLAKES CEREAL for KIDS

False needs

are instilled in some while others go without (the need for mansions, luxurious clothes, and gourmet excesses), or the instillment of economic needs in the masses whose real goal is not satisfaction but profit for the privileged owning class (planned obsolescence:

light bulbs that burn out in a month, razors that go dull and are to be thrown away, automobiles whose bumpers collapse in collisions at five miles per hour). Second, the foundations of social production (natural resources, means of production, means of distribution) must not be privately owned but must be socially owned and democratically controlled. Third, social production must be such that individual workers are not forced to enter into streams of specialization that constrain the natural abundance

Karl Marx inspects a triumph of capitalism.

of the creative urge. No one may be objectified in a specific role — become <u>the</u> waiter, <u>the</u> teacher, <u>the</u> janitor, <u>the</u> physicist, or even <u>the</u> neurosurgeon. This does not mean that no one can <u>specialize</u>. (Who wants to have one's brain operated upon by one's hair-

dresser or by one's philosophy teacher?) A person may spend years training to learn neurosurgery, but still, one does not become <u>the</u> neurosurgeon. (In today's America, perhaps one also becomes <u>a golfer</u>?)

In a famous passage in which Marx announces the abolition of "the division of labor," he says :

> ... in communist society, where nobody has one exclusive sphere of activity but each can become accomplished in any branch he wishes, society regulates the general production and thus makes it possible for me to do one thing today and another tomorrow, to hunt in the morning, fish in the afternoon, rear cattle in the evening, criticize after dinner, just as I have a mind, without ever becoming hunter, fisherman, shepherd or critic. [3]

Under these conditions, the motto of justice will be "From each according to his ability, to each according to his need." Here we will have the recovery of true human nature, the release of the human creative potential, and for the first time, _true_ individuality because true individuality requires "true consciousness" (recognition that the needs of the individual and the needs of the society are identical) and unconstrained creativity — which is really where individual differences come into play. Marx has no trouble handing these new humans over to a democracy.

Criticisms of Marx's View

Many of Marx's ideas are impressive. In my view, he is right that much of the history of the world has been characterized by the power and privilege of a few, supported by the misery of many; and I think he is also right that any complete theory of the just society must include the concept of "distributive justice" (the fair distribution of socially produced wealth or the fair distribution of scarcity). But Marx's system is itself fraught with problems.

First, consider Marx's tremendously optimistic picture of human nature. As opposed to pessimists like Freud and Hobbes, Marx thought we are naturally social and naturally workers. (Freud thought we were natural egoists and natural bums, so our

414

Doc, I'm a greedy bum.

true nature would have to be suppressed if civilization was to flourish.) According to Marx, we are naturally cooperative. Competition and selfishness are primarily the result of unhealthy social arrangements. Now, one can _hope_ that Marx was right about all this, but the evidence available to you and me is not always on the side of his argument. His response to this charge is that such evidence comes to us from cultures of alienation and is being evaluated through a fog of alienation (your fog and my fog). But because all cultures _have_ been alienated to one degree or another, according to Marx, what evidence can he point to in order to establish that people are basically "good" (other than to Hegelian metaphysics, that is,

Trying to see through the fog of alienation

which is hardly _evidence_)?

A second and similar concern is Marx's apparent identification of "the good" as _social creativity_. One might agree with him that this is a necessary condition for happiness and well-being, but why should we think that it is a sufficient condition for them? As one critic of Marx, Professor Alan Brown, asks, couldn't we also consider "bodily and mental health, the development of cognitive faculties, of certain character traits and emotional responses, play, sex, friendship, love, art, religion" as possible candidates for the full and happy life?[4]

A third, and still related, objection concerns the mystification of the working class. Why should we accept Marx's claim that the destiny of the human race is the destiny of the working class? Why should a particular class of oppressed, alienated, and unhappy people contain the hidden meaning of human history? (And are we sure that human history has a _meaning_, a _telos_?)

A fourth criticism concerns Marx's essentially Platonic claim that, in the truly human society, the interests of the individual and those of society will be identical. Certainly, Marx is right that every effort must be made to reduce the opposition between these two, but isn't there a suspicion, as

Does history have a _meaning_?

416

Alan Brown says, that

> the only way in which the individual interests can be reconciled with collective interests is for those collective interests to <u>replace</u> the individual's own self interests in his own consciousness? ... Consider the problem of congested traffic in rush hours. There is a collective interest in everyone using public transport, since this would be so much more convenient. The individual has to curtail his own behavior to achieve a <u>second-best</u> solution — he would prefer that he should use his car and everyone else the bus.[5]

Civic mindedness

And finally, what about Marx's willingness to accept democracy as valid only "after the revolution"? He would reject as factitious the Western democracies of the contemporary world on the grounds that the voters in them are all alienated ideologues in a state of false consciousness who misunderstand their own interests and those of the human race. The vote will be given only to those nonalienated communalists in true consciousness who will be the second or third generation product of the revolution; yet their creation will depend on an interim "dictatorship of the proletariat" — an absolute totalitarianism that will guide the newly-revolutionized society for several generations until the "new human" has been fully hatched. Because, at that point, social classes will be no more, and class struggle, exploitation, and the need for the state as an instrument of exploitation will have disappeared, the dictatorship of the proletariat will

simply "dissolve itself," voluntarily stepping down and handing its absolute power over to "the people." Doesn't one have to be a bit <u>naive</u> to accept all this? Is one simply a capitalist lackey if one observes that, unfortunately, Lord Acton was probably more accurate than Marx? (Acton: "Power corrupts; absolute power corrupts absolutely.")

The newly hatched true human being

   The reason that all this matters has to do with Marx's organicism. He believed that no piecemeal corrections of injustice can succeed. If the <u>game</u> is rotten, then every possible move in the game is rotten. The whole thing most be swept away, or there will be injustice forever. So, according to Marx, we must accept his judgment on all these issues or be ourselves condemned eternally as reactionaries, lackeys, and mouthpieces of the forces of injustice.

The Minimal State

At the opposite pole from Marx's communist society (or "communalist" society) is the idea of the "minimal state." This would be a state that has the legitimate power to prevent the use of force and fraud and to punish such uses, but could not have the legitimate power to tax or confiscate property in order to perform any actions above and beyond these minimal duties. No public works or systems of aid to the needy would be justified.

Such a minimal state has recently been defended in a much-read and greatly discussed book by Harvard philosophy professor, ROBERT NOZICK, in <u>Anarchy, State and Utopia</u>. The starting point for Nozick's defense is Locke's "state of nature," in which, as we have seen, individuals have a natural right to "life, liberty, health, and property." Nozick begins by seriously considering the anarchistic charge that the move from "the state of nature" to the "political state" is illegitimate. The anarchist's view is that "in the course of maintaining its monopoly on the use of force and protecting everyone within a territory, the state must violate individuals' rights and hence is intrinsically immoral."⁶ The state would violate individuals' rights

if it taxed them against their will for the protection it offered them, according to the anarchists' line of reasoning. After pondering this anarchistic argument, Nozick concludes that the anarchist is wrong to think that the minimal state would violate individual rights. In fact, he tries to prove that an anarchy itself would evolve into a minimal state automatically. In the former, individuals would hire bodyguard agencies to protect

I'm protecting you against robbers. That will be $20,000 please.

their rights and to punish abuses of those rights. Competing agencies would finally be beaten out by the most efficient agency — the biggest agency, the one offering the most protection — and this agency itself be-

Competing bodyguard agencies

comes identical to the minimal state.

The reason the minimal state is the maximum state allowed is that any more extensive state must finance its projects through taxation, and if this taxation is not consented to by some individuals, it will violate their rights. According to Nozick, unconsented taxation is on a par with forced labor. It makes the government part owner of you (because on the Lockean principles from which Nozick's argument proceeds, you own yourself, and your labor is an extension of yourself) and is indistinguish-able from semislavery.

Nozick criticizes both socialism (of which communism is a version) and liberalism (which, like socialism, claims that fairness demands some kind of redistribution of wealth) on the grounds that they are what he calls "patterned" theories of justice rather than historical theories. That is, they impose a certain kind of pattern on the distribution of goods (e.g., Marx's "from each according to his ability, to each according

420

to his need") that has nothing to do with the <u>history</u> of the goods distributed. This would be fine, says Nozick, if goods fell from heaven like manna. But, in fact, most goods come to us with a history. They are already encumbered, already owned, — purchased, traded, earned, or received as a gift. Those goods, or "holdings," are covered by an

absolute right to them by their owners — a right whose overriding would be unjust. These rights pertain if the initial acquisition was just and if all subsequent transactions with it are just (e.g., if I own an object by virtue of having made it or purchased it with money that is legitimately mine, etc.). Furthermore, there is a right to transfer holdings. I can

Goods falling like manna from heaven

421

trade or give away things I own. (This means there is a right to inheritance.) Finally, there is a right to demand rectification. In an anarchy (the "state of nature"), I have a right to defend myself and my property against those who would injure me or my holdings, steal from me or defraud me; and I have a right to exact punishment from those who do so. In a minimal state, I give up the right to punish others personally, by my own hand, but I do have the right to demand that the state perform these protective and punitive functions (though there are no other demands I can make on the state).

The implications of all this are that <u>only</u> an unlimited capitalism can produce a just society and that any state that prohibits "capitalist acts between consenting adults" is a tyranny. Nozick seems to recognize that it is a consequence of his view that some will amass great wealth and power while others will struggle in poverty. But he believes that this unfortunate side effect of his system is nevertheless consistent with justice. On the first page of his book, Nozick says that he knows that many readers will reject his conclusions, which are "so apparently callous toward the needs and suffering of others." Throughout his argument, he does little to alleviate this concern, though he does make a gesture in its direction by subscribing to Locke's proviso that, in acquiring property, "one must leave enough

for others." Says Nozick:

> Thus a person may not appropriate the only water hole in a desert and charge what he will. Nor may he charge what he will if he possesses one, and unfortunately it happens that all the water holes in the desert dry up, except for his. This unfortunate circumstance, admittedly no fault of his, brings into operation the Lockean proviso and limits his property rights (p. 180).

In a footnote, Nozick adds, "The situation would be different if his water hole didn't dry up, due to special precautions he took to prevent this" (p. 180).

Not surprisingly, Nozick's theory has delighted a number of people whose political posture is decidedly to the right. But most of the literature that his book has inspired has been critical. Still, the sheer volume of this literature is an impressive testi-

Pleased by Nozick's views

mony to the significance of Nozick's book. It's as if political writers see Nozick's arguments as important enough to require a response.

Numerous critics attack the notion of <u>rights</u> on which Nozick's libertarian utopia is based. The first sentence of his book is, "Individuals have rights, and there are things no person or group may do to them (without violating their rights)." These rights are the right against coercive interference in one's affairs and the right to property. Where did one get these rights? Nozick does not really tell us; yet for him they are absolute and override any other moral claims. A typical strategy against Nozick is to insist that the existence of such rights cannot be merely presupposed, but must be demonstrated.

One group of critics simply denies that such absolute rights exist at all. For example, Alasdair MacIntyre, a prominent British philosopher, says, "... belief in them is one with belief in witches and unicorns."

Another British philosopher, Alan Brown, says that claiming that I have a <u>right</u> to something is just an elliptical way of saying that, "all things considered, there is a good moral reason to respect or promote my freedom in this case."[7] Therefore, rights

Once upon a time in a far distant land there existed witches, unicorns, and natural rights....

cannot be absolute or foundational; rather, they are derived from other moral deliberations. Other philosophers have agreed with Nozick that there are basic rights but claimed that <u>his</u> list of them is arbitrary. For instance, Ronald Dworkin says:

> It is true that the idea that people have a right not to lose anything they possess without their consent has a certain intuitive appeal. But other ideas also have intuitive appeal, such as the idea that people in a desperate situation have a right to the concern of others ... I agree that rights ought not to be violated. But sometimes claims of rights conflict, and I see no reason why Nozick's right to property is exclusive of other rights, or why it is necessarily more important than others.[8]

Another kind of criticism attacks the purely utopian (hence impractical) nature of Nozick's argument. For example, Nozick

424

claims that only a _historical_ theory of acquisitions can be truly just and also claims that _current_ entitlement to holdings is just only if original acquisition was just. But what is original acquisition? Adam's and Eve's? Certainly, most current holdings are historically traceable to items that were once the spoils of war or of other forms of removal by force or intimidation. My county was once the territory of the Miwok Indians. I don't know if the Miwoks wrested that land from an earlier prehistoric people, but I do know that the Miwoks did not simply bestow their land on the European settlers who are my ancestors. In today's world, does _anybody_ have just entitlement to his property derivable from an original acquisition? Amazingly, Nozick seems to admit that these historical facts undermine

Adam and Eve, and the original acquisition

425

his historical theory and force us to accept some form of " patterning."
He says, "Although to introduce socialism as the punishment for our sins
would be to go too far, past injustices might be so great as to make

Nozick goes to hell.

necessary in the short run a more extensive state in order to rectify
them" (p. 231). Critic Alan Brown concludes from all this:

> So Nozick's theory is essentially Utopian in the worst sense of the
> term: it has no practical relevance. Like the Garden of Eden
> before the Fall it can offer no insight into the problems of what
> we are to do here and now, since we are left ignorant of what
> principles are to inform our choice. The theory has application
> nowhere.[9]

Liberalism

Somewhere in the theoretical spectrum between the communistic
utopia of Marx and the minimalist utopia of Nozick can be found
the idea of what we can call " the liberal state." It has been
heartily defended by Nozick's colleague at Harvard, JOHN RAWLS,
in his book, <u>A Theory of Justice</u>. The liberal state is pretty much

what exists today in the Western democracies: a large degree of free enterprise, with capital and many of the natural resources in private hands, but regulated by the state in order to foster low inflation and high employment. Tax-financed social security tries to control poverty for those who cannot work or for whom no work exists. The presupposition behind liberalism is that society is necessarily much more complex than it is seen to be in either Marxian or Nozickian utopias — that it is necessarily a cooperative enterprise and that therefore its products and wealth are partially the result of cooperation (and that therefore all members of the cooperation have a claim to a fair share of the products and the wealth, as in Marx), but also that there will necessarily be competition both in producing and obtaining the goods (and that, therefore, some members of the cooperative — those who contribute most to it — have a claim to

Cooperation but also competition

unequal portions of the products, as in Nozick). Any adequate theory of justice will have to balance these legitimate claims and find a formula for dismissing illegitimate claims. Rawls thinks that such a theory, once formulated, could apply to a democratic capitalist society or a democratic socialist society. In any case, society must have a public school system, must be dedicated to equality of economic opportunity, must have Social security, and must define a minimum standard of living below which its citizens will not be forced to exist.

Rawls' conception of justice is "justice as fairness." Besides guaranteeing that all citizens will get a rational share of the social goods, the doctrine of fairness consists in a set of constraints on what people may do to each other in the pursuit of those goods. On the one hand, Rawls thinks that no <u>theory</u> of justice can be justly forced down people's throats — the correct theory would have to be one that rational people would somehow arrive at by themselves. On the other hand, Rawls is pretty sure he knows what such a theory would look like. Justice would be whatever was chosen by rational, self-interested, un-

A piece for you,... a piece for you,... and a piece for me!

Justice as fairness

envious people who knew that they would have to inhabit the society created by their mutual agreement but who did not know what personal characteristics they would bring to that society (i.e., they wouldn't know their race, their physical and mental abilities, their inheritances, or their social backgrounds). Such people, Rawls says, would choose the following principles in the following order:

> I know that $e = mc^2$, that Charlemagne was crowned Holy Roman Emperor on Christmas day, 800 A.D., that the first person singular of the present subjunctive of the Spanish verb "hacer" is "haga." ... I know _everything_ (except my name, age, weight, race, parents, bank account, IQ, friends, and education).

A Rawlsian citizen

1. Equal and maximum liberty (political, intellectual, and religious) for each person consistent with equal liberty for others.

2. Wealth and power to be distributed equally except where inequalities would work to the advantage of all and where there would be equal opportunity to achieve advantageous positions of inequality.

If this is true, then it follows (unlike in Nozick's theory) that the only society that can be just is a liberal society that partially distributes wealth and income for the benefit of its most disadvantaged members.

Rawls tries to show that there are certain "socially primary goods," which any rational person would want. He says, "it is rational to want these goods whatever else is wanted, since they are in general necessary for the framing and the execution of a rational plan of life." [10] These goods are, as we have seen, liberties, income and wealth, and opportunities, but also the bases of self-respect. In fact, the most important of these socially primary goods, according to Rawls, is self-respect, which is "a person's sense of

My worth = $ $ $ $

Self-respect

his own value, his secure conviction that his conception of his good, his plan of life, is worth carrying out." " (Critics have pointed out the bias [Can we call it a bourgeois bias?] in Rawls' list of primary goods. Some forms of self-respect would require a rejection of income and wealth, for example, ascetic Buddhism or Christianity.)

Notice that Rawls' theory, like Plato's, begins with a political myth — a "noble lie." In Plato's myth, people are told that their memories of their past are really only memories of a dream and what they believe of themselves is in fact false. Similarly, Rawls' myth establishes what he calls a "veil of ignorance," in which the facts we know about ourselves are set aside (our psychological, physical, social, and racial characteristics). The myth also supposes that we

Students wearing the veil of ignorance (proudly)

430

are not envious and we rationally pursue our own self-interest. If you tell Rawls that his myth is <u>only</u> a myth, that none of it is true, he will respond that it is merely a philosophical device to be used as an analytic tool to demonstrate the rationality of a certain kind of society. (In this respect, his "original position" [as he calls the status of his mythical negotiators behind their veil of ignorance] is very much like the "state of nature" in traditional contract theories.) It allows the political philosopher to acknowledge the intuitive fact that some inequalities in a naturally evolving society are unjust because they are undeserved. It is unjust that some should have to suffer through life because they were born with less and that others are surrounded by excessive amounts of goods due to the mere accident of birth. It allows Rawls to arrive rationally at a conclusion that he intuits to be true, namely, that a society can be just only if it partially redistributes wealth for the benefit of its most disadvantaged. In short, it shows how a just society requires that we all be transformed from Hobbesian egoists into Kantian universalists. It does this by purporting to show that if we were forced to enter into a society that we would negotiate with others, denuded of all the characteristics that were ours merely

The transformation from Hobbesian egoist to Kantian universalist

by accident of birth, we would choose the liberal society.

Though Rawls' theory strikes a responsive chord in many of

its readers, you will not be surprised that it has also found its share of critics. Many are suspicious of any theory that sets out to determine the most rational of all possible societies and concludes that it just happens to be the type inhabited by the author of the theory. The specific criticism very often centers on the arbitrariness of Rawls' myth. For instance, he has received much flack for his assumption that, in the "original position," people would not be envious. (An "envious man" in this context would be one who would prefer that others not receive advantages over him even if their doing so would mean that his situation would also improve.) Rawls has argued that in his just society, there would be little incitement or occasion for envy. But critics have pointed out that Rawls himself has said that "self-esteem" is the highest social good, and a person's self-esteem is deflated when new inequalities reduce his power and wealth relative to the power and wealth of others who benefit by the new inequalities. This is true even if in some absolute sense the situation of the less advantaged is improved by the introduction of these inequalities.

Another criticism says that Rawls ignores our natural gambling nature. Rawls thinks that his liberal society is superior to a utilitarian society because the latter is compatible with slavery (a _few_ miserable, hard-working slaves

might produce the greatest amount of happiness for the greatest number of people), but slavery is incompatible with liberalism because negotiators in the "original position" would not risk opting for slavery because they themselves might end up as slaves. But, ask the critics, wouldn't some risk the low odds of being designated a slave if the odds for a great benefit from such a system were high enough?

Yet another criticism is that no contract is legally binding if the signers of it are kept in ignorance of their own real interests; yet _all_ signers to Rawls' social contract are ignorant of even their personal identity. So, on this account, Rawls' contract, produced behind the "veil of ignorance," is invalid. Finally, we should remind ourselves of Nozick's main criticism of Rawls. Nozick says that it would be okay to divide the goods according to some patterned formula of equality "if goods fell from heaven like manna." But it is unjust to divide up the pie equally when it is known who contributed to it and who in fact owns it. Nozick asks, how do the people in the "original position" get the _right_ to divide up the pie as they do? (But of course it could be asserted that _the_ _right_ _to_ _fair_ _treatment_ is as basic as Nozick's _right_ _to_ _property_.)

Conclusion

My own conclusions here are not offered up as being trouble-free. Any position one takes on this important topic involves its author in serious problems. Still, that does not excuse us from thinking this problem through to the best of our ability and reaching some tentative conclusions; here are mine. I agree with Marx when he says that a just society cannot be one in which an oppressed majority is constrained to support a system of privileges for a nonproductive minority. Everyone who hopes to benefit from social productivity should contribute to it. But Marx (in contrast to Mill) needs to be criticized for his view that the individual has no legitimate rights vis-à-vis society, and he was wrong to think (if he did think) that society must be founded on <u>one</u> view of human good — that of productivity. Liberalism (Mill and Rawls) is to be applauded for its view that the state must be open to as many views of human good as are compatible with each other. Nozick correctly reminds us that the goods that offer themselves to us for consumption, purchase, or trade do not fall from heaven like manna. We cannot create justice by simply taking away from some to give to others without considering entitlement — that is, without considering that some people have legitimate claims of ownership or control of certain goods by virtue of having legally produced them, purchased them, or inherited them. But "entitlement" is not an absolute category.

I find Rawls convincing when he sides with Marx against Nozick in holding that a just society cannot be based on entitlement alone, but that claims of entitlement must be balanced with claims of need or social victimization, and that therefore the just society must be committed to an ongoing partial redistribution of wealth to guarantee that the least advantaged in society do not fall below a certain agreed-upon standard of living and are provided with opportunities to rise above their position of disadvantage — not only because it is morally right to do so, but because otherwise that vicious (Hobbesian) side of human nature that can make human relations dangerous for all may be activated.

Notes

1. Karl Marx, _Economic and Philosophical Manuscripts_, in Erich Fromm, _Marx's Concept of Man_, T.B. Bottomore, trans. (New York: Frederick Ungar, 1969), p. 97.

2. Marx, _Economic and Philosophical Manuscripts_, pp. 98-99.

3. Karl Marx, _German Ideology_, in Fromm, _Marx's Concept of Man_, p. 42.

4. Alan Brown, _Modern Political Philosophy: Theories of the Just Society_ (New York: Penguin, 1986), p. 126.

5. Brown, _Modern Political Philosophy_, pp. 117-118.

6. Robert Nozick, _Anarchy, State and Utopia_ (New York: Basic Books, 1974), p. 180. Unless otherwise stated, all subsequent quotes from Nozick in this chapter are from this source.

7. Alasdair MacIntyre, _After Virtue_ (Notre Dame, Indiana University of Notre Dame Press, 1981), p. 67; Brown, _Modern Political Philosophy_, p. 106.

8. Interview with Ronald Dworkin, in Bryan Magee, _Men of Ideas: Some Creators of Contemporary Philosophy_ (London: British Broadcasting Corporation, 1978), p. 254.

9. Alan Brown, _Modern Political Philosophy_, p. 99.

10. John Rawls, _A Theory of Justice_ (Cambridge, Massachusetts: Harvard University Press, 1971). p. 433.

11. Rawls, _A Theory of Justice_, p. 440.

Chapter 11

But Is It Art?

Philosophy of Art

The urge to produce art seems as old as the human race. If you compare the thirty-thousand-year-old representations on the walls of the caves of Altamira or Lascaux to the images of the typical prime time TV production — or worse, to the graffiti on the walls of the men's room in the bus depot (or even worse yet, if anything worse is possible, to the drawings in this book) — you may think that there has been a downward spiral since the times of our Cro-Magnon ancestors.

But at least there have been some great moments in between!

What are human beings doing when they create "art"? Are their works frivolous or even dangerous distractions, or do they exhibit something deep

Early graffiti

and essential about human nature? And what is the relationship between art and "reality"? Is art a poor imitation of reality, as some philosophers have held? Or is art a spiritualization and enrichment of nature — an improvement upon the world — as other philosophers have asserted? These are some of the big questions in the philosophy of art. Whatever answers there are to these questions, it is not surprising that for thousands of years people have been provoked to philosophize about art because, for better or for worse, art has been such a pervasive part of human experience.

Plato and Freud

You were advised earlier that our discussion of art, like so many of our discussions, would begin with Plato's views. However, you may or may not have anticipated that those views would be decidedly negative. His indictment of art, based on the metaphysics of the Simile of the Line (see "The Philosophy of Plato" in Chapter 2), can be stated in three parts. There is an _ontological_ objection, an _epistemological_ objection, and a _moral_ objection. The ontological objection has to do with Plato's view that art is imitation (_mimesis_). This was the standard Greek view, and it went unchallenged by all the greatest Greek thinkers on the subject.

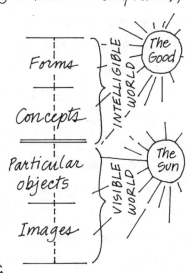

Review of Plato's Simile of the line

But what is art an imitation _of_? Well, according to Plato, art must be imitating the world as it _appears_, not the world as it _is_. Artists imitate "particular objects." If this is so, then art itself must be consigned to the realm of "images" (being a copy of "particular things," which are themselves but copies of higher things). In Book X of _The Republic_, Plato says that art is "thrice removed from the truth." It is a copy of a copy of a copy.

Because most of us today do not approach art under the influence of the Simile of the Line, and because we are no longer satisfied with the view that art is simply imitative, we probably do not feel that Plato's ontological objection is very forceful. Therefore, to be able to understand his point better, consider the following example. Imagine a novel by someone like Charles Dickens that begins with this line, "It was a foggy day in London." Now, precisely _what_ day was a foggy day? June 21, 1836? August 7, 1829? Obviously, the sentence does not refer to _any_ real day. Strictly speaking, the sentence is false, or at least, its status has nothing to do with the truth. Such is the case with _every_ sentence in the novel, even those that coincidentally could correspond with the facts. (For instance, if Dickens had said, "September 26, 1782, was a foggy day in London," we might check the records and discover that that day really _was_ foggy, but it wouldn't matter to the work of art whether that was so. The work is no better or worse as a work of art if that sentence is true. Similarly, medieval and renaissance paintings of Jesus would be none the worse off as paintings even if it were proved that Jesus never lived.)

It follows that works of art are what they are by virtue of being _illusions_. The success of Dickens' novels depends upon his creating the illusion that he is describing real events and real

people, just as the
success of a painting
depends upon the
artist's creating the
illusion that these
blotches of color are
clouds, mountains,
houses, people, etc.
So, for Plato, the
function of art is
always to deceive.

It always draws attention away from reality (the Forms) and toward illusion (images). Plato did not deny that an art whose function
was more noble might be ontologically justifiable, but it seemed to
him that almost all art was deceptive in the way just described.

Plato's epistemological objection is directed both against the
work of art and the artist. The work of art, being false, does not
give us any true knowledge of the world, and the artists do not

Art whose function is more noble

439

know what they are doing. They cannot give the _logos_.

Plato's moral objection is multifaceted. First, if Plato has established that the pursuit of knowledge is the pursuit of the Good, and if art produces ignorance, then art is immoral. Second, art seems to concentrate on the flaws in human and divine nature and often depicts great men and gods doing immoral things. (Here Plato had in mind Homer and the Greek tragedies. How much respect can you have for a god like Zeus, who cheats on his wife, then lies to her when she asks him where he's been? Or can he be admired when on other occasions he is henpecked and even cuckolded by her? And what about the story of Odysseus in the underworld? When Odysseus meets the ghost of Achilles, Odysseus tells this honored hero of the Trojan War how much he envies him as prince among the dead. Achilles responds despairingly:

Achilles and a horrified Odysseus

"I'd rather be a serf or labouring man Under some yeoman on a little farm Than be king paramount of all the dead." How can you inspire courage in young men so that they will fight to defend their country if an idol like Achilles says that it is better to be a live coward than a dead hero? If the people have flawed gods and heroes to imitate [even _tragically_ flawed ones], the people themselves cannot be expected to try to achieve perfection.) And because we forget that art is illusion, we do appeal to it for examples of ideal cases. Ask yourself how many times in the past week some of your own teachers have used an example from fiction to make a point.

"A perfect example of madness is, of course, Don Quixote," "Hamlet exemplifies the feelings of indecision from which we all suffer," "Picasso's <u>Guernica</u> analyzes the horrors of war." But in truth, there never was a madman named Don Quixote, nor did Hamlet have any <u>real</u> feelings of indecisiveness, not even bombed horses look like Picasso's horse, and real tygers do not burn in the forests of the night.

A real tyger burning in the forests of the night

This brings us to the third and most important of Plato's moral objections against art. Art does not appeal to the highest faculty of the soul, Pure Reason. (How could it? It must deal with <u>images</u>.) Rather, it appeals to the basest part of the soul, the emotions. Plato, like Freud after him,

Philosophy appeals here. → REASON

Action appeals here. → COURAGE

Art appeals here. → PASSIONS

The structure of the soul

was very suspicious of the irrational passions. Both Plato and Freud believed that in the darkest recesses of the soul there is a cauldron of unruly emotions of sexuality and violence. These passions are antisocial and destructive of the individual. One of the most difficult jobs we face is to see that these passions are under our control rather than our being under their control. It is interesting that both Freud and Plato point to dreams as proof of the existence and as a demonstration of the content of this part of the psyche, which Freud calls "the id" and Plato calls "the appetitive soul." You will remember from Chapter 7 that in The Republic, Plato presents the following exchange between Socrates and his friend Glaucon:

Soc: See here, this is what I want to look into.... I feel that some of the unnecessary desires and pleasures are lawless: they are born in everyone....
Glau: What are these, pray?
Soc: Those which are aroused in sleep, whenever the rest of the soul, all the reasonable, gentle and ruling part, is asleep, but the bestial and savage, replete with food or wine, skips about and, throwing off sleep, tries to go

and fulfil its own instincts. You know there is nothing it will not dare to do, thus freed and rid of all shame and reason; it shrinks not from attempting in fancy to lie with a mother, or with any other man or god or beast, shrinks from no bloodshed, refrains from no food – in a word, leaves no folly or shamelessness untried.[1]

According to Plato, the way to control this part of the soul and thereby to prevent dreams of violence and sex is to live moderately, eat and drink little before retiring, think philosophical thoughts before sleeping, and, above all, <u>avoid art</u>! Precisely the reason we like art is that it titillates the passions and provokes us. Sophisticated people

Preventing violent and sexual dreams

are provoked by Bach, the unsophisticated are provoked by James Bond movies, but in some strange sense, the content is identical. We could almost say in Plato's name, all art is pornographic.

Before you condemn Plato's view, ask yourself where you stand on this controversial claim from a contemporary debate of our own: "Violence on television perpetuates violence in society. Children who spend a great deal of time watching TV are less sensitive to violence and are more prone to solve their

443

own problems by resorting to violence." If you agree with that passage, you are siding with Plato, for television is the contemporary art form; and all of Plato's objections, ontological, epistemological, and moral, apply vividly to the bulk of what we see on our screens. This does not exclude the "commercial messages." (Does McDonald's really "do it all for you"? And what is the "it"?)

Before leaving Plato and his objections to art, let's return for a moment to the comparison between Plato and Freud. You may have noticed earlier that there is a striking similarity between Plato's doctrine of innate ideas and parts of Freud's psychoanalytic theory. For both thinkers, liberation comes when we remember the past, a past buried deep in our unconscious. Also, both men divided the soul into three aspects: for Freud, the id, the ego, and the superego, for Plato, the appetitive, the spirited, and the rational portions. Now, in their suspicion of art, we have found another similarity. Freud's theory of art is interesting in itself, but a brief discussion of it will also shed light on Plato's similar theory. It will also prepare us for a twentieth-century attempt to solve the problem of art, that of Herbert Marcuse, to be introduced shortly.

Freud's theory of "instincts" ("_Triebe_," better translated as "drives" or "impulses") changed substantially over the forty-year period of his authorship, but I'll try to present a representative version of that theory. The sexual and aggressive drives contained

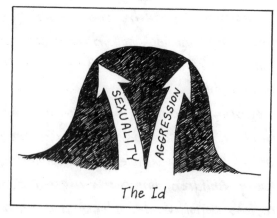

The Id

444

in the id are irrational and antisocial. If rationality and society are to survive, these passions must be controlled. The rational component of the psyche (the ego) is not capable by itself of containing the explosiveness of the id, so it must ally itself with the harsh irrationality of the superego. (For this alliance, the psyche pays a high price in terms of unconscious guilt.) Together they form a barrier that blocks the animal drives and returns them to their source. There they are "deanimalized" and redirected into socially acceptable forms of creativity: art, religion, philosophy, law, science, and morality — "higher culture." Freud calls this process "sublimation." It produces a cultural product that is a substitute gratification for the primary aim from which the drive was deflected. Yet the cultural product never completely loses its original (sexual or violent) nature. For example, imagine a little boy with a particularly strong aggressive drive. His idea of fun is to tear flesh, maim, and make people bleed. We can't afford to let him loose on the streets, so we send him to medical school, where he may sublimate his hostility into science and become a surgeon. He is now able to tear flesh, maim, and make people bleed, and thereby he receives wealth, prestige, and respectibility. Freud believed that one could successfully sublimate one's animality into science (he believed that he and Einstein, at least, had done so), but apparently Freud was suspicious of artistic sublimation, even

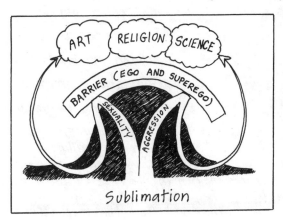

Sublimation

445

though he personally had a great reverence for art. His investigation of two of his favorite artists, Leonardo da Vinci and Michelangelo, did not alleviate his suspicions. Arnold Hauser has summarized Freud's most pessimistic estimation of art in this passage:

Both neurosis and art are essentially purposive; they are not only the expression of a failure and resignation in the face of reality, but also a kind of escapism. They represent partly an outcome of, partly a means of withdrawal from the real. "Every neurosis," says Freud, "has the result, and therefore probably the purpose, of forcing the patient out of real life, of alienating him from actuality." As far as the work of art is concerned, there can be no doubt about the existence of such a purpose. Neurosis and art equally reject reality, but neurosis does not deny it; only tries to forget it; art, on the other hand, tries both to deny and to replace it. The artist's attitude is, therefore, in this respect at least, more akin to insanity than to neurosis.[2]

Furthermore, the artist's product, unlike the scientist's, doctor's, or

446

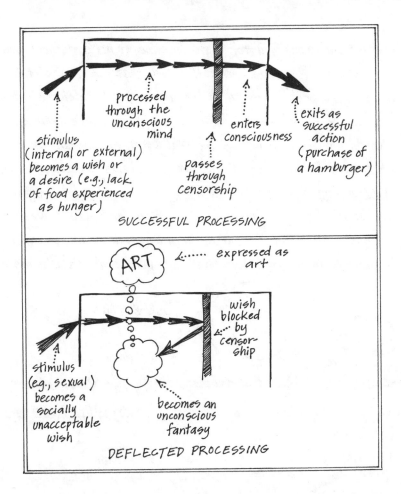

SUCCESSFUL PROCESSING

stimulus (internal or external) becomes a wish or a desire (e.g., lack of food experienced as hunger)

processed through the unconscious mind

passes through censorship

enters consciousness

exits as successful action (purchase of a hamburger)

DEFLECTED PROCESSING

ART

expressed as art

wish blocked by censorship

stimulus (e.g., sexual) becomes a socially unacceptable wish

becomes an unconscious fantasy

lawyer's, is still too close to its source in unconscious fantasies. Fantasies are guided by the infantile "pleasure principle" and have refused to submit to the "reality principle." Therefore, art is not a rational response to the demands of reality, but an irrational denial of reality. This is just another more complicated way of stating Plato's objection to art.

Aristotle

In spite of Plato's tremendous influence on Western philosophy, very few of his followers have agreed with his condemnation of art. In

447

fact, the first philosopher after Plato to come to art's defence was Plato's most important student, Aristotle (384-322 B.C.). Aristotle, though in many respects faithful to his master, ultimately rejected Plato's doctrine of Forms as too "otherworldly." Aristotle believed that the world we are born into *is* the real world and is not just a shadow of a more ultimate world. He brought Plato's philosophy down to earth by claiming that the Forms must be "imbedded in matter." He believed that the distinction between Form and matter was only an <u>intellectual</u> distinction, a distinction that could be drawn in theory but not in reality. We shall not pursue Aristotle's meta-

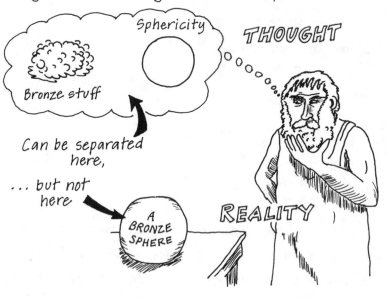

physics further here, but we will take note of the fact that his theory does not have the bias against "the visible world" that we saw in Plato; thus, Aristotle could accept Plato's claim that art deals in mimetic images without thereby condemning art.

There is another comment about Aristotle's metaphysics

that is pertinent here. The late British philosopher Sir Isaiah Berlin liked to apply the story of the fox and the hedgehog to philosophers. The hedgehog has one <u>big</u> idea, and the fox has many small ideas. If that is so, then Plato is a hedgehog, and Aristotle is a fox. (Berlin said that the Russian novelist Tolstoy was a fox who wanted to be a hedgehog.) That is to say, Aristotle's metaphysics is more piece-meal than Plato's. This means that his discussion of art was less under the domination of some central, over-riding philosophical <u>idea</u> and that therefore Aristotle could consider art more as an auton-omous activity

The hedgehog and the fox, and their respective collection of ideas

(though not completely autonomous because no Greek would consider <u>any</u> activity as independent of moral and political implications).

So Aristotle met Plato's ontological objection to art by rejecting Plato's hierarchical ontology. Yet he never denied that art is <u>mimesis</u>, imitation. Then what is art an imitation <u>of</u>?

Aristotle, who was particularly interested in poetry and drama, tells us that art imitates an <u>action</u>. But it does not imitate an action in the way that the writing of history imitates actions, simply recounting particular events (the second stage on Plato's line). Art is superior to history because it <u>theorizes</u> about actions (the third stage on the line). It does not tell us what <u>has</u> hap-pened; rather, it tells us what <u>can</u> happen. Art deals with universals and not with particulars, so it is more philosophical than history. So we see that Aristotle has also answered Plato's epistemological objection to art. Nevertheless, it must be pointed out that, for Aristotle, art is still inferior to philosophy. It is, as it were, on the third level of the line and cannot achieve the fourth level. As in Plato, that level can be achieved only by philosophy.

What about Plato's moral objection to art? Aristotle agreed with Plato's claim that art appeals to the passions, and, even though Aristotle was less suspicious of the passions than was Plato, he too believed that they can be wild, unruly, and dangerous. However, rather than art encouraging the passions to take control away from reason, art _purges_ the passions. Let's read Aristotle's famous passage about this purgation (_catharsis_).

> An emotion which strongly affects some souls is present in all to a varying degree, for example pity and fear, and also ecstasy. To this last some people are particularly liable, and we see that under the influence of religious music and songs which drive the soul to frenzy, they calm down as if they had been medically treated and purged. People who are given to pity or fear, and emotional people generally, and others to the extent that they have similar emotions, must be affected in the same way; for all of them must experience a kind of purgation and pleasurable relief. In the same way, cathartic (songs and) music give men harmless delight. We must therefore make

Greek audience

450

those who practice <u>mousikê</u> [poetry and music] in the theater perform these kinds of tunes and songs. [3]

Keep in mind that, unlike the more domesticated audiences of today, when Athenians went to the theater, they laughed, moaned, shrieked, beat their chests, and tore their hair as the drama unfolded. It is easy to see what Aristotle claimed to be the function of art in such a context, but before you decide between him and Plato, ask yourself again whether you think that watching violence on television and in the movies <u>replaces</u> real violence or causes it. And perhaps you'll be even more confused when you ask yourself the same question concerning sex in films and literature. Does pornography replace sexual activity or stimulate it? Does it replace sexual crimes or provoke them?

Regardless of your opinions concerning these topics, I think you may be somewhat disappointed with parts of Aristotle's defense of art when you read the passage that follows his description of catharsis:

> There are two kinds of spectator: the one kind is a free and educated man, the other, the vulgar kind, is made up of mechanics and general laborers and other such people; these too must be provided with contests and spectacles for their recreation. Their souls are perverted from their natural state; so there are perversions of melody and songs that are tense and corrupted. Every man takes pleasure in what is naturally akin to him, and we must therefore allow the performers to use this kind of <u>mousikê</u> with this kind of spectator in view. [4]

We see here that the experience of catharsis is most needed by "mechanics and general laborers" and other such "vulgar" people. Plato had worried about the effects of art on the aristocracy as well as on the plebeians. Aristotle seems to see the production of art as a way of pacifying the masses (another "opiate of the

"So can you fix my car now?"

"I'm afraid I'll have to step outside and have a cathartic experience first."

Catharsis and the working class

masses"?). This appears to conflict with his claim that art is philosophical.

There is a final point. In spite of Aristotle's defense of art against Plato's attack, it is clear to any reader of both authors that Plato has much more feeling for art than does Aristotle. In fact, ironically, Plato is a poet and artist par excellence, but no one will ever accuse Aristotle of being that. Aristotle never felt the stirring of passion produced in the sensitive soul by the confrontation with art. Plato had done so and was fearful of it. When he drummed the artists out of the Republic, he said he did so with tears in his eyes.

The Interlude Between Aristotle and the Nineteenth Century

We have treated the Freudian theory of art as a twentieth-century adjunct to Plato's theory. Shortly we will leap from Plato and Aristotle in the fourth century B.C. to Karl Marx in the nineteenth century A.D. But I do not want to leave the impression that nothing significant was thought about art in the intervening twenty-two hundred years. During the long medieval period, a number of views were expressed, but the overriding one was that art should only be a form of worship or be conducive to worship. During the renaissance, art theoreticians were mainly "neo-Platonic." This does not mean that they condemned art, as did Plato, but that they were Platonic revisionists, seeing art as expressing higher truths about beauty and sensuality.

The association between art and pleasure came to a head in the eighteenth century with the work of Alexander Baumgarten, who coined the term "aesthetic." He believed that the perception of "forms" (with a small "f") in art and nature produces "changes in the soul" that are experienced as delight or repugnance. This hedonistic "formalism" became a powerful influence in the early nineteenth century through the work of Johann Herbart and Robert Zimmermann. (This school may have reached its point of absurdity with Zimmermann's remark, "The large beside the small pleases, the small beside the large displeases.") Immanuel Kant, in his great Critique of Judgment, saw art as a moral symbol. G.W.F.

The large beside the small

The small beside the large

Hegel defined art as "nature passed through spirit." John Ruskin (1819 - 1900) understood art to be the expression of emotion or instincts. Some of the Romantic poets combined Ruskin's view with a return to the medieval idea that art is religious service. Leo Tolstoy (1828 - 1910) claimed that art was the communication of feeling and saw its function as the unification of humanity in a universal brotherhood. Nineteenth - century artists like Flaubert, Baudelaire, Poe, and Wilde were members of the school of "art for art's sake," which claimed that art had _no_ function; it was valuable in and for itself. These samples demonstrate that, although traditional philosophy of art may have been kicked off by the debate between Plato and Aristotle, it was by no means restricted to their polemic.

Marx

The debate about the relation between art and justice, initiated by Plato, was reopened in the work of Karl Marx. Marx never wrote a treatise on art, but he was obviously fascinated by it and very concerned over it because there are references to art and art theory scattered at significant places throughout his philosophical, sociological, and economic works. The attempt to reconstruct his ideas about art is complicated by the fact that there are two separate strands of thought concerning art running through Marx's writings, and these two strands sometimes seem at odds with each other. On the one hand, there is his claim that the need for artistic expression and aesthetic enjoyment is an _essential_ aspect of human nature. On the other hand, there is his assertion that art and aesthetics are components of "ideology" and as such are political captives. The first assertion sides with those traditional authors, such as Kant and Tolstoy,

who extoll art. The second claim sides with Plato's condemnation of art. We shall examine both strains and see whether they can be made consistent with each other; then we shall briefly look at the theory of Herbert Marcuse, a contemporary philosopher in the Marxian tradition who believed that the tension between Marx's views can be relieved and art restored to its correctly exalted position by, ironically, infusing a bit of Freudian thought into Marxism. (The irony has to do with Freud's own ambivalence toward art, which we have just noted, and with the fact that, in general, Freud and Marx seem so incompatible.)

Marx's view is that human beings cannot be studied in a vacuum, but must always be studied in their relation to the world. The world of human beings is composed of relations to nature, to fellow humans, and to the products of their hands and minds. Under optimum conditions, these relations are positive. They are productive, artistic, aesthetic, and creative. Wherever those relationships are ruptured, humans are alienated from their world and hence from themselves. (In Chapter 10, we took a look at "alienated labor.") Marx wrote that man is independent only "if he affirms his individuality as a total man in each of his relations to the world, seeing, hearing, smelling, tasting, feeling, thinking, willing, loving — in short, if he affirms and expresses all organs of his individuality."[5] For Marx, the fully _human_ being is essentially an artist who approaches the world aesthetically and forms things "in accordance with the laws of beauty."[6] From the point of view of this concern, we can say that the goal of communism (at least as envisioned by the _young_ Marx) was the liberation of _homo artisticus_, the human being as artist. Robert Tucker has characterized this aspect of Marx's conception of communism in the following passage:

> What will remain is the life of art and science in a special and vastly enlarged sense of these two terms. Marx's conception of ultimate communism is fundamentally _aesthetic_ in character. His utopia is an aesthetic ideal of the future man-nature relationship, which he sees in terms of artistic creation and the appreciation of the beauty of the man-made environment by its creator. The acquisitive and therefore alienated man of history is to be succeeded by the post-historical aesthetic man who will be "rich" in a new way. . . .
> Economic activity will turn into artistic activity, with industry as the supreme avenue of creation, and the planet itself will become the new man's work of art. The alienated world will give way to the aesthetic world.[7]

However, this general theory, which turns all truly human productivity into artistic and aesthetic acts, does not tell us anything about the difference between artistic production and non-artistic production in history up to Marx's own time. When we look not to Marx's future communist society, where all are artists, but to the present and the past, where only some are artists, we run up against Marx's theory of ideology. To understand this theory, we must first draw Marx's distinction between the _foundation_ and the _superstructure_ of society. Marx says:

> In the social production of their means of existence men enter into definite, necessary relations which are independent of their will, productive relationships which correspond to a definite stage of development of their material productive forces. The aggregate of these productive relationships constitutes the economic structure of society, the real basis on which a juridical and political superstructure arises, and to which definite forms of social consciousness correspond. The mode of production of the material means of existence conditions the whole process of social, political and intellectual life. It is not the consciousness of men that determines their existence, but, on the contrary, it is their social existence that determines their consciousness.
>
> . . . .
>
> Then an epoch of social revolution opens. With the change in the economic foundation the whole vast superstructure is more or less rapidly transformed. In considering such revolutions it is necessary always to distinguish between the material revolution in the economic conditions of production, which can be determined with scientific accuracy, and the juridical, political, religious, aesthetic or philosophic — in a word, ideological forms wherein men become conscious of this conflict and fight it out. [8]

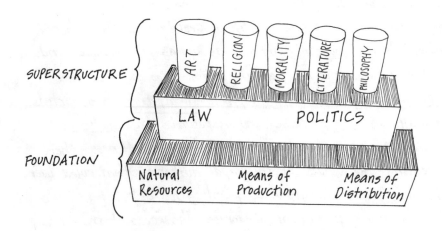

457

Furthermore, Marx added: "The ideas of the ruling class are in every epoch the ruling ideas." [9]

"Ideology" is Marx's term for the myth of self-aggrandizement that each socioeconomic system necessarily (if unintentionally) creates by monopolizing and controlling the form and content of

"The ruling ideas of each age..."

the spiritual productions of its creative members. These products become a form of unconscious political propaganda. The theory of ideology clearly applies to artistic as well as philosophical and political ideas. This means that the artists too express the values of the ruling class which supports them; therefore, artists, intentionally or not, endorse and perpetuate the status quo. Medieval art glorified God and condemned worldliness, thereby reflecting the values of the papal authority that ruled over the Christian world. Renaissance painting too depicted religious themes, but also mythological allegories, the faces of the Medici,

PORTRAIT OF
LOUIS XIV

(after Hyacinthe
Rigaud)

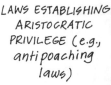

LAWS ESTABLISHING
ARISTOCRATIC
PRIVILEGE (e.g.,
antipoaching
laws)

PROPERTY
OWNERSHIP
BY THE
NOBILITY

Art as ideology

and great military victories, thereby affirming the values of the ruling elite who provided the artist's livelihood. The amazing treatment by Vermeer and the northern baroque artists of light and air in Dutch drawing rooms, kitchens, and studies was the celebration of the values of the bourgeoisie who bought those paintings. The lovely nineteenth-century English landscapes of Constable left one with the feeling that all's well with the (bourgeois) world. Constable's beautiful _Dedham Vale_ shows the lush English countryside leading down the valley to the peaceful village of Dedham, whose church spire we see glimmering in the sun. We do <u>not</u> see the jute factories in which tubercular children are slaving twelve hours a day in order to be able to add a few pieces of bread to their parents' table and add their "surplus labor" (profit) to the sumptuous table of the capitalist owner of the mill. Again, art, like religion, is an opiate. Even the most beautiful art, the greatness of the classics, is "ideology."

But we must add a further complication. For Marx, the material foundations of society, from which all art emerges, are fractured

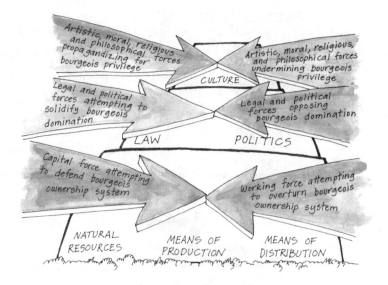

Inside the diagram:

Artistic, moral, religious, and philosophical forces propagandizing for bourgeois privilege

Artistic, moral, religious, and philosophical forces undermining bourgeois privilege

CULTURE

Legal and political forces attempting to solidify bourgeois domination

Legal and political forces opposing bourgeois domination

LAW   POLITICS

Capital force attempting to defend bourgeois ownership system

Working force attempting to overturn bourgeois ownership system

NATURAL RESOURCES   MEANS OF PRODUCTION   MEANS OF DISTRIBUTION

in terms of antagonistic classes. That is, there is a class that owns the material wealth of the society, and there is a dispossessed class that must sell its labor to the owning class. The interests of the one class are not the interests of the other. The interests of the ruling class will always be expressed as the dominant ideas in any historical period, but the interests of the disadvantaged class may find cultural expression too. So for every expression of the socioeconomic foundation in terms of a cultural form, there can be a counterexpression as well. After all, the morality of the aristocrat is not the morality of the serf, nor are their ideas the same, nor their religion, nor their art. Cultured art may be the portrait of the king; "counterculture" art may be a caricature of him, drawn on a wall accompanied by scatological graffiti or, among the working class imbued with class consciousness, a political poster or a mural by José Orozco or Diego Rivera. But apparently from the point of view of the theory of ideology, it must be admitted that "counterculture" or "revolutionary" art, like mainstream art, is propaganda. (Of course, Marx would say that the propaganda of the revolutionary working class is not "ideology" because ideology is always a form of illusion, and the proletariat is the one class that does not need illusion. But this claim itself seems to be ideological. Left-wing propaganda can be as "ideological" as right-wing propaganda.)

As if all this were not bad enough for art, Marx held that some socioeconomic systems were inherently antagonistic to art. This is specifically the case with capitalism. Marx says, "Capitalistic production is hostile to certain branches of spiritual production, for example, art and poetry." [10] Capitalism is hostile to art because "The bourgeoisie has stripped of its halo every occupation hitherto honored and looked up to with reverent awe. It has converted the physician, the lawyer, the priest, the poet, the man of science, into its paid wage-labourers." [11] In capitalism, says Marx:

> Only that wage-labour is productive which produces capital.... For example, Milton, who wrote *Paradise Lost* for £5 sterling, was an *unproductive labourer*. On the other hand, the writer who turns out stuff for his publisher in factory style, is a *productive labourer*. Milton produced *Paradise Lost* for the same reason that a silk worm produces silk. It was an activity of *his* nature. Later he sold the product for £5 sterling. [12]

In capitalism, to be productive is to produce a commodity. But art is not a commodity. It is a necessary expression of the true human essence. Therefore, art and capitalism are incompatible.

Another sense in which capitalism is hostile to art has to do with the division of labor. Marx and his collaborator Friedrich Engels say:

> The exclusive concentration of artistic talent in particular individuals, and its suppression in the broad mass which is bound

Well, paradise lost, but $12.50 gained....

John Milton

up with this, is a consequence of the division of labor . . . . [The issue is not] that each should do the work of Raphael, but anyone in whom there is a potential Raphael should be able to develop without hindrance . . . . In a communist society there are no painters but at most people who engage in painting among other activities.[13]

So far, Marx's theory seems to be the following: The artistic impulse is a natural and necessary expression of human nature. In a truly human and humane community (i.e., in communism), each individual would find an artistic form of expression "according to the laws of beauty," some reaching great heights of artistic excellence, but all achieving a satisfactory expression of the aesthetic urge. However, historically the artistic impulse has sometimes been co-opted and sometimes suppressed. The artistic urge has been corrupted and twisted into a conduit of political propaganda. The artistic form of expression will be liberated only in a postrevolutionary communist society, where humankind's creative birthright will be restored to it.

But there is a problem with this interpretation (not to mention the problem of deciding whether there is any good reason to think Marx is right). If we look at Marx's actual examples, we see

462

that he extolls the very artists whom, as it would seem, his theory should condemn. Obviously, Milton and Raphael, the two artists referred to in the preceding passages, are not being denigrated by Marx; rather, it is implied that he holds them in high esteem Yet these are two artists whose work is essentially religious. Furthermore, if we look at the list of names of artists Marx admired (Balzac, Dickens, Cervantes, and Heine) and consider the fact that every year Marx reread the complete works of Goethe, Shakespeare, and Aeschylus, we discover that his own taste in art was decidedly traditional.

Karl Marx contemplates Raphael's <u>Madonna Del Granduca</u>.

How does Marx's personal preference in art square with his theory of art as ideology? Marx himself seems to have realized that there was some tension between his general theory of culture as ideology and his personal aesthetic taste. He explained the apparent inconsistency by saying that, in some epochs, art is more in bondage to the economic substructure than in other periods. Art can have a relative autonomy if the economic system is not

463

highly developed, if it is not especially hostile to art, and if there are a number of intermediary connections between material production and artistic production. Marx uses Greek art and Shakespeare as examples of the possibility of the uneven development of economy and art. Apparently, Marx felt that neither the form nor the

content of the works of Aeschylus and Shakespeare could be explained purely in terms of the structure of the socioeconomic relations of their day. Such an admission seems to amount to a major qualification of the theories of materialism and ideology.

Romeo, Juliet, and the profit motive

Some might even pose the question as to whether it marks a total abandonment of those theories. Indeed, after Marx's death in 1888, his collaborator, Friedrich Engels, admitted that perhaps he and Marx had overstated the dependence of culture on economics. And Marx himself was so upset by the exaggerations of certain French Marxists that he uttered to Engels, "All I know is that I am not a Marxist."

But perhaps Marx's general theory of culture can be maintained if certain corrections are made to the theory of art. So

thought the contemporary Marxist philosopher, Herbert Marcuse. We
will turn briefly to his work now.

Marcuse

Herbert Marcuse (1898-1979), who
came to America fleeing Nazi per-
secution, was a controversial figure
in the American Left. He was very
influential in Europe and the United
States during the activist period of
the late sixties and early seventies.
During one demonstration in Rome In
1968, the radical students chanted
"M-M-M" (Marx, Mao, Marcuse).
Though ultimately there was a
falling-out between Marcuse and the
student activists because of his re-

Herbert Marcuse
(1898-1979)

fusal to endorse the dismantling of Columbia University in 1972,
there can be no question as to his impact on intellectual developments
in the West. The work that will chiefly concern us here is Eros
and Civilization (1955). In spite of its subtitle, A Philosophical
Inquiry into Freud, this book deals basically with the problem of
art as raised by Plato and Marx and in fact represents a valiant
attempt to synthesize Freud and Marx. This attempt is complicated
by the fact that these two architects of the modern mind seem to
disagree fundamentally on so many important issues (which may
partially explain why the modern mind seems so schizoid).

We can begin our discussion of the pertinent themes in Marcuse's
book by reminding ourselves of one of the basic disagreements

between Marx and Freud. The anarchistic side of Marx envisions a world in which all restraints and all forms of repression are ultimately removed. In that world, the true artistic nature of the human being will flower in ways that heretofore have been possible in only a handful of unique individuals. Freud, on the other hand, saw art as possible only in a world of repression. The doctrine of sublimation holds that only under the repressive conditions established against libidinal energies by the authority of the ego, the superego, and the harshness of reality can those energies be redirected into the field of art. As opposed to Marx, Freud felt that the abolition of repression would not result in a flowering of art, but in a reversion to our murderous, rapacious past of the primeval jungles.

How in the world can Marcuse synthesize this dialectic of extreme opposites? He does so in truly Hegelian fashion by finding truth in both views. Freud is right (and Marx is wrong) to say that society without repression is inconceivable. There will always be restraints and requirements backed up with the implied threat

466

of force. (Someone has
to plant and reap the
corn, slaughter the
fowl, and keep the
sewers open.) This
Marcuse calls "neces-
sary repression." But
Marx is right (and
Freud is wrong) to
recognize that the
bulk of social repres-
sion does not serve
the purpose of meet-
ing basic biological

and social needs; rather, it serves the purpose of guaranteeing the
privileged position of the elite classes. This domination Marcuse calls
"surplus repression." In short, we can say that for Marcuse, the
goal of philosophy (and of political action) is to eliminate "surplus
repression" and to reduce "necessary repression" to an absolute
minimum.

So far, Marcuse's argument has leaned more heavily on Marx
than on Freud, but his "Marxism" is decidedly qualified. For
example, Marx thought that the dialectical laws of history would
guarantee progress and the ultimate success of socialism, but
Marcuse demonstrates that the "dialectic" has broken down. Marx
had held that history would resolve itself into the two ultimate
classes, the bourgeoisie and the proletariat; and the clash between
these two would end the class system as such and result in a
classless society, the initial stage of his true communism. But
Marcuse believed that, rather than clashing with the proletariat,

PUTOOEY

The confrontation between capitalism and the working class, according to Marcuse

the "cunning of capitalism" (far more cunning than Marx gave credit) simply opened its jaws, swallowed the proletariat, chewed it up, and spat it back out as its own best representative. In Marcuse's day, especially in America, the best spokesperson for capitalist values was not the executive of the corporation, but members of the working class itself, who owned stock in the corporations, who marched in hard hats <u>against</u> the peace movement, and whose most radical demand was that they be given the opportunity to consume even more goods. Today, too, all walks of American life have accepted uncritically the view that they are "the consumers." Even the "good guys," the protectors of the people, are called "consumer advocates." We consume movies, lectures, education, and even landscapes. As Erich Fromm, Marcuse's erstwhile ally on the Freudian Left, puts it: "He (modern man) is the eternal consumer; he 'takes in' drink, food, cigarettes, lectures, sights, books, movies; all are consumed, swallowed. The world is one great object for his appetite: a big bottle, a big apple, a big breast."[14]

_If_ the Marxian dialectic were in fact operational, we could expect that this "thesis" would spawn a negative "antithesis," which would fundamentally oppose and eventually destroy the prevailing consumer world. But the "cunning of capitalism" (or really, the cunning of advanced technocracy)

The consumer

has been such as to preempt all possible opposition. So argued Marcuse in _One-Dimensional Man_ (1964). Nothing counts as opposition to the "system." It has become totalitarian, not in the Stalinist or Hitlerian sense, but in that it has "totalized" itself. Everything is, or becomes, a version of the system. In the sixties, the "flower children" concocted a kind of antiestablishment, psychedelic art, which soon found its way to billboards and TV commercials, advertising the useless products spewed out by the system. The "V" sign, which was a symbol of the antiestablishment peace movement, became the victory sign of Richard Nixon.

I am not a crook!

Me neither.

469

The peace symbol itself was quickly available as a decorative embellishment on the checks of a large national bank whose investments in South Vietnam helped bolster the makeshift government there. The symbol was also found on the packages of one of the largest cigarette companies. The growing of long hair as an antiestablishment gesture was so successful that the establishment itself took it over. Patched jeans and farmers' overalls were similarly quickly co-opted. In fact, soon jeans made _entirely_ of prefaded denim patches were available at all the most fashionable, expensive shops. It became obvious to Marcuse that the enemy was no longer Wall Street, but Madison Avenue. Capitalism had not only become cunning; it had gone "cool."

Capitalism: old style, new style

Other apparently antiestablishment activities met the same fate under Marcuse's scrutiny, sometimes to the annoyance of his would-be followers. Smoking marijuana was not a revolutionary activity, nor were the demonstrations to legalize it. Similarly, the so-called sexual revolution came in for criticism. It was no revolution at all, but a new form of manipulation orchestrated by Madison Avenue, or at least quickly co-opted by it. "The pill" was not invented by a hippy, but by a pharmaceutical company. It was not revolutionary fervor that lowered women's necklines, tightened men's trousers, removed "modesty shields" from the front of desks, put full-frontal nudity in the cinema, steamed up prime-time TV, and created such entities as "sexy floorwalkers." Capitalism was not going to be consumed by the fire from burning brassieres or overturned by young people tumbling in and out of each others' beds. Rather than calling all this a sexual revolution, Marcuse called it "repressive de-sublimation." It is the act of reifying ("thingifying") sexuality, turning it into yet another commodity. Marcuse wrote:

> The most telling illustration is provided by the methodological introduction of sexiness in business, politics, propaganda, etc. To the degree to which sexuality obtains a definite sales value or becomes a token of prestige and of playing according to the rules of the game, it is itself transformed into an instrument of social cohesion. [15]

So not only was the sexual freedom of the flower child generation incapable of threatening the foundations of the commodity world; it itself has been transformed into a commodity.

It is finally time to return to our discussion of art. Did Marcuse find any hope in the antiestablishment art that abounded in the sixties and seventies? According to the Marxian theories of the dialectic and of ideology, this kind of art ought at least to provide some ideological opposition to the established powers. But the dialectic has been neutralized, and antiestablishment art has also been co-opted and has simply become avant-garde capitalism. The "living theater," the "guerrilla theater," and rock music (or at least white rock music) all came in for their share of abuse. (To demonstrate that the goal of rock music is not revolution but "noisy aggression," Marcuse enjoyed quoting Grace Slick of the Jefferson Airplane. "'Our eternal goal in life,' Grace says, absolutely deadpan, 'is to get louder.'"[16]

Where, then, if anywhere, is there any hope? Now comes the surprise (if it is still a surprise). In traditional art — in the art that Marx himself loved but could not easily explain! In order to understand Marcuse's rationale here, we will have to return to Freud. It will be recalled that both Freud and Plato found the source of art in fantasy. It was for precisely this reason that both of them were suspicious of art. For Freud, fantasy, particularly un-

It's beautiful! (Its beauty is supposed to lull me into complacency and convince me that all is well with the world, thereby draining me of my revolutionary fervor.)

It's beautiful! (Beside its beauty, my own world looks stale and hollow. This beauty angers me. It makes me demand changes that would bring more beauty into my own world.)

Marx and Marcuse contemplate Constable's _Dedham Vale_.

conscious fantasy, was still guided by the "pleasure principle." It was the one realm that had escaped the "reality principle." Marcuse accepted the Freudian account of art, but not Freud's judgment of it. Art indeed has its source in fantasy, and fantasy, deriving from infantile memories and hopes, indeed escapes the reality principle. But Marcuse came to associate Freud's reality principle with what Marcuse called "surplus repression." Fantasy,

and the art
deriving from
it, is the one
component of
the contempo-
rary psyche
that has re-
fused to accept
the domination
of surplus re-
pression or, for

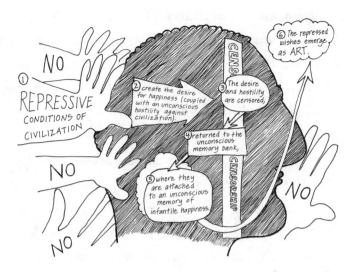

that matter, <u>any</u> repression. Art is indeed a hallucinatory realm.
It is based on the infantile promise of happiness found, perhaps, at the mother's breast, a promise that was betrayed. Therefore, Marcuse calls art too "the promise of happiness" — <u>la
promesse du bonheur</u>, and he calls its beauty "the sensuous
appearance of the idea of freedom." Art, as Freud's "return of
the repressed," is the "negation of the commodity world."
Marcuse says, "The <u>return of the repressed</u> makes up the tabooed
and subterranean history of civilization." [17] It haunts repressive civilization as the memory of happiness that civilization
denies us — a memory from our own individual infancy and perhaps from the infancy of the human race. The value of psychoanalysis is that it has elevated memory to a status of supreme
importance. Of psychoanalysis, Marcuse says:

> Its truth value lies in the specific function of memory to pre-
> serve promises and potentialities which are betrayed and
> even outlawed by the mature, civilized individual, but
> which had once been fulfilled in his dim past and which
> are never entirely forgotten. . . . The psychoanalytic liber-
> ation of memory explodes the rationality of the repressed
> individual. [18]

When we look at a work of classical art, such as one of Vermeer's bourgeois drawing rooms or Constable's English countrysides, we enter into the source of utopian thinking. Rather than these works serving ideologically to convince us that all is well with the world (as a perhaps oversimplistic "Marxist" reading would have it), instead they indict the world. When we return from the realm created by Gauguin, whether it be the softness of the Breton countryside or the lushness of Tahitian eroticism, we must again occupy our own hollow world of dreary _things_ to be consumed. The person who correctly enters into the spirit of art will be disturbed by the fact that his or her world is not what it could be or should be. He or she will be moved to do something concrete about this fact. All great art, art that refuses to be co-opted by the prevailing reality, is revolutionary. It is subversive. It reactivates the dialectic. It is what Marcuse calls "the power of the negative."

Notice that Marcuse's solution to the problem of the status of art never really denies one of Plato's main criticisms. Art lies. It promises a happiness that cannot be achieved. We shall never recline among the green, yellow, and purple shadows of Gauguin's tropical world, nor shall we stroll through the sensuous density of Constable's vale of Dedham. A totally nonrepressive world is impossible. Still, if we do not believe in these possibilities, do not believe in "the noble lie" (Plato's term), we shall never be able to overcome that great surfeit of suppression that is irrational and that _can_ be overcome.

A final critical note here: I believe that Marcuse's synthesis of Marx and Freud has given us an interesting and plausible account of what is exciting in great art. But his account is problematical, for it seems untestable. What would count as evidence for or against Marcuse's interpretations? This is a difficult question to answer. But perhaps Marcuse's theory is no more problematical than other theories of the nature and status of art. Aesthetic theories are often more like recommendations concerning the proper way to view art than they are like scientific theories that could be verified or refuted through careful attention to empirical detail.

Existentialism

Existentialism is a twentieth-century philosophical movement that has had a great interest in art. The term "existentialism" was coined by Jean-Paul Sartre (see "Existential Freedom" in Chapter 6), but the philosophy itself derives from certain currents in the nineteenth century, especially from the thought of Friedrich Nietzsche and Søren Kierkegaard. The task of defining existentialism is complicated by the great variety of philosophers who are called existentialists and by the many discrepancies among their views. One can sympathize with those who finally abandon in exasperation the task of defining existentialism as a philosophy, settling for

Existentialism: A shared mood

calling it "a shared mood" or "an attitude," but I think the task is really not that hopeless. Sartre himself has tried to define existentialism in a simple, relatively successful manner. We will follow his lead.

Sartre says that an existentialist is any philosopher who has as a guiding idea the view that, in the case of human beings at least, "existence precedes essence." Now, traditionally in philosophy, it has been held that the opposite is so, that "essence precedes existence." To sort out this debate between Sartre and the tradition, we have to return to Plato and Aristotle. In Greek thought, "essence" is associated with "nature" (as when we ask, "What is the nature of the beast?") and with "Form" in the Platonic sense. The Platonic doctrine, with which we are familiar, holds that a natural object or a human being exists only as a copy of a Form, so for Plato, "essence precedes existence." As we saw, Aristotle tried to bring Plato's Forms down to earth, pointing out that "Form" with a capital "F" was really "form" with a small "f." In other words, the Form of a knife is actually its <u>shape</u>, which is related to its <u>function</u>. (What would a knife with flabby edges be like? Well, it wouldn't be a knife, because it couldn't function as a knife.) So to say that "essence precedes existence" is to say that first

Fig. 1

the nature and function of a thing exist; then the thing exists.

Sartre agrees that this formula is true of artifacts, such as knives, and seems to agree that it is true of natural entities, too. For instance, in the case of a knife, first the human being conceives of a <u>function</u> (fig. 1). He <u>needs</u> something that will cut the bread. Then he creates an object that fulfills this function (fig. 2). It is perhaps less clear how this analysis applies to natural objects, such as oak trees, mountains, and pussycats, but I suppose we can say that there really is a thing called the species "cat" (i.e., there is a "cat

476

nature") and that, to be a cat, a thing must fulfill certain criteria of "catness." (This all sounds very Platonic.) Now, the _old_ picture of the human being, that is, the preexistential picture, treats the human being the same way as it treats the cat or knife. First, there is God. He conceives of the human being. ("What I need is one like me, only smaller, weaker, and dumber" [fig. 3].) Then, Michelangelo style, he creates one (fig. 4). The creature is truly human only insofar as it fulfills certain divine criteria. Actions falling outside these criteria will be viewed as "inhuman," or even "insane." Then along comes Friedrich Nietzsche with his bad news, "God is dead!" If we erase God from the picture, all we get is the scene in fig. 5, which is the human condition according to the existentialists. The human being is, as Kierkegaard said, in "absolute isolation" and as Sartre says, "abandoned." Sartre asks:

what is meant here by saying that existence precedes essence? It means that, first of all, man exists, turns up, appears on the scene, and, only afterwards, defines himself. If man, as the existentialist conceives him, is indefinable, it is because at first he is nothing. Only

Fig. 2

Fig. 3

Fig. 4

Fig. 5

afterwards will he be something, and he himself will have made what he will be. Thus there is no human nature, since there is no God to conceive it. [19]

This account seems to make existentialism essentially atheistic and would appear to rule out Kierkegaard's inclusion in its ranks. And indeed, Nietzsche and Sartre, along with many other existentialists, are radically atheistic; but a few pages beyond the passage just quoted, Sartre himself says, somewhat contradictorily perhaps, "... even if God did exist, that would change nothing." [20] And, like Kierkegaard, Sartre uses the case of Abraham as an exemplification of the human condition. For Kierkegaard, the human condition is one of absolute isolation. In his despair, he calls out for God's help, but the answer is — as the Kierkegaardian, Ingmar Bergman, says in the title of his movie — _The Silence_. For Kierkegaard, this would be bad enough if there were no God. But it is worse because there _is_ a God. A qualitative abyss gapes open between man and God. As in Sartre's philosophy, the human is left alone, forlorn, dreading the total freedom that is his, despairing over the immense task of assuming the responsibility for the world he must create. If you agree with this picture, you are an existentialist.

From its first moments in the writings of Kierkegaard and Nietzsche, existentialism has always been fascinated by art. However, contemporary existentialists do not simply philosophize about art in a technical manner; many of them actively

478

produce art. Sartre, Simone de Beauvoir, and Albert Camus produced systematic treatises on philosophy but also wrote novels, short stories, and plays. Nietzsche wrote poetry; Miguel de Unamuno wrote novels, plays, and poetry. And the novelists Franz Kafka and Fyodor Dostoyevsky are often included in the ranks of the existentialists. In order to see how existentialism theorizes about art, we will briefly inspect the work of two contemporary American existentialists, Arturo Fallico and Maurice Natanson. I have selected them because their books are readable and at the same time representative of the technical philosophizing about art that emerges from the phenomenological-existential school.

In Arturo Fallico's book, _Art and Existentialism_, he says, concerning the possibility of an existentialistic aesthetic, "we must try to see what we can learn about the condition of man from the art phenomenon, and about the art phenomenon from the existential condition of man."[21] One of the main themes in his book is that there is a sense in which the world confronts us like a work of art, but there is also a sense in which the world confronts us quite differently from a work of art, and there is something about art and human existence that we can learn from each of these phenomena. The sense in which the world confronts us like a work of art is that our lived-in world is fundamentally aesthetic rather than scientific. The hegemony of science over the modern mind may make us forget this fact, but actually the world presents itself in terms of experienced qualities of the type better described in terms of the language of the art critic than in terms of the language of the physicist. To the unjaded eye, the world presents itself like a spontaneous work of art. Under the impact of this insight, Fallico, with Nietzsche, talks about the possibility of "the aesthetic transformation of our experience"

479

becoming our individual existential project. He approvingly quotes Nietzsche, who said, "To the extent that man is artist, he is already delivered from his ego and has become a medium through which the true subject celebrates his redemption in illusion." In _The Birth of Tragedy_, Nietzsche tells a story, which he calls "an old legend," about King Midas, who

The world confronts us like a work of art.

hunted a long time in the woods for the wise Silenus, companion of Dionysos, without being able to catch him. When he had finally caught him the king asked him what he considered man's greatest good. The daemon remained sullen and uncommunicative until finally, forced by the king, he broke into a shrill laugh and spoke: "Ephemeral wretch, begotten by accident and toil, why do you force me to tell you what it would be to your greatest boon not to hear? What would be best for you is quite beyond your reach: not to have been born, not to _be_, to be _nothing_. But the second best is to die soon."[22]

In the context of Nietzsche's version of existentialism, the moral of the story is that the demon Silenus is correct _unless_ an individual does something to prove Silenus wrong. Unless one _creates_

something, and
for Nietzsche,
creation itself
is artistic, then
it would be better
that one had
never been born.
For Nietzsche,
existence can
be redeemed
only artistically.

Having asserted
the similarity between art
and the world and the significance of this similarity for us
humans, Fallico then turns to the <u>difference</u> between the world
and the work of art. The difference inheres in the fact that in
its spontaneity, the world presents itself to us as "not-done-
and-having-to-be-attended-to." The art work, in contrast,
presents itself as a totality, a completed unity, a fullness, and
a completeness that
is unavailable
anywhere else
in existence.
The "still life"
is the exem-
plar of all
art. "In
art," says
Fallico,
"everything

The world as not-done-and-having-to-be-attended-to

Art reveals our homeless condition.

_is_, nothing is becoming or has need to become." Only art conquers time. Like Faust, in Goethe's great drama of the same name, we cry out to time, "Stay!" But time does not stay. In art, time _does_ stay. Art shows that "human existence is a lack rather than a plenitude of being and meaning."[23] It is a testimony of "man's homeless condition and his lack of essence." So once again, according to Fallico, art shows us that we must _create_. "Art places on exhibit a way of validating existence."[24] Art shows us what value, in its pure possibility, is.

Another American author in the phenomenological-existential tradition is Maurice Natanson. The title of his book, _The Journeying Self_, also emphasizes our homeless nature. We are told by Natanson that the confrontation with art affords the individual the opportunity of passing from the typical to the symbolic, or from the familiar to the transcendental. In art works, we find represented the great "metaphysical constants of human existence, Birth, Aging, Inter-subjectivity and Death." Of course, in daily life, we continually run up against these great constants too, but precisely because they are so enmeshed in our day-to-day existence, we are unable to isolate these themes in terms of their true significance. In art, I confront birth, sociality, and death in a way that is "primordially unlike all my acquaintance with individual births and deaths." Here, "the

482

naive attitude of daily life is forced to the edge of its limits" as
"the symbolic cuts a gash in common sense and draws its hot blood."[25]
The radical confrontation through art with the ultimate themes of
birth, sociality, and death forces the individual to philosophize ex-
istentially as he or she struggles to construct the foundations of his
or her own world. The existentialistic point might best be expressed
by relating an anec-
dote told of the
German poet, Rainer
Maria Rilke, who,
after spending an
afternoon contem-
plating the beauty of
the statue of Apollo
in an Athenian
museum, returned to
his hotel and made
the following single
entry in his journal:
"You must change
your life."[26] This
demonstrates a

common denominator in existentialism and the theory of Herbert
Marcuse. According to both, art can and should provoke us into action
and creation.

Wittgenstein

We will now turn to a very different kind of discussion of art from those
we've seen so far. It will be somewhat less dramatic than some of the

material we have looked at to date, but it contains interest in its own right. It stems from the work of the Viennese philosopher LUDWIG WITTGENSTEIN (1889-1951), who studied and taught at Cambridge. Wittgenstein is hardly a household name among the general public. You probably had not heard of him before taking a philosophy class. But many people believe he will prove to be one of the two or three greatest philosophers of the twentieth century, and certainly one of the most influential.

Wittgenstein's work is usually divided into two periods, one centering on his _Tractatus Logico-philosophicus_, written early in his career, and the other on his _Philosophical Investigations_, a much later work (published posthumously). The first book is a strange combination of a variation on the theme of "logical positivism" and mysticism. The second book apparently abandons these strains and concentrates on the subtle workings of everyday thought, language, and action.

In the _Tractatus_, there is only one passage that could be construed as dealing with art. Characteristically, it is an obscure passage. Wittgenstein says, "Ethics and aesthetics are one and the same." Because in that book

Wittgenstein had put ethics outside the realm of language ("It is clear that ethics cannot be put into words"); it follows that the object of aesthetics (philosophical meditation on beauty) is part of the mystical and that nothing intelligible can be said about it. [27] In the Tractatus, Wittgenstein followed his own advice and said nothing about art. (His admonishment at the beginning of the book had been, "Whereof one cannot speak, thereof should one remain silent!") However, the later Wittgenstein had a number of things to say with implications for art theory, some of which have proved to be quite provocative and have become

Was sich überhaupt sagen lässt, lässt sich klar sagen; und wovon man nicht reden kann, darüber muss man schweigen.

the grist for the mills of later philosophers. We will examine two areas of the later Wittgenstein's thought on art that have proved to be especially instructive. One of them has to do with Wittgenstein's discussion of the "open-endedness" of certain concepts; the other concerns his notion of a language as a "form of life." As can be seen, neither of these two topics contains any specific reference to art; yet their application to the problems of the philosophy of art has generated much interest and much controversy of late. However, before we can apply Wittgenstein's ideas to the topic of this chapter, art, we will have to spend a couple of pages

485

developing the key Wittgensteinian notions.

Open Concepts

Wittgenstein believed that over and over again in the history of philosophy, thinkers had been deceived by taking a particular, successful model of clarity and trying to force all of language and thought into the mold of that one model. He called this error a form of linguistic bewitchment of the intellect. A clear example of this kind of error is the attempt to come up with a general theory of meaning based on certain examples from mathematics or logic. For instance, take the definition of a triangle: "A triangle is a three-sided closed figure." Now assuming standard meanings for words like "side" and "closed," this definition is exhaustive. Any candidate for the term "triangle" must meet this criterion. There can be a variety of kinds of triangles (isosceles, right, obtuse), but each one must nevertheless be a three-sided closed figure. Then this feature, which can be called "the essence of triangularity," is the feature common to all possible triangles. A similar kind of analysis can be performed on such concepts as "brother" (a brother is a male sibling) or "bachelor" (a bachelor is an unmarried, eligible male). Inspired by this kind of clarity, many philosophers, especially philosophers of a Platonic bent who are looking for "essences," have claimed that a word is meaningful only if it is the name of a certain feature common to all members of a class, and in fact it is possible to view Socrates as spending his whole life trying to force all concepts to behave the way mathematical concepts behave.

In order to destroy the illusion that a successful theory of meaning can be based on such a model, Wittgenstein asks us to consider the concept of "game." However, he does not ask us to _philosophize_ about the concept; rather, he asks us to _look_ at all the activities we call

486

"games" in order to see whether we discover anything they all have in common.

Consider for example the proceedings that we call "games". I mean board-games, card-games, ball-games, Olympic games, and so on. What is common to them all? — Don't say: "There *must* be something common, or they would not be called 'games'" — but *look and see* whether there is anything common to all. — For if you look at them you will not see something that is common to *all*, but similarities, relationships, and a whole series of them at that. To repeat: don't think, but look! — Look for example at board-games, with their multifarious relationships. Now pass to card-games; here you find many correspondences with the first group, but many common features drop out, and others appear. When we pass next to ball-games, much that is common is retained, but much is lost. — Are they all 'amusing'? Compare chess with noughts and crosses. Or is there always *winning and losing*, or *competition* between players? Think of patience. In ball games there is winning and losing; but when a child throws his ball at the wall and catches it again, this feature has disappeared. Look at the parts played by *skill and luck*; and at the difference between skill in chess and skill in tennis. Think now of games like ring-a-ring-a-roses; here is the element of amusement, but how many other characteristic features have disappeared! And we can go through the many, many other groups of games in the same way; can see how similarities crop up and disappear.

And the result of this examination is: we see a complicated network of similarities overlapping and criss-crossing: sometimes overall similarities, sometimes similarities of detail.[28]

Notice what Wittgenstein means when he refers to characteristics like "amusing," "winning and losing," "competition," and "skill and luck." Take the term "amusing." Is it the case that everything that is amusing is a game and that all games are amusing (or "fun" or "enjoyable")? Exactly who must be amused? Must the players be amused as well as the spectators, if there are spectators? Imagine a professional baseball game on the last day of the season between the two last place teams. Only a handful of spectators has made the mistake of showing up to see what turns out to be the most sloppily-

played game of the season in the most miserable weather of the year. It is quite possible that you could interview every person in the stadium and discover that nobody was enjoying himself. Neverthe-less, it certainly would not follow that, because no one was having fun, no game of baseball was being played. (And the fact that the game was a _professional_ game doesn't keep it from being a game either.) In fact, I am sure that I have played games of Monopoly that went on so long that, toward the end, no one was enjoying the game. It was just that no one wanted to be the first to admit that the game was not fun. Finally, it is simply absurd to say that the only way of establishing that a particular activity is a game would be to interview people to find out whether anybody was having a good time.

Similar fates await any attempt to define games in terms of "winning and losing" or "skill and luck." Just look at ring-around-the rosy. There is no winning or losing there, and how much skill or luck do you need just to fall down? (Ring-around-the-rosy, by the way, is one of those games whose <u>origins</u>, at least, are hardly amusing. It probably derives from the period when the Black Plague swept England. The "rosy"

is the red ring around the mortal sores, or, on some theories, the rosary. Thank goodness, the sinisterness of the last line, "Ashes to ashes, we all fall down," usually escapes our children.)

What about "competition"? Consider the game my son invented when he was five years old (probably along with every other five-year-old boy) called "hit-the-ball-against-the-wall." With whom was he competing? Perhaps he was competing against himself? But surely there is a difference between the case of the boy who plays to see how many times he can hit the ball without missing and the case of the boy who first pretends he is Tom, then Bill. When "Tom" misses the ball, it is "Bill's" turn to hit it. In this latter case, the boy really is competing against himself. When I was small, my cousin talked me into playing a game _he_ invented. He called it, "push-the-boy-down-the-stairs." There may or may not have been competition involved in that game.

Push-the-boy-down-the-stairs

It might be suggested that all games have <u>rules</u> in common by virtue of which they are called games. It is probably true that all games have rules (a possible exception is "the Caucus race" in <u>Alice in Wonderland</u>), but so do all sorts of things that are not games — crossing the street, giving a lecture, attending a movie, etc. In fact, there is a significant sense in which all recognizable human activities are rule governed. In the face of this fact, some of my students like to say that, after all, everything <u>is</u> a game, especially school. (To this I usually reply that Aztec jai-alai was also a game, and the loser was decapitated; some games are more serious than other games.) And in fact, it is curious that almost any activity can be <u>made</u> into a game. (When I was a kid and had to mow the lawn, I used to pretend that the unmowed grass was "the Nazis." I still shave that way sometimes. I knew a

man who
drove home in
the commuter
traffic pre-
tending he
was a pilot in
a bombing
squadron. I
found this out
once when he
forgot I was with
him; as he pulled into

his suburban driveway, he put his fist to his mouth as if he was
talking into a microphone and muttered, "Lame Duck, Lame Duck;
clear runway number five for a crash landing!") The fact that
any activity can be made into a game proves that not all activities _are_ games. Eric Berne's book, <u>Games</u> <u>People</u> <u>Play</u>, was a
success precisely because the activities he listed were not really

games. My favorite in his list was the "game" he called "See-what-you-made-me-do!" There _is_ a ritualized, game-like quality in the activities of people who scapegoat, but if you buy a book called Party Games, in it you will never find "See-what-you-made-me-do!" If you could find such a game, then Berne could not have included it in _his_ book.

See what you made me do!

Games people play

As we saw in Chapter I, Wittgenstein's conclusion concerning the undefinability of the concept "game" in spite of the many similarities among games is this:

> I can think of no better expression to characterize these similarities than "family resemblances"; for the various resemblances between members of a family: build, features, colour of eyes, gait, temperament, etc. etc. overlap and criss-cross in the same way. — And I shall say: 'games' form a family.[29]

"Game," then, is an "open concept." That means that we could never close the concept with a specific definition, in the way that we _can_ do with "triangle," because it is always possible, and even likely, that at a later date we will want to include a new activity under the concept "game."

You may have already guessed what all this has to do with art (or have deduced it from the few comments concerning this issue in Chapter 1). Those who seek an exhaustive definition of the word "art" may be in the same bind as those who seek to define the word "game." Wittgenstein himself only hinted at this conclusion. It has been explicitly drawn by a follower of his, Morris Weitz, in an influential article, "The Role of Theory in Aesthetics." Professor Weitz defines the term "open concept" in the following way:

> A concept is open if its conditions of application are emendable and corrigible; i.e., if a situation or case can be imagined or secured which would call for some sort of <u>decision</u> on our part to extend the use of the concept to cover this, or to close the concept and invent a new one to deal with the new case and its new property. If necessary and sufficient conditions for the application of a concept can be stated, the concept is a closed one. But this can happen only in logic or mathematics where concepts are constructed and completely defined. It cannot occur with empirically-descriptive and normative concepts unless we arbitrarily close them by stipulating the ranges of their uses.[30]

According to Weitz, then, questions like, "Is Andy Warhol's 'Elvis' art?" cannot be answered by appealing to an already established definition; rather, a <u>decision</u> is called for. Shall we extend the concept "art" to cover this case? Apparently the

Hmm. This calls for a decision.

GENUINE ELVIS ART ON BLACK VELVET

reasons one can give to justify one's decision to apply or withhold the title "art" must have to do with what Wittgenstein calls "family resemblances." (Is "push-the-boy-down-the-stairs" similar enough to other activities we call games to justify our extending the term "game" to cover this case also?)

If Weitz's Wittgensteinian account of the concept of art is correct, at least he will have explained what is surely one of the most puzzling features of contemporary art. He will have explained why the current crisis in art need not undermine the very concept of art itself. Only in our day could an event like the one described in Chapter 1 take place (a dump truck backs into an art museum and dumps a pile of gravel; the driver places a small embossed card by the pile bearing the title The Gravel Pile; people seriously interested in art read the card and slowly circle the pile, gazing studiously into it, arguing among themselves about its artistic merit). Old Socrates would have said that if one could not define art in such a way as to give its essence, and thereby give absolute reasons for calling something "art" or for declaring it not to be art, then one had no right to claim to know anything about art. But Weitz's analysis allows all the museum visitors to be certain that Vermeer's Woman Reading a Letter Beside a Window is art, and it also allows them to argue rationally about the status of The Gravel Pile.

A Form of Life

It is perhaps ironic that the most serious challenge to Morris Weitz's Wittgensteinian analysis of the concept of art comes from a group of philosophers who are themselves deeply influenced by Wittgenstein. They base their challenge on an aspect of Wittgenstein's philosophy different from the one that has inspired Weitz. The basic position of these philosophers of art was laid down in articles by Arthur Danto and George Dickie. It is called "the institutional theory of art." It was Dickie who actually formulated the theory, but his formulation is based on this line of Danto's: "To see something as art requires something the eye cannot de(s)cry — an atmosphere of artistic theory, a knowledge of the history of art: an artworld"[31] Professor Dickie takes Danto's idea of "an artworld" and interprets it in the light of the following remark of Wittgenstein's: "And to imagine a language means to imagine a form of life."[32] Wittgenstein insisted that we always consider language as a _social_ activity. Similarly, Dickie stresses the social context of art and of the discourse about art. He believes that if we _do_ place art in its social context, we will be able to define art adequately in spite of Weitz's assurance of the wrongheadedness of such attempts. Here is Dickie's definition: "A work of art in the classificatory sense is (1) an artifact (2) upon which some person or persons acting on behalf of a certain social institution (the Artworld) have conferred the status of candidate for appreciation."[33] Dickie's definition is based on an analogy between the institutional nature of "the Artworld" and other social institutions. For example, a particular round, white, hideboond pellet becomes a "strike" when it has that status conferred upon it by an umpire; an adult male human and an adult female human become "married" when they have that status conferred upon them by a clergyman or justice of the peace; the author of a particular action becomes "guilty" when that status is conferred upon him by a jury or a judge. Similarly, a particular object becomes "art" when the title is conferred upon it by some member of the artworld, usually the artist who created the artifact, but sometimes the "artist" can confer that status

on "ready-mades," as the twentieth-century French Dadaist artist Marcel Duchamp did in the case of urinals and snow shovels. (In fact, Dickie tells us that it is the work of Duchamp and his followers, Rauschenberg, Warhol, and Oldenburg, that inspired his new definition of art.) Professor Dickie summarizes his argument, saying, "The main point I am trying to make is that something is art because of the place it has in a certain social system."[34]

Dickie's view has been influential among contemporary aestheticians, but not all of them are satisfied that he has refuted Weitz's claim that art is an open concept. For example, B.R. Tilghman implies that Dickie's definition really comes down to claiming that "it's art if the artist says it's art," and he claims that such a definition "is altogether wide of the mark; the real issue of understanding and appreciation is not touched."[35] Nevertheless, Tilghman agrees with Dickie in stressing the social nature of art. Tilghman quotes Wittgenstein's *Lectures and Conversations*, where Wittgenstein says, "The words we call aesthetic judgments play a very complicated role, but a very definite role, in what we call the culture of a period. To describe their use or to describe what you mean by a cultured taste, you have to describe a culture."[36]

Finally, I want to report on a contribution to this discussion of art made by Timothy Binkley, another contemporary philosopher deeply influenced by Wittgenstein. Binkley completely disarms Dickie's definition by making the following stipulation: "I hereby create a prodigious class of pieces of art by specifying everything to be art."[37] If Dickie's definition allows everything to be art, what is the point of drawing the distinction?

(Compare Binkley's stipulation with the piece of "conceptual art" alluded to in Chapter 1, to which Binkley refers, created by Robert Barry: "All the things I know but of which I am not at the moment thinking — 1:36 P.M., 15 June 1969, New York.")

So Binkley wants to return to Weitz's Wittgensteinian claim that art is undefinable. However, he finds that Weitz's specific account makes art seem too tame. Binkley says that the family resemblances of "games" allow us to discriminate clear cases of games from clear cases of nongames, but the recent history of art indicates that this is not the case with art. He says that art is "radically open, radically indefinable,"

Conclusion

Even if we accept the Wittgensteinian view about art—that it is a "radically open concept," and that art is always a part of the social fabric of any culture—we can still appreciate Plato's perplexity about art. We can recognize its seductive and manipulative features. Because art, as Freud and Marcuse point out, is extrarational and grounded in fantasy, it pulls us away from reality and "the reality principle." There is good news and bad news here.

The bad news: the pull is toward phoniness, frivolity, danger, and even madness. All art is, as Arnold Hauser has said, a version of Quixotism.[38] (You will recall that Don Quixote abandoned real life for the life of romantic novels and went mad in the process. And of course the delicious irony here is that Don Quixote himself is merely a character in a novel [and what a novel!]. We readers are the Don Quixotes who escape our real world for his. Art always offers an alternative reality, hence the possibility of madness, or sometimes a substitute for the madness that is the everyday world [the title of Freud's book: The Psychopathology of Everyday Life].)

The good news: but art also pulls toward philosophy (as Aristotle and the existentialists have it), and toward joy and the celebration of life (as Nietzsche has it) — the large beside the small pleases!

Plato and the Greeks called art a form of mimesis (imitation). The very term connoted for Plato a kind of simulacrum - a replacement for reality by something not as rich as what it replaced. This Platonic concept is too narrow (what do a painting by Jackson Pollack, a musical composition by John Cage, or James Joyce's Finnegan's Wake imitate?), but not so far off after all. Art does not imitate the world, but it represents it. However, what it represents is neither Plato's icy, timeless Forms (though it does formalize and

498

arrest what it represents, and in that sense rescues it from time),
nor does it represent mere "things." It represents the world in all of
its actual and possible aspects. And in doing so, it reveals itself as
being a kind of infinite regress, as art represents itself representing
itself. (Most paintings are influenced more by other paintings than
by the natural world, and most books [including this one] are about
other books.) The nature of art, then, is not so different from the nature
of the mind, whose nature it also is to represent the world and to
represent itself to itself. So if art offers the possibility of madness
and degradation, it also offers the possibility of insight, joy, progress,
sophistication, and redemption. Once again, in this respect, it is
like the human mind itself.

Notes

1. Plato, The Republic, in Great Dialogues of Plato, Eric H. Warmington and Philip G. Rouse, eds., W.H.D. Rouse, trans. (New York:
New American Library, 1956), pp. 369-370.

2. Arnold Hauser, The Philosophy of Art History (Cleveland, Ohio:
Meridian Books, 1963), p. 56.

3. Aristotle, Politics, in Aristotle: On Poetry and Style, G.M.A.
Grube, trans. (New York: Liberal Arts Press, 1958), pp. xv-xvi.

4. Aristotle, Politics, pp. xv-xvi.

5. Quoted by Erich Fromm, ed., Marx's Concept of Man, T.B.
Bottomore, trans. (New York: Frederick Ungar, 1969), p.38.

6. Karl Marx, "Alienated Labor," in Fromm, Marx's Concept of Man,
p. 102.

7. Robert Tucker, Philosophy and Myth in Karl Marx (New York:
Cambridge University Press, 1965), pp. 157-158.

8. Karl Marx, "Preface to a Contribution to the Karl Marx Critique of

Political Economy," in Fromm, <u>Marx's Concept of Man</u>, pp. 217-218.

9. Karl Marx, "The German Ideology," in Fromm, <u>Marx's Concept of Man</u>, p. 212.

10. Karl Marx, "Theories of Surplus Value," quoted in Adolfo Sánchez Vázquez, <u>Art and Society: Essays in Marxist Aethetics</u>, Maro Riofrancos, trans. (New York: Monthly Review Press, 1973), p. 155.

11. Karl Marx and Friedrich Engels, "Manifesto of the Communist Party," in <u>Marx and Engels: Basic Writings on Politics and Philosophy</u> (Garden City, New York: Doubleday, 1959), p. 10.

12. Karl Marx, "Theories of Surplus Value," quoted in Sánchez Vázquez, <u>Art and Society</u>, pp. 200-201.

13. Karl Marx, "The German Ideology," quoted in Sánchez Vázquez, <u>Art and Society</u>, pp. 282, 285, 286.

14. Erich Fromm, <u>The Dogma of Christ and Other Essays on Religion, Psychology and Culture</u> (New York: Holt, Rinehart and Winston, 1963), p. 96.

15. Herbert Marcuse, <u>Eros and Civilization: A Philosophical Inquiry into Freud</u> (New York: Vintage Books, 1955), pp. IX-X.

16. Herbert Marcuse, <u>Counterrevolution and Revolt</u> (Boston: Beacon Press, 1972), p. 115.

17. Marcuse, <u>Eros and Civilization</u>, p. 15.

18. Marcuse, <u>Eros and Civilization</u>, p. 18.

19. Jean-Paul Sartre, <u>Existentialism and Human Emotions</u> (New York: Philosophical Library, 1957), p. 15.

20. Sartre, <u>Existentialism</u>, p. 51.

21. Arturo B. Fallico, <u>Art and Existentialism</u> (Englewood Cliffs, New Jersey: Prentice-Hall, 1962), p. 52.

22. Friedrich Nietzsche, <u>The Birth of Tragedy</u>, Francis Gollfing, trans. (Garden City, New York: Doubleday Anchor, 1956), p. 29.

23. Fallico, _Art and Existentialism_, pp. 74-75, 65.

24. Fallico, _Art and_ Existentialism, pp. 66, 81.

25. Maurice Natanson, _The Journeying Self: A Study in Philosophy and Social Role_ (Reading, Massachusetts: Addison-Wesley, 1970), p. 122.

26. Quoted by Arthur Danto, _Mysticism and Morality: Oriental Thought and Moral Philosophy_ (New York: Harper & Row, 1972), p. 77.

27. Ludwig Wittgenstein, _Tractatus Logico-Philosophicus_, D.F. Pears and B.F. McGuinness, trans. (London: Routledge and Kegan Paul, 1961), sec. 6.421, p. 147.

28. Ludwig Wittgenstein, _Philosophical Investigations_, G.E.M. Anscombe, trans. (New York: Macmillan, 1964), pp. 31-32.

29. Wittgenstein, _Philosophical Investigations_, p. 32.

30. Morris Weitz, "The Role of Theory in Aesthetics," in _Philosophy Looks at the Arts: Contemporary Readings in Aesthetics_, Joseph Margolis, ed. (New York: Charles Scribner's Sons, 1962), p. 54.

31. Arthur Danto, "The Artworld," in _Culture and Art_, Lars Aagaard-Mogensen, ed. (Atlantic Highlands, New Jersey: Humanities Press, 1976), p. 16.

32. Wittgenstein, _Philosophical Investigations_, p. 8.

33. George Dickie, "The Institutional Conception of Art," in _Language and Aesthetics_, Benjamin R. Tilghman, ed. (Wichita: University Press of Kansas, 1973), p. 23.

34. Dickie, "The Institutional Conception," p. 30.

35. Benjamin R. Tilghman, "Artistic Puzzlement," in Aagaard-Mogensen, _Culture and Art_, p. 80.

36. Tilghman, "Artistic Puzzlement," in Aagaard-Mogensen, _Culture and Art_, p. 80.

37. Timothy Binkley, "Deciding About Art," in Aagaard-Mogensen, _Culture_ _and_ _Art_, p. 109.

38. Hauser, _The_ _Philosophy_, p. 55.

Glossary

(An asterisk* indicates that a term is cross-referenced within the Glossary.)

A POSTERIORI. A belief, proposition,* or argument is said to be _a posteriori_ if its truth or falsity can be established only through observation. Classical empiricism* was an attempt to show that all significant knowledge about the world is based on _a posteriori_ truths.

A PRIORI. A belief, proposition,* or argument is said to be _a priori_ if its truth or falsity can be known independently of observation. Definitions, arithmetic, and the principles of logic are usually held to be _a priori._ Classical rationalism* was an attempt to show that all significant knowledge of the world is based on _a priori_ truths, which most of the rationalists associated with innate ideas.*

AESTHETICS. The philosophy of art or sometimes the philosophy of beauty.

AGNOSTICISM. A view that holds open the possibility that God exists, but that claims we do not know, or cannot know, whether he exists in fact.

ANALYTIC GEOMETRY. The branch of mathematics created by René Descartes in which algebraic procedures are applied to geometry.

ANALYTIC PROPOSITION. A proposition* is analytic if its negation leads to a self-contradiction. For example, "squares have four sides" is analytic because its negation, "squares do not have four sides," is a self-contradiction. See also TAUTOLOGY,* CONCEPTUAL TRUTH,* and A PRIORI.*

ANARCHISM. The political doctrine according to which the state is both unnatural and unjustifiable because it necessarily violates the rights of individuals.

ANOMIE. A sociological term designating a condition in individuals or societies characterized by a loss of direction, meaning, values, and norms.

ATHEISM. The view that there is no God.

ATOMISM. As an ontological* theory, the view that the ultimate building blocks of reality are basic, irreducible particles of matter — atoms. (This view is a version of materialism.*) As an epistemological* theory, the view that the ultimate building blocks of knowledge are basic, irreducible, perceptual units — sense-data.* (This view, called "psychological atomism," is a version of empiricism.*)

BAD FAITH. A technical term in the philosophy of Jean-Paul Sartre naming a state of human inauthenticity, a flight from responsibility, freedom,* and anguish. A kind of willful self-deception in which one tries to convince oneself that one is not the sole source of one's being and actions.

BEHAVIORISM. The theory that only observable, objective features of human or animal activity need be studied to provide an adequate scientific account of that activity. See also HARD BEHAVIORISM,* SOFT BEHAVIORISM,* and LOGICAL BEHAVIORISM.*

BEING-FOR-ITSELF. A term in the philosophy of Jean-Paul Sartre designating human reality.

BEING-IN-ITSELF. A term in the philosophy of Jean-Paul Sartre designating nonhuman reality — "being" as it is prior to human intervention.

CATEGORICAL IMPERATIVE, the. The name given by Immanuel Kant to a purported universal moral law: in one form,

504

"So act that the maxim of your action could be willed as a universal law," in another form, "So act as to treat humanity ... always as an end, and never as merely a means."

CATEGORY MISTAKE. A key philosophical error noted by the British "linguistic philosopher"* Gilbert Ryle wherein a term that belongs to one logical category is mistakenly categorized as belonging to another. Then faulty questions are asked based on the miscategorization. For example (according to Ryle), Descartes' assumption that the mind is a <u>thing</u> in the same way that the body is a thing, then asking how these two "things" interact, is a category mistake.

CAUSAL EXPLANATION. A mechanical kind of explanation in which the object or event to be accounted for is rendered intelligible by demonstrating how that object or event follows necessarily from antecedent objects or events. Causal explanations are usually represented in terms of natural laws. Contrast with TELEOLOGICAL EXPLANATION.*

COGNITIVE DISSONANCE. A state of perceptual confusion caused by the experience of sensations that are different from those anticipated.

COMMUNISM. The political theory that advocates the abolition of private property and asserts that goods must be held in common and that the ideal social unit is the commune. See also MARXISM.*

CONCEPTUAL ART. A late twentieth-century art form in which concepts rather than objects are designated as works of art.

CONCEPTUAL TRUTH. A proposition* expresses a conceptual truth if that truth is based on a merely logical relationship rather than on an empirical fact. For example, "widows are female" is a conceptual truth. See also ANALYTIC PROPOSITION,* TAUTOLOGY,* and <u>A PRIORI</u>.*

CONCEPTUALISM. The epistemological view that concepts are generalized ideas that exist only in the mind, but they are derived from real similarities and distinctions in nature from which the mind is capable of abstracting.

CONTINGENT (or CONTINGENCY). A relation between two objects or ideas is contingent if one of the terms of the relationship could exist without the other; if term A is dependent on term B, but term B is not dependent on term A; or if neither term A nor term B depends on the other. For example, Descartes says that the relation between the soul and the body is contingent because the soul can exist without the body, and bodies can exist without souls. Contrast with NECESSITY.*

COSMOLOGICAL ARGUMENT. An attempt to establish God's existence by deducing it from some observable facts in the world. For example, Thomas Aquinas' claim that from the observation of causal chains in the world we can deduce the necessity of a "first cause," or God.

DADA (or DADISM). From the French word for hobbyhorse, a Continental art movement conceived as a protest against the mechanized slaughter of World War I. It manifested a nihilistic* irrationality calculated to inform the public that all established moral and aesthetic values were meaningless after the horrors of the war.

DECONSTRUCTION. The intellectual creation of the contemporary French philosopher Jacques Derrida, based on his eccentric but provocative reading of the linguistic theory of Ferdinand de Saussure, deconstruction is a theory of <u>texts</u> (philosophical, fictional, legal, scientific) according to which, due to the very nature of thought and language, almost all traditional texts can be shown to "deconstruct" themselves, to undermine and refute their own theses.

DETERMINISM. The view that every event that occurs does so necessarily. Every event follows inevitably from the events that preceded it. There is no randomness in reality; rather, all is law governed. Freedom * either does not exist (HARD DETERMINISM*) or exists in such a way as to be compatible with necessity * (SOFT DETERMINISM*).

DIALECTIC. In the philosophies of Hegel and Marx, the dialectic is a mechanism of change and progress in which every possible situation exists only in relation to its own opposite. This relationship is one of both antagonism and mutual dependency, but the antagonism (a form of violence) eventually undermines the relationship and overthrows it. (However, sometimes the term "dialectical" is used only to emphasize a relationship of reciprocity between two entities or processes.)

DISTRIBUTIVE JUSTICE. According to some social theories, a "just society" must be one in which there is a fair distribution of the wealth and opportunities created within that society. Only then does distributive justice exist.

DUALISM. The ontological* view that reality is composed of two kinds of beings, usually (as in Descartes) minds and bodies.

EFFICIENT CAUSE. A term from Aristotelian philosophy designating one of the four kinds of causes in the world — the physical force operating on the object undergoing change (e.g., the sculptor's chiseling of a piece of granite). (The other three Aristotelian causes are "the material cause" [the piece of granite], "the formal cause" [the idea of the statue in the mind of the sculptor], and "the final cause" [the ultimate purpose of the statue].)

EGOISM. A theory of motivation according to which the motive behind all acts either is self-interest ("psychological egoism") or ought to be self-interest ("moral egoism"). See also HEDONISM.*

ELIMINATIVE MATERIALISM. A materialistic* theory of mind according to which sentences that seem to refer to nonmaterial conscious states (such as "I have a headache") will be capable of being eliminated in favor of more accurate sentences referring to material states (such as "My C-fibers are firing").

EMPIRICISM. The epistemological view that true knowledge is derived primarily from sense experience (or, in "purer" strains of empiricism, exclusively from sense experience). For these philosophers, all significant knowledge is a posteriori,* and a priori* knowledge is either nonexistent or tautological. The "classical" empiricists were the seventeenth- and eighteenth-century Britons (Locke, Berkeley, and Hume), all of whom denied the existence of innate ideas* and conceived of the human mind as a "blank slate" at birth.

ENLIGHTENMENT, the. A philosophical movement of the eighteenth century characterized by the belief in the power of reason to sweep away superstition, ignorance, and injustice.

EPISTEMOLOGY. The theory of knowledge that answers questions such as: What is knowledge? What, if anything, can we know? What is the difference between opinion and knowledge?

EROS. The name of the Greek god of love, which in psychoanalytic* theory becomes the name of a purported "life instinct" and is opposed to Thanatos,* the "death instinct."

ETHICS. Moral philosophy: the branch of philosophy that answers questions such as: Is there such a thing as the Good? What is "the good life"? Is there such a thing as absolute duty? Are valid moral arguments possible? Are moral judgments based only on preference?

EUGENICS. The advocacy of controlled breeding in order to improve the human race.

EXISTENTIALISM. A twentieth-century philosophy associated principally with Jean-Paul Sartre but also thought to encompass the work of Karl Jaspers, Martin Heidegger, Gabriel Marcel, Albert Camus, and Miguel de Unamuno, among others. More of a shared attitude than a school of thought, it can nevertheless be roughly defined by saying with Sartre that existentialists are those who believe that, in the case of humans, "existence precedes essence." This is the thesis that there is no human nature that precedes our presence in the world. All humans individually create humanity at every moment through their free acts.

EXPERIENCE. As a technical term in empiricistic epistemology,* the name of the data provided directly by the five senses. See also SENSE-DATA.*

EXPERIMENTAL. A theory or proposition* is experimental if observable evidence is pertinent to its confirmation or falsification. See also A POSTERIORI,* SYNTHETIC,* and PRINCIPLE OF FALSIFIABILITY.*

FALSIFIABILITY. See PRINCIPLE OF FALSIFIABILITY.*

FORMS. Usually associated with the philosophies of Plato or Aristotle. For Plato (in whose philosophy the word "Form" is capitalized), everything that exists in the physical or conceptual world is in some way dependent upon Forms, which exist independently of the world but are the models (essences, universals, archetypes) of all reality. Forms are eternal, unchangeable, and the ultimate object of all true philosophizing. For Aristotle, forms are also the essences of things, but they exist _in_ things and are not independent of them. The form of an object and its function are ultimately related.

FREEDOM. Freedom exists if there are such things as free acts and free agents, that is, if some acts are performed in such a way that the authors of those acts could be held responsible for them. Some philosophers (called "libertarians"*) say that these acts _do_ exist, that some acts are freely chosen from among genuine alternatives, and that therefore determinism* is false. ("I did X, but under exactly the same circumstances, I could have done Y instead. Therefore X was a free act.") Other philosophers (called "soft determinists"*) also say that free acts exist but define "free acts" not in terms of genuine alternative choices, but in terms of voluntary acts. ("I wanted to do X, and I did do X; therefore X was a free act.") Still other philosophers (called "hard determinists"*), while agreeing with the definition of "free act" given by libertarians, deny that any such free acts or agents exist.

GESTALT PSYCHOLOGY. The theory according to which perception does not occur as the result of the summation of a number of perceptual parts; rather, these perceptual parts themselves are derived from the general perceptual field, which has properties that cannot be derived from any or all of the parts.

HARD BEHAVIORISM. The view that there are no minds and that, therefore, psychology can study only "behaviors" — an ontological* view, as opposed to the merely methodological view of "soft behaviorism."*

HARD DETERMINISM. The view that determinism* is true and that therefore freedom* and responsibility do not exist. Contrast with SOFT DETERMINISM.*

HEDONISM. A theory of motivation according to which the motive behind all acts either _is_ pleasure (psychological hedonism) or _ought to be_ pleasure (moral hedonism). See also EGOISM.*

HYPOTHETICAL IMPERATIVE. The name given by Immanuel Kant to the nonmoral use of the word "ought." This use of "ought" can always be stated in a hypothetical form (e.g., "You ought to be nice to people if you want them to like you.").

IDEALISM. The ontological* view that, ultimately, every existing thing can be shown to be spiritual or mental (hence, a version of monism*), usually associated in Western philosophy with Berkeley and Hegel.

INDETERMINISM. The view that there are such things as uncaused events and that therefore determinism* is false.

INNATE IDEA. An idea present at birth, hence a priori.*

LEGAL POSITIVISM. The view that justice and legal legitimacy are defined exclusively by the established political powers.

LIBERALISM. The political view that advocates a democratic government and asserts that the state has a legitimate right and an obligation to set standards of living below which none of its citizens may be forced to live and to enforce laws providing equal opportunity and distributive justice.*

LIBERTARIANISM. The view that freedom* exists.

LINGUISTIC PHILOSOPHY. A loosely-knit twentieth-century philosophical school according to which apparent philosophical problems can be traced to misconceptions about language.

LOGIC. The branch of philosophy that studies the structure of valid inference. A purely formal discipline, interested in the structure of argumentation rather than in its content.

LOGICAL BEHAVIORISM. The epistemological* view that all meaningful mentalistic terms must ultimately be capable of being traced back to some observable behavior and not back to some purely mental facts. For example, the term "intelligent" must ultimately be related to certain observable capacities, not to a mental state called "intelligence."

LOGICAL CONSTRUCT. A term from twentieth-century empiricism* naming an entity that can be inferred from sense-data.* For example, the belief that a table exists independently of our perceptions is based on an inference drawn from our perceptions. In this view, only sense-data can be known directly. Logical constructs can be known only indirectly.

LOGICAL EMPIRICISM. See LOGICAL POSITIVISM.*

LOGICAL POSITIVISM (or LOGICAL EMPIRICISM). The name of a school of philosophy that flourished between the two world wars according to which the only cognitively meaningful utterances are those of science. All other utterances can be shown under analysis to be merely expressions of emotions or to be nonsense.

LOGICAL POSSIBILITY. Something is logically possible if its idea contains no self-contradiction (such as the idea of a one million-sided figure). Conversely, something is logically impossible if its idea does contain a self-contradiction (such as the idea of a four-sided circle).

LOGOS. (1) A Greek term meaning "word" or "study," from which is derived the English term "logic" and the "...logies" of "biology," "sociology," etc. (2) In Plato, a term designating the rational justification of beliefs. (3) As opposed to "mythos,"* logos designates a scientific or philosophical account of the world.

MARXISM. A political or philosophical doctrine based on the writings of Karl Marx: politically a form of communism,* philosophically a form of materialism* known as "dialectical"* materialism.

MATERIALISM. The ontological* view that all reality can be shown to be material in nature (e.g., that "minds" are really brains).

MENO'S PARADOX. An epistemological* paradox set forth by Meno in the Platonic dialogue of the same name: How is it possible to seek knowledge? If one does not know what one is looking for, one will not recognize it if one finds it. If one does recognize it, then one already knew it and did not need to seek it.

METAPHYSICS. The branch of philosophy that attempts to construct a general, speculative worldview: a complete, systematic account of all reality and experience, usually involving an epistemology,* an ontology,* an ethics,* and an aesthetics.* (The adjective "metaphysical" is often employed to stress the speculative, as opposed to the scientific or common-sensical, features of the theory or proposition* it describes.)

511

METHODOLOGICAL DOUBT (or **RADICAL DOUBT**). The name of the philosophical method employed by Descartes to discover the absolutely certain foundations of all knowledge. Every belief that can be doubted should be doubted until one arrives at a belief that itself is indubitable.

MINIMAL STATE, the. The social ideal of certain theorists such as Robert Nozick according to which the only rights and obligations a government has are those of protecting the persons and property of its citizens, punishing offenses against those citizens, and taxing its citizens to finance these activities. The state has no other legitimate obligations or rights.

MODE. A property of an essential property. For example, for Descartes, "thought" is an essential property of "mind" and "understanding" is a property, or mode, of thought.

MONISM. The ontological* view that only one entity exists (e.g., as in Spinoza) or that only one _kind_ of entity exists (e.g., as in Hobbes and Berkeley).

MYTHOS. The whole body of myths, legends, and folktales that attempt to make sense of the world by placing it in a narrative context tracing things back to their supernatural origins. Sometimes contrasted with LOGOS.*

NAIVE REALISM. The prephilosophical epistemology* attributed to the "person in the street," according to which the perceptual data in the mind accurately duplicate the external world as it actually is.

NATIVISM. The psychological or epistemological* view that there are certain innate ideas,* principles, or structures in the mind that organize the data of consciousness.

NECESSARY CONDITION. X is the necessary condition of Y if Y cannot exist in the absence of X. For example, oxygen is a necessary condition of fire. See also SUFFICIENT CONDITION.*

NECESSITY. A relation between two things or ideas is _logically_ necessary if the existence of one logically entails the existence of the other. For example, the relation between triangularity and three-sidedness is logically necessary.

512

(Contrast with CONTINGENCY.*) A relation between two things is _physically_ necessary if the existence of one always results physically in the existence of the other. For example, death is the necessary result of the destruction of the brain.

NIHILISM. As an ontological* view, the theory that nothing exists; as a moral view, the theory that there are no values or that nothing deserves to exist.

OCKHAM'S RAZOR (or OCCAM'S RAZOR). A principle of simplification derived from the medieval philosopher William of Ockham according to which if there are two competing theories, both of which account for all the observable data, the simpler of the two is the preferable theory. "Do not multiply entities beyond necessity."

ONTOLOGICAL ARGUMENT. An _a priori_* attempt to prove God's existence by showing that, from the very concept of God, his existence can be deduced. This argument has been defended by a number of religious philosophers in the Platonic tradition. It was first formulated by St. Anselm and appears in one form or another in the work of Descartes, Spinoza, Leibniz, and Hegel. It has some able contemporary defenders (eg., Charles Hartshorne and Norman Malcolm). But it has been rejected by some notables, too, including St. Thomas, Hume, Kant, and Kierkegaard.

ONTOLOGY. Theory of being. The branch of philosophy pursuing such questions as What is real? What is the difference between appearance and reality? What is the relation between minds and bodies? Are numbers and concepts real, or are only physical objects real?

OPERANT CONDITIONING. A method of behavioral control in which habits are created by positive reinforcement (reward) or negative reinforcement (punishment) of the responses to certain stimuli.

ORGANICISM. The ontological* view that reality is organic — that the whole is more real than any of the parts and that the parts are dependent upon the whole for their reality.

PARADIGM SHIFT. A moment in intellectual history when the key conceptual apparatus of an age gives way to new ones, as when the essentially theological view of reality in the medieval world gives way to a more secular one involving new standards of judgment and criteria of evidence.

PHENOMENALISM. A radical form of empiricism.* As an epistemological* view, the theory that all knowledge can be constructed exclusively from sense-data.* As an ontological* view, the theory that only sense-data exist.

PHENOMENOLOGY. A philosophical school created by Edmund Husserl employing a method of analysis that purports to arrive at the pure data of consciousness and thereby provide the foundation for epistemology* and ontology.* The method involves "bracketing" certain features of experience, stripping them of all assumptions and presuppositions, and laying bare their essence.

PLURALISM. The ontological* view that reality is composed of a multiplicity of things or different kinds of things and that this multiplicity cannot be reduced to one or two categories.

POLITICAL PHILOSOPHY. The branch of philosophy that explores questions concerning the justification of political entities and political relationships.

PRAGMATISM. An American philosophy that claims that the meaning of an idea can be established by determining what practical difference would be produced by believing the idea to be true and that the truth of an idea can be established by determining the idea's ability to "work."

PRIMARY QUALITIES. A term from seventeenth- and eighteenth-century epistemology* designating properties that inhere in material bodies independently of our perception of them (e.g., size, shape, location, and divisibility). Contrast with SECONDARY QUALITIES.*

PRINCIPLE OF FALSIFIABILITY. A criterion of scientific meaning set forth by Sir Karl Popper according to which a proposition* or theory is scientific only if it is framed in such a way that it would be possible to state what kind of evidence would refute or falsify the theory, if such evidence existed.

PROPOSITION. As employed in this text, a proposition is whatever is asserted by a sentence. The sentences "It's raining," "Es regnet," and "Llueve" all assert the same proposition.

PSYCHOANALYSIS. The name given by Sigmund Freud to his method of psychotherapy, eventually becoming a theory of the mind, of selfhood, and of culture, in which psychological and social phenomena are traced to their origins in the unconscious mind.

RADICAL DOUBT. See METHODOLOGICAL DOUBT.*

RATIONALISM. The epistemological*view that true knowledge is derived primarily from "reason" (or <u>exclusively</u> from "reason" in the purer strains of rationalism). Reason is conceived as the working of the mind on material provided by the mind itself. In most versions, this material takes the form of innate ideas.* Therefore, for the rationalists, <u>a priori</u> * knowledge is the most important kind of knowledge. In rationalistic ontologies,* the mind and the world are seen to be in conformity — the real is the rational. The classical rationalists were the seventeenth-and eighteenth-century Continental philosophers (Descartes, Spinoza, and Leibniz), but the concept is broad enough to include such philosophers as Plato and Hegel.

REIFICATION. The result of illegitimately concretizing that which is abstract, that which is general, or that which defies concretization. From the Latin <u>res</u> (thing), hence, to "thingify."

REPRESENTATIVE REALISM. An empiricist*epistemology,* usually associated with John Locke, according to which the data of perception <u>represent</u> the external world without literally duplicating it, very much the way a photo or a painting does.

SECONDARY QUALITIES. A term from seventeenth-and eighteenth-century epistemology* designating perceived qualities (such as colors, tastes, odors) that appear to be real properties of material objects but in fact actually exist only in perception and are caused by the properties that do exist in material objects, viz., by "primary qualities."*

SENSE-DATA. A sense-datum is that which is perceived immediately by any one of the senses, prior to interpretation by the mind. Sense-data include the perceptions of colors, sounds, tastes, odors, tactile sensations, pleasures, and pains. Classical empiricism*based itself on the supposedly epistemologically* foundational nature of sense-data.

SKEPTICISM (or SCEPTICISM). A denial of the possibility of knowledge.

General skepticism denies the possibility of _any_ knowledge; however, one can be skeptical about specific fields of inquiry (e.g., metaphysics*) or specific faculties (e.g., sense perception) without denying the possibility of knowledge in general.

SOFT BEHAVIORISM. The view that there is no need to include "minds" in the scientific study of humans, whether or not minds exist. The study of "behaviors" and their physical causes is sufficient for a complete psychology. Contrast with HARD BEHAVIORISM.*

SOFT DETERMINISM. The view that determinism* is true but that freedom* and responsibility can exist in spite of the truth of determinism. Contrast with HARD DETERMINISM.*

SOLIPSISM. The view that the only true knowledge one can possess is knowledge of one's own consciousness. According to solipsism, there is no good reason to believe that anything exists other than oneself.

STRUCTURALISM. Based on the philosophical anthropology of the contemporary French theorist Claude Lévi-Strauss (but also finding followers in all the human sciences), structuralism is the view that the human mind is universal in that everywhere and in every historical epoch, the mind is structured in such a way as to process its data in terms of certain general formulas that give meaning to those mental data.

SUBLIMATION. A term central to psychoanalysis* that names the process whereby certain antisocial drives are directed away from their primary goal (the satisfaction of sexual or aggressive desire) and transformed into the production of socially valuable higher culture — art, religion, philosophy, law, science, etc.

SUBSTANCE. In philosophy, "substance" has traditionally been the term naming whatever is thought to be the most basic independent reality. Aristotle defined a substance as whatever can exist independently of other things, so that a horse or a man (Aristotle's examples) can exist independently, but the _color_ of the horse or the _size_ of the man cannot. The seventeenth- and eighteenth-century rationalists* took the idea of substance as _independent being_ so seriously that one of their members, Spinoza, claimed there could be only one substance in the world (i.e., only one _thing_), namely, God, because only God could exist independently. Under Berkeley's criticism of material substance and Hume's criticism of spiritual substance, the concept of substance was very much eroded. It turned up again in Kant, but only as a "category" of knowledge, not as a basic reality itself.

SUFFICIENT CONDITION. P is the sufficient condition of Q if the presence of P guarantees the presence of Q. For example, the presence of mammary glands in an animal is a sufficient condition for calling that animal a mammal. (It is also a "necessary condition"* for doing so.)

SYNTHETIC PROPOSITION. A proposition* is synthetic if its negation does not lead to a self-contradiction. For example, "Jupiter has a square moon" is synthetic because its negation, "Jupiter does not have a square moon," is not self-contradictory (usually associated with "a posteriori* propositions; the opposite of "analytic"* propositions).

TABULA RASA. Latin for "blank slate." Empiricism*from John Locke forward assumed that the mind is a _tabula rasa_ at birth and that all knowledge must be inscribed on that blank slate by experience.

TAUTOLOGY. A proposition* is a tautology if it is in some way repetitive or redundant. For example, definitions are tautological because their predicates are equivalents of the term being defined. See also ANALYTIC PROPOSITIONS.*

TELEOLOGICAL ARGUMENT. An attempt to deduce God's existence from the fact that there is purposeful behavior in nature on the part of nonintelligent beings. (E.g., the "purpose" of the sharp point on the bottom of an acorn is to break the surface of the ground when the acorn falls.)

TELEOLOGY. A teleological explanation is an explanation in terms of goals, purposes, or intentions (from the Greek _telos_ = goal). For example, "John closed the window because he didn't want his budgie to escape" is a teleological explanation because it explains John's behavior in terms of his intentions. Contrast with CAUSAL EXPLANATION.*

THANATOS. The Greek god of death, which in psychoanalytic* theory becomes the name of a purported "death instinct" inherent in all organic matter and that is somehow more basic than its opposing instinct, "eros,"* the life instinct.

THEISM. Belief in the existence of God or gods.

THEORETICAL ENTITY. A term from twentieth-century empiricism*
naming entities that exist only as parts of theories, not
parts of reality. For example, "the average American housewife" is a theoretical entity.

TRANSFORMATIONAL GRAMMAR. A system of grammatical
analysis that uses a set of algebraic formulas to express
relations between elements in a sentence or between different
forms or tenses of a phrase, such as active, passive, future,
and present.

UTILITARIANISM. The moral and social philosophy of Jeremy
Bentham and John Stuart Mill according to which the
value of any action or legislation can be derived from the
"principle of utility," which advocates "the greatest amount
of happiness for the greatest number of people."

Credits

Index